T0339981

When We Deal With Children

Fritz Redl

WHEN WE DEAL WITH CHILDREN

Selected Writings

THE FREE PRESS
A Division of Macmillan Publishing Co., Inc.
NEW YORK

THE FREE PRESS
A DIVISION OF MACMILLAN PUBLISHING CO., INC.
866 Third Avenue, New York, New York 10022

ISBN 0-02-9258804

First Free Press Paperback Edition 1972

Library of Congress Catalog Card Number: 66-13599

printing number
6   7   8   9   10

To Helen

Preface

There is nothing wrong with specialization as such. In fact, all the progress that has been made so dramatically in recent decades in fields such as physics or surgery, for instance, could never have happened without it. However, we may pay a price for rapidly stepped-up degrees of specialization. It may isolate us from each other; we may become more and more unaware of what it "feels like" to work in the other guy's domain, we may even become estranged.

In the children's field, for example, it is obvious by now that whoever spends his life as a classroom teacher, psychiatrist, group worker, case worker, house parent, "children's worker" of some sort or another, or even as a research-psychologist or -sociologist may have a chance to familiarize himself with some of the findings of his "neighbor discipline." But it usually takes between 50 to 80 years for the exciting conceptual and theoretical formulations of a given period to translate themselves into the taken-for-granted commonplace knowledge of today, accessible to the nonspecialist in a given field. This means he remains doomed to operate with the conceptual discards of the epoch just passed, and when he finds himself making statements in the other specialist's domain, he may easily look like somebody who walks around in the clothing seen in 1890 family albums or in some of those amazing film strips of beach scenes of 1910.

The parent—and the "intelligent layman in general"—is even worse off. Your child may finally get around to teaching you some of his "New Math," but you could hardly expect him to give you a reliable glimpse of "New Psych."

Immersing oneself into the literature published in periodicals and books of one field or another, is only a partial solution. At best, it gives us some acquaintance with theoretical progress and some of the "findings," but it hardly offers more than a ringside view. For, by the time we publish something considered respectable enough to be printed under headlines such as "research," we usually have omitted the exciting details that might give a picture of what we went through to get those "findings," and what it felt like to be exposed to all this to begin with. The written—and unwritten—diaries of our professional daily lives usually remain inaccessible to those who are not "in it" themselves.

Few of us are thrown, for long enough stretches of time, into one field of specialization after another, with the result that we become "marginal men." With all the disadvantages this implies, it does give us a chance to "be it" for the duration of such professional specialization and to know what it does to us and to those under our care. Even what we produce under those conditions is usually dispersed over a dozen or so professional periodicals and books of widely differing disciplines, and is hardly accessible for casual consumption by those who stay in their field—or to the educator or parent at large.

The book is an attempt to help bridge this gap. Through the chance of my personal case history—and also my personal quirks—I have wandered, not only as a theorist, but also as a practitioner through a variety of disciplines and of "settings" in which we try to be helpful to growing youngsters—healthy or sick—and have had the opportunity to be stunned by the theoretical excitement as well as the stumbling blocks of each. I have selected from my writings, lectures, and speeches those stuffed with enough concrete illustrations of daily events in my professional role in the lives of children and adolescents as to achieve not only a considerable spread among the professional disciplines involved, but also to retain some of the flavor of daily struggle with concepts as well as with child behavior in the raw.

It is unavoidable, of course, that this book will bear some of the imperfections and disadvantages of such an enterprise—occasional repetition of the same basic theme in different contexts being only the most obvious one. All I can hope is that the reader may be generous enough to tolerate these limitations and to find stimulating, for his own life with the young, whatever glimpse I may be able to offer from those settings and goal-frameworks that are markedly different from his own.

Acknowledgments should go to all those professionals from whom I learned most of what I know, and to all the youngsters who so vigorously kept reminding me of what I don't know. Such a list, unfortunately, would become unmanageable. I have even refrained from adding a proper chapter on references and bibliography—it would counteract the very purpose for which this selection is being offered. One person, though, needs to be listed, for the reader will be most appreciative of what she did for him: Miss Estelle Whelan, my editor, who so bravely struggled with the task of improving my English without destroying the feeling of what I wanted to convey.

F.R.

Contents

Preface   vii

PART ONE
Crisis in the Children's Field   1

    Crisis in the Children's Field   3

PART TWO
A Challenge to Concepts and Theories   33

    The Life-Space Interview—Strategy and Techniques   35

    The Concept of a "Therapeutic Milieu"   68

    Improvement Panic and Improvement Shock   95

    Ego Disturbances and Ego Support   125

    Psychoanalysis and Education   147

PART THREE
And What About Groups?   153

    Group Emotion and Leadership   155

    The Phenomena of Contagion and "Shock Effect"   197

    Resistance in Therapy Groups   214

    The Psychology of Gang Formation and the Treatment of Juvenile Delinquents   224

    The Art of Group Composition   236

    Discipline in Classroom Practice   254

Psychoanalysis and Group Therapy: A Developmental
Point of View   309

PART FOUR
Talking It Over with My Staff   329

Just What Am I Supposed to Observe?   333

What Is There to "See" About a Group?   338

How Do I Know When I Should Stop It?   346

This Time We Should Not Interfere—But Why?   349

Framework for Our Discussions on Punishment   355

What Do We Do About the "Facts of Life"?   378

How Good or Bad Is It to Get Angry?   386

PART FIVE
Serious, But in a Lighter Vein   391

Preadolescents—What Makes Them Tick?   395

Our Troubles with Defiant Youth   409

Who Is Delinquent?   418

Sex Education: Unfinished Business   427

Psychopathological Risks of Camp Life   440

The Furious Children in the Library   452

The Virtues of Delinquent Children   461

"Disadvantaged"—and What Else?   467

Publications by Fritz Redl   489

Index   495

When We Deal With Children

Part One

Crisis
in the
Children's Field

Crisis in the Children's Field

"The Crisis in the Children's Field" is clearly what it was meant to be: a utilization of the wonderful opportunity that the president of a professional organization has to open his mouth wide without the usual restraints tied to the task of "reading a scientific paper" on a specific piece of research. The limitations that come with such a rare privilege also have to be kept in mind, though. Time is limited to what a speech audience can possibly bear at the opening of a richly menu'd professional meeting; the audience itself is selective, so that one can take many things for granted that, in a different framework, would have to be spelled out in detail; and there is a limit to the number of "challenges" one can possibly squeeze into a single appearance. Yet I anticipate no difficulty for readers from neighboring professions and for thoughtful parents and community organizers in accepting those limitations as unavoidable and in stretching the issues raised here far into their own domains by their own creative thought.

In short—I am convinced that the issue of a "crisis in the children's field" is as acute now as it was in 1962 and that the additions needed to complete the list here are as vital as they were then. Only a few comments need be made to make sure that a recent flurry of large-scale promises and beginning programs in the fields of education and child care do not seduce us into getting prematurely complacent again.

Nothing has as yet changed in the clinical field. The state of underimplementation of all the actual services so vitally needed is still as ridiculous as it was before, and the manpower shortage in terms of appropriately trained personnel seems to be even more desperate.

In the field of community mental-health services of a "preventive" nature and in the field of education, considerable sums of money are likely to become available in the not too distant future. At this writing, most of this is still in the planning stage, but what is visible in the first tries, after one penetrates the rubble of administrative squabbles, political excitement, and bureaucratic snafu in which most of them are enveloped, makes me feel like adding to my previous list of "crisis issues" the following points:

Let's be sure we get rid of the faint odor of antiprofessionalism that new
    enterprises, which have to produce a lot of visible action fast, are likely
    to get insensitive to.

Let's be sure we don't fall into the temptation of quality sacrifice beyond
    what is decent, toward which the pressures of large numbers, wide geo-
    graphical spread, and the need to spend much money fast are likely
    to seduce us.

Let's get rid as fast as we can of the false stereotype of our new customer,
    which already seems to fill many of our blueprint pages, the over-
    simplified image of the "children of the poor."

In short—let's not swap the crisis of underimplementation for that of
    pseudo-abundance; let's tackle either of these crises where it needs to
    be hit.

*I*NTRODUCTORY REMARK 1. I am eager to announce
the items to which I hope to address myself. I am not sure that I can
elaborate on all of them in as much detail as I may wish, but I want
at least to be sure you know what I hope to get you excited about.

Underdeveloped Country Type II: United States of America
Love of Kids, Neglect of Children, Hatred of Youth
Implementational Psychopathy and Other Forms of Community Disease
Let's Put the "Search" Back into "Re-Search"
The Obsolete Model and the Latest Fad
The Ghost of the Lay-Therapy Issue and How It Gums Up the Works
Treatment into What? And Why Don't We Like Mental Health?

Introductory Remark 2. This must sound like a funny outline—
and it is! However, you are stuck with it. For it is my perception of a
presidential address that it should not be a market stall for my personal
wares but a challenge to the professional field. I have only one ambition here: not to make a speech myself but to make *you* talk. So this is
really a "go out and tell them" session.

I have no aspirations to offer a scholarly paper. I assume that I will

"The Crisis in the Children's Field" is based on the article by the same title
that appeared in *The American Journal of Orthopsychiatry* (October 1962), ©
1962 by the American Orthopsychiatric Association.

not tell you anything that you don't already know. I could hardly think of a group of people who collectively have more complete knowledge of what the lives of kids with problems are like and what the deficiencies even in our best communities really are and what we ought to know more about in terms of needed research. But it is my impression that we need to be reminded from time to time of what we know very well but ought to talk somewhat more loudly about, so that communities can go into action about the issues we know they need to face but frequently neglect to do anything about.

It is also my conviction that, as professionals, we usually do not talk loudly enough to others until we talk plainly to ourselves first. All the impressive knowledge about children and their service needs, so easily "taken for granted" by ourselves, does not come close enough to the "action scene," unless we bring it forcibly to the attention of those who have the power to translate it into well-implemented reality. Uncomfortable fact? Yes. And I hope to make you as uncomfortable as I possibly can about it.

Underdeveloped Country Type II: United States of America

I know that this is a rather strong statement, and I have deliberated its possible misinterpretations. But I have to make it, and I can back it up. I want you to know, however, that the typology I am using is entirely mine, so I had better explain it. There are two types of what I would consider "underdeveloped countries"—and, remember, I am talking about the children's field—and I am not talking about degrees of underdevelopedness now, but of types: Type I includes countries that are underdeveloped and have good excuses for being so. Type II includes countries in which the services for children are sorely underdeveloped but that haven't the slightest excuse for that sordid state of affairs.

For example, in an underdeveloped country of Type I, the people might have miserable conditions and inadequate services for children because they are run by a benighted autocrat whose main interest in life is having his kids drive around in golden Cadillacs—never mind starvation and all that. Or the services for children might be underdeveloped because the country may be run by a Fascist or any other type of totalitarian regime in which people who know what is needed have to keep their mouths shut and cannot afford to mention in the open items or defects adverse to state propaganda. Or a country may be underdeveloped in spite of being really eager for progress, because its people are actually very naïve and way behind in insight and know-how. They may, for instance, be just in the process of discovering that there are things like child psychology, psychiatry, and mental health; that schools can be served by clinics with special methods and designs; and that all this could bring them much closer to the chance for prevention of whatever ails their children most. They may even have caught on to the fact that some of the diseases that were previously considered "innate" and were accepted as unavoidable destinies are not that at all but can be tackled with the knowledge we have right now. However, they have trouble translating such dim emerging awarenesses into politically and officially backed-up action. Or countries might be underdeveloped simply because they have just recently emerged from incredible hardship. They may have had to give "priority" to the rebuilding of bombed-out cities, the replacement by playgrounds and schools of mass cemeteries for the battle dead or the politically slaughtered, and the production of the bare necessities of life.

In all these cases, regardless of the degree of whatever underdevelopment there is, I consider it underdevelopment with a reasonably good excuse.

Underdeveloped countries of Type II, in my terminology, are those with no excuse at all. They are countries that are free and proud of being free. They are countries with long experience in community planning and with clearly developed and refined patterns for public action and service that have proved themselves effective in other fields. They are countries with plenty of evidence throughout their history that people who want to do so can bring about change if they know what is wrong and if they speak loudly enough. In these countries, citizens do not have to be afraid of speaking up, for the voice of progress is laden with status, even though it may have trouble getting itself heard and followed. These countries, too, are so far advanced in technical progress that even the most miserably programed and poorly staffed detention home, if recently built, still has the most elaborate plumbing of the latest design. These are countries where the best services known to mankind are in existence and could easily be used for models of what is needed and what can be done for those areas that don't yet have such services. These are countries where the possibility of reducing disease and tackling previously untreatable sickness in the physical field has been clearly established and demonstrated and where the concept of the complexity of modern disease prevention has become a commonplace item even in the thinking of those without very elaborate educational backgrounds. These are countries where people know that to provide what is needed to do a job well is more appropriate to a concept of "sound financial realism" than is a silly penny-pinching cost count, which frequently is palmed off on an unalert public under that label—at least as long as the thinking is directed at gadgets and at problems of bodily disease. In short, these countries have well-paved roads to progress and also well-paved roads to research, as well as back from research to engineering and action. There is, accordingly, no excuse for not applying consistently and universally such principles in the mental-health field, even when "only" our kids are at stake.

I could now spend all the remaining space to give you some of the facts and figures about what is needed, compared with what we have. This could easily be done; in fact, most of this knowledge is probably assembled among this readership. However—why waste our time? In this group it isn't necessary. The trouble is not that we don't know and need "proof" of the issue. The trouble is that we don't always remember what we know at the moment when it counts most.

Just a few reminders to make sure that we are all looking in the same direction right now: When did you last try to find a placement for a fifteen- or sixteen-year-old severely disturbed, "acting-out type" of kid—even with a lot of money behind him? How many places can you even think of, in terms of solid long-range residential therapy and individual treatment, that you could possibly imagine "selling" him to? When did you last visit a children's ward? I am sorry, I am ahead of the times. I mean a mental hospital with, say, two or three kids crowded into a ward with gobs of psychotic adults in all stages of deterioration —one of those hospitals in which the administrators have finally decided that maybe the children should have a place of their own. When the administrators got to the point, they remembered what trouble would be involved in getting it staffed and equipped and keeping it small enough to be run. The result would only get the kids out of one place that is unfit for them into another just as poorly designed for what they need but more troublesome to run. When did you last try to count the kids that any schoolteacher in a large class could point out as needing something beyond what they are getting? In large cities, the teacher might even know exactly what help they need. But the teachers have given up asking for it, for they only get laughed at or labeled "unrealistic fools" if they do. When did you last inquire how long the waiting line is for those special services we have even for the kids everybody agrees need them right now?

Enough for now. A well-documented publication on all that would be easy to do. This is not the moment to do it. All I want is to get you stirred up about what you already know and run into in your daily work.

Even all this, however, would only prove that we have wide areas of hardly pardonable neglect. It would, in itself, not yet justify the term "crisis." I personally think that we have more than vast pockets of neglect. The reason I think we are confronted with something more in the nature of a crisis is the basic attitude we show, even as professionals who are "in the know," when faced with this type of neglect.

For, collectively, we have developed two most efficient defenses against the discomfort of our professional and public conscience. One is the shoulder shrug, which sometimes actually gets us twitchy and twisty with all the shrugging off we have to do. "After all, there is nothing *I* can do about it. Don't ask me. I know it is wrong and very unfortunate and wish it were different." The other defense is an even better one: a convulsive fit of condemnation or glorification of somebody else. The first one is better known and easier to manage. If we get mad enough because we can't do anything in a given case of obvious need for service, we are likely to pin it on somebody else who, we know, "is no good anyway"—preferably picking for that purpose someone who originally reminded us of what should be done. The other defense is somewhat subtler and harder to describe. Sometimes we can find an excuse for not having what we should in terms of services by overglorifying other groups. They are so wonderful; they have and do everything we don't have and do. We can get to feel so good about what is being done elsewhere that the sting is taken out of the fact that we don't do it and that overpraise of "the others" allows us to forget what we should and could do right here. The best illustration for this latter defense is what I would like to call the "sputnik neurosis" that has hit us so visibly in recent years. I find us spending an undue amount of time talking incessantly about "how excellent the Russian schools are, how even their sixth graders know all about arithmetic already. Isn't that wonderful? Of course *our* schools aren't teaching them anything; *our* teachers are interested in nothing but fads and frills. There isn't any learning going on in the American school anymore. We better run fast and do as the Russians do."

I wish I had the space to puncture that one, but good. At this moment I must confine myself to highlighting it as the handy mechanism of defense that such statements all too frequently are. By glorifying— and overglorifying far beyond what the traffic bears—some isolated issue that seems to us well taken care of somewhere else, we can readily get mad at our own kids and, preferably, their teachers, instead of facing the stench of neglect that is a frequent cause for what messes up the learning atmosphere in classrooms and coming to grips with what really needs to be done about it.

If a whole country, forward-looking and free and well-heeled on top of that, allows itself to drift into regression to defenses as primitive as the ones I have mentioned, then, indeed, the term "crisis" seems challengingly appropriate.

Love of Kids, Neglect of Children, Hatred of Youth

This I consider a really serious form of pathology, which sometimes hits us as a community. The first part of the heading, "love of kids," I will not have to defend. Everybody knows Americans "love kids"; in fact, we are not only credited with this characteristic, but it is sometimes mentioned in a not altogether complimentary way. It then often has in it the flavor of "overcultivation" and "overpermissiveness." As to "neglect of children," I have just been at that one, though perhaps I should add that the issue is not only a problem with disturbed children. I think we have as many problems of neglect when we look for support for the services the normal and healthy child needs too. Even in the realm of regular planning for appropriate implementation of our educational facilities, the educator could easily add his lament to that of the clinician.

I want to dwell on the third part of the heading, "hatred of youth," which I know will make you mad because it is hard even to bring it into self-awareness.

I really think that, during the last fifteen or twenty years, we have drifted into a stage of development that encourages—when we talk as members of the larger community—a highly ambivalent or even a downright hateful attitude toward the "youth of our time." Of course, I am not talking about us as individuals. Obviously, we all still love kids, and I am sure we would happily admit that "some of our best friends are teen-agers." But as soon as we talk as members of a committee, as part of a profession, including that of psychiatry, I find an uncanny amount of negative attitudes and stereotypes smuggling themselves into our discussion—attitudes I am sure we wouldn't allow ourselves to harbor if we knew we were harboring them. In fact, the phenomenon as such is well-enough known to all of us, especially when it hits those we treat or their parents. Remember how often it is quite clear that either Junior or his father or mother is aware only of the positive part of his or her relationship to each of the other two, whereas the hostile components, though obvious to everyone else, seem submerged or even repressed to the point of personal nonrecognition? Such a phenomenon of partial denial or repression of hostile components in a relationship is natural and, in minor degrees, normal enough. If it smuggles itself in large doses into the thinking processes of the whole generation of adults against the youth of our time, it assumes dangerous proportions. Yet this seems to me to be exactly what all too often takes place.

I find people who quite obviously love the kids entrusted to their care, as teachers or parents, or to their treatment, as therapists, who are caught in the trap of negative stereotypes when they talk as representatives of their professions or of their communities before they even know what hit them. All of a sudden, the kid whose behavior they discuss is not Johnny or Mary and more, or their child or client or student. He becomes a "youth" who must not be allowed to get away with "such behavior toward us adults." Even the term "teen-ager," by the way, which was not current when I came to this country in 1936, reflects that inclination toward hostile stereotyping. It is true that the older term "adolescent," which was more in vogue at that time, also had the problem of generalization built into it; but at least it had more of the odor of a discussion of "developmental phases." The teen-age label has since assumed the character of a downright prejudicial stereotype. By this I mean that we deprive people of their personalities and individuality, of their roles as "persons" in our lives, and make them into something that just happens to remind us of the undesirable imputed characteristics of a group we don't really like. As is the case with all prejudicial stereotypes, the teen-age label also carries with it the implication that the teenager is guilty until proven innocent. The mere fact that we have to reassure ourselves that we are still capable of making exceptions because "some of our best friends are teen-agers" only proves how deeply we distrust the group as such.

Fortunately, we know by now, as social scientists, how this machinery of displacement of issues onto prejudicial stereotypes works. We know to what pathological distortions of perception and thought it leads in the areas of racial, religious, national, and political issues. We should therefore be able to recognize in time how it fools us in our attempt to face the problems of services to our youth. It is all too easy to use the undeniable misbehavior of individuals or groups to help us overlook the fact that much youthful misbehavior and sick action occurs because we frequently load the lives of our children and youth with unpardonable degrees of mishandling, neglect, inaccessibility of needed services, and delay of appropriate treatment when needed. It is easier to get mad than to face the real issues collectively as a challenge to positive action.

As professionals, we must first squarely face this problem of a negative stereotype and a basically hostile component of dangerous proportions in our attitudes to the youth of our time. It is not enough to know that such sick deviations of thought happen to those we treat or plan for under the stress and strains of life and to discover and treat them in our clinics. It is up to us to admit and show just how this may and does happen to the best of us, as soon as we ourselves are confronted not with that child or patient of ours but with a public stance toward the youth of our country. We know what it is like when our patients are caught up in unconscious hostilities they don't really want to be ridden by but that nevertheless get in the way of appropriate handling of their children's behavior. I think the fact that this happens to us on a nation-wide scale as representatives of public opinion comes as close to the danger of a collective disease as any other that community psychiatry has pointed up in the past. I think that it is time for us to detect this disease in ourselves, to point it out to others, and to search for ways of helping all of us to cope with it more wisely than we have done in the past.

Implementational Psychopathy and Other Forms of Community Disease

I don't like the term "psychopathy" too well, and I am quite aware of the possible oversimplification that an all-too-old-fashioned regression to this label might imply. However, after all is said about the complexity of the phenomenon, there is at this time no other word that would so briefly designate what I hope to underline here. Again, by the way, I am not talking about ourselves as private and highly individual personalities. I am talking about an attitude that hits us when we do our thinking and planning as members of the "community at large."

As members of our communities, we are all very ambitious and eager to have the highest quality, the best, and the latest available in our service designs. If somebody points out to us in disgust that we "don't have this type of clinic, service, hospital, and so forth," in our towns, either we hurry to prove him wrong, or we nearly die with shame at having to listen to such insults. If there is something that's better, newer, and recognizedly more up to date, we'd better see that we have it too. Nothing but the best will do for our towns.

It seems to me, on closer view, that this terrific pride in having the latest and best is paralleled by an amazing lack of interest in whether or not two other equally important issues are taken care of: whether or not the service thus prized is available in sufficient quantity to serve numerically all those who need to be served and whether or not the service thus coveted is available in sufficient social and geographic spread to be accessible to those for whom it is intended. Let's just use one simple and well-known illustration to illuminate this point. As soon as a community finally gets itself a really well-designed child-guidance clinic, even having at least a part-time psychiatrist to administer the operation, it is rightfully proud of that fact and justifiably tickled pink. At the same time, for months to come, you would have no luck trying to point out that it needs at least twenty such clinics to reach the kids that need them; some of those needing those services most live in geographical or social environments that make the use of that clinic impossible, even though it is "physically" in existence; thousands of kids are still sitting around in jails with adults, in mental hospital wards of the "snake pit" variety, in detention homes that are too poorly staffed or equipped to offer anything but "detention," and thousands more are simply names on the pages of year-long waiting lists for children's institutions, foster-home placements, special services for retarded, delinquent, epileptic, or what have you—a mass of children for whom even the best and latest model of a child-guidance clinic obviously is not the answer, only the referral source. It is amazing how vigorously the justified pride in the achievement of that one model clinic seems to eradicate beyond recognition any possible guilt for not doing anything for all those others.

Or do you remember how often it happens, if you are in the therapy field, that you get a letter from a children's institution, reformatory, or similar enterprise begging you to get it at least that part-time psychiatrist it has wanted for so long or a part-time person to run at least one "therapy group" for the institution, because some of the kids might be amenable to that? Do you also remember what trouble you have, the moment it gets what it asks for, if you try to tell it that it doesn't do to dump the kids the rest of the time in large masses into unfit mass dormitories; that the special therapist, group worker, or caseworker cannot possibly make up for the fact that the kids' program is on a starvation basis? If their living room cannot ever be used for anything but "waxing" by those with penalties to work off, that their two-hour therapy on Wednesday cannot make up for the fact that forty children sit idly around a cottage punitively supervised in the evening hours by an untrained substitute in a state of panic and despair? The fact that everything else is still so inappropriate suddenly doesn't seem to bother anybody very much. People are so proud of the one "high-level service" tagged onto their outfit at last that the voice that tries to remind them what else is just as important sounds like the nasty intrusion of an uncooperative cuss who just doesn't "want to play ball" and is spoiling their fun with a new toy.

The same thing may happen even in settings where, in their clearly body-related services, the staffs wouldn't dream of regression that far, as for instance in psychiatric hospitals that want to undertake special projects for the care of children. Obviously, the standards that an over-all treatment design for a residential-therapy tool of this sort is supposed to meet are well established by now. Yet if children are exposed to "total living" in any institutional setting, the part of treatment that needs to be "implemented" may well greatly transgress popular concepts—even medical ones. To be on a high level, certain conditions of staff training for the top positions and plumbing for hygiene are—thank heaven—taken for granted. But you cannot help severely disturbed children grow out of their desperate pathologies into the more or less healthy autonomy of those functioning in open society on their age level, unless you also can provide appropriate design of the living spaces they are supposed to grow out of and into; appropriate staffing, not only on the medical and nursing, but also on the group-work, casework, and therapeutic-learning levels; and several other elements.

The type of "program for living" needed by psychiatrically sick children of various disturbance types has a wide range of equally essential ingredients too long to mention here. Even when you start treating them out of the worst, you especially need provisions for convalescence—a supportive form of life you want to treat them into and through. Although we know all this—and ample research is available in printed form about it—I am constantly amazed at the ease with which our professional consciences stop being worried just a few lines down from the line of top staff and medication. The fact that the "ward" is usually predesigned on an entirely unfit basis for the purpose, that program implementation and contemplated staffing are far short of minimum standards even before we open the place, seems to fall way below the threshold of guilt about responsible standards. It is hard to get money or permission even for the most clearly essential parts of the basic design, by now clearly demonstrable as nonluxury items, simply because all guilt is tied up with the over-all idea of high-level list items, whereas the question of appropriate "implementation" of what we said we were going to do is beyond the reach of responsible concern.

Such attitudes are very different from the one we have reached, as communities, in the simple "gadgetorial" field. If I intended to build a plant for the production of atomic energy, for instance, nobody would come around and call me a fool because I insisted on getting uranium or whatever it takes instead of being nice and cooperative and doing it with strawberry juice, which is much more "reasonable" because it grows right here, is cheaper, and supports the local industry to boot. My demand for just the type of material—and just the type of container and storage atmosphere—I need would be considered, although admittedly exorbitant, quite "realistic." In a parallel case in the field of services to emotionally sick children, I would much more likely be called an "unrealistic fool who probably thinks money grows on trees." The result of our widespread disease of "implementational psychopathy" is that we are often not really doing what we said we would undertake and that we are all too elegantly hopping over our implementational sins, just because we don't think we really have to care.

With respect to "other forms of community disease" I shall mention only three once over lightly: the "resurrection of agency guilt," the "dog-bone complex," and "reticence neurosis"—an affliction of the clinical field. As for the first, no matter how many communities I get involved with—either directly or as a "consultant"—in the development of new and badly needed services, I find that the following steps are taken with uncanny regularity time and again.

Step 1. There is a universal complaint. Everybody—but *everybody* —chimes in: "We are flooded with children who do not fit our services. We don't have the places that we need to take care of them." This is terrible, for, not only do the children get no help, but also they mess up treatment channels for those who could make use of what is available.

Step 2. Somebody finally gets the money and opportunity to develop exactly that type of service for that type of child, even though, in the beginning, on a small and numerically modest scale, of course.

Step 3. There is a referral "freeze-up"—no more kids. It then takes at least nine to fourteen months before the other agencies eventually come through with some referrals, and the first ones are invariably of the nature of "punitive referrals" anyway, by which I mean the agency refers kids it hopes that at least somebody else will fail with too. Besides, the new agency usually has to face the accusation of undue luxury and snobbism because it seems fancier, makes claims the original agencies did not make, and is usually temporarily highlighted a little beyond what jealousy-coping capacities can tolerate. This phenomenon, which I have observed as it hits communities time and again, is understandable enough, once one comes to think of it. Yet it is basically a sick phenomenon, which would block us from progress even were we ready to incur some of the price one always has to pay for a new move.

In connection with the "dog-bone complex," I think it was Winnicott or Soddy of the Tavistock Clinic in London who mentioned this term a few years back at a World Health Organization workshop in Copenhagen. Anyway, it struck me as so well fitted to some of our problems that I cannot help but describe it here. My description may be somewhat off the original model, but this is what it then seemed to me to imply: Sometimes some old bone, which doesn't amount to much, lies lonely in the street; no dog even bothers to sniff at it. All of a sudden, one dog, out of boredom or for reasons known only to his analyst, starts idly worrying it. In no time all the other dogs in the neighborhood come around and want it too. A fight ensues, in which the possession of this bone seems to have become a matter of life and death. Somehow the fight peters out—or maybe somebody bothered by the noise breaks it up. Gone are the dogs. The bone is left lying there, untouched and alone and forgotten once again.

If that doesn't remind me of some of the problems we have with services for children, especially for those who are hard to manage, I don't know what would. It reminds me, especially, of some of the changes in contemporary service fashions. The delinquency issue, for instance, was quite fashionable a while back; in the meantime other afflictions have caught the public fancy. Now again it seems to be somewhat revived, and various agencies in our communities and in the nation have started wondering again: To whom does delinquency belong? Not that anybody wants these kids to smell up their offices or to swear up their playgrounds, but somehow we are again faced with conflicting claims. Maybe all research money on delinquency should go to psychiatry, for is it not another form of mental disease? Or maybe delinquency is the domain of the sociologist, for isn't he the one who knows most about urban and community disorganization? Of course his training doesn't really include the skills of working with kids individually or in groups; but then there is no doubt that environmental factors and status issues are often involved. Or perhaps delinquency should be claimed by the educator? For where but in the schools do we find most kids most of the time and most clearly visible in their emerging malfunctioning, at least until we have to kick a few hundred of them out every year because they make it too hard to live with them in classrooms and still get some teaching done? Let me stop this rather lengthy chain—I haven't even brought the churches into the fracas yet. What I want to avoid is seeing that bone lying there, lonely and unwanted again, after the fight and excitement are over. Maybe we can some day get over the fracas solution into a really concerted, saturated, and joint interdisciplinary effort, instead of elevating the dog-bone complex from a local to a national level.

As for the third community disease, reticence neurosis—an affliction of the clinical field, here is what I have in mind: If you become a clinician of any kind, you had better be equipped with a heavy dose of reticence—never mind who calls it what. You can't constantly blab what you know all over the place. In fact, if I get somebody on my staff who is hit by pride in reticence even to a mildly neurotic degree, I am happy indeed; I couldn't do without him or her. But will you please keep your reticence ambitions within the clinical part of the operation? I mean within the realm of your work with patients, clients, teachers, children, parents, and so forth? As soon as we think we have to retain an unusual degree of reticence when we go into the open market of interpretation of community and service needs and when we act as citizens whose job it is to wake the larger community up to what needs to be done and implemented, then reticence—such a virtue in our clinical practice—becomes indeed a serious affliction that stifles progress and community growth.

Let's Put the "Search" Back into "Re-Search"

This point is purposely somewhat overstated, to make sure that the basic theme in which I want to get you interested receives proper attention. These are the four points for my illustrative departure: carelessness in feeding the counting machines; the control group—an intimidation device against imaginative research; the hypothesis complex versus the search for treatment-relevant facts; research versus service —divide them and it will be easier to dominate both.

CARELESSNESS IN FEEDING THE COUNTING MACHINES

This issue seems to me clear enough and should not need much elaboration here. Of course I am not objecting to the counting machines—in the shape of the human brain or of other gadgets. Nor am I objecting to the terrific eagerness and pride that go into the production and preservation of appropriate and really decent and clean mathematical operations. Without them no research would be worth its salt. That I take for granted, and I don't expect to be misquoted on this one. In short, it is obviously important to be as conscientious or, if you want to, even as compulsive as can be when it comes to mathematical procedures by which we extract special findings from the data we have. However, I find all too often that our nearly compulsive conscientiousness in the mathematical area is not at all coupled with an equally conscientious concern about what "facts" we put into the counting machinery to begin with. I find that we are sometimes downright lighthearted not to say psychopathic, showing little worry about how closely the data we count are related to the issues we hope to study. Even in research efforts with which I have personally been closely connected I have, time and again, run into situations in which somebody approaches me and says, "Listen, can you quickly tell me—I am working on a questionnaire or some such—what are the three most frequent reasons for 'acting out' in children?" Whereupon I shudder and tremble and mumble: "What do you mean three? There are at least eighteen that I can reel off right now without thinking twice. And what do you have in mind, and which kids are you talking about when you say 'acting out'?" Little good does that do me, though. For my assailant counters in disdain: "Listen, brother, don't be nasty. I only have three lines left on my IBM card, so what's the matter with you?"

Unfortunately, although somewhat exaggerated here, this is more than a joke. It is an attitude that I meet time and again. And those of us who are looking for more than something to be fed into a counting or tabulating machine are invariably the losers. In fact, the implication seems to be that it is better for us to be ashamed of ourselves for being that fussy; that maybe there *should* be only three types of acting-out children, for how can one be so unfair to counting machines? My colleague in the episode just described may even sympathize with me. But after all, if there are only three lines left, let's be "realistic" and just put three things in there—as though this wouldn't be a distortion of the complexity of nature way beyond what should be considered decent.

THE CONTROL GROUP—AN INTIMIDATION DEVICE
AGAINST IMAGINATIVE RESEARCH

Please understand me correctly. I am *not* against control groups. I know that there are some types of research and some research issues for which control groups are so important that it would be silly to do anything without them. However, I am definitely bothered by frequent instances in which I have noticed that the administrative bodies giving out money for research are not really considering the control group as an essential research device for a given research theme but are using it to intimidate the one who wants to do the job. I could quote many cases in which, in my conviction, the view that a control group is a "must" has nothing to do with the nature of the research project; or in which the pretense of using a control group seduces the researcher into downright indecent claims about what can and cannot be controlled. In order to meet respectability criteria in mid-air, researchers are induced to mess up their data-finding designs, especially in the study of problems about which we do not know enough to produce really relevant sets of controllable variables and in the realm of exploratory clinical research. I think that, simultaneously with a search for better knowledge about the development of control groups where they belong, we need to develop more spine and courage to defend ourselves against the control-group pressure when it is used, in the disguise of a symbol of research respectability, as a bureaucratic tool for intimidation against imaginative design.

THE HYPOTHESIS COMPLEX VERSUS THE SEARCH FOR TREATMENT-RELEVANT FACTS

Again I hope that you are well aware that I am not talking against hypotheses or against the importance of the wide variety of themes we strike by this term. What I am pleading against is the frequently quite inappropriate demand for a neat sentence under the deceptive heading of "hypothesis," which gives the impression that, from here on in, it is all merely a matter of well-known and well-defined steps before the last of the testable variables is caught, duly processed, examined, and found wanting or usable as "evidence" that we supposedly knew exactly what we were looking for.

There are areas of research in which such "hypothesis neatness" is obtainable and worth striving for. In the field of clinical knowledge, however, few issues are that neat. In this area, we may have to limit ourselves for a long time to come to painstaking efforts to pile up naturalistic observation upon naturalistic observation. The need to "listen to nature"—and human nature is nature too—takes priority over the somewhat premature demand to classify it. Now, in theory, most research-minded people go along with this statement. In my own experience, for instance, I have been liberally encouraged to go ahead with a modest "collection" of observations and to gather whatever an experientially well-calibrated mind might see and hear and observe when thrown into the midst of raw life. In practice, though, I find that those who are supposed to support research financially and by their administrative powers soon tire of this generous gesture—or that they do not allow younger researchers the liberties granted me. I have seen many a most ingenious and promising research design rejected, simply because those who supported it could not be made to pretend, upon demand, that they had a neat hypothesis for situations in which clinical virgin land was as yet too dense to allow such simplification. All officially mouthed reassurances notwithstanding, it seems to me that the real "respectability test" still lies in the surrender to the hypothesis cult, at the expense of the frankly admitted complexity of clinical reality.

RESEARCH VERSUS SERVICE—DIVIDE THEM AND IT WILL BE EASIER TO DOMINATE BOTH

This problem especially bothers me, as I am convinced there isn't really any "versus" in it at all. However, I have seen too many organizations and projects in which, officially, no such "either-or" attitude was mentioned or intended, yet they invariably ended up that way. This usually happens on two levels: One is seduction into dishonest financing. Yes, I mean just that. Example? Easy—I could deliver them a dime a dozen. One may suffice: a children's service, clinic, hospital unit, residential home, or community project, has been developed with a grandiose and honestly intended plan. The agency financing it falls way short of what it really takes to "implement" such service or finds out soon enough that the service runs into more money than had been realized. It ends up with a good service but one woefully lacking in staff or in time for staff to do high-quality recording and supervision or to serve the parents as elaborately as necessary. The original planners thought this would be an easy addendum and could be submerged under the children's-service budget without trouble. In short, they soon realize that they need much more than they had thought in order to raise the service to the high quality it set out to reach or to cover the additional requirements not fully recognized at the outset. It happens that national money and foundation money may be available for "research only." Those bodies and foundations expect the communities to take care of "direct service needs." It also happens that the given community won't—or simply can't—come through with the goods. Result: "Let's start doing some research. Maybe in that way we can get somebody to give us what we need." Needless to say this method ends up in mayhem, for the research-financing outfit will, rightfully, have none of it. The service organization will resent whatever research may have been built in, and it turns out to be, obviously again and again quite justifiably, not only no answer to the service problem but simply an additional burden on everybody. The lessons turn out to be easy: don't force decent people to ask for what they need under false pretenses. And if you do, don't be surprised if neither of the intended jobs gets done. Also, if you want good research in and out of a service operation, you had better give them what they clearly need to provide proper service. And don't mind paying for it; how can you do research on data obtained to begin with in a messy service outfit?

The other level on which this problem of "research versus service" becomes a festering sore is one that hits the researcher where it hurts. Let's assume that a good research operation has been built into a reasonably decent service operation. The pressures on it frequently mount beyond what anybody seriously doing research can possibly endure. For not only the service-engaged people but also the community at large expect the mere existence of a research department to provide the practitioner with all the answers to his problems right here and now; otherwise the researcher gets into ill repute for being "ivory tower," impractical, and probably an expendable luxury item to begin with. The researcher will soon have to fight for his long-range or depth-oriented research design, and in the course of that battle both sides, research and practice, get more estranged from each other. What started as a happy interdisciplinary enterprise ends up in research-*versus*-practice mayhem. The researchers either feel so guilty for not solving all the immediate problems of their practicing pals that they come through with premature and totally phony recommendations and water down their research designs; or they get so defensive about having them watered down that communication between the two sides stops. On the other hand, the practitioners, having been misled into believing that their investment in the research operation can pay off for them in terms of immediate relief, get more and more hostile to the research—or, worst of all, want themselves to become "little researchers" and abandon the job that the kids need them to do.

At the moment, it seems to me, we as a nation are caught in a miserable attitude on this point. There seems to be no question that "research money" is much easier to obtain than service moneys, especially as even a skimpy and very limited little research project, if well designed, can be made to look so much more respectable and "scientific" than can the most justifiable request for the improvement or extension

of service. Thus, the incentive for those eager for the improvement of
service needs to bolster their operations by "pseudo-research" projects
will remain strong. The disgust with this situation among sincere
therapy- and service-oriented workers and administrators is bound to
land eventually on the innocent shoulders of "research as such." It
seems to me high time that we say this out in the open, even at the risk
of losing a "research project" or two, for neither serious research nor
properly implemented service can profit as long as the house remains
divided by unsound policies of financial support.

The Obsolete Model and the Latest Fad

If we talk about "obsolete models," we should separate them into
two categories: obsolete models of service and obsolete models of
theory. I have plenty of complaints about both but will confine myself
here to those of service. Let me breathe in passing only my complaint
that I really think even the best "models of personality" with which we
operate today are very obsolete, indeed—and that includes the ones I
myself favor. Watching the change in the complexity of our concept of
the model of an atom that has taken place in my lifetime and comparing it with the still two-dimensional proportions of most of our theories
of personality, I feel that we have a long stretch to make up for.

However, that is too large a topic to treat here, so let me hurry on
to just a few illustrations of what bothers me about the service models
that seem to me totally obsolete and that we hang on to with a tenacity
worthy of a better cause.

First of all, though, let me remind you again of what I mean when
I call something "obsolete." Maybe reference to the more commonly
understood military situation might help to keep straight our lines of
thought. It is my impression that military men in the highest strategic
positions are never so much afraid of an enemy as they are panicked
by the idea that the equipment they have may be found obsolete at the
moment when they need it. No matter how brave and courageous they
may be, they are desperately worried that something that may be in
itself quite wonderful may simply prove to be not enough or obsolete
at the time when it is needed. It seems to me that in the field of human
behavior we have not yet reached as wise, frank, and clean a point of
view. Let me add to that: When somebody says, for instance, that the

institution of foot soldiers, in modern warfare, must be considered obsolete, he does not mean that his soldiers are cowards or no good or that the men in uniform don't know what to do. He doesn't even mean that they are poorly trained. He means to say that our foot soldiers need to be even better and more marvelous than ever and that all glory should go to them. He also means, though, that the total danger situation implied in the term "warfare" can no longer be met by the institution of foot soldiers, no matter how well trained. I remind you of this point because we are likely to think less clearly when we apply the term "obsolescence" to the field of mental health and child service. When I say that certain of our institutions are "obsolete," it is in this spirit that my remarks are made.

THE HOLY TRINITY OF THE CHILD GUIDANCE TEAM

For professionals, this point should need little clarification, though it may be a painful one to contemplate. I grant you that the original model of the trinity of psychiatrist, social worker, and psychologist as "the" orthopsychiatric team—under the leadership of a medically licensed psychiatrist, no matter what the issue might be—has become classic. It was a good beginning and still has a place in our over-all service designs. In fact, most child-guidance clinics are still designed that way. This model has not become wrong. It still serves a wonderful purpose for the kids who need it. I even venture to say at least 3,000 more institutions on this model are needed right now, with no alteration at all. However, as a "model" for treatment services for the youth of our time, this holy trinity with its clear-cut "inside" status is totally obsolete. There are loads of kids whose disturbances are so different from the one for which this model was designed—and is still adequate —that new patterns are also needed for them. That we produce such new mixtures of disturbances is neither the fault of the trinity nor of the kids who show them. Some of the types of pathology we produce need services in closer proximity to the daily-life situations of the kids than the "clinic" concept allows, and other disciplines and professions are just as necessary as are the three original ones.

Other people—and their professional skills—must be involved in the "team" effort, even though they do not sit in on the clinic discussions and are not paid out of the same till. The need for team members has spread from the "psychiatric caseworker" to the caseworker to the social group worker, recreation worker, nurse, nurse's aid, and even the clinically sophisticated attendant who remains with the kids on a ward long after everybody else has gone home. The idea that the psychiatrically sophisticated nurse, the pediatrician, the public-health nurse, the teacher, and the educational therapist should never be included and the fact that even organizations committed to the interdisciplinary approach are still struggling with this idea is a hangover from obsolete concepts beyond what we can afford. We have begun to respond to the impact of these facts of life, and the struggle to incorporate "other than trinity" professions into the concept of the treatment team has made some progress during the past years. It is an arduous job to confront the original team members with the awareness that most kids spend major parts of their lives in classrooms; that the healthy learner is as important a commodity, whose mental health needs to be preserved, as is the one on your waiting lists; and that those who regulate the children's learning experiences are "psychiatrically" as important partners in our efforts as is the clinic's paid staff. I complain bitterly that we have not gone far enough at all in coming to grips with the changed reality with which we have to deal. If there is a job to be done in correcting obsolescence we have a wonderful chance to go right ahead and do it. Not tomorrow, right now. The old and "classical" trinity has become obsolete as a model for mental-health services to children. Let's not be seduced by the classical simplicity of the lines of the model into hanging on to it when it has outlived its usefulness. It takes more than "three" professions to give our kids what they need.

THE GOOD OLD ORPHANAGE—WHERE HAS IT GONE?

As you know, we ran out of orphanages, simply because we ran out of the type of orphans that nice people who finance their care would enjoy watching at a Christmas performance. The orphanage was a wonderful model in its time. There probably is no other institution that has saved the miserable lives of as many children as a really well-run good old orphanage did. Right now, though, it is no good as a model for the institutional care of children—even of undisturbed children. I hope you are with me when I insist that the claim of not wanting a bad institution for children has long ceased to be a good excuse for having none. With the new pathologies we produce and with our increased insights into the processes of institutional care, we know that we need more rather than fewer residential institutions for children. We also know that, by the time they need institutions, some of the youngsters are already too messed up for regular ones, no matter how "good," and that they need specific additions of therapy, therapeutic and remedial tutoring, special education, and so forth. Most of the children need well-implemented residential treatment centers, even though the physical facts of their lives still make it possible to list them as "orphans." How many such institutions do we have?

THE FOSTER HOME—FAST BECOMING A FRAUD

Beyond dispute is the fact that there is a need for foster homes and that there are children for whom such placement is a good answer. The idea that disturbed children are really taken care of in large numbers in our present communities by foster-home placement seems to me to come close to a fraudulent claim, however. I happen to have some close involvements with projects in this direction, and what I see happen scares me stiff and makes me foam at the mouth. It is downright grotesque that the sight of a child of ten who has already breezed through eight or nine foster-home placements doesn't remind us that he may need something else and does not destroy our naïve assumption that "a foster-home placement is still the best" thing for him. We know for how many children, who might benefit from foster-home placement, it simply is not available, especially if they belong to minorities that are discriminated against or to social classes in which foster-home placement is not considered an acceptable way of life. We also know that for many children the chances of sticking it out in a regular foster home are totally nil and that the support foster homes get financially, in consultation, and in aid is greatly limited. The support they get is totally inadequate to make them really work. The people who know this best are those who bravely and desperately work in the agencies that deal with foster-home placements. I am as depressed by their despair as I am by that of the children. The staffs, too, suffer under having to ward off feelings of deepest depression for not being able to act on what they know better at "first hand" than does anybody else—what Johnny needs and is not getting. What they have to observe about well-known and manageable misery that is not being solved but shelved and about hopeless waiting lists for what is really needed should be written up as a document in its own right. So many very disturbed children, of the degrees and variety of disturbance we happen to produce en masse in our society, are so far beyond the grip of the old concept of "foster-home care" that we can safely say: As an institution for the safeguarding of the mental health of vulnerable children, the foster home of yesterday is either extinct or not sufficient any more. It is an obsolete answer to a current problem of huge proportions. Why, then, don't we who know this become more vocal about it? Just because we have to hang on to the obsolete slogan that, even for a very disturbed child, after the neighbor's dog a "foster mother" is still the child's best friend?

Let me break off this list of obsolete models right here, and, among the "fads" that I also promised to hit at, let me, for lack of space, pick just one. I want to say something about a fad that I am especially incompetent to talk about—and maybe that is why I can afford to say it so loudly. Among the "modern fads" that have hit us so hard recently is that of using pharmaceutical products in the management of child behavior. As far as the issue of drugs is concerned, I have no quarrel about it. I know nothing about this, but this much I know and want to say: I respect the importance of the use of drugs as an issue in its own right. I am impressed with some of the wonderful possibilities they may open up in the line of support for therapy. But I want to maintain, in spite of many impressive claims, my right to raise my voice and say this much: There is a difference between the thoughtful and judicious use of drugs within the therapeutic process, on the one hand, and chemical warfare against the American child on the other. The two are not the same.

The Ghost of the Lay-Therapy Issue and How It Gums up the Works

Which organization could more appropriately raise this issue than one that so clearly believes in an interdisciplinary-team approach? Who, as a person, would have a chance to speak up on this point with as little likelihood of being called "prejudiced" as I? I guess this is a pretty strong statement—so permit me to become autobiographical for a minute, in order to put this matter into the right perspective and to make you understand why I open my mouth so wide about it.

Personally, I have no quarrel on the "lay issue" account. Rather, the fact that I do not have an M.D. degree has been a real blessing in my life. For instance, I never had to face the nightmare of immigration-conditioned exams that others had to go through in order to re-establish themselves with medical degrees. Actually, you know, I am really a privileged character in that area; every Thanksgiving Day I remember to be grateful for having only a PH.D. Besides, I am probably the only person in this country and in this field who, in spite of not having a medical degree, has been quite happily entrusted with the running of a children's psychiatric ward in a huge government research hospital. In case some of you should worry, let me hasten to add that this, of course, does not mean that adequate provisions were not made to supplement what I obviously was not equipped to do. I had plenty of psychiatrists on my staff, around me and above me, who would see to it that the medical issues for which I am not competent would not be neglected and that those provisions and securities that are legally part of hospital practice would be well taken care of. Beyond that, however, I can assure you that my leadership in determining what we would try to do was clearly accepted, and I was permitted to run the outfit, with none of my troubles coming from the issue of "degree." Don't think I am trying to say I had no troubles. On the contrary, I had plenty of them. But the troubles I had were those anybody would have who ran the type of therapy project I was running and who dragged in the type of hard-to-manage child patients we catered to. There are plenty of medical psychiatrists around and probably in this audience who could describe to you what these troubles are. Anybody who brings action-prone child patients into a hospital would have these troubles, even if he had twenty medical degrees or were president or ex-president of the American Medical Association itself.

In short, of all the people who quite obviously have no personal axes to grind, I am probably the one with the biggest responsibility to speak up on this issue.

Remember the heading? It is the *ghost* of the lay-therapy issue I want to talk about—the issue itself is too complex a theme to be raised in the remaining time. That ghost of the lay-therapy issue is sitting at our banquets; it is even sitting with us at board meetings. It is this ghost that keeps us from bringing issues out in the open, often simply because people are too tactful and polite to do so. My proposition is this: Let's stop being polite. We can't afford it any more, for there are points beyond which politeness is a worse block to progress than is hostility itself.

I think the ghost of the lay-therapy issue sitting in on our clinical feasts blocks us most on two levels. One level is better known: psychotherapy—or something close to it—done by people who have no medical degrees. On one hand, we are talking about people whom we consider well trained for the job, well equipped to do it. We have no qualms about their professional competence for psychotherapy with children. On the contrary, we are desperate for them, we wish there were more of them, for to whom would we send the kids we don't want to take on ourselves or our own children when they need help? We know, in private, but don't whisper it too loudly, that we couldn't even run our clinics without their doing a lot of the work.

The other level of the problem of lay therapy is equally important, but I find it usually swept entirely under the rug: psychotherapy with children, done by people who happen to have medical degrees and who are suddenly required to do what they really don't want to do simply because they have not been trained for it. They have had no exposure to the normal teachings in child development that any teacher or social worker would be automatically expected to go through. They have had no opportunity to get experience with children in different age groups and in open settings where children live and learn. They have had no opportunity for appropriate intensive psychotherapy with a wider range of child patients than the usual hospital clinic naturally harbors. Many of those doctors I am referring to have actually been screaming for this kind of training, but either it is not available to them or whatever "children's work" they can get into has been tacked on as a low-status item at the tail end of their training. In short, medical degree or not, these people are laymen in the field of psychotherapy with children on all but the legal counts. This is even true of some who may be well trained for psychotherapy with adults but who have never been checked on the additional characteristics and skills that go with psychotherapy with children. Many of these "lay therapists," for reasons of legality and practicality, are lured or forced into positions not only of doing but also of supervising, administering, and legitimizing psychotherapy with children beyond what, by their frank admission, their previous training has really equipped them to handle.

The ghost of the lay-therapist issue gums up the works on both these levels of the concept of lay therapy. It gums it up by reducing the training facilities for both groups that are so much needed. It gums it up for the nonmedical student by blocking the proper training of people with well-developed skills in children's work for specific forms of psychotherapy that by now we could well describe and isolate. It gums it up for the medical student because there are so few places and chances for getting the appropriate experience. The medical schools usually are far behind in their recognition of psychotherapy and counseling skills with children as a sufficiently important technical specialty in its own right. In addition, medical schools by themselves are not automatically equipped to provide the type of training and experience that "skill for children's work" demands, especially skill for work with the wide range of children's problems on which the community will later need the psychiatrist's advice.

At this point I feel impelled to add one more remark, in protection and defense of my younger medical colleagues and especially of the students. I find that public opinion has developed, for some reason, a nasty stance while implying that it is so hard to get enough psychiatrists to go into training and work primarily with children. The general implication seems to be of two varieties: that the reason for this difficulty is financial greed or financial need. One assumption is that young psychiatrists don't want to go into work with children because they can't live on it and can earn more in practice with adults. The other assumption is that young people don't go into psychotherapy with children because they can't afford it. By the time they are through the amount of economic frustration and infantilization that medical and especially psychiatric training requires, they can't afford the luxury of doing what doesn't help them pay back the money they had to borrow in order to get trained.

I personally know very well that both statements have some "reality" in them. However, as stereotypes they are wrong. I know plenty of young medical students or young psychiatrists who are finished with their training and who, even knowing that the financial sacrifice they have to make to go into child psychotherapy is a heavy one, would willingly make it. The reason they hesitate is not that they overemphasize the importance of economics but that they are too decent and conscientious to want to do something for which they know they have not been adequately trained. In fact, some of them are desperately searching for the kind of institutional setting, the kind of therapy project, the kind of counseling chance with a representative portion of the teen-age population in which they could really learn what they need to know to be helpful to the youth of our time, to their parents and the teachers who are screaming for help in the task of raising them. The thin experience offered the young doctors for a few months, frequently in a very messy, poorly staffed, and miserably programed service, and the limitation to only a few special types of pathology that hospitals can traditionally house in connection with their adult schizophrenic populations do not give my young friends the feeling of competence they want—never mind the legal privileges that come with their degrees.

This is what I mean by the "ghost of the lay-therapy issue." I think we need to ban that ghost and bring the real issues into open discussion. The lack of new people in adequate numbers for services to our children and youth is so serious that it needs to be tackled from all sides.

Treatment into What? And Why Don't We Like Mental Health?

Because this issue so frequently gets wrapped up in so many other issues, I feel like pulling it out into the limelight it needs all by itself. In a nutshell, this is what I want to say again: For much that we do and support under the term "mental health," the use of this label comes close to terminological insincerity or even terminological fraud. Much that is being carried on under that name—and financed out of its appropriations—is primarily concerned with "mental disease" as we have always understood it. Even our praised and appreciated report on mental health needs is haunted by that problem, to say nothing of the fact that support for the mental-health of children didn't seem to bother that project much.[1] In short, the symptom droppage, cure, and eradication of mental diseases, which have filled textbooks for the past seventy-five years, are good, decent, and important jobs in their own right. But there is more to the fostering and protection of mental health. The closer a project stays to the well-entrenched disease entities in their more extreme form, the easier it is to be "respectable" and to hire all those involved out of mental-health appropriations. If you do something with children who still happen to run around in classrooms or who are sick in "different" ways from those of the established mental-hospital categories, your trouble will increase. For in-

1. *Action for Mental Health: Final Report of the Joint Commission on Mental Illness and Health* (New York: Basic Books, Inc., 1961).

stance, the people essential in their treatment may be "just teachers, parents, group workers, house parents"—none of which categories rises to the height of "mental-health worker." On the other end of the line, many studies and activities are supported that are, again, perfectly important and respectable in their own right. However, they seem to me to be rather far from "mental-health" concerns. Lots of mental-health money goes into rat mazes, monkey cages, and pigeon feed. I don't mind dogs, cats, and any other animals getting all that fancy air-conditioning and well-trained care, which I have trouble requisitioning for my child patients. I am sure all this work needs to be done. In fact I consider it so important that it should be done under its own quite respectable name rather than being smuggled in under the "mental health" disguise. In short, I don't think it is good practice to cover everything that is "also important and of possible eventual benefit" under the mental-health label, for I see the areas that have closest meaning for mental-health problems and are most closely related to the places where children live and grow getting thinned out to the point of neglect.

One more word I want to say. I am worried about the fact that we still seem to be so much more comfortable with what we are treating children out of than what we are supposed to treat them into. In short, even our concept of what constitutes "improvement" frequently remains dependent on what we can count as "symptoms dropped." When we get beyond that our whole field of mental health and clinical endeavor seems to be still rather confused. It seems to me that we give more thought to what our kids are like than to what the world into which we educate and treat them is really like and to what the "reality" into which we want to reimmerse them actually holds in terms of health-supportive and health-destructive ingredients. How can we ever trust our statistics on recidivism, for instance, if we do not know what threw or supported them in their later life situations as exactly as we now know what we expose them to in corrective experiences or in therapy? Also, one concept that the public has learned to take for granted in the field of physical ailments still seems rather under-developed in our own domain, that of the requirements and importance of well-implemented convalescence.

In the field of physical diseases, the complexity of appropriate postsurgical care, to mention just one variety, has been well established and has become as respectable an endeavor as the original surgical intervention. It is not considered "sissy stuff" to help a kid for weeks after a bone operation to use the limbs that have been operated on. In the mental-health field, that is not so. The youngster is hardly out of his therapist's office or out of that special class or treatment cottage when most everybody is supposed to take care of him and decide what he is and what he isn't supposed to be able to do. The concept of a carefully designed convalescence experience, with reference to the specific therapeutic operations that have to be performed on a youngster, still needs much more specific elaboration. Worse even, the number of "settings" available for judicious discharge or transitional support of our improving kids is still unduly thin.

Something seems to me to be wrong even with the self-concept we have developed in the clinical field. If somebody fixes up a kid after a skiing accident and then somebody else comes and hits him with a sledge hammer, nobody insinuates that the previous doctor probably did a poor job. In the field of mental health, unfortunately, this analogy does not quite hold. I find us constantly bothered out of our wits and sometimes discouraged about our clinical know-how, if somebody reminds us that one of our patients or clients didn't seem to hold up so well after several years had elapsed, without much concern about the question of just what really "did it" to begin with, what the situation was really like that renewed the trauma, or whether or not the problem did lie after all in an incomplete recovery.

To make such evaluations, however, another issue first needs more study—a thorough assessment of the psychological ingredients inherent in life experiences to which children are exposed. Not only does the "life-space interview" as a device for bringing treatment situations closer to the daily scene of children's experiences need further development. We also need to bring into much sharper focus our skill at sizing up settings, environmental givens, and child-care practices in terms of those properties that have high relevance to the ego's capacity for maintaining mental health. This, however, would lead us far beyond what we can hope to contemplate right now.

Part Two

A Challenge
to Concepts
and Theories

The Life-Space Interview—Strategy and Techniques

There is no need at all for a new "school of thought" in child therapy. But there invariably arises a need for modification of existing techniques of any given school of thought, so as to fit them to the changing range of child disturbances a given society produces at a given time and to changing life conditions and the changing social scene.

When I introduced the concept of the life-space interview at the first printing of this article, I knew I was in for it. Much work has been done since, and many tryouts in clinical and school situations have been discussed in many workshops and research meetings.

With the enthusiasm about the possibilities this concept has opened up for us, I also notice the danger of its overestimation—by friends as well as enemies of the thought—or, worse still, the temptation to make an "either-or issue" out of it all or to rigidify into a memorizable list of items what was meant to be a wide-open challenge for exploratory try-out. As an example of the latter, I have found attempts to "straitjacket" my comments, which were made on basic "goal" potentials within interview situations, into a prescribed sequence, implying that any one child should be subjected to the torture of "reality rub-in," "symptom estrangement," "massaging numb value areas," and so forth down the line until finally the poor victim would certainly need the "emotional first aid" described in the subsequent pages. I hope it is clear that nothing could be further from what I am trying to convey than such nightmarish applications and that the article that follows will suffice to dispel such ideas for good. The life-space interview is really meant only as an adaptation to specific disturbance syndromes, to specific situations and specific tasks. It was not intended to displace any other techniques and was never conceived of in opposition to individual therapy, counseling, or group therapy of any sort.

"The Life-Space Interview—Strategy and Techniques" is based on "Strategy and Techniques of the Life Space Interview," *The American Journal of Orthopsychiatry* (January 1959), © 1959 by the American Orthopsychiatric Association; and on "Why Life Space Interview?" in Ruth Newman and Marjorie Keith, eds., *The School-Centered Life Space Interview*.

By the way, neither is this article meant to offer a ready-made tool but only a challenge to produce such a tool.

Child Analysis, Milieu Therapy, and the Missing Link

*L*ET US LOOK for a moment at the model of the most classical type of psychoanalytic therapy, with a patient suffering from the most classical neurosis we can possibly think of—then it seems to me that we can well make the following statements.

The peculiar ritual and the behavioral prescriptions to which the patient is bound, as well as the variety of technical tools with which the therapist arms himself, make sense only when viewed as steps to the following goals:

to isolate the patient enough from the pressures of adjustment he finds in his daily life to create purposely an atmosphere that more nearly resembles the conditions under which the roots of his neurosis developed;

to get the patient to re-create around the therapist the emotional relationships he experienced with focal people in his life at that time;

through skillful manipulation of these emotional relationships—especially those of transference—and through skillful reactions to the patient's fantasy productions and behaviors (a) to enable the patient to bring unconscious material into open manifestation (this applies not only to the id but also to unconscious ego and superego elements); (b) to help the ego recognize and handle previous experiences as well as to reorganize its own techniques so that pathological symptom formation or character distortion is not any longer necessary; and (c) to give some aid to the ego in reorienting the healthier personality thus emerging to the actual present-day tasks of life adjustment, so that dependence on therapy can safely cease.

What the therapist needs in order to accomplish all this can be well condensed into the image of a pressurized cabin. I hope you will not expect me to carry this analogy too far, but, with a model as complicated as that of psychoanalytic therapy, even a half-way usable analogy may be permissible for the purpose of abbreviated summary.

With this much speculation behind us, I should like to refer to the classical style of long-range psychoanalytically oriented therapy as therapy in the pressurized cabin, considering the establishment of such a pressurized condition of life for the patient an essential part of the model for analytic treatment. But now we had better get ready for a surprise, which, if misunderstood, might well throw our speculations off the conceptual beam, for, if we should happen to take a sound movie of what happens during a sequence of actual psychoanalytic hours with a patient in that pressurized cabin, we should be quite puzzled to find, for long stretches of time, little of what we have postulated in our model just now. Instead, we find both patient and therapist engaged in such an amazing array of activities and experiences that it would be hard to say how this relationship is supposed to be much different from what child and mother, teacher, or play leader, would do together at any other time or place. Let's hasten to add—this is only as it should be, for conceptual models are meant to extract from reality the structural lines of basic dynamics; they are not meant to mirror it. But more important, not only does the actual pattern of events in a psychoanalytic hour not look like its conceptual model; it actually contains many procedures that also do not belong in the conceptual model. Yet, without them, analytic therapy in its purer form could never be made to occur. To become specific, let's simply remember what Anna Freud[1] reminded us of in her description of what it takes to establish those moments of "real psychoanalytic work" with the child and how, sometimes for many months, even six weekly hours may be filled with activities that she terms "preparatory" to the main event.

Among those "preparatory" activities there are many that deal with the *transition* of the child from schoolroom and breakfast table at home to the "pressurized cabin" of the analytic hour and back again; others are intended to help parents and teachers understand and react to this process. Others of the therapist's "preparatory" manipulations, over and beyond his techniques used during the "pressurized hour," include "milieu manipulation" in the wider meaning of the term and contain issues all the way from safeguards against traumatic handling to the arrangement for more vitamin-rich recreational experiences in the child's natural habitat. Anna Freud's emphasis, besides, is heavy on the demand that the phases of child development and their specific needs be well planned for, and that the educational needs in a child's life be given as careful attention as the strategy of the analytic hour itself.

1. Anna Freud, *The Psycho-Analytical Treatment of Children* (London: Percy Lund Humphries & Co., Ltd., 1954).

All these "precautions" about the wide range of tasks a child analyst must not forget about, though, must not deceive us about the nature of the most "classical" therapeutic event in an analysis itself, which has to take place in the pressurized atmosphere that remains characteristic of the model of full child analysis throughout. On the other end of the continuum from the classical concept of child analysis in its "pressurized-cabin style" is the concept of total milieu therapy. In its more modest claims, this concept urges us to take all the things Anna Freud has listed under "preparatory" jobs of the child analyst more seriously and to elevate them to a therapeutic and preventive stock of interventions in their own right. In its more calculated and elaborate forms, the idea of "total milieu therapy" ranges all the way from the supportive use of specific influences and experiences in the child's life to the belief that sometimes the impact of "milieu ingredients" in its own right may bring about a "therapeutic move." We have to refrain from the challenge of offering even an abbreviated picture of "milieu therapy" in this paper[2] and only hasten to add that we, personally, can see no conflict between the pressurized-cabin style of classical analytical work and the demand for total milieu therapy as another treatment design. In fact, in the very project from which the illustrations in this paper are largely gained, a combination of both is planfully attempted.

To reap the benefit that we hoped to get from our detour through a sketch of the model of child analysis and that of milieu therapy, the following statement might be made: Different though they are from each other, the two have one thing in common—the need for taking care of a "missing link." Starting with child analysis, it is obvious that, even for a child in classical analysis six days a week, a lot of "experiences" and "issues" have to be picked up, handled, and "talked about with the child" by people other than the child's analyst. Jumping from there to the "total milieu therapy" situation, no matter how highly we treasure the influence of "environment," we cannot rely on the "environment's" always doing its job by itself. For the *experience* that exposure to a given milieu factor creates in a child is not only a function of environment but also of the readiness of this child to perceive it correctly and to deal with it in an appropriate way at the time it happens. Thus, although some milieu impacts do their job in their own right and without mediation by anybody else, more often than not

2. Further details are given in "The Concept of a 'Therapeutic Milieu,'" p. 68.

the educational or clinical adult has to become mediator between environment and child. To use but one purposely crude illustration to prepare the ground for more subtle ones:

The shower offered children as a routine requirement upon admission in many hospitals, detention homes, or other institutions may be *intended* by the institution as a relaxing support, as a gesture of friendly ablution, to make it easier to start a comfortable day in a decontaminated environment. Or it may have been introduced especially as a face-saving device, so that a less fortunate newcomer would not be conspicuous by his need for a shower, as everyone gets it anyway, routinely; or it may be planned to secure the child against exposure to hurt feelings, through the insinuations of less tactful peers that he stinks. The way this experience may be perceived by the child, however, may have no similarity whatever to its original intent. It may be experienced as a hostile accusation that the modest social background from which he comes is "dirty"; it may be perceived as the forerunner of a whole host of forcibly demanded routines that violate the spontaneity of his own need-fulfillment schedule; it may be experienced as a sharp inroad on his privacy.

It is clear, then, that even for ordinary environmental influences, in order to have the intended effects, interpretation of some sort is a *link* that cannot be omitted in this chain. Now as we all know, the correct perception of the intent of a given experience may be conveyed through many means. More often than not, the very way the adults act in a given situation is already clarifying enough. At other times, one expects a certain amount of original misinterpretation by the child but one also assumes that it will correct itself automatically in the course of time, without too many words about it. In other cases, it seems obvious that the adult has to do some talking about it.

In all those cases in which the adults find it necessary to surround a youngster's experience at a given time with some form of verbal communication that has the purpose of regulating the impact of this experience on the child, we have before us what we have begun to call the "life-space interview."

The Concept of the Life-Space Interview

It is our contention that life-space interviewing plays an important part in the lives of all children. All adults in educational roles in children's lives find themselves in many situations that can correctly be thus labeled.

It is our contention that the life-space interview assumes a mediating role between the child and what life holds for him, which becomes just as important as the interviewing that goes on within the pressurized cabin.

It is our contention that in work with seriously disturbed children, even if they are not exposed to the special type of pressurized-cabin therapy in addition to their exposure to milieu therapy, the strategically wise use and the technically correct handling of the life-space interviews held with the children are of foremost clinical importance.

It is our contention that, even when children are exposed to clearcut pressurized-cabin therapy for special phases of their problems, the wisdom and techniques used by their natural home or school-life personnel in mediating life experiences for them are of major strategic relevance in their own right.

It is, above all, our contention that what goes on in a life-space interview, even though it is held with the child by somebody not his therapist in the stricter interpretation of the term, involves as subtle and important issues of strategy and technique as do the decisions the psychoanalyst has to make during the course of a therapeutic hour.

It is our contention, last and not least, that any application of total milieu therapy in support of individual therapy or undertaken in its own right will stand or fall with the wisdom and skill with which the protectors, teachers, and interpreters in the children's lives carry out their life-space interview tasks.

It is for this reason that we shall try to subject some of the occurrences during the process of a life-space interview to the same type of scrutiny that psychiatric therapy techniques have for a long time been exposed to in our technical seminars. By the way, one more word about the term:

What we have in mind when we say "life-space interview" is the same thing that my staff, my friends, and my coworkers in our earlier Detroit projects referred to under the name of "marginal interview." The reasons for the change in term are many and seem to me so strong that they outweigh the equally obvious disadvantages of the switch. When I, and many of us in the same type of work, started talking about the marginal interview, it was pretty clear from our own context of operation and to us personally what we felt it was "marginal" to. We meant, at first, the type of therapy-like interview that a child may need around an incident of stealing from the "kitty" in his club group but that would be held right around the event itself by the group worker in charge of that club, rather than by the child's therapist—even though the same material would probably later come up in therapy too.

So, it was "marginal" in two ways: marginal in terms of the rest of the life events around which it was arranged and marginal in terms of the over-all job expectation of a group leader who used casework or therapy technique even while functioning in his group-leader role.

When I moved into the operation of a residential-treatment design[3] within a huge hospital setting, the term "marginal" lost the clarity of its meaning entirely, in addition to other disadvantages that the low-status sound of the word "marginal" seems to assume for many people.

In changing to the term "life-space interview," we apologize for the possible confusion that may be created because we are using the term here with an entirely different meaning from the one Kurt Lewin had in mind. In spite of this disadvantage, we feel that the term is at least frank in its emphasis on the major characteristics of this type of interview: In contrast to interviewing in considerable detachment from the "here and now" of Johnny's life, like the psychoanalytic play-therapy interview, the life-space interview is closely built around the child's direct life experience in connection with the issues that become the interview focus. Most of the time, it is held by a person who is perceived by the child as part of his "natural habitat or life space," with some pretty clear role and power in his daily living, as contrasted to the therapist, to whom he is sent for "long-range treatment." We are fully aware that none of the similarities or differences implied here is truly characteristic of the two operations; in fact, to find similarities

3. Whenever the "children on our ward" are mentioned, I mean children in a closed ward on the premises of the National Institute of Health, a large research hospital. The children referred to here were a carefully selected group of six boys ranging in age from eight to ten years at the time of intake, chosen as representatives of "borderline" disturbances commonly referred to as "explosive, acting-out type." They were children of normal IQs however, and were expected to be free from traceable physical pathology, characterized in their behavior by rather extreme aggression, extreme forms of reckless destruction, and an amazing array of learning disturbances and character disorders to boot. The ward on which the children lived was staffed and operated more along the lines of a camping program, with the hospital as a base, but not ultimate limit, for the activities. At the time of the presentation of this material, the movement of the children into a newly constructed open residence was imminent. The treatment and research goals of the operation included the study of the impact of intensive individual psychotherapy (four hours per child per week), of observations in our own school setting (individual tutoring as well as group school), and exposure to "milieu therapy" in their lives on the ward.

and differences is the goal, not the starting point of our research. For the time being, and until someone with more imagination and linguistic know-how gives us a better clue, we think the term is as good or bad as any we could think of to connote what we have in mind. Frankly, we aren't quite used to it ourselves, and you may find us slipping back into calling the whole thing by its old name of "marginal" more often than we may be willing to admit.

Goals and Tasks of the Life-Space Interview

First, I want to select for discussion two major categories of goals and tasks for life-space interviewing: (a) clinical exploitation of life events and (b) emotional first aid on the spot. The difference between these two categories does not lie in the nature of the events around which the need for the life space-interview arises—we shall in the future refer to this event as the "issue"—but in our decision about what we want to do with the interview. It is also defined, of course, by the question of just what the situation itself allows.

Let's assume that a group of children is just about ready to go out on that excursion it has anticipated with eagerness for quite a while. Let's assume there is, through our fault, some delay at the door because of a last-minute search for lost shoes, footballs, and so forth, so that irritability mounts in the gang that is already assembled and raring to go. Let's further assume that in the ensuing melee of irritated bickering two of our youngsters get into a flare-up, which ends with Johnny's getting socked more vehemently than he can take, furiously running back to his room, cursing his tormentor and the world at large and all educators in particular, and swearing that he will "never go on no trip no more in his whole life." We find him just about to soak himself in a pleasurable bath of self-pity, nursing his grudge against people in general, and adding up new evidence for his theory that life is no good, people are mean "so-and-so"s anyway, and autistic daydreaming is the only safe way out.

Well, most of us would feel that somebody ought to move into this situation. The staff member who tries to involve the sulking child in a life-space interview at this time has a choice of doing either of two things.

He may want to be with John in his misery and to assist the child in disentangling the complicated web of emotions in which he is so hopelessly caught, simply in order to "get him over it" right here and now, to get him back into his previous anticipation of enjoyment. This situation seems to be quite comparable to the concept of "first aid"; the organism is capable of taking care of a wound produced by a minor cut, but it might be wise to help it.

On the other hand, depending on how much time there is and how Johnny reacts to the adult's interview strategy, the adult may suddenly find that this opportunity gives him a long-hoped-for chance to help John come to grips with an issue in his life that the staff has so far had little opportunity to bring to his awareness. He may forget about his intention to get John back to his original cheerful excursion-anticipating mood; he may even give in to his sulky insistence that he "wasn't going to go nohow," but he may decide to use this special opportunity to start on an interpretational job. He may begin to tie this event up for John with many similar previous ones, hoping to help John see how he really "asks for it" many times, even though he has no idea that he does so, how his irritably rude provocation or lashing out at other children often gets people infuriated, or whatever the special version of this perennial theme may be. In short, half an hour later our interviewer may be driving after the rest of the group with a somewhat sadder but wiser companion at his side, or he may at least have laid the groundwork for some such insight to sink in at a future opportunity or to be picked up by the boy's therapist at a later opportunity in case John happens also to be "in individual therapy" of the more classical style.

By the way, most of the time we can't be sure before an interview under which of the two goal categories it will eventually have to be listed, for we may in the middle of an interview find good enough reason for a switch from the original intent with which we entered the scene.[4]

This differentiation between "emotional first aid on the spot" and "clinical exploitation of life events," however, still leaves us with two rather comprehensive categories before us. I feel that the practitioners among you would like it better if we broke those wider concepts down into smaller units and thus brought them closer to the observational scene.

4. More detailed illustrations for this concept of "clinical exploitation of life events" can be found in *Controls from Within* (New York: The Free Press, 1952), where this concept was first developed; and in an unpublished paper by Joel Vernick, "Illustrations of Strategy Problems in Life Space Interviewing Around Situations of Behavioral Crises."

The Clinical Exploitation of Life Events

Our attempts at pulling out of a life experience, in which a given child is involved, whatever clinical gain might be drawn from it for our long-range treatment goals, may assume some of the following special forms.

REALITY RUB-IN

The trouble with some of our youngsters, among other things, is that they are socially nearsighted. They can't read the meanings of events in which they get involved, unless we use huge script for them and underline it all in glaring colors besides. Others are caught in such well-woven systems of near-to-delusional misinterpretations of life that even glaring contradictions in actual fact are glided over by their eyes unless their views are arrested and focused on them from time to time. More fascinating even are the youngsters whose preconscious perceptions of the full reality are all right but who have such well-oiled ego skills in alibi-ing to their own consciences and rationalizing to any outside monitor's arguments that the pictures of situations that can be discussed with them are already hopelessly repainted by the time we get there. It is perhaps not necessary to add how important it is, strategically speaking, that such children have some of this "reality rub-in" interviewing done right then and there, preferably by persons who themselves have been on the scene or are at least known to be thoroughly familiar with it.

SYMPTOM ESTRANGEMENT

In contrast to those of their more clearly neurotic contemporaries, our children's egos have, in part at least, become subservient to the pathological mechanisms they have developed. They have learned well how to benefit from their symptoms through secondary gains and are therefore in no way inclined to accept the idea that something is wrong with them or that they need help. A large part of the "preparatory" task at least, without successful completion of which the magics of the more classical forms of individual therapy are rather lost on these children, consists in alienating their egos from their symptoms. Hopeful that there must be, somewhere, parts of their ego functions that have not been swallowed by pathology, that are waiting for a chance to speak up, we use many of their life situations to try to pile up evidence that their pathologies really don't pay or that the children pay too heavily for what meager secondary gains they draw from the pathologies, or that the glee they are after can be much more regularly and reliably drawn from other forms of problem-solving or pursuit of life and happiness. By the way, the assumption in all this is not that one can simply argue such children, through well-placed life-space strategy, into letting go of their symptoms; part of the job has to be tackled, in addition, by many other means. However, we can enlist part of their insights into helping their egos want to liberate themselves from the loads of their pathologies. To make it possible for them, even after they want to, to shuffle off the unconscious coils of their neuroses is an issue in its own right. We also ought to remember at this point how important it is that symptom estrangement be pursued consistently by all the staff all the way down the line. It would do little good to talk in interviews about the inappropriateness of their symptomatic actions if the social reality in which they live made it too hard for them to let go of those very symptoms. Our actions definitely have to be well attuned to our words in this task more than in any other.

Massaging Numb Value Areas

No matter how close to psychopathic our children may sometimes look, we haven't found one of them yet who didn't have lots of potential areas of value appeal lying within him. But, although the arm is still there, circulation has stopped. Value sensitivity for which a child's inner self has been liberated still needs to be *used*, and something has to be done to get circulation going again. Admitting value sensitivity, just like admitting hunger for love, is quite face-losing for our youngsters. There are, however, in most youngsters some value areas that are more exempt from peer-group shame than others. For instance, even at a time when our youngsters would rather be seen dead than overconforming and sweet, the appeal to certain codes of "fairness" within their fight-provocation ritual is quite acceptable to them. Thus, in order to ready the ground for "value arguments" altogether, the pulling out of issues of fairness or similar values from the debris of their daily life events may pay off handsomely in the end.

New Tool Salesmanship

Even the most classicism-conscious therapists confess from time to time that they spend quite some effort helping youngsters see that there are other defenses than the ones they are using and that doing this may at least partially widen the youngsters' adaptational skills. The therapist, however, who operates in the "pressurized cabin" of a long-range, classical, individual-therapy design cannot afford to waste too much of his effort in this direction, or he will puncture the pressure-safe walls he has spent so much time building up to begin with. So, as soon as the potential to use such mechanisms has been liberated in individual therapy, the adults who "live" with those children can begin to use many of their life experiences to help them draw visions of much wider ranges of potential reactions to the same messes. Even the seemingly simple recognition that seeking out an adult to talk it over with is so much more reasonable than lashing out at nothing in wild fury may need to be worked at hard for a long stretch of time with some of the children I have in mind.

The life-space interview offers a chance to leave the more general level of propaganda for better adjustment tools and to become quite specific in the demonstration of the all-too-obvious inadequacy of the special tool previously chosen by the child. In this respect we feel the same advantage that the salesman may feel who, beside having leaflets to distribute, is given the opportunity to demonstrate.

MANIPULATION OF THE BOUNDARIES OF THE SELF

From time to time one invariably runs into a child who combines with the rest of his explosive acting-out type of borderline aggressive pathology, a peculiar helplessness toward a process we like to refer to as group-psychological suction. Quite vulnerable to even mild contagion sparks, he is often discovered by an exceptionally brilliant manipulator of group-psychological currents, and then he easily drifts into the pathetic role of the perennial "sucker" of an exploitation-happy subclique.

The life-space interview, of course, offers a strategic opportunity to begin to move in on this. To illustrate what we mean by this concept of "manipulation of the boundaries of the self"—and leaving out all details of life-space strategy employed in the case—the following example may serve:

Several months ago, we felt that the time was ripe to "move in" on the problems of one of our youngsters around "group-psychological suction," so we decided to exploit incidents of this sort wherever they might happen, through an increased use of "life-space interviews." We felt good when eventually the following incident occurred one day in school: Two boys of the subclique that enjoyed exploiting this youngster were hard at work to get him to "act up" for them. This time their wiles didn't seem to get them anywhere; in fact, in the process of accomplishing their job they got out of hand themselves and got themselves "bounced." They were hardly out of the room when the youngster in question turned to the teacher, with a relieved look on his face, and declared, "Gee, am I glad I didn't get sucked into this one."

Many of our children are more ready than one would assume at first sight to expand their concepts of the wider boundaries of their selves to include other people, benign adults, their groups, the whole institution to which they feel a sense of belonging, and so on. In an entirely different direction, again, we may want to use life incidents to help youngsters with the problem of acceptance of their selves, or of hitherto split-off parts of them. Anything that educators describe under terms like "encouragement" or "inculcating a feeling of worth and pride," anything that betrays confused attitudes of the children toward their "selves" in the form of despondency coupled with megalomanic illusions, and so forth, might well be grouped under this heading.

In summary, we should underline the implication that these five goals for the use of the life-space interview are meant to be illustrative rather than system-binding. In all the instances we have raised so far, the real goal of the life-space interviewers was the clinical exploitation of given life events. It meant making use of momentary life experiences in order to draw out of them something that might be of use for long-range therapeutic goals.

Emotional First Aid on the Spot

Although children are exposed to therapeutic long-range work on their basic pathologies, it is important to remember that they are still forced to live with their symptoms until they finally can shed them and that child development is also still going on. For, although it is true that our children are sick enough to deserve the term "patients," we must never forget that child patients are still growing youngsters. This means that the adults who accompany them during the various phases of their growth are also needed as aides on the spot in those adjustment demands of daily life that they cannot well manage on their own. It is our contention that this in itself is an important enough task to deserve special technical attention and that the opportunity for such "aid in conflict" includes the situations we term "life-space interviews." The emphasis here lies on the fact that emotional first aid in itself is a perfectly valid reason for a carefully planned life-space interview, even when the special issue around which the interview is built promises no long-range gain of the kind described in the previous section. As illustration of the first-aid goals a given life-space interview may set itself, we should like to enumerate again five randomly assembled subcategories.

DRAIN-OFF OF FRUSTRATION ACIDITY

Even normal children easily experience as something quite infuriating the interruption of the pleasurable exploits in which they happen to be engaged. This is especially unfortunate with our type of child who has such low frustration tolerance, for he is overaggressive and hostility-projective to begin with. It is here that the life-space interview has an opportunity to serve as an over-all hygienic device. In sympathetic communication with the child about his anger or justified disgust at the discomfort of having been interrupted, we can drain off the surplus of intervention-produced hostility and thus avoid its being added to the original reservoir of hate. Such situations offer themselves especially when something has gone wrong with a planned enterprise or when the mere need to maintain a schedule may force interruption.

SUPPORT FOR THE MANAGEMENT OF PANIC, FURY AND GUILT

The trouble with many children is, not only that they have more feelings of anxiety, panic, shame, guilt, fury than they should or than the normal child would experience, but also that they don't know what to do with such states of mind when they get into them. We have already complained, in *Children Who Hate*,[5] about how difficult it is to help such children react correctly even if they do feel guilty when they should. It is important, then, that the adult intervene and give first aid as well as therapeutic support whenever heavier quantities of such emo-

---

5. Redl and Wineman, *Children Who Hate* (New York: The Free Press, 1951), or in the combined edition, *The Aggressive Child* (New York: The Free Press, 1957), pp. 488–517.

tions hit the child or the group. In our own over-all strategy plan, for instance, we consider it important that an adult always stay with the child, no matter how severe his tantrum attack may become. The knowledge that we are just as interested in protecting him from his own exaggerated wishes as from the bad intents of other people has been found quite ego-supportive in the long run. By being with the child right after the excitement of a blowup abates, the adult can often help the child "put things back into focus and proportion" again. He can also aid him in the return to the common course of activities or social life of the day without the sour aftertaste of unresolved hurt.

COMMUNICATION MAINTENANCE IN MOMENTS OF RELATIONSHIP DECAY

There is one reaction of our children to experiences of emotional turmoil that we fear more than any other they may happen to produce —and that is the total breaking off of all communication with us and full-fledged retreat into an autistic world of fantasy into which we are not allowed to penetrate. We get scared because, with children at the borderline of psychotic withdrawal from any and all reality, this weapon of defense against help from us is the most efficient one.

It is used especially frequently when events force us to a clear-cut form of intervention in a youngster's behavior, the nature of which seems, at first sight, to offer an especially "clear-cut" point of argument or interpretation to the child. Yet at this very moment he is liable to drop all relationships with us and thereby to make us quite helpless in our attempt to offer sympathy, explanation, or support. Often, for instance, after a particularly vicious attack upon another child, a youngster will misperceive the motives for the intervention of a protective and battle-interrupting adult to such a degree that he interprets even the most well-handled interruption of the fight as rude and hostile "betrayal." To this he reacts with such resentment that the breakdown of all previously established relationships with that adult seems imminent. It is important that this process be stopped right then and there and that we prevent the next step in the youngster's defensive maneuver, the withdrawal of all communication and the total flight into autistic daydreams. Often, in such a moment, it is obvious that nothing we can do will make any impact on the hopelessly misconceived image in the youngster's mind. However, our attempt to involve the youngster in some form of communication may prevent the next level of retreat from us right then and there. So we surrender any plan to "talk to the point" but simply try to keep communication flowing between child and adult, no matter on what theme and no matter how trivial or far removed it may be from the issue at hand.

REGULATION OF BEHAVIORAL AND SOCIAL TRAFFIC

This specific task of the life-space interview doesn't look like much, and we have become painfully aware that people have a tendency to consider it too "superficial" and undignified to be included in items of such high status as the discussion of "interview techniques." Yet our respect for the clinical importance of our service as a social and behavioral traffic cop has gone up, if anything, over the last ten years. The issue itself is simple enough and doesn't need much explaining. The performance of the task, however, may get so difficult that it is easily comparable to the most delicate problems that may emerge in individual therapy with either children or adults.

The facts of the situation are these: The children know, of course, what over-all policies, routines, and rules of the game of social interaction are in vogue in a given place. But, no matter how well they "know," to *remember* the relevance of a given issue for a given life situation is a separate task, and to muster enough ego force at the moment to subject impulsivity to the dictates of an internalized concept of rules is still another. Thus the service they need becomes very similar to the job the traffic cop, when functioning at his best, performs for adults, and even the most law-abiding ones among us may need help from time to time. He reminds us of the basic rules again or warns us of the special vicissitudes of the next stretch. He may point out to us where we deviate dangerously even though we happen to be lucky this time. As people do not necessarily learn even from dramatic experience unless they are aided by benign and accepted guides, it may be important to go, in a subsequent session, through a stretch of behavioral confusion and to use it for reinforcement of our over-all awareness of the implications of life. As our children are especially allergic to moralizing or preaching or lecturing of any kind, it would not do to offer them a condensed handbook of behavioral guidelines. It is important to subdivide that phase of their social learning into a number of aids given on the spot when needed most.

For example, we have a clear-cut policy on our ward about the child's going to our school sessions and about the reasons for this, as well as the course of events that will take place if a child gets himself "bounced" temporarily. We have spent great effort to have everybody live up to this policy consistently so that the unanimous attitude of all adults involved can ·rve as an additional nonverbal reinforcer of the basic design. Yet, in order for all this to become meaningful and finally incorporated and perceived as part of the over-all structure of "life in this place" for our children, it took hundreds of life-space interviews surrounding school events.

UMPIRE SERVICES—IN DECISION CRISES AS WELL AS IN LOADED TRANSACTIONS

The children often need us for another function, which may sound simple though the need for it may be emphatic and desperate: to umpire. This umpiring role in which we see ourselves put may be a strictly internal one. It assumes the flavor of our helping them decide between the dictates of their "worse or better selves." For those instances, our role resembles that of a good friend whom we ourselves might take along shopping, hoping he would help maintain more vision and balance in the weighing of passionate desire versus economic reason than we might be capable of in the moment of decision-making. However, we wouldn't want to restrict this term to its more subtle, internal use. We envision it as going all the way from the actual umpiring of a fight or dispute, of a quarrel about the game rules in case of conflict or confusion, to the management of "loaded transactions" in the children's social lives. Into the last category fall many complicated arrangements about swapping, borrowing, trading, and so forth, the secondary backwash from which may be too clinically serious to be left to chance at a particular phase. Many such situations, by the way, offer wonderful opportunities to do some "clinical exploitation of life events." But, even if nothing else is obtained in a given incident of this kind, the hygienic regulation and the emotionally clean umpiring of internal or external disputes are perfectly legitimate and most delicate clinical jobs in their own right.

Summarizing all this, we should like to emphasize what we have tried to imply all along: All these "goals"—the strategic exploitation type, as well as the moment-geared emotional first-aid ones—may be combined sometimes in one and the same interview, and we shall often see ourselves switching goals in midstream. We probably need not even add that the type of goal we set ourselves at a given time in our project would also be strongly influenced by the phase the children find themselves in in their individual therapy and, of course, just where they are in their movement from sickness to mental health. In fact, "stepping up" and "laying off" in respect to selecting special issues for life-space interviews are in themselves important parts of the over-all coordination of individual therapy and the other aspects of our thera-peutic attack on the pathology of a given child.

Speculations about Strategy and Technique

The importance of a clinically highly sophisticated concept of strategy and technique in regard to the life-space interview is taken for granted in this discussion by now. That this short paper cannot hope to do more than open up the issues and point at the need for more or-ganized research seems equally obvious. In view of this, it may seem most advisable to concentrate on one of the core problems of all dis-cussions on strategy and technique, the question of indications and counterindications, and to draw attention to some of the most urgent aspects that need further elaboration soon. When we say "indications and counterindications," by the way, we mean both indications and counterindications for the holding of life-space interviews to begin with, as well as indications and counterindications for specific tech-niques or for establishing or abandoning specific strategic moves. The question "Should I keep my mouth shut, or should I interpret this dream right now?" which is an issue so familiar to us from discussions of individual therapy, has its full analogy in life-space interview work.

The following criteria seem to turn up most often in our own discussions of technique.

CENTRAL THEME RELEVANCE

By this term we mean the impact of over-all strategy in a given therapeutic phase on the question of just what situations we should move in on and what issues we should select for life-space interview pickup. It would not do to surround the children with such a barrage of attempts to exploit their life experiences for clinical gains that it would disturb the natural flavor of child life that must be maintained; and too much first aid would contain the danger of overdependency or adult-intervention oppression that we certainly want to avoid. As an example, at certain stretches we purposely keep away from "talking" too much about our previously mentioned youngster's proneness to allow himself to be played for a sucker. It is only after certain over-all therapeutic lines have emerged that we decide in unison that such inci-dents should from now on be exploited more fully. It is felt, at such a particular time, that the child's individual therapist will welcome such supportive rub-in from without.

EGO PROXIMITY AND ISSUE CLARITY

The first is an old standby, well known from clinical discussions in classical psychoanalytic work. One simply does not sail interpretively into material that is at the time so "deeply repressed" that stirring it up would only unnecessarily increase resistance or lead to marginal problems in other areas. On the other hand, material of high ego proximity had better be handled directly, else the child might think we are too dumb or too disinterested to notice what he himself has figured out long since on his own. The same issue remains, of course, an important criterion in life-space interview work.

The item of issue clarity is a more intricate one and becomes especially complex because of the rapidity with which things move on the behavioral scene of children's lives and because of the many factors that may crowd themselves into the picture. Just one brief illustration of what we are trying to point out:

Johnny has just attacked another youngster viciously, really undeservedly. The other child's surprise and the whole situation are so crystal clear that this time we are sure that even our insight-defensive Johnny will have to let us show him how he really asked for it all—so, here we stand, our clinical appetites whetted while we watch the fight. But—wham—a third child interferes. He happened to run by and couldn't resist the temptation of getting into the brawl, and he is a youngster Johnny has a lot of hostile feeling about anyway. Before anybody quite knows what has happened, Johnny receives from that interfering youngster a blow much too heavy and unfair for anybody's fight ritual, and so, of course, Johnny leaves the scene howling with fury, pain, and shame at losing face. Obviously, we had better assist Johnny in his predicament, but the idea of using this life-space interview for a push in the direction of Johnny's insight into the provocativeness of his behavior seems downright ridiculous at this point.

ROLE COMPATIBILITY

Children who live in an institutional setting do not react to individual people as "persons" only. There is also a direct impact brought to bear on them from the very "role" they perceive a particular adult to be in. This issue has long been obscured by the all too general assumption that the personal relationships between child and adults are the only things that count. To illustrate this point:

When a camp counselor finds her whole cabin up on the roof where they know they shouldn't be, she may have trouble getting them down no matter how much the children may all love her. I, as the camp director walking in on that scene, may find it much easier to get them off the roof; in fact, they may climb down as soon as they see me coming along. This does not mean that they have less good relationships with their counselor or better ones with me. It simply means a difference in their role expectations. The counselor is seen by them in the role of the group leader, which has a heavy flavor of one who plans happy experiences with them. It is true that on the margin of this role they do know that the adult counselor also has certain "overgroup-demanded" regulations to identify herself with and to enforce. However, that part of her role—and for the sake of a happy camp experience we hope so—is less sharply in focus than the program-identified one. In fact, if that counselor gets too fussy or too indignant about the youngsters' not responding immediately or uses the argument of the overall camp regulations against her gang too fast, she would create resentment and a loss of subsequent relationship for a while. The role of the camp director, no matter how cordial individual feelings toward him may be, is much more clearly loaded with the expectation that it is his job to secure overall coordination of many people's interests. The children therefore expect the director to demand that they get off that roof and do not hold it so much against him that he does interfere with the pleasure of the moment or considers the whole camp more important than Cabin 7 at this time.

The compatibility of the major role of a given adult with the role he is forced into by the life-space interview is an important strategic consideration. In our present operation, for example, we felt, during the first year or so, that it was quite important that the role of the counselor be rather sharply set off from that of the ward boss, the teacher, the therapist. During that phase it also seemed important for us to protect the counselor from too many unnecessary displaced hostilities, as she had enough to do to handle those that would naturally come her way. In short, during that period of time we felt it important that all requests to go home or for special prolonged week-end visits, and so forth be steered to the psychiatrist, who was seen as the ward boss by the children. The transference character of many of these requests and the terrific ambivalence of the children about them, on top of all the aggression manipulation a counselor has to cope with anyway in her daily play life with the children, would have increased the ensuing confusion. The arrangement we created allowed the ward boss to absorb some of the extra frustration acidity unavoidably generated during such interviews, whereas the counselor was, so to speak, "taken off that hook." At the same time, however, we did feel that the counselor was the most natural person to assist the child in first aid interviews around his concern about home, his mother's not turning up for a visit, and so forth.

MOOD MANAGEABILITY—THE CHILD'S AND OUR OWN

With due respect to all the clinical ambition any staff member can have to manage his own mood, there is a limit beyond which he cannot be forced any further. Such limits should be recognized. Oversimplifying the issue for purposes of abbreviation:

If I work for an hour in order to get the children finally in shape to be quite reasonable and have a good stretch of quite happy and unusually well-modulated play with me, I can't possibly act concerned enough if one of them does something that needs a more serious "reality rub-in" for good measure. This is especially the case when I allow a child to perform his "cute antics" for the service of everybody's entertainment and when he suddenly begins to go too far. Even a serious talk with someone who quite visibly found the same antics cute two minutes ago will not have the same strategic chance as a talk with one who was not involved in the original scene.

The item of mood manageability is, of course, an even more difficult one as far as the moods of the children are concerned. The issue may be clear enough and the event beautifully designed to draw some learning out of it. If a youngster in the meantime gets over-excited, bored, tired, or grouchy, the best laid-out issue will be hopelessly lost, and we had better look for another occasion for the same job.

ISSUES OF TIMING

One of the great strategic advantages of the life-space interview is the very flexibility in timing that it offers us. We don't have to hope that the child will remember from Friday noon until his therapy hour next Wednesday what was happening just now. We can talk with him right now. Or having watched the event that led to a messy incident, we can quite carefully calculate how long it will take the youngster to cool off enough to be accessible to some reasonable communication with him, and we can move in on him at that very calculated time. Or we may even see to it that he gets enough emotional first aid from us or from our colleagues so that he can be brought into a state in which some insight-focused discussion is possible at last. One of the most frequent dilemmas that aggressive and explosive children force us into is the fear of waiting too long to talk about something, because we know how fast they forget, as opposed to the need to let some cooling off take place, lest the interview itself be shot through with the aggression debris left over from the original scene. Sometimes external things happen, and the "time" aspect may often work against us. I shall never forget a painful experience several years ago when I finally had succeeded in working a bunch of quite recalcitrant delinquents into a mood conducive to my talking with them about an issue they didn't want to face. Just then the swimming bell put a rude end to my efforts. To keep them one minute longer while they heard and saw everybody else running down for the beloved free swim would have made a shambles out of my carefully built up role as interpreter of the rules of life.

THE IMPACTS OF TERRAIN AND PROPS

Both the life-space interview and the more classical styles of individual therapy recognize the importance of terrain and props. In long-range therapy, after we have figured out the most goal-supportive arrangements, the problem of terrain and props loses its importance because it can easily be held constant or can at least be kept under predictable control. Although the most favorable terrain is always the one in which both partners feel most comfortable, in life-space interviewing the terrain may be terrifically varied, and neither it nor the selection of props is often within our power.

In fact, more often than not, terrain and props are on the side of the child's resistance, rather than on our side. This is, of course, especially true when we move in on a situation involving extreme behavioral conflict.

For the child, the most comfortable place may be the one behind his most belligerently cathected defenses. From bathtub to toy cabinet, from roof or treetop to "under the couch," his choice of terrain seems endless. In all cases the problem of what emotional charges the surrounding props may suddenly assume remains of high technical relevance. Beside what is going on between the two people, what is going on between them and space and props can be highly relevant.

In summary, the choice of a given technique must be dependent on the specific goal we have in mind within a given setting with a specific type of child in a given phase of his therapeutic movement.[6] There is no "good" or "bad" technique in itself. The very procedure that "made" one situation all by itself may be the source of a mess-up in another or may be irrelevant in a third. This reminder, although disappointing, should not be too hard to take, for we have learned that lesson from the development of concepts of strategy and techniques for the psychiatric interview long ago. Rather than relearn it, we simply need to remember the difference between a pseudoscientific technical trick bag and a more complex, but infinitely more realistic, concept of multiple-item conditioned choice of criteria for the selection of strategy as well as of techniques.

Why "Life-Space Interview"?

OUT OF WHICH ROOTS?

The roots of the techniques lead us back into four separate directions.

INDIVIDUAL THERAPY

We are by now in possession of a well-developed and fairly well-established instrument for the treatment of disturbed children, which is frequently referred to as the psychiatric interview technique. Basically, we subsume under this name at this moment a wide range of endeavors, all the way from the most orthodox, restricted psychoanalysis of children with classical neuroses through psychotherapy and play therapy. We include psychiatric casework or casework treatment, and indeed, addressing ourselves to school people, we include any form of thorough and depth-oriented counseling—never mind who is doing it. For all these efforts have in common the awareness that talking with kids or playing with them is not enough if you hope to help them with the disturbances by which they—or you—are plagued.

6. Many of the illustrations used in this paper must be understood as limited by the specific conditions under which the observations were made. For their full evaluation, a detailed description of the over-all program and ward policies for the clinical management of the children and the guidance of staff behavior would have to be added here. It is, therefore, expected that most of our illustrations will have to be read with this reservation in mind. Although literal translation into practice with other children in different settings is not intended, we do imply emphatically that the basic principles we are trying to illustrate here should hold for a wide variety of designs.

There is a plan in this madness; a whole cluster of well-developed interview techniques can be described, delineated, and demonstrated, and people can be trained in them—and must be, if the kids are to be helped. Of course, the range of what is implied under the challenge of "interview technique" is wide indeed. It varies with the specific theoretical orientation and professional affiliation of the person who is attempting it. It varies, too, with the age, developmental phase, social background, and disturbance type of the child or youth being treated. Equally it varies with the setting in which the child is to be treated, as well as with the over-all societal value system into which the child is supposed to fit. But never mind all this right now. For the moment, and for the point I am trying to make, it is enough to remember that there is a whole tool shed full of strategies and techniques that are being used in talking or playing with kids in such a way that their disturbances, hopefully, will be forced to disappear.

There is one other thing the various schools of thought and training have in common. When we talk about individual therapy on any one of these levels, we take for granted that somebody is clearly in the role of the therapist and that the setting in which this process operates is a reasonably private tête-à-tête between adult and child. Also, we hope that whoever does the job will be permitted exemption from any other roles in that child's life. At least he must be exempt from any role that might conflict with the therapeutic goal.

CLINICAL GROUP WORK WITH DISTURBED CHILDREN
OR GROUP THERAPY

Which of the two terms you prefer will depend on how fussy about legal rights to the term "therapy" you or the specific outfit engaged in seeing the children happen to be.

The assumption here is that we are still talking about disturbed children and that their disturbances are well-enough ingrained so that some special process has to be added to whatever else we do with them, in order to bring about a cure.

Let me substitute for a lengthy elaboration of this theme just one confession out of the long chain of painful dilemmas with which those of us who are guilty of the development of the life-space interview were confronted.

Scene. The scene was the "Detroit Group Project" in the late Forties or early Fifties, a club of about eight nine-to-twelve-year-old boys and girls, all referred to us by a child-guidance clinic, social agency, or school social worker (visiting teacher). Most of these children had also been worked with intensively by their own therapists or caseworkers within the frameworks of the referring agencies. Referral was based on the assumption that the specific disturbance syndrome of these kids made it mandatory that, beyond the treatment they were getting in individual therapy or casework, they also be provided with a group-psychological atmosphere of a certain type and with a clinically guided and carefully designed activity group.

In charge of such a group was a well-trained group worker who had appropriate sophistication about individual casework and who also had the type of information provided by most psychiatrically oriented schools of social work.

Situation. Mary was not really a delinquent, but from time to time swiping stuff had been one of her ways to deal with some of her personal problems and childhood neurotic trends. Recently, things had begun to disappear from the club and money from the club kitty. Although nobody could say for sure, the rest of the group had a strong inkling that Mary might be the reason.

Result. There emerged an irritability on the side of both parties—the group and Mary—and a trend in the group toward the exclusion and scapegoating of Mary. On Mary's part there was perceptibly greater orneriness and downright meanness and a marked increase in incidents that required handling by the group leader.

Incident. One day the situation finally came to a flare-up. The kids apparently challenged Mary about the disappearing money. Mary ran out of the room and slammed the door. There she was outside. She was crying at first, then sulking, and, of course, she refused ever to go back in there again. Meanwhile, back in the room, the rest of the group wavered between triumphant sneers and downright gleeful threats of "Let's go after her."

Predicament. It was obvious that something had to be done. *Right then*—not the following week when the child would see her therapist again. The group leader, extraordinarily well trained in individual casework, clinical group leadership, and designing activity programs, found herself in a serious dilemma. She did the right thing and handled all phases of it superbly. But what a conflict for her between her role as she thought she ought to conceive it and her imagined intrusion on the role of Mary's therapist! So, of course, in the next supervisory staff session she questioned her own procedure.

Questions. "I *had* to talk with Mary, myself, then. How else could I get her back into the room, no matter how well I had prepared the group for her re-entry? I had to talk to *her*. But Mary has a therapist of her own. As I, too, am doing such work with other kids, I know how her therapist might feel about my intruding on Mary's psychic life. But, on the other hand, in order to get anywhere with Mary, I need to apply the best I know from psychiatric interview technique. Yet it is obvious that I do not want to overlap or interfere with what Mary's therapist might want done. But, of course, what I want to use my technique for is not to deal with the whole problem of Mary's neurosis but primarily to help her in her momentary predicament. And I mean her internal predicament as well as the external one of helping her back into the group.

"How can I know how far to interpret to her what she has done and why she is doing it? How far can I make open use of what I know about her case? Which of these themes of her life patterns and psychodynamics am I free to refer to; which of them must I be careful to stay a mile away from?"

It is obvious that, in this case at least, our group worker could not have waited until Mary had her next therapy appointment. The state of mind Mary was in had to be handled right at that moment, in as delicate and thoughtful a way as possible and using as technically skillful an approach as any required in an individual therapy session.

In short, somebody had to use depth-oriented interview techniques with Mary right there and then. In this particular case it had to be done by the very person who also played an important part in the club group in which Mary's symptom of swiping had occurred. This is just one instance in which we could not wait until a child returned to the confines of a hygienically constructed private cabin. We have to act at the moment when the conflicted behavior occurs. The same person who is involved in other relationships in the child's real life has to do the interviewing. Furthermore, the interview has to be held in close proximity to the life events that lead up to the open conflict.

THE CASE OF THE "MALADJUSTED DISEASE"

No, this is not a joke; I really mean it. And it is not a misprint. I did *not* want to say "the case of the maladjusted patient." I really meant the maladjusted disease.

Even in straight medical history, there are always times when given disease entities fit exactly the types of knowledge, implementation, and skill that medicine happens to have available at that moment. For example, a simple case of acute appendicitis is a very well-adjusted disease. We know all about it; we know exactly how to take the appendix out; we have hospitals, surgical instruments, lots of well-trained surgeons, and lots of assistants who are well aware of the basic laws of hygiene and convalescence so that they can take good care of the patient and his wound while healing proceeds. Of course, a patient with appendicitis is still sick, but it is a nice sickness that politely bows to the contemporary state of our knowledge, implementation, and personnel. Compare with the accommodating appendicitis the sudden appearance of a new virus that creates a new type of pneumonia. What a maladjusted disease that is! All the medication we have brewed, which is so good for other types of pneumonia, doesn't work. The new variety of disease does not fit the tools we have ready and waiting.

But let's go back to the children, where things get even worse. We don't even have what we need for the "well-adjusted" mental disorders, that is, for good classical cases of hysteria or anxiety neurosis. They are well-adjusted diseases in terms of our present knowledge. We know enough about them to know exactly what to do. The only trouble is we don't have enough psychiatrists available to do it. Nor do we have enough money for those people who can't afford to have such expensive diseases. In contrast to such comfortably familiar neuroses, we are now producing ever-increasing quantities of disease entities for which our psychiatric tools are not designed.

These new diseases consist of syndromes for the treatment of which even the most elaborate "classical" interview technique is hardly an answer. Some of the children don't remember long enough and distort too fast. What good does it do to talk with them next Wednesday about feelings they may have had last Friday? Some of the childhood disturbances we produce are accompanied by severe disabilities to conceive of cause, effect, and time. Neither past nor future means much to Billy. All that has meaning to him is what happens right now. Even just five minutes before or after is already too long. Or some of the disturbances we produce in such quantities are also accompanied by peculiar inabilities to relate to people in artificial situations, either too remote from the here and now or too different from the aura of "home base." Some kids just cannot develop therapeutic relationships in the office or consultation room of the clinic or guidance center. To become meaningful to a child with such a disease, an adult must be perceived as part of daily life: as someone like a teacher, play leader, camp counselor, uncle, or even cop, provided he is a decent one. This form of disturbance is diametrically opposed to that of the classical neurosis.

In a classical neurosis, the therapeutic relationship works exactly the other way around. Any therapist who acts in the role of mother, father, teacher, counselor, or cop contaminates the relationship beyond hope of successful treatment for the child, whereas, in the pathology just described, any absence of a real-life role makes a meaningful relationship totally unlikely. In short, we are now producing children who need their interview work done right now, close to where and when things happen, and by the very people they are familiar with anyway.

Uncooperative diseases are the ones for which we prescribe heavy doses of the kind of on-the-spot interviewing that is built right into the patient's life space. We prescribe this treatment even in cases in which the child also needs (and perhaps is getting) intensive individual therapy, classical style. For this kind of child the therapy room or clinic office is not enough. He needs to have some of his troubles handled and talked over right now, right here, or else no dice.

FIRST-AID AND EGO SUPPORT FOR THE HEALTHY CHILD IN MOMENTS OF UNUSUAL STRAIN

The idea that normal and healthy children don't need any therapy is basically correct. The further assumption that being normal and healthy also means being free from the danger of being overwhelmed by the complexities of life is a naïve illusion. Most healthy and normal kids are equipped with considerable amounts of resilience. They can handle a lot of experiences in their stride that would send their more disturbed compatriots into psychotic blowups or neurotic convulsions. This, however, does not mean they can manage all of them. Take any child, no matter how well endowed, how healthy, how wonderful, even in the best conceivable classroom. At some time during some phase of his life he will find himself in two kinds of predicament in which he will need the adult at hand to stand by. Indeed, during such a time it will make a lot of difference just how well this adult handles himself in this task.

The first predicament is that of a child overwhelmed by internal confusion or conflict from within. Even well-put-together children have moments when they are suddenly filled with rage, fear, shame, fury, embarrassment, or anger. They may be disgusted with what adults have done or not done. They may experience flare-ups of impulses to do or say things that they would not ordinarily consider acceptable. The moods of most normal children sometimes swing from depressed to elated, from apathetic and bored to "high" and overexcited.

Take for example last Monday. Something must have happened between Bobby and Jim. By the time you entered the classroom they had sailed into each other in furious battle, so excited they didn't even notice that you had appeared on the scene. And they are both quite normal kids, neither delinquent nor psychotic nor really the type one would call "acting-out." It was just one of those things. Yet, if you had appeared just one moment earlier you would have had to try to talk to these two customers, and you would most certainly have found they could not hear you. At that moment, would they not have resembled their prepsychotic pals more than their own "better selves"?

In short, sometimes kids need to be given some immediate ego support by an adult who is in an important role in their lives, regardless of therapy-hour schedules that they may neither have nor need.

The second predicament involves the child overwhelmed by experiences and events from without. All children find themselves, from time to time, overwhelmed by life situations that are unusual. They may not be prepared for such events. Indeed, such events may be more than anyone could expect even a well-developed and healthy ego to cope with. Consider the degrees of regression one may find even in a perfectly healthy child when he suddenly gets a new little brother, loses an old friend, experiences the trauma of divorce or death in the family. Consider what contortions of behavior even well-brought-up kids may get into when they suddenly have to cope with the pressure of a group manipulator. In a bored classroom in which the manipulator is working hard to get the other kids to clown, a self-respecting normal child may well feel he has to take the dare. Recall what occurs when a child meets with his first disappointment—a friend who betrays him, an admired hero who ridicules him. In such a case a child may well fall apart temporarily. Recall children's reactions to that painful period of suspended time before an exam or right after an exam or before a performance in front of an audience. Certainly it is usual for children to be exposed to all these experiences. Although much of this kind of stress and strain can well be taken in stride, destiny does not use clinical judgment about just how much a given child can manage on his own at a given time. Just as in our own lives, in theirs, too, things sometimes pile up. The point is, if the pile-up comes to a certain child at a certain age, it is important that an adult be nearby to help the child cope with these overwhelming experiences.

Regardless of how basically healthy or normal the youngster is, during the onslaught of some experiences, just as in times of confusion and conflict from within, normal youngsters are much more similar to the legitimately disturbed ones than to their own normal selves. The same child who can listen respectfully to preaching and teaching under ordinary circumstances may be hard to reach while in tears, in a sulk, or under the impact of an excited flare-up. The same words and gestures that may ordinarily be used for his benefit won't do the trick in crises. To talk with a child in moments of strain necessitates an approach more similar to that of the clinician, therapist, or psychiatrist than to the usual "civilian" approach of a classroom teacher.

In summary, there are moments in every child's life when he needs something that is very close to what we call a "psychiatric interview technique" if only he were sick enough to need therapy. In this case, emergency depth-oriented interviewing may have to be done right then and there by the adult at hand. One cannot always wait until the doctor comes, and often a doctor is not what is actually needed.

LIFE SPACE—WHAT'S IN IT?

One of the most urgent questions raised about the life-space interview is precisely what we do and do not subsume under such a peculiar term. This question reminds me of a philosopher who used to comment that it is funny how people enjoy being happily surprised at the many things that come out of a stuffed goose once it is served on the dinner table. He observed wittily that it shouldn't be too difficult for them to get over their surprise if they wish. All they have to do is go out into the kitchen and see what is stuffed into that goose to begin with. The point of comparison for our philosopher was, of course, the "content of concepts," which he likened to the stuffing of a goose.

In fact, as the concept of the life-space interview is being stuffed right now, one certainly has a right to come and watch what is being packed into it. My coworkers and I used to discuss it under the heading of "marginal interview," for we still had to deal with a relatively clearly and artificially structured situation: the same person in a marginal role between caseworker and group worker vis-à-vis one and the same incident with one and the same child. It became obvious, however, that, in a hospital or school setting, the term "marginal" was meaningless, for the great number of people, the variety of tasks, the diversity of situations in a day's time would no longer make it clear when such interviews were "marginal" and when they were intrinsic. It was at that time that I adopted the term "life-space interview." I was fully aware of the problems this change in terminology would bring down on my head.

The term is an unfortunate one and a clumsy one at that. All I hoped was that it might help us get away from the even bigger ambiguity of the old term "marginal interview." I wanted to suggest the idea of the greater proximity of this type of interview to the actual life experience of the child, the more true-to-life role of the person who does it, and the proximity in time and space to the child's natural life.

Several cautions should be remembered about this term, as about any coined phrase. Our aim is to indicate what the child perceives as part of his normal living, in contrast to artificial environments. What children consider their natural life space, compared to artificial situations, varies from child to child, from neighborhood to neighborhood, and from culture to culture. For instance, it is well accepted by a child that sometimes one is given a physical checkup. At those times the child understands he may have to undress and the doctor may go through manipulations that are important and, within this specific situation, appropriate, although the procedure may be mildly embarrassing or exciting. On the other hand, the same child does not consider it part of his regular life to be handled in this way outside the examining room. It is important to keep in mind how variable this factor may become. What is natural and therefore acceptable and what is artificial and therefore unacceptable change with the child and the situation. In some schools, going to the visiting teacher's office may be much like going to a special tutoring session. It has become part of school. In others, the idea of anybody talking with a child as a social worker might, especially during regular school hours and especially in the school building at that, is unheard of. The question of where this interview takes place is not the only issue. In the Child Research Branch at the National Institute of Mental Health, the therapy rooms were geographically close to the living and school quarters of the children. Yet, at later stages in their treatment, the atmospheric difference between the hours spent with the therapist and those spent on the ward was very sharp indeed. Sometimes even a straight "therapy session" might be held geographically somewhere between doorways or in a corner on the ward where a child had happened to take refuge. The therapy session was, however, sharply different from a life-space interview, in content as well as in the child's perception. On the other hand, a life-space interview might move from the original position under the table to the comfortable surroundings of a staff member's office, still continuing to retain the flavor and technical implications of a life-space interview, as contrasted to a therapy session.

All I am trying to underline is that the life-space interview is a concept meant to contain a variety of issues of technical relevance. Even though the words "space" and "life" are used to convey greater proximity to a child's natural habitat than the usual therapy concept embodies, this point should not seduce us to oversimplify the issue or define it too rigidly.

What Is Particularly New about This Technique?

On one hand, there is the question of how it differs from classical interview techniques; on the other, there is the question of how it differs from ordinary talks with children held daily by teachers, principals, parents, and camp counselors.

These questions are easy to answer: The life-space interview is new in some ways and draws on past experience in others. Words and playing are used by many people in a child's life—mother, teacher, anybody. The psychiatric-interview technique also involves talking or playing with kids. What makes it a technique is its planned strategy, its thoughtful basis of observation, theoretical conceptualization, and well-formulated policies based on long experience. All these specially designed and purposeful elements underlie its use of play and words. And this point is exactly what we have in mind. What's new about the life-space interview is that it is basically as depth oriented and strategically important an intervention into a child's life as other forms of therapy may be. The mere fact that sometimes people other than bona fide therapists have to administer it or that it occurs outside the confines of the office or therapy room should not obscure the multifaceted complexity it involves.

What has been so refreshing for us in our laboratory experiences is that life-space interviewing can be learned and taught. It can become an important adjunct to other forms of therapy and an important preventive ingredient in moments of stressful living, even for the undisturbed child.

THE LIFE-SPACE INTERVIEW IN THE SCHOOL— A QUESTION, NOT AN ANSWER

As usual, newly introduced terms or procedures contain the lure of "either-or" oversimplification. The life-space interview is not meant to substitute for any other form of clinical or educational intervention. It is not necessarily better or worse than anything else. It is an *additional* potential in the armamentarium of ego support for the disturbed as well as the healthy child. Obviously, there are numerous similarities and differences between the life-space interview and other forms of interview techniques or between it and clinical and educational interventions.

Rather than list these similarities and differences, it is more urgent to discover the potential advantages, as well as the pitfalls, of this strategy. We need to explore the rich varieties of issues raised by questions of timing, terrain, role confusion, symptomatic and pathological affinity, developmental appropriateness, feasibility, and indications and counterindications for use.

The Concept of a "Therapeutic Milieu"

If you are not directly involved in running a psychiatric children's hospital or a residential treatment center of some sort, you may be tempted to skip the following pages, for isn't milieu therapy a rather specialized business, quite remote from the usual channels of child therapy, to say nothing of normal school and family life?

My suggestion: Please don't. For the issues of just what constitutes a supportive life experience for a child, of what we should look for in order to make a realistic assessment of what his "life space" holds, require exactly the types of thought and conceptualization that have been applied here to the residential-treatment milieu. With increasing emphasis on the need to help others help kids, to design school life and community experiences in such a way as to support "mental health," the adult's sensitivity to what constitutes powerful "environmental givens" in a child's life has increased in importance way beyond the specialized field.

Now, the issues used in this article in order to open up the concept of "therapeutic impact of milieu ingredients" have admittedly been taken from the experiential framework of psychiatric-treatment institutions. The implications of those issues, however, reach far beyond that. It might pay, as it has done in physical medicine, to learn from the problems that emerge in the treatment of the sick what needs to be known in order to plan the life of the healthy.

$\mathcal{S}$PECULATIONS about the therapeutic value of the "milieu" in which our patients live are neither so new nor so revolutionary as the enthusiasts, as well as the detractors, of "milieu therapy"

"The Concept of a 'Therapeutic Milieu'" is based on the article of the same title that appeared in *The American Journal of Orthopsychiatry* (October 1959), © 1959 the American Orthopsychiatric Association.

occasionally want them to appear. If I may risk shocking you so early in the game, the most extreme degree of "holy respect" for the tremendous impact that even the "little things" in an environment can have is represented in the original description of the conditions for a Freudian psychoanalytic hour. The ritual of interaction between patient and therapist is certainly sharply circumscribed. Even conditions like the horizontal body posture and geographical placement of the analyst's chair are considered important. Of course, the "basic rule" must be strictly adhered to; there should be no noises from the analyst's children coming through from the next room, and one should worry about whether or not patients might meet one another on the way out or in. The idea that months of solid work even by the greatest genius of transference manipulation might be endangered if doctor and patient should happen to meet at the Austrian equivalent of a cocktail party, instead of in the usual office terrain, is certainly impressive evidence of the great impact classical psychoanalysis has ascribed to factors like time, space, and other "external givens."

If you now want to argue with me by reminding me that all this is true only for the duration of the fifty-minute hour and that other "milieu" factors in the patient's wider circle of life have not been deemed so relevant, then I might concede that point. But even so, I should like to remind you that we have always had a holy respect for two sets of "milieu" factors, at least in child analysis: We have always lived in the terror that the parents or teachers of our child patients might do things to them that would be so traumatic that we could, of course, not analyze them while it was all going on; and we have insisted that we cannot touch a case unless we can get the child out of the terrain of parental sex life and into a bed of his own or unless the parents stop some of the more extreme forms of punitive suppression at once. These are only a few of the illustrations we could think of. You will find a much more impressive list of "milieu variables" that certainly need to be influenced by the therapist in Anna Freud's classic *Introduction to the Technique of Child Analysis,* though not under that heading, of course.

The other case in point of my argument that even classical psychoanalysis has not neglected concern with "milieu" influences as much as it is supposed to have relates to our evaluation of failure and success. At least in our informal appraisals, I have time and again observed how easily we ascribe the breakdown of a child analysis to the "negative factors in the youngster's environment," and I have found in myself an inclination to do the same with the other fellow's successes. If my colleague seems to have presented an unusual therapeutic "break-through," I find the temptation strong to look for the good luck he had with all the supportive factors that were present in his case and that, to my narcissism, seem to explain his success much better than the technical argument he has put forth.

Now, seriously, if we secretly allow "milieu particles" to weigh so strongly that they can make and break even the most skillfully developed emotional therapy bridges between patient and doctor, hadn't we better look into this question some more?

The fortunate fact that the answer to this question has, historically, been an enthusiastic "yes," however, has started us off in another problem direction. As more and more of us become impressed by more and more "factors" that in some way or other can be subsumed under the term "milieu," the word has assumed such a variety of connotations that scientific communication has been overstimulated and at the same time blocked in its development toward precision.

Because avoiding the traps of early concept confusion is an important prelude to a more rigid examination of meanings and their appropriate scope, we might allow ourselves the luxury of at least a short list of "dangers we ought to watch out for from now on," provided we keep it in telegram style, so as not to take too much attention from the major theme. As space for argument is dear, I shall be presumptuous enough to confront you simply with my personal conclusions and to offer them as warning posts, without further apology.

Traps for the Milieu Concept

First, the cry for *the* therapeutic milieu as a general slogan is futile, and in this wide formulation the term doesn't mean a thing. No milieu is "good" or "bad" in itself—it all depends. And it depends on more factors than I want to list, though some of them will turn up as we go along.

Second, it won't do to use our own philosophical, ethical, or political convictions or our taste buds, in order to find out what really has or has not "therapeutic effects." Even the most respectable clinical discussions around this theme drift all too easily into A's trying to convince B that his setup is too "autocratic" or that what he called "democratic" group management isn't really good for those youngsters. Whether or not a ward should have rules, how many, and which must not lead to an argument between those who like rules and those who don't; I have seen many a scientific discussion end up in the same personal taste-bud battle that one otherwise finds acceptable only when people talk about religions or brands of cars.

Third, even a concept of "total milieu therapy" does not imply that all aspects of a given milieu are equally relevant in all moments in clinical life. Every game, for instance, has some kind of "social structure" and, as part of it, some kind of "pecking order," which determines the power positions of the players for the duration of the game. Whether or not the specific pecking order of the game I let them play today had anything to do with the fact that it blew up in my face after five minutes is a question that can be answered only in empirical terms. I know of cases in which the pecking order was clearly it; I had to look no further. I know of others in which it was of no clinical relevance at the time. The boys blew up because they got too scared playing hide-and-seek with flashlights in the dark. In short, the scientific establishment of a given milieu aspect as a theoretically valid and important one does not substitute for the need for diagnosis on the spot. Such diagnosis alone can differentiate between potential milieu impacts and actual ones in each case.

Fourth, the idea of the "modern" and therefore social-science-conscious psychiatrist that he has to sell out to the sociologist if he wants to have his "ward milieu" studied properly is the bunk. Of course, any thoughtful appraisal of a hospital milieu contains many variables that the mother discipline of a given psychiatrist may never have dreamed of. On the other hand, the thing that counts is not only the description of a variable but also the assessment of the potential impact on the treatment process of a given group of patients. That is basically a clinical matter, and it remains the clinician's task. The discipline that merges social science with clinical criteria in a balanced way still has to be invented. There is no short cut to it either by psychiatry's stealing particles of social-science concepts or by selling out its own domain to the social scientists.

Fifth, the frequently voiced expectation that the discovery of what "milieu" one needs would automatically make it easy to produce that style of milieu in a given place is downright naïve. An instrumentology for the creation of "ward atmosphere," of "clinically correct policies of behavioral intervention," and so forth has yet to be created, and it will cost blood and sweat to get it. The idea that all it takes to have a "good treatment milieu" is for a milieu-convinced ward boss to make his nurses feel comfortable with him and to hold a few gripe sessions between patients and staff is a daydream, the simplicity of which we can no longer afford.

"Therapeutic"—In What Respect?

The worst trap that explorers of the milieu idea are sometimes goaded into is the ubiquitous use of the term "therapeutic," coupled as an adjective with the noun "milieu." I have described the seven most common meanings squeezed into this word in scientific writings and scientific discussions elsewhere,[1] but I must at least point out this possible confusion before we go on. Whenever people demand that a really good "therapeutic milieu" have this or that quality, they may be referring to any one—or any combination—of the following issues:

"Therapeutic," Meaning Don't Put Poison in Their Soup

Not only is the adjective "therapeutic" often used in such a wide way to cover anything that is "good for a patient"; it is also made to serve as an umbrella for all demands that "damaging influences" be excluded.

Example.

Any "therapeutic milieu" in which children are supposed to be treated would certainly pride itself on an absence of stupid punishments and of cruel and thoughtless handling by disinterested or poorly trained employees; it would have to guarantee protection against exposure to too many "traumatic experiences" either from staff or from the other children. In fact, often enough we find this negative request upon a milieu sufficient to distinguish one setting proudly as a "residential-treatment home" from another, which is then relegated to the lowly connotation of "just a children's institution."

In short, on this level, the term "therapeutic" usually is confined to the request made upon the people who design a milieu not to do to their patients what they wouldn't do to people anyway—any people—and to keep injurious substances out of their diets.

1. Fritz Redl, "The Meaning of 'Therapeutic Milieu,'" in Walter Reed Army Institute of Research, *Symposium on Preventive and Social Psychiatry* (Washington, D.C.: U.S. Government Printing Office, 1958), pp. 15–7.

The questions, of course, of just what is or is not "good for people" and of how we know whether the specific impacts of living arrangements, atmosphere, patient handling by staff, and so forth are "therapeutic" or not in a given case provide a story in their own right and go far beyond the scope of this discussion. May I be allowed to add at least the demand that we become more specific about this point and stop confusing our own recreational taste buds, philosophical convictions, and habits of social interaction with objective assessments of what is or is not useful in the treatment of a given patient at a given time?

"THERAPEUTIC," MEANING YOU STILL HAVE TO FEED THEM

Widening this heading to the concept of "basic-need coverage," we can easily remember that patients in a hospital—or children in any institution—are a "captive audience." They have come there not only with the special pathological conditions on which the institution's therapy hopes to focus and for the sake of which they were referred to begin with. They also bring with them all the other "basic human needs" of a given person in a given developmental phase with a given cultural background, regardless of whether or not such basic needs are closely related to the problems for which they were sent or even have anything to do with them. Once we declare a given need "basic," it must be well taken care of, or else some serious damage is done to the patient, no matter how well the specific therapy for which he was referred may look for the time being.

It is this fact that speakers often have in mind when they raise the question of the "therapeutic value" of special features in their institutional settings or their ward programs. In short, when we use the term this way, we refer to the conviction that it is important not only "not to put poison in their soup" but also to see that their psychological nourishment contains all the vitamins individuals of a given age need —beside the medication administrated for specific subgoals. Just what, in a hospital setting for instance, should be considered a "basic need" is, of course, dependent on the nature of pathology, age, previous life habits, developmental phase, and many other factors related to the specific patient in question.

By the way, the form in which such "basic needs" must be taken care of is as important as the content and varies greatly, especially in terms of developmental phase, pathology, and social background. What might be called "good basic-need coverage" in terms of an occupational-therapy program for a group of young adult neurotics may have little relevance to the activity program that has to be developed for a group of hyperaggressive twelve-year-olds of the borderline variety, and both programs may be downright unrecognizable as such by anybody who is used to catering to the art needs and activity tastes of a normal population in a given neighborhood. It seems to me that this issue especially is frequently neglected in the planning of milieu designs. The expectation, in all this, is not that "basic need coverage" in itself will bring about the desired therapeutic change. It is, rather, that, without its guaranteed provision, the intended therapy will be counteracted or that damage in other areas of the patient's life will be produced while we are busy blindly treating the one for which he was admitted.

Examples.

Even with six hours of intensive individual therapy guaranteed each child per week, one would not consider a milieu "therapeutic" in which the children are expected to sit on benches waiting for their therapy hours, living in large groups with staff not trained to discover damaging influences of one patient upon another, bereaved of the basic ingredients of activities, and thrown into a group atmosphere heavy with hatred, fear, boredom, lethargy, and social strain.

Looking at the activity program of our six boys at the Bethesda project —youngsters selected for their "borderline, acting-out type of behavior disorders"—during the first few months after their admission, one would hardly have recognized much similarity between it and what is customarily considered a "good youth program" in the open community or on the school playground. Yet it was, at that time, most important to administer to those children the basic recreational vitamins that they needed in forms that, in spite of their illnesses, could make them "go down and stay down." For instance, organized athletic-team competition had, for a long time, to be carefully excluded, as it would only have produced a new chain of disruptive hostility. The essential experience of "participation in group living" had to be smuggled in through all sorts of deviously planned games with special care for proper dosage of all ingredients all the way through.

"THERAPEUTIC," MEANING DEVELOPMENTAL-PHASE APPROPRIATENESS AND CULTURAL-BACKGROUND AWARENESS

This item is, of course, especially urgent in work with children. The very style of adult-child relationships that is normally expected to convey the impression of "cared-forness" and warmth is quite different for a five-year-old than, for instance, for an adolescent. Squeezed into a group of adolescents, three five-year-olds might find themselves entirely out of focus in this important aspect. Their play-therapy hours might be as frequent as those of the older group and as well planned, but they would still find the "milieu" in which they lived very puzzling and strange. To limit myself to one issue picked from a hundred possibilities: The very adult behavior that the five-year-old might consider most reassuring would produce spasms of hostile rebellion in the adolescent, who could never tolerate such a gush of infantilizing motherly care. On the other hand, the more matter-of-fact "palsy" style of the young adult with the young-group client, well suited for the older group, would badly scare the little ones: They would be traumatized by the panic produced in them by watching the "loose" give and take between the adult and the adolescent group.

Obviously, subcultural and other differences would complicate the issue even further.

Example.

It would not be "therapeutic" to keep adolescents in an infantilizing "little boy and little girl" atmosphere. A "fine lady" fussing over a little boy's hair grooming might convey "warmth" to a neglected middle-class child but would simply be viewed as a hostile pest by a young toughie from the other side of the railroad track.

Just what "developmental-phase appropriateness" means in different "socioeconomic, subcultural, racial, and national strata" is, of course, in itself an issue in need of much more elaborate and specific exploration.

"THERAPEUTIC," MEANING CLINICALLY ELASTIC

Not only what facilities or program provisions a potential milieu contains, but also how adaptable it is to the whims of clinical movement and therapeutic exigencies, makes one setting more "therapeutic" than another. I mean by "clinical elasticity" the ability of a given milieu aspect or ingredient to yield to specific therapeutic demands, without the over-all structure getting entirely lost in the shuffle.

In so many discussions, I have noticed people swept away by "flexibility demands" to the point at which it is not even clear any more just what there is to be "flexible" about anyway. Such terminological preference may, however, be based on my chance experiences only and may not be of real importance, as long as we remain aware in our demands for either elasticity or flexibility that they are not values in their own right and that there has to be some clear-cut issue of structure, or else there is nothing left on which to base these adjectives to begin with. More specifically, the following demands by clinicians seem to me to fall into this category.

First, there is the ability of all milieu features to allow a wide leeway for "exceptions" for the partial toleration of downright "regression" even at high prices in other milieu features, whenever it is indicated.

Second, there is the ability of milieu features to absorb the surplus of pathological behavior that a given treatment technique may require or that a given treatment policy may demand and to provide safe handling of such surplus pathological behavior by the respective milieu areas outside their own domains (school, O.T., ward program, and so forth).

Examples.

The teachers of the children on our closed ward, during the earlier phases of their stay with us, had to be able to hold back their ambitions to exploit learning potentials they might have discovered, if over-all clinical policy on a given child demanded such restraint. The same teachers also had to know what to expect and what it meant when, on certain days, a child came in to their classrooms straight from an exciting therapy session and hit them with "transference spillover" far beyond what they had learned to consider customary. They also had to be able to deal "hygienically," but clearly, with some of this surplus wild behavior in their classrooms, even though it came from different areas of the therapeutic space. In the same vein, the therapist, even while going through a phase when unleashing of the child's aggression was his basic main line, had to retain enough sense of proportion to slow down the rate at which he worked, so as not to destroy other ego-supportive life experiences for the child in school and elsewhere by unleashing more action-geared destruction than the rest of the outfit could cope with at the time or more than was compatible with the ward's concept of "group-psychological hygiene."

"THERAPEUTIC," MEANING ENCOMPASSING FRINGE-AREA TREATMENT GOALS

Beyond the outspoken "auxiliary" aspects of a milieu design, many speakers and writers also ascribe to certain parts of the milieu a much more direct impact on treatment in a much more sharply focused use of the term. That puts it somewhere between "real therapy" and "important, but not really therapy-focused, basic-need coverage." We frequently find the idea expressed that, although the main part of the more basic pathology of the patient was to be tackled by the psychiatrist in his own individual or group-therapy sessions, many other things that are also "wrong" with this same patient should be corrected somewhere else, at some other time, by some other people in the institution. In short, those other areas of the patient's problem are also viewed as part of his "sickness," and what these "auxiliary" people are expected to do is also a "repair job" in its own right. But it should not be confused with the therapy done as the major clinical task. In this way, the recreational and social parts of the design of a milieu are often emphasized way beyond their function just for "basic-need coverage" and are elevated to regular jobs of "therapy." Or it may be considered a well-established treatment task to open up for a patient expressional channels like art and music, thus affording him access to an enriched life, just as soon as the psychiatrist is through unlocking the major door. On this level, we expect the psychiatrist to be busy with a frontal attack on the most "deeply rooted" phases of a patient's illness, but we also find him quite frankly relegating the other and also therapeutic jobs to other people on the team, to other phases of residential life, to other props and ingredients than those of the individual or discussion-group therapy room. In short, when we examine a milieu for its "therapeutic" properties on this level, we raise the question: "Who else treats other parts of the patient's disease, and how far do the setting and the over-all design of the place allow such work?

Examples.

Johnny is here for treatment of his kleptomania, and his therapist works hard on that in individual therapy. Johnny also has a severe deficiency in school learning and is clumsy in his play life with his contemporaries. Even though the therapist is not yet in a position to pull any of these factors in, some other aspects of the milieu to which Johnny is exposed must give him corrective experiences in this direction, or else the place to which we sent him is not considered "therapeutic enough."

A therapist works hard at removing the unconscious hurdles in a child's ability to read during his work with him in his play-therapy hours. There are cases in which something else is needed beside. For some of our children it is important that somebody else, not his therapists, be loaded with the task of remedial work on the youngsters' reading problems. Beyond this, the production of an atmosphere indulgent to curiosity, even during the moments of a child's life on the ward, may be of equal importance.

"THERAPEUTIC," MEANING THE MILIEU AND I

Some lecturers and authors go beyond this concept of "supportive milieu therapy as a fringe task, a relevant but not focal repair job to be done," as outlined under the previous section. They ascertain that there are ingredients in a good therapeutic milieu that could accomplish a specific therapeutic task directly—either all by themselves or at least as indispensable and equal partners in the major therapeutic task. These claims range all the way from repair jobs that a good therapeutic milieu alone is able to perform through tasks for the performance of which the "milieu" as such is claimed to be superior to other more specialized and long-term efforts to the more modest demands for a partnership arrangement of some sort.

In all those cases, however, whatever dynamic forces emanate from the milieu aspects mentioned are forces in their own right, well suited to be brought to bear on a "treatment" task of major proportions, and no more fooling about that! Enough of the pussy-footing about "auxiliary values." We are not discussing the issue of right or wrong here; we are merely outlining the conceptual content of a term. Though the verbiage used on the various levels previously listed may be misleading, it is quite clear that this one cannot be reduced to any of the other five—it is a claim in its own right.

Example.
Among the kinds of therapeutic help the children on our ward are badly in need of is that of at least partial "superego repair." No matter what else ails them, something went wrong in the building and development of the type of value sensitivity or conscience children normally develop over the years. It is our impression that the more serious cases of superego damage can never be tackled by any kind of individual therapy alone; it must also be accompanied by an all-out total life-space engulfing approach, well attuned to this job, with plenty of "clinical resilience" built in, in order to guarantee a long-range focus on this major task.

Beyond what the individual therapist can do for such a child, it is our impression that we must provide living space for that child in which he can afford to let go of distorted defenses and allow himself the necessary emotional ties that have to precede any primary value identification whatever. It also seems clear to us that all experiences of daily life have to be geared to avoid guilt-flooding panic and more paranoid interpretations of daily life events than are compatible with an already heightened sibling rivalry—and that the roles of adult figures around whom value sensitivities are supposed to accrue or to be rearranged are protected from overlapping and from confusion that would make a mess of the clinical scene. In addition, for some children, there is a need for something like the tie to a "depersonalized group code," which alone can open the path to value incorporation, all previous personalized channels of that sort being hopelessly contaminated for a long time to come. In those cases, the "milieu" and what it begins to mean for the individual patient becomes as strong a force in therapy as the "therapist's relation with the patient" is customarily assumed to be.

"THERAPEUTIC," MEANING IN TERMS OF RE-EDUCATION FOR LIFE

Even though all the previous criteria for a "therapeutic milieu" are checked out and found proper, we may want to give the term yet another twist. On this level, we are not satisfied with the appropriateness of the milieu for the present repair job to be done. We also want it to contain enough of the ingredients that the later, normal, open life situation will contain and to which the patient will have to adjust after his release.

In short, we measure our milieu in terms of its resemblance to "life for real." We find "nontherapeutic," on this basis, a milieu that contains no challenge to the patient to grow away from his disease and from the place in which it is meant to be cured. We consider a milieu "therapeutic" if it only aspires to "outlive itself" and if it builds into the hospital as many life experiences as the patient will have to meet later, hopeful that their taste may whet his appetite for more normal living rather than be obliterated by the smell of psychological detergents so importantly surrounding him now.

It seems to me that this use of the term "therapeutic" constitutes one of the most important problems in our usual debates. In fact, aren't we somehow drifting into a paradox? Isn't this demand to contain the "normal situations and experiences of life" really contradictory to the very idea of using a "special" milieu at all? For how is one and the same milieu supposed to provide maximum leeway for regression and at the same time to offer the patient all the challenges of life in the open community, with its rich rewards but even more frightening punishments? How are we to provide for Johnny a classroom experience with only two other children present and a highly trained teacher who also has time and skill to sit out five tantrums in a school hour without becoming punitive or disillusioned and at the same time to provide for the youngster the fascinating experience of watching more well-adjusted children happily at work, cheerfully succeeding, and smilingly accepting criticism if they fail, and at the same time taking all the aggression and disturbance he is liable to put out? It seems to me that, on this level, the term "therapeutic" requires the most careful examination of all, for the custom of making demands out of both sides of our salvation-greedy mouths, requesting opposites that cannot be delivered in one package at one time and place, is all too widespread already.

However, short of such abuse of our desire to have our clinical cake and to eat it with the normal life sauce too, the demand that a really therapeutic milieu contain enough ingredients to be supportive of growth and change beyond the present level of pathology-geared design is of great importance indeed. In fact, if we look at most of what comes close to the model for hospitals or "communities" emphasizing the therapeutic milieu, we may easily find that it ranges all the way from demanding protection and dependence as prime requisites to insistence on the patients' leading a nearly normal communal existence "even though they are all schizophrenics." Fortunately, things get that bad only when we leave the facts of daily life too far behind us. For in reality the issues are rarely that extreme. Rather, for any group of patients or any special therapeutic task, we can well define just which aspects of a given milieu should be emphasized for the immediate clinical job and which should be guaranteed and maintained out of the awareness that ingredients of later life must be inserted along the way. A community that would not create special milieu conditions for the therapy of the very sick could hardly be called a therapeutic community anymore, and a hospital that found no place at all to retain and build in essential ingredients of later open life in which patients will need and use such elements would lose its claim to doing "treatment." Sometimes the answer is that there is a limit to what one milieu design can possibly encompass and that the patients would be better off if they could move from one to the other, thus achieving consistency but at different locations or even under different staffs.

Example.

In our children's ward at the Clinical Center, it was obvious from the start that we would have to anticipate problems of this nature. Although the "closed" section constituted an advantage at the beginning of therapy, especially as it was, of course, endowed with a rich and appropriate program design and with ample staff, it was to be expected that the children would outgrow the advantages of our milieu as soon as their ego functions were repaired to a certain point. Whereas protection in terms of the first six levels we have discussed constituted a great asset from the start, it would, at a certain point in the children's clinical advances, become important to substitute a design allowing much more opportunity for moving away from the highly supervised dependence we first had to lure them into. We would then have to insert the opportunity for a much more community- and real-life-related style of existence for them.

With this point in mind, the construction of an "open cottage" in a sort of "half-way house" style was begun and became available as a next step in their therapy. It becomes important for such children to move into a milieu that exposes them to a much higher degree of independent choice in conflict situations—though exploitation of such experiences by trained staff interviews and continuation of many of their other therapies still have to be provided.

Enough of this dissection of an adjective. I hope I am understood correctly: Any one of these meanings of the term "therapeutic" is justified in its own right. Any one of them may, in a given case, assume priority or may fade out in relevance to the zero point. All I am trying to convey is the importance of remembering who is talking about what —and about which patients—when we use the term in a scientific "free-for-all." So far I haven't been too impressed with our ability to do so.

By the way, even in all seven cases, the term "therapeutic" may still be used in a double frame of reference: Was it therapeutic for a given patient—if so, how do you know? Is it expected to be potentially "therapeutic"—meaning beneficial for the treatment goal—from what I know about the basic nature of the issue under debate? These two frames of reference should be kept asunder too.

A Milieu—What's in It?

Obviously I am not going to use the term in the nearly global meaning that its original theft from the French language implies. For practical reasons, I am going to talk here only of one sort of milieu concept, of a "milieu" artificially created for the purpose of treating a group of youngsters. Within this confine you can make it somewhat wider if you want, and you can think of the "children's psychiatric unit" on the fourth, eighth, or ninth floor of a large hospital, or you may hold before your eyes a small residential-treatment home for children that is not part of a large unit. Of course, I know that the similarity of what I am talking about to other types of setups may be great, but I can't cover them all. Therefore anything else you have in mind you keep strictly at your own risk.

So, here we are on the doorstep of that treatment home or at the keyhole of that hospital ward. And now you ask me: If you could plan things the way you wanted to, which are the most important "items" in your milieu that will sooner or later become terribly relevant for better or for worse? The choice is hard, and only such a tough proposition gets me over the guilt feeling for oversimplifying and listing items out of context.

THE SOCIAL STRUCTURE

This is some term, and I have yet to see the psychiatrist who isn't stunned for a moment at its momentum—many would run and hire a sociologist on the spot. Being short of space, I have no choice, but let me hurry and add: This term in itself is as extendable and collapsible as a balloon. It doesn't mean much without specifications. So let me list a few of the things I have in mind.

First, a hospital ward is more like a harem society than a family, no matter how motherly or fatherly the particular nurses and doctors may feel toward their youngsters. The place I run at the moment is purposely shaped as much as possible after the model of an American camp, which is the only pattern I could find in which children would be familiar with a lot of adults walking through their lives in older-brother and parental roles without pretending to an equivalent of family life.

Second, the role distribution among the adult figures can be terrifically important for the amount of clarity with which children perceive what it is all about. Outspokenly or not, sooner or later they must become clear about just who can or cannot be expected to decide what; otherwise, how would one know when one is getting the run-around?

Third, the pecking order of any outfit does not long remain a secret to an open-door, neighborhood-wise toughie, no matter how dumb he may be otherwise. He also smells the "pecking order" among the adults who take care of him, no matter how carefully disguised it may be under professional role titles or civil-service classification codes.

Fourth, the communication network of any given institution is an integral part of its social structure. Just who can be approached about listening to what is quite a task to learn; and to figure out the real communication lines that are open and those that are secretly clogged in the adult communication network is usually an impossible task except for the suspicious outside researcher.

I mentioned only four illustrations of all the things I wanted included under "social structure." There are many more, and I have no quarrel with the rich inventory many social scientists have invented for it. The quarrel I have is against oversimplification, and if you tell me that social structure is only what goes into a power-line drawing or a sociogram or that social structure is the only important variable in "milieu" that psychiatrists have neglected in the past, then you have me in a mood to fight. By the way, if I list "social structure" as one of the important milieu variables, I'd better add in a hurry: A mere listing or description of the social structure extant on a given ward is of no interest to me at all if it doesn't go further than that. From a clinical angle, the excitement begins *after* the sociologist tells me what social structure I have before me. Then I really want to know: What does it do to my therapeutic goals? What does it imply for my choice of techniques? In which phase of the therapy of my children is it an asset, and in which other phase does it turn into a serious block? To use just one example of the clinical question to be added to the social scientist's answer: The kind of ward I have run—harem-society style—makes individual attachments of child to worker difficult to achieve; on the other hand, it pleasantly dilutes too-excited libidinous-attachment needs into more harmless distribution over a larger number of live props. Question: Is that good or bad and for whom during what phase of the treatment?

THE VALUE SYSTEM THAT OOZES OUT OF OUR PORES

Some people subsume this point under "social structure." I think I have reasons to want a separate place for it here, but let's not waste time on the question why. The fact is that the youngsters not only respond to what we say or put in mimeographed writing; they also smell our value feelings even when we don't notice our own body odor any more. I am not sure how, and I can't wait until I find out. But I do have to find out which value items are there to smell. Does the arrangement of my furniture call me a liar while I make a speech about how much at home I want them to feel, or does that gleam in a counselor's eye tell the child: "You are still wanted," even though he means it when he says he won't let him cut up the tablecloth? By the way, in some value studies I have missed one angle many times: the clinical convictions of what is professionally correct handling, which sometimes even questionnaire-clumsy workers on a low salary level may develop and which themselves become motivating sources for their behavior, beside their own personal moral convictions or their power drives.

ROUTINES, RITUALS, AND BEHAVIORAL REGULATIONS

The sequence of events and the conditions under which people experience certain repetitive maneuvers in their life space can have strong impacts on whether or not they can keep themselves under control or whether or not their impulse-control balance breaks down. Since Bruno Bettelheim's classic description of the events inside a child while he seems engaged in the process of getting up or getting himself to sleep, no more words should have to be said on this point. Yet many "therapeutic milieu" discussions still waste time on arguments between those who like regularity and those who think the existence of a rule makes life unimaginative drudgery. All groups also have certain "rituals" by which members get back into the graces of the group if they have sinned and others that the group has to go through when an individual has deviated. Which of those ceremonial rites are going on among my boys, thinly disguised behind squabbles and fights, and which of them do adult staff people indulge in, under the even thinner disguise of discussions on punishment and on the setting of limits? Again, the mere discovery of phenomena fitting into this category is not what I am after. We are still far from having good research data on the clinical relevance of whatever specific practice may be in vogue in a specific place.

THE IMPACT OF THE GROUP PROCESS

We had better pause after pronouncing this weighty phrase—it is about as heavy and full of dodges as the phrase "social structure," previously pointed out. And as this one milieu aspect might well keep us here for a week, let me sink as low as simple word listing at this point. Items that I think should go somewhere under this name: over-all group atmosphere, scapegoating, mascot cultivation, subclique formation, group-psychological role suction, exposure to group-psychological intoxication, dependency on contagion clusters, leadership tensions, and so forth. Whatever you have learned from social psychology, group psychology, and group dynamics had better be written in right here. The point of all this discussion is: These phenomena are not simply interesting things that happen among patients or staff, to be viewed with a clinical grin, a sociological hurrah, or the curious stares of an anthropological slumming party. These processes are forces to which my child patient is exposed, as real as the Oedipus complex of his therapist, the food he eats, and the toys he plays with. The forces producing such impacts may be hard to see or even to make visible through X-ray tricks. But they are there and as much part of his "surroundings" as the unbreakable room in which he screams off his tantrum.

THE TRAIT CLUSTERS OTHER PEOPLE WHIRL AROUND WITHIN A FIVE-YARD STRETCH

I first wanted to call this item "the other people as persons," but I know this would only call forth a long harangue about feelings and attitudes—isn't it people anyway who make up a group?—and so forth. From bitter experience, I am trying to duck these questions by this somewhat off-beat phrase. What I have in mind is this: My youngsters live as part of a group, true enough. But they are also individuals. And Bobby, who shares a room with John, is within striking distance of whatever personal peculiarities John may happen to throw at others. In short, we expect some children to show "shock" at certain colors on a Rorschach card. We expect children to be lured into excited creativity at the mere vision of some fascinating project outline or plane model seductively placed before their eyes. Well, the boy with whom Bobby shares his room is worse than a Rorschach or a plane model. His presence and the observation of his personality do something to Bobby, for John not only has character traits and neurotic syndromes; he also swings them around his body like a wet bathing towel, and they are going to hit whoever gets in their path, innocent or not. In short, personality traits remain psychological entities for the psychologist who watches them in the youngsters. They are real things that hit and scratch if you get in their way, for the roommate and all the other people on the ward.

We have learned to respect the impact of certain extremes in pathologies upon one another, but we are still far from inspecting our milieus carefully enough for what they contain in "trait clusters" that children swing around their heads within a five-yard range. Let me add: Not all traits and syndromes are "swung"; some stay put and can only be seen or smelled, so they become visible or nuisances only to the one who shares the same room. Also we are far from knowing what this all amounts to clinically. For the question of just what "milieu in-gredients" my ward contains, in terms of existent trait clusters of the people who live in it, is still far removed from the question of just which ones *should* coexist with one another and which others should be carefully kept asunder.

THE STAFF, ITS ATTITUDES AND FEELINGS—BUT PLEASE LET'S NOT CALL IT ALL "TRANSFERENCE"

This one I can be short about, for clinicians all know about it; sociologists will grant it to you, though they may question how heavily it counts. In fact, the attitudes and feelings of staff have been drummed up for so long now as "the" most important aspect of a milieu, often even as the only important one, that I am not afraid this item will be forgotten. No argument is needed; it is self-evident. Only two issues I should like to battle over: First, although attitudes and feelings are very important indeed, they are not always all that counts, and sometimes other milieu items may obliterate their impact. Second, attitudes and feelings of staff are manifold and spring from many different sources. Let's limit the term "transference" to those phenomena for which it was originally invented. If nurse's aid A gets too hostile to Bob because he bit him too hard, let's not throw all of that into the same terminological pot. By the way, when I grant "attitudes and feelings of staff" a place on my list of "powerful milieu ingredients," I mean the attitudes and feelings that really fill the place, that are lived—not those that are only mentioned in research interviews and on questionnaires.

BEHAVIOR RECEIVED

I tried many other terms, but they won't work. There just isn't one that fits. In a sentence I would say: What people really *do* to one another counts as much as how they feel. This statement would then force me into a two-hour argument in which I would have to justify why it isn't "unpsychiatric" to say such a thing. For isn't it the underlying feelings that "really" count? That depends on which side of the fence your "really" is. The very fact that you use such a term already means you know there is another side to it; but you don't want to take it as seriously as yours. In short, there are situations in which the "underlying feelings" with which adults punish children count so much that the rather silly forms of punishment that were chosen are negligible. But I could quote you hundreds of other examples in which this is not the case. No matter what your wonderful motive, if you expose child A to isolation with more panic in it than he can stand, the effect will be obvious. Your excuse that you "meant well and love the boy" may be as futile as that of the mother who gives the child an overdose of arsenic not knowing its effect.

This item of behaviors received in a day's time by each child should make a really interesting line to assess. We would have to look about at "behaviors received" from other boys, as well as from staff, and see what the implications of those behaviors are, even after deducting from them the mitigating influences of "attitudes that really were aiming at the opposite." The same point, by the way, should also be taken into consideration in hiring staff. I have run into people who really love "crazy youngsters" and are quite willing to sacrifice a lot. Only they simply cannot stand more than half a pound of spittle in their faces a day, professional attitude or no.

In order to make such an assessment, the clinician would of course be interested especially in the *forms* that are being used by staff for intervention (limit-setting), expression of acceptance and love, and so forth. The prevalence of certain forms of "behavior received" is not a negligible characteristic of the milieu in which a child patient has to live.

ACTIVITY STRUCTURE AND THE NATURE OF CONSTITUENT PERFORMANCES

Part of the impact a hospital or treatment home has on a child lies in the things he is allowed or requested to do. Any given activity that is halfway influential enough to be described has a certain amount of structure to it—some games, for instance, have bodies of rules, demand splitting into two opposing sides or staying in circles, and have certain assessments of roles for the players at least for the duration. At the same time, they make youngsters "do certain things" while the games last. Paul Gump introduced the term "constituent performances" into our Detroit Game Study and referred by this term to the performances required as basic within the course of a game. Thus running and tagging are constituent performances of a tag game, guessing word meanings is a constituent performance in many a charade, and so forth. We have plenty of evidence by now that—other things being equal—the very exposure of children to a given game, with its structure and demands for certain constituent performances, may have terrific clinical impact on the events at least of that day. Whenever we miscalculate the overwhelming effects that the seductive aspects of certain games may have (flashlight hide-and-seek in the dark just before bedtime), we may ask for trouble, whereas many a seemingly risky game can safely be played if enough ego-supportive controls are built into it (the safety zone to which one can withdraw without having to admit he is tired or scared and so forth). In short, although I hardly limit the job of total treatment of severely disturbed children in a mental hospital ward to that factor alone, I certainly do want to figure on it as seriously as I calculate the mental-hygiene aspects of other factors more traditionally envisioned as of clinical concern. What I say here about games goes for many other activities patients engage in— arts and crafts, woodwork, outings, overnight trips, cookouts, discussion groups, musical evenings, and so forth. Which of these things takes place, where, with which feeling tones, and with what structural and activity ingredients is as characteristic of a given "milieu" as is the staff that is hired.

SPACE, EQUIPMENT, TIME, AND PROPS

What an assortment of names. But I know as yet of no collective noun that would cover them all equally well. As I have made such a fuss about this point for years, I may try to be shorter about it than seems reasonable. Remember what a bunch of boys do when running through a viaduct with an echo effect? Remember what may happen to a small group that is supposed to discuss plans for its next Scout meeting and is required to hold this discussion unexpectedly in a huge gym with lots of stuff around, instead of in its usual clubroom? Remember what will happen to a baseball that is put on the table prematurely while the children are still supposed to sit quietly and listen, and remember what happens to many a well-intended moral lecture to a group of sloppy campers if you have timed it so badly that the swimming bell starts ringing before you have finished? Do I still have to prove why I think that what an outfit does with arrangements of time expectations and time distribution, what prop exposure the youngsters are expected to stand or avoid, what space arrangements are like, and what equipment does to the goals you have set for yourself should be listed along with the important "properties" of a place where clinical work with children takes place? So far I have found that in hospitals this item tends to be left out of milieu discussions by psychiatrists and sociologists alike; only the nurses and attendants have learned from bitter experience that it may pay to lend an ear to it.

SEEPAGE FROM THE WORLD OUTSIDE

One of the hardest "milieu aspects" to assess in a short visit to any institution is the amount of "impact from the larger universe and the surrounding world" that actually seeps through its walls and finds its way into the lives of the patients. No outfit is airtight, no matter how many keys and taboos are in use. In our own little children's-ward world, for instance, there were the following "seepage ingredients from the world outside" that were as much a part of our "milieu," as it hit the boys, as anything else: adult visitors and the "case history" flavor they left behind; child visitors and the "sociological body odor" of the old or new neighborhoods that they exuded, excursions that we arranged; old haunts from prehospital days that we happened to drive through unintentionally on our way to our destination; plenty of purposely pulled-in outside-world movies, television, pictures, and stories we may have told them. And, of course, school was a full-view window hopefully opened wide for many vistas to be seen through—if we only could get our children to look.

There was the "hospital impact" of the large building that hit them whenever they left the ward floor in transit and the physically sick patients they met on the elevator who stirred the question up again in their minds: "Why am I here?" There were the stories other boys and staff told, the secrets we were believed to be hiding from them whenever we seemed eager to divert attention to something else. As soon as the children moved into the open cottage, the word "seepage" wasn't quite so correct any more. Suffice it to say: The type and amount of "outside world" particles that are allowed or even eagerly pulled in constitute a most important part of the lives of the captive population in an institutional setting and should be given attention in an appraisal of just what a given "milieu" holds.

THE SYSTEM OF UMPIRING SERVICES AND TRAFFIC REGULATIONS BETWEEN ENVIRONMENT AND CHILD

Those among you who have sharp noses for methodological speculations may want to object and insist that I am jumping category dimensions in tagging on this item and the next one on my list. In some ways they still belong, for whether or not there are any umpiring services built into an institution and what they are like are certainly important "milieu properties" in my estimation. What I have in mind here has been described in more detail in a previous paper. In short, it runs somewhat like this: Some "milieu impacts" hit the children directly; nobody needs to interpret or translate. Others hit the children all right but to make sure the proper impact is achieved someone has to do some explaining. It makes a great difference whether or not a child who is running away unhappy after a cruel razzing received from a thoughtless group is left to deal with the problem all by himself, or whether or not the institution provides interpretational or first-aid services for his muddled feelings. Some of our children, for instance, might translate such an experience, which was not intended by the institution, into additional resentment against the world. With sympathy in the predicament offered by a friendly adult who tagged along and comforted, this same experience might well be decontaminated or even turned into the opposite. A similar item is the one I had in mind in using the phrase "traffic regulations." Much give and take can follow naturally among the inhabitants of a given place. Depending on the amounts of their disturbances, though, some social interactions that normal life leaves to the children's own resources require traffic supervision by an adult. I should like to know whether or not a given milieu has foreseen this problem and can guarantee the provision of some help in the bartering among the youngsters and whether or not a new youngster will be mercilessly exposed to the wildest blackmail, with no help from anyone, the moment he enters the doors to my ward. In short, it is like asking what medical first-aid facilities are available in a town before one moves into it. Whether this problem belongs to the concept of what makes up a "town" or should be listed under a separate heading I leave for a later exploration. All I want to point out now is that the nature and existence or nonexistence of umpiring services and social-traffic regulations are as "real" properties of a setup as are its walls, kitchen equipment, and clinical beliefs.

THE THERMOSTAT REGULATING CLINICAL RESILIENCE

If it is cold in an old cabin somewhere in the midst of "primitive nature," the trouble is obvious: Either there isn't any fire going, or something is wrong with the stove and the whole heating system, so they don't give off enough heat. If I freeze in a building artificially equipped with all the modern conveniences, such a conclusion might be off the beam. The trouble may simply be that the thermostat isn't working right. This, like the previous item, is a property of a given milieu rather than a "milieu ingredient" in the strict sense of the word.

However, it is of such utmost clinical relevance that it has to go in here somewhere. In fact, I have hardly ever participated in a discussion on the milieu concept without having this item come up somehow or other. The term under which it is more often referred to is actually "flexibility," which most milieu-therapy enthusiasts praise as "good," whereas the bad men in the picture are the ones who think "rigidity" is a virtue. I have more reasons to be tired of this either-or issue than I can list in the remaining time. It seems to me that the "resilience" concept fits better what most of us have so long tried to shoot at with the "flexibility" label. A milieu certainly has to be sensitive to the changing needs of the patients during different phases of the treatment process. It has to "tighten up"—lower the behavioral ceiling—when impulse panic looms on the horizon, and it may have to lift the ceiling when self-imposed internal pressures mount. Also it has to limit spontaneity and autonomy of the individual patient in early phases of intensive disorder and rampant pathology; it has to insert challenges to autonomy and even the risking of mistakes when the patient goes through the later phases of recovery. Especially when severely disturbed children are going through an intensive phase of "improvement," the resilience of a milieu to make way for its implications is as important as its ability to "shrink back" during a regressive phase.

Just How Does the Milieu Do It?

Listing these twelve variables of important milieu aspects that can be differentiated as explorable issues in their own right is only part of the story. I hold no brief for this list, and I am well aware of its methodological complications and deficiencies. The major value of listing them all lies in the insistence that there are so many of them and that they can be separately studied and explored. This point should at least help us to secure ourselves against falling in love with any one of them to the exclusion of the others and of forcing any discipline that wants to tackle the job, whether it be psychiatry, sociology, or what not, to look beyond its traditional scope and directly into the face of uncompromisingly multifaceted facts.

As the major sense in all this milieu noise is primarily the impact of these variables on the treatment process of the children we are trying to cure, the question of clinical assessment of the relevance of each of these items is next on the docket of urgent jobs. This one we shall have to skip, but we may point to the other question leading into the most important core of the problem: If we assume that any one of these milieu ingredients, or whatever you want to call them, may have positive or negative impacts on our therapeutic work—how does it do it? Just what goes on when we claim that any one of those milieu givens "did something to our youngsters"? This question gets us into one of the most noteworthy gaps in our whole theory of personality, and frankly I don't think even our most up-to-date models are quite up to it. True enough, we have learned a few things about how pathology is influenced in the process of a specific form of psychiatric interview, and we know a little about the influence of human over human, here or there. We are not so well off when we come to the impact of more abstract-sounding entities like "group structure." We have even more trouble figuring out just how space, time, and props are supposed to do their jobs, whenever we claim that they have the power to throw an otherwise well-planned therapeutic experience out of gear. One phase of this problem sounds familiar—when psychiatry first began to take the impact of "culture" seriously, we were confronted with a similar puzzler: Just where, within the individual, is what going on at the moment when we say a "cultural" factor had some influence on a given behavior of a person?

This problem is far from solved. I think it might help, though, to introduce a thought that might lead to greater specificity in observation and ultimately to more "usable" forms of data collection. Frankly, I have never seen the "milieu" at work. My children are never hit by the "milieu" as such. It always hits them in a specific form and at a given time and place. I think the researchers who play with the concept of "setting" have a technical advantage over us in this field. Of course, the setting alone doesn't interest me either. For what it all hinges on is just what experience a given setting produces or makes possible within my child patient and what this child patient does with it.

Rather than studying the "milieu" per se and then the "reactions of the children," how about making a four-step plan? Let's keep the "milieu" as the over-all concept on the fringe; its basic ingredients come close to my youngsters only insofar as they are contained in a given setting. For example, my children on the ward can be found engaged in getting up and eating meals or snacks. They can be found roaming around the playroom or in a station wagon, with all their overnight gear, on the way to their camping site. They can be found in their arts-and-crafts room or schoolroom engaged in very specific activities. Enough of illustrations. The point is in all those settings the whole assortment of milieu aspects hits them in very specific forms: There is an outspoken behavioral expectation floating through the arts-and-crafts room at any time. There are spatial characteristics, tools, and props. There is the potential reaction of the other child or adult, the feeling tone of the group toward the whole situation as such; there is the impact of people's goal values and attitudes, as well as that of the behavior of a child's neighbor who clobbers him right now with his newly made Viking sword. In short, I may be able to isolate observations of milieu ingredients as they "hit" the child in a specific setting during a specific activity. On such a narrowed-down level of observation, I may also be able to trace the actual experience that such a concrete situation in a given setting produced in the child; and if I know what the child did with the experience, it may make sense, for I have both ends of the line before me: the youngster's reaction to his experience and the nature of the ingredients of the "setting" on both ends of the line, plus plenty of good hunches on the child's experience while exposed to its impact.

It seems to me that much more work has to be done with the concept of "setting" to make it clinically more meaningful and that sharper observational techniques, capable of catching "implied milieu impact," as well as "child's coping with" the experience produced by the setting, have to be developed.

One more word. It is time that we take Erik Erikson's warning more seriously than we have done so far—and I mention him because he represents a point of view that many of us have been increasingly impressed by. If I may try to say what I think he would warn us about after all this discussion of "milieu impacts" on therapy of children, it would run something like this: Why are we still talking most of the time as though "milieu" or "environment" were some sort of rigid structure and the individuals were good for nothing but to "react" to it? How does some of that "environment" we talk about come into being, after all? Couldn't we reverse the story just as well and ask: "What do your child patients do to their milieu?"—not only "What does the milieu do to them?" Mine, by the way, are doing plenty to it, and I have little doubt that many of the items we describe as though they were fixtures on the environmental scene are actually products of the attitudes and actions of the very people who, after they have produced them, are also exposed to their impact in turn.

I, for one, want to exclaim loudly what I didn't dare whisper at the beginning of this paper, as I would have scared you off too soon. I should like to find out, not only what milieu is and how it operates, but also how we can describe it, how we influence it, and by what actions of all involved it is, in turn, created or molded. At the moment I am convinced of only one thing for sure—we all have quite a way to go to achieve either of these tasks.

Improvement Panic and Improvement Shock

It is a commonly held assumption that life with children ought to grow easier once they begin to improve—at last. In fact, we are even convinced that this is true for the children too. Not only will we have an easier time of it, but they too will be happier and have more fun, once they get "out of the worst." For isn't it natural that increased health ought to bring increased happiness in its wake?

Unfortunately, this only holds for certain very simple "part skills" in daily living, like the gain to be had from improving one's skill in reading or in baseball. It is not true for children with severe psychiatric afflictions or for those who have to be treated or educated out of severe characterological deviations. It is time that we shed this illusion of an easy way out or up. For the adult the task of catering to improved persons contains a terrific challenge of change of method as well as implementation; for Junior it is even worse—he is in for the painful discovery that nothing is tougher than to live with a partially improved self.

If you don't believe me, read the following account.

Why Don't We Like Mental Health?

THE WAVE of furious resistance with which Freud's early discoveries and theories were greeted by the contemporary world is by now a matter of cool historical record, fantastic as it seems to have been in its gory details. His statements about infantile sexuality, the subsurface existence of death wishes in children and parents, and the impact of Oedipal fantasies, even his very assertion of the existence and power of unconscious feelings and thoughts, brought forth a wave of moral indignation, accusation, contempt, disbelief, and slander that seems hard to comprehend in an era in which many of these very same concepts have found entry into high-school texts on guidance and human behavior and have been given a promising place in the daily diet of the consumers of *The New Yorker*.

Yet there is one concept left, resistance to which is no less intensive in our day and age: the concept of mental health. If this statement seems startling to you, let me remind you of the well-known fact that resistance doesn't have to be openly angry and furious in order to be strong. Remember the patients who plague you, not by their outspoken hostility, doubt, and disbelief, but by overcompliance, overexpectation, and semiphony hero worship before they unleash from their various couches the most vehement spectacles of ambivalence and all the other fireworks so well known by now in clinical literature? The general public too—scientific as well as lay—has a very effective weapon at its disposal in its desperate defense against the implications of demands for research and action in the field of mental health. This term, no matter how loudly it is being uttered, doesn't get anybody's dander up at all. All it does is put everybody to sleep. In an age in which admission of one's own feelings of hostility has become akin to a societal cult, what more effective defense could one invent? And of course, as usual, "defense" mechanisms rarely operate alone in mid-air. They are well reinforced by "assertions to the opposite" as safeguards against detection and insight. In consequence, the official outcry is rather in favor of the very thing that is being so effectively defended against. To make a long story less long—let me make three statements to arouse you properly for the benefit of this discussion—and, as arousal is my only objective at this point, I shall not add any evidence to any of them.

First, the recent trend in general "public opinion" toward voicing enthusiasm for prevention and mental health—in indignant contrast to a "morbid and costly interest in the sick"—is about as sincere as a stage magician's assertion that he wants everybody to look closely at what he does. The facts, if we had time to enumerate them, would make it quite clear that, in actuality, lectures and speeches on the "normal" put audiences to sleep, that we are all at heart avid consumers of the psychiatric mystery story. While loudly protesting against too much talk about the morbid, it is the morbid we are primarily ready to consume with glee. By the way, I have no objection to this type of fun. I only wish we admitted more frankly what we are doing.

Second, the scientific world isn't much better in this respect. Most of the mouthings about "research focus that should be directed toward matters of prevention and mental health" are about as sincere as campaign promises. Most of the money appropriated under that slogan still goes into the study of the same old disease processes that have been under scrutiny for decades. In fact, we haven't even got a decent definition of mental health, and we don't even know how to describe "normal behavior" without falling into the drowsy stereotypes of moral or "preachy" terms ourselves. It could easily be seen—if we had the time to point it out—that we know much better what to treat our children out of than what to treat them into. In fact, as soon as we leave the comfortable field of listing the "dropout" of symptoms of extreme and well-known pathology, we grow vaguer and vaguer in our terms and more imprecise in our statements until we finally begin to hope that somebody will take those more and more uninteresting cases off our hands and hand them over to a lower-status discipline.

Third, thousands of children are in trouble right now, not because the treatment they have received hasn't done them any good, but because we don't know how to nourish the improvement potentials we have produced in them. I really mean this; it is a new hypothesis of mine. I think a well-designed study could easily show that more recidivism in kids is due to the inability of our communities to create the leeway needed for further unfolding of the healthy parts of their personalities than to the unapproachability of the old pathologies for which they were referred to begin with. The link between pathology and health, on which I plan to focus in this discussion, is usually marked by the label "improvement," a term all too undramatic in its natural flavor and therefore frequently replaced by more sophisticated language for the more choosy consumer—for example, "therapeutic movement" and the like. No matter what labels we use, it all boils down, though, to the problem of transition from a state of disturbedness, disease, or pathology to a state of comparative normality or mental health. As this transitional phase—and its transitional term—promises to contain elements of both the states of mind between which it marks a transit, it may well pay off to have a closer look at it and at what it does to us.

The Phenomenon of Improvement Panic

The objective of this paper is not to crow about, rationalize, defend, or even describe improvements of the children we shall be discussing. In fact, whether they did or did not actually improve or how well such improvements may hold up is totally irrelevant to this discussion. The objective of this paper is exclusively to try and come to grips with some of the clinical implications of this multifaceted concept. The motivation, however, for getting so excited about it does come from a rather unique experience that my staff and I went through in the course of our work with a group of long-term patients at the Child Research Branch, with whom we worked for six years. The peculiarity of the setting, the nature of our children, and probably also the fact that we had an opportunity to stick with one very small group of children, with no turnover, through several years have forced us to experience with a bang and in condensed form what staff usually goes through more gradually and with only a few children from a larger group at a time. Maybe at this stage I'd better confess just which experience in our interdisciplinary life has led us into this detour of conceptual speculation to begin with.

If one starts out on a venture in which one asks staff to survive and live with the most disorganized, destructive, hate-filled, inaccessible, and, *in toto,* rather disgusting bunch of child patients one can scrape up, then it becomes obvious that a considerable effort must go into the preparation for such an experience for the staff. In line with such an expectation, we spent about a year or so primarily geared to just this task. We worked hard on the objective of creating a staff team and a treatment atmosphere that could allow the children and us to survive under the impact that therapy invariably holds for all partners in such a venture. To list only a few of the essential "givens" that must be guaranteed if such a venture is to have any chance for success at all, we tried to help each other

to develop tolerance of a wide array of frightening, disgusting, offensive, and painful behavior, without becoming naively overpermissive or even covertly pathology-identified in the process;

to learn very specific and clear-cut skills for the limiting of out-of-bounds child behavior, ranging all the way from inventing clear but hygienic rules for conduct to using special skills in holding a patient without becoming punitive or angry, including learning how to cut a contagion chain without becoming petty or overrestrictive in the process;

to learn how to differentiate on the spot between child behavior that is the unavoidable outcropping of a warped mind and that nearly identical behavior that is actually the result of milieu factors or of our own mistakes;

to find our peace with the fact that for years to come rewards for all our suffering and effort might be nil, that the real subsurface effect that counted might lie in exactly the opposite direction from the superficial results of our endeavor, that the awareness that regression is part of the show and that the inability to know whether we are coming or going had to be borne with equanimity;

to learn to resist the temptation to lure the children into premature though good-looking "improvements," to resign ourselves to the fact that most of the program and child-care techniques so effective with other children would be totally unusable with this patient group, to swallow our pride and realize that no harvest for patience or love in terms of gratitude or even change could be expected for a long stretch of time;

to surrender all enjoyment of competitive pride within our team group, in favor of a full-fledged team spirit of resignation to the unrewarding task, with no hope of ever knowing who really did what, as long as the ball was carried forward eventually.

If you spend a few years in training yourself and your staff team to do reasonably well in all these items, then you will earn the gratification of having a clinical operation that is a delight and a staff that is proud of being frank about failure, remains gracious in defeat, and survives even under the impact of hard blows without losing its clinical grace, one that remains protective of the nature of the children's diseases even when confronted by outside criticism, lack of visible success, and total unclarity about the eventual outcome.

At one point I think we had such a staff. I think we were in such a frame of mind. Then came the day that threw us into turmoil of a new kind. At least this is my impression of what happened to us.

Condensing into a few bold and obviously somewhat exaggerated and oversimplified statements what took us several months to discover and come to grips with, I can now outline the phenomenon of "improvement panic" I have in mind:

The children, being the hostile cusses we knew them to be, would gang up on us by improving before we knew why. For a project that draws most of its *raison d'être* from research, this is a nasty blow indeed.

The adults, all of us, though of course in varying forms and varying degrees, were stunned into cautious silence at first, and the following phenomena began to unfold.

Recording of critical incidents in nursing and other child-care-staff notes decreased in volume and degrees of specificity.

There was a discussion dry-up in case conferences among the very people who were closest to the daily lives of the children and had been among the richest contributors of relevant detail.

There was also an increase in covert—and sometimes not so covert—inter-disciplinary tension, especially when people of different disciplines also played roles in the children's lives that were unclear, overlapping, or uncustomary in the mother disciplines.

Vehement debates took place over whether Johnny was *really* getting better or such statements were just the naive illusions of clinically not-sophisticated-enough staff.

Violent rejection followed, especially among the clinically most sophisticated staff, of my suggestion that we launch a study of improvement processes as a major part of our research—and this objection from staff that was otherwise research-minded and basic-research proud.

Finally, there was anger at all this and a certain nostalgia for the good old days when we had all been united in desperate survival under the impact of the kid's unquestionable pathologies and could be so justly proud of how well we stood up together under battle conditions.

In short, it became quite clear to me that the sudden improvement in the children had made life miserable for us. The strength we had all developed to deal with the onslaught of the children's pathologies, was not the same type of strength it would take to nourish their improved traits. Living with traces of mental health seemed to imply different joys and different sorrows, seemed to require different types of skill and "atmosphere" than had catering to the demands of pathology well entrenched.

What hit me most in all this, however, was the resistance to a study of improvement processes, in fact secret shudders at the very term "improvement," which I seemed to detect, of all places, among the most sophisticated clinical and research staff.

Long ago, Freud made the casual remark that, if an especially brilliant patient uses obviously especially stupid arguments for his defense, then it is a sure sign that there is more to the resistance than meets the eye. If a bunch of people on our level of clinical endurance are thrown into frenzy by a process of "improvement"—the very thing we are actually working and living for day and night—then there must be angles that might well stand exploration beyond what we are aware of right now.

Our first interest, of course, might well be directed to the unconscious roots of our improvement panic. Also, we should, of course, expect that, beside an over-all collective theme, there would be a wide difference in personal factors involved, which would probably demand breakdowns from staff member to staff member and would in part go beyond the pale of a professional theme. In fact, with just a little self-analysis, I can detect in myself about fifteen major reasons why I shuddered in the face of the concept of improvement. I am sure I can detect some of these fifteen unconscious resistances against the improvement concept in others as well, and I am sure nobody would mind my listing them. Only such an effort would burst the framework of this paper way beyond what I can possibly justify. It will have to be reserved for another time and place. Simply to list a few illustrations, though, I suspect among my unconscious motives for discomfort at a concept like "improvement" my own narcissistic investments. I should really like to think that most improvements can be traced to my contribution to the treatment of the children, but how can I maintain such a claim in the face of such obvious evidence of the opposite? I really can't allow myself as much hope for omnipotence or lack of appreciation of my teammates' work as I am now getting away with or as much open admission of my primitive envy as an organized assessment of the contributions to success by the rest of the staff might force me to face. I might find myself shuddering at the implications of improvement because it really means I am not needed any more or, on the other hand, because I am really afraid that the fun I had working with these kids and the pride I gained from the difficulty of the task might well have hidden my mistakes from me and that a study might reveal the full shape of my fear of failure—or of success, as the case may be. Beside these "personal resistances," there are, of course, also a lot of other factors that I am sure had a part in the production of improvement panic. Some of those elements lay in the over-all administrative design of our project, the dynamics of an interdisciplinary group process, and some of them are sheer displacement of the daily wear and tear of trying to run a kid-treatment-oriented program in the line-authority-oriented administrative design of a huge governmental hospital. Some of the studies by our sociologically more sophisticated colleagues seem to show ample evidence of this reaction. At this point, however, I want to dwell neither on the unconscious roots of our individual troubles nor on the dynamics of administrative-group pathology. There is, beside all this, enough in it that confronts us on the conscious level within the realm of our direct task orientation, and I want to confine myself to that level of exploration for the rest of this paper.

Improvement—What Do We Really Mean?

If anything became clear to us during those months when we tried to come to grips with our collective improvement panic, it was the fact of multiple meanings with which this term is bandied about in discussion. This isn't much of a discovery, of course, but, as the hesitation—or resistance—in coming to grips with this multiplicity of meanings seems to be very strong, it might help future discussants if we lay bare the major traps in concept formulation right here. When people argue about improvements, the following four meanings seem to be involved—and confused.

IMPROVEMENT, MEANING A SPECIFIC FUNCTION IN MID-AIR

One hears claims that children can read better now than before; that they are able to stick to assignments, to fulfillment of tasks; that they can participate in competitive games without being thrown by failure or success; and that they can now "allow themselves to learn" how to swim, paint, spell, or what have you.

Such claims by the various disciplines involved in the cultivation of such skills are frequently met by the therapists with uneasy frowns and polite nods in the direction of the sister disciplines, followed by hot debates over whether or not this "really" constitutes improvement—but that one we shall come back to soon.

IMPROVEMENT IN OVER-ALL MENTAL HEALTH

In this respect, staff argues over whether or not a given child is getting "better"—usually referring to a rather specific part of his well-known pathology. Most frequently though this type of statement ends in a list of "symptoms dropped" or in harder-to-formulate statements about desirable attributes customarily described in our American culture as signs of well-being: less tenseness, more relaxedness, more freedom to react to reality, less "drivenness" by irrational impulse, and so forth.

IMPROVEMENT FROM THE POINT OF VIEW OF THE CONSUMER

By this I mean all the adjustment demands that are made on a child by the surrounding universe, many of which have primarily to do with the comfort and taste buds of those who are on the receiving end of the line of child behavior. Thus one finds statements like "He is less rough on trips outside, sticks within rules better, is much quieter, has fewer tantrums, and then they aren't quite so hard to live through; when in a sulk it doesn't take quite so long to get him out of it" and so forth.

IMPROVEMENT AS A "HUMAN BEING"

Into this category falls a variety of statements that do not seem to be quite founded in either psychiatric theory or any special educational creed and frequently mark themselves quite clearly as different from strictly clinical statements. People get easily embarrassed while making them in the course of case discussions and frequently also apologize for them with the kind of pride one usually displays when apologizing for something one really deems more important than what happens to be on the official agenda.

Thus staff would refer to our children as "more lovable" than before, would insist that Bobby was more of a *Mensch* and seemed to be a more "decent" human being, more responsive to over-all expectations or just in terms of plain human charm.

Needless to emphasize any one of these four different meanings may actually be contained in a given statement in mixture with the other three, and, as in other aspects of clinical life, apologies for the phenomenon of overdetermination hardly have to be made in a paper like this one.

The moral of the story that we want to lead up to today lies in the impact of these multiple connotations on staff discussion among an interdisciplinary team. Several chance observations may be of interest.

First, individual staff members lose, under the impact of improvement panic, whatever level of conceptual astuteness they really possess, at least for the duration of a case conference. You may find a therapist who knows very well that a given teacher who said that Bobby has improved in reading does not for a moment delude herself that this might mean he is cured; you may find a therapist going, in spite of this knowledge, into a long harangue about how "improvements" are often really in "the service of resistance" and so forth, which then in turn leads to a somewhat angry insistence by the teacher that skills do count also, after all.

Second, members of disciplines that have reputations for being "clinically more sophisticated" than some others (psychiatry versus teaching, art therapy versus nursing, and so forth) have a tendency to get irritated beyond reason by even modest statements of improvement of part functions or skills and on the whole pride themselves in somewhat overostentatious pessimism—as though even the mention of improvements would throw them back into a lower-status field. The representatives of more part-skill oriented disciplines have a tendency to hide their improvement observations, for fear of being deemed unpsychiatric or clinically too naïve for words. The debate thus avoided usually breaks out in displaced areas of clinical or technical issues.

Third, on a good team, members of the same discipline who meet the children in their daily lives in different roles or at different times have a tendency to hide their observations of improvements if their revelations might seem as though they took undue credit for them. Thus, in our case, a lot of quite clear-cut improvements remained unmentioned for a while simply because a given counsellor was afraid his teammates might interpret his statements about Bobby's new relationship of trust as though it was meant to tell the others on the team how skillful the speaker was. Such is the price of good battle-morale after return to civilian life.

Fourth, a frank discussion of these issues and an encouragement to record observed improvements, never mind what they might imply, bring about an increase in recording and observations offered, but the effects of such "medication" never last very long and must be repeated more often than one might assume.

Improvement—How Do We Know It Is "Real"?

What people are most afraid and ashamed of on a high-level interdisciplinary clinical team is to appear overconfident, overoptimistic, too naïve in their expectations about human change, too rash in their claims, and "too easily fooled." Working with child patients whose very pathologies seem to lay traps for such weaknesses with special wile and skill, this "countersuspicion" among adults in battle with child motivations seems to assume an even higher force.

In discussions, this theme usually comes up under the guise of questions of whether a given claim of improvement is "real" or not. Some of this way of putting it is actually only a concession to the amenities of middle-class conduct—for you can't very well tell a teammate that he is a fool who doesn't know what he is talking about and sees improvements where there are none. Rather, one can concede the appearance of the improved behavior claimed, as long as he shifts his incredulity to the question of the substance it might hold.

In actuality, the question "but is it real?" seemed, in our struggles at least, to cover six rather discrete issues that should be carefully kept apart.

Is It "Real" or Only a Defense Against Treatment or Change?

Examples.

The tough kid who becomes quite "goody-goody" for a few weeks after arrival because he wants to stall for time to "size up the joint."

The originally obstreperous youngster who suddenly becomes more amenable to adults because he has changed tactics: He takes revenge on them by manipulating the behavior of his peers into antiadult escapades behind the scenes.

Is It Ready for Transfer?

In this respect, we do not doubt the appearance of improvement where it is claimed but question whether or not it would stand up if situations were even slightly changed.

Examples.

A youngster suddenly opening up in a real friendship with one counselor—does this mean he is reducing his hostile warfare against the adult world, or does he simply reserve this attitude to this one person alone, thus even reinforcing his warfare against the rest of the world?

Bobby shows more interest in activities on the ward, gets involved in much more complex art projects there—does this mean now he is ready for prolonged interest spans in his work in school?

Is It Retraumatization-Proof?

What we really question in this case is not the clarity of improvement but just how much of the old bad stuff the youngster can take without a relapse. It should be noted, by the way, that I have found many clinicians falling into the trap of general public opinion on this score. I find therapists blushing at the thought that somebody might come around a year—or two foster-home placements—away and say: "See, I told you it wouldn't last," regardless of the question of whether or not the new breakdown isn't perhaps due to totally unacceptable traumatization of the child. In no other field of medicine do I find people that untrusting in their own domain. A cured pneumonia remains cured as far as the physician goes, and nobody expects retraumatization-proofness for the rest of the patient's life.

Example.

Bobby has made tremendous strides in trust, is capable of accepting reprimands or even punishment if handled wisely and with proper care. But what will happen if he runs into a sadist of a teacher, a drunken fool of a foster-home parent, a stupid antediluvian practice of rule enforcement in another institution?

Is the Basis on Which Behavior Rests "Genuine"?

In this frame of reference, we do not really doubt the factualness of an improvement claim. What we wonder, however, is how much improved behaviors or attitudes flow from real "personality changes from within" and how far they are actually maintained only through unusual pressure from without.

Examples.

Some children suddenly get scared we might abandon them if they are too bad. Under the impact of that separation panic, their surface behavior seems to "improve." However, does that mean that the "real problem" has been solved?

Under the impact of a momentary enthusiasm for a special project or a newly found adult friend, youngsters sometimes act and promise way above their means. The way they act and feel during that phase is quite visibly an improvement over what we saw before—how solid, though, is the basis on which such improvements are erected?

IS THIS IMPROVEMENT WORTHWHILE MEASURED AGAINST THE PRICE WE MAY PAY?

This problem is especially difficult when our ambitions lead us to squeeze out of youngsters levels of operation that are developmentally premature, thus cramping the styles of life they ought to have in order to complete their developmental phase at ease.

Examples.
   A preadolescent who is trapped into displaying a lot of "Emily Post" adaptations to adult taste patterns on how a little lady or a little gentleman should act, thus missing the rough-and-tumble play that this age phase ought to have a large dose of.

An adolescent who is trapped into premature job or vocational ambitions becomes a much more "serious" youngster and is actually postponing an important shift in adolescent psychosexual growth to a much later phase; or he forces himself into a "compulsion-neurosis-like" state of pseudomaturity.

ARE WE JUST HAVING LUCK FOR A WHILE?

Often our improvement statements are obviously well rooted, and we are sure we haven't done anything to force the children into higher levels of operation. But we soon discover that all that happened was that we had a special piece of luck. Sometimes it just happens that we hit a day of unusual relaxedness for the program we had in mind or one of those situations in which a "positive mood" is simply in the air from the first waking hour or in which a lucky surprise, an unusual event, sets the tone so well that even disturbed children, with that much supportive luck, can really live above their means for a while. But it would be premature to expect their continued function on that level or to forget what price in regressive interludes we may have to be taxed for after a while.

Example.
   A skillfully designed school or play hour often turns out unexpectedly well. Seduced by such luck, the adults may try to make such planning part of the regular and prolonged diet of the group. If premature, the result is a throwback or regression to or beyond the original level and the insight

that the experience of such happily "improved reactions" was just a piece of unusual good luck.

By the way, this element of "living above their means" should not be ignored entirely. The ability to do so for certain stretches seems to be one of the safest signals of imminent ego change.

In summary, all these six interpretations of the question whether a given phenomenon of "improvements" is "real" or not raise valid issues in their own right. They should be viewed separately, though, and confusion among them is one of the most dreaded pitfalls in staff debate.

We made a number of observations on these issues from our own "improvement-panic phase." First, in interdisciplinary team discussions, disappointments on the question of whether it was "real" or we were simply having luck for a while and was the improvement ready for transfer seemed hardest for the staff to take with grace. They frequently led to "I told you so" debates, rather than realistic reappraisal of the scope of improvement exploitability; or they led staff members to withdraw all their previous improvement statements, rather than simply to admit that they are not so sure how much improvement will remain "transferable" after all.

Second, regardless of realities in the picture, therapy staff in the stricter sense of the term, was inclined to suspect all program and school staff of overexploiting mild improvement cues beyond what the treatment traffic could bear; child-care and teaching staff had a tendency to suspect and accuse therapy staff of being "overfussy" and holding the kids back from experiences for which they were quite ready.

Third, faced with predictions as forerunners of a widening scope of community contact of the child patients—whether partial (changing rooms, moving from hospital school to community school) or total (impending home, foster-home, or after-care placement)—all staff tended to become panicky and ended with predictions much more negative than it really thought the improvements themselves amounted to. In short, trust in the transferability of improvement went down, and panic about retraumatization vulnerability went up. In fact, sometimes it even looked as though we hoped or at least expected that the subsequent handling of the child would be traumatic in nature, for only then could we have an alibi for having discharged him to begin with, in case it didn't work out.

Improvement—At What Cost?

In the preceding discussion we mentioned the case in which we think that improvements can be obtained at "too high" a price in terms of other areas of the child's life. Of course, such mistakes have to be avoided. But, let's face it, all improvements give us a rough time, at least for a while. Of course we somehow know this, and in specific case discussions the problem is invariably raised. Yet I do not find that the literature has given enough emphasis to the very specific problem it constitutes for the child to run around with an improved personality in the same old stable, for the adult to live with a child who has improved program readinesses, and for the institution that has to maintain a disease-protective atmosphere for some of its patients while others should be put on the path to the outside world.

In the following pages, I shall try to list a few of the thoughts that forced themselves upon us during those months of improvement panic and have been with us ever since.

PRECISELY WHAT DOES IT IMPLY FOR THE CHILD?

The ego of a child who allows himself to "improve" while under our treatment and care—and let's forget for a moment which aspects of "improvement" we may be talking about, as the problem is there in all of them to some degree—has added complications to face and needs a lot of resilience to bear the burden of improvement with courage.

EXTRA ELATION AND DEPRESSION LOAD

Children of the type we are talking about remain for a long time quite incapable of dealing with even normal quantities of elation or depression, excitement or emptiness. Both extremes of emotion throw them into frantic ego gesticulation instead of eliciting the usual coping mechanisms children have available for such events. Therefore, for a long stretch of time, the therapeutic team has to avoid any planning that contains too much chance for either, and the adult has to substitute for coping mechanisms his controls from without if either experience should hit a child too hard. Under the grip of improvements occurring within—even partial ones—such protection from elation or depression can no longer be maintained. Widening the scope of the children's experiences in areas in which they are ready also implies the exposure to elation and triumph, sudden insights into the distance between where they think they are and where they really are, and sudden onslaughts of depression. For all practical purposes, then, an ego that is exposed to the right diet of experiences challenging enough to bring elations also has to take in its stride accompanying accidental depressions and has to be ready for both. But often enough the movement in skill or personality area of improved functioning is not necessarily well coordinated with the development of such coping mechanisms. The result is that the children's egos experience more failures with coping with either depression or elation than before, which makes life for and with those children more tumultuous than it was when they were still in the grip of their old pathologies.

INCREASED PROBLEMS IN DEALING WITH FAILURE AND
SUCCESS, CRITICISM AND PRAISE, PUNISHMENTS AND REWARDS

For years we had to learn to avoid exposing our child patients to any of these elements, as their egos' incapacity to cope with such experiences or educational techniques was among their primary characteristics. Astounding ingenuity had to be developed by staff to find a way of life that would spare the children's egos the necessity for such coping, to find forms of child handling and child care that would substitute for the challenges such experiences and techniques involve.

With the emergence of new improvement potentials, this state of affairs also could no longer be maintained. Expanded exposure to a life of more complexity makes use of such techniques unavoidable. Growing into normal life makes learning of how to deal with such experiences paramount. Hardly freed from the onslaught of their old pathological impulsivity, therefore, these children had to practice new ego techniques in coping with the consequences of their widened areas of potential functioning.

INCREASE IN "NEWNESS" PANIC AND ADDITIONAL FEAR
OF LOSS OF CONTROL

More "newness" also brings with it an increase in the anxiety that goes with exposure to new situations—a liability from which we had to protect these children for quite a while. Exposure to trying themselves in situations of increased scope also implied increased fear of loss of control, of being overridden by onslaughts of impulsivity. In fact, as these children, along with improved functioning, also usually developed some level of increased insight into their selves, their own awareness that they *might* be suffering loss of self-control in new situations also went up. It seems paradoxical but is an important fact of clinical life that, with movement toward mental health, these children's perceptions of actual weakness of their internal controls become more realistic, which increase in internal realism brings in its wake new waves of anxieties about loss of control. This kind of a chain reaction probably poses one of the most delicate clinical-policy problems of all.

FEAR OF COMMITMENT AND NOSTALGIA FOR PATHOLOGY FUN

This phase of the improvement curve has been better documented in reports on individual therapy with children and adults than have the others. It nevertheless introduces new challenges in the children's daily lives. We refer to the well-documented fact that the emerging awareness of a healthier ego and of what life in health implies also brings with it the dawning recognition of the price one pays for freedom and health and of the demands society—and oneself—is likely to make once one has left the dreary but relatively safe refuge of mental disease. Also newly tasted gratifications are still wobbly, and the secondary gain extorted from old pathology-geared gratification, although spurious is at least safely predictable and well known. The "improvement-prone" child thus travels a road that is more challenging but also much emptier of the known and much more unpredictable in terms of the nature of the gratifications to be expected.

THE DIVERSION OF IMPROVEMENTS AS BARGAINING
TOOLS WITH ADULTS

Of all the pitfalls, this one is probably the worst, at least in therapy with the type of children we have in mind. For, once improvement on several levels has been tasted, these children are not slow in detecting their terrific bargaining power over the adults on the behavioral scene. And once a given piece of improvement becomes a bargaining tool in the battle with the surrounding universe, its value, *clinically speaking,* has been nullified. In fact, the improvement we produce, once it is in the service of such a battle against change, is but an additional weapon in the child's hand. We shall go into the problem of keeping staff from playing into this vicious and perverse process shortly. At the moment, what we are referring to is the tendency and skill of children on the way to health to bribe and blackmail those in their surroundings with the very issue of health itself. Only after they have improved enough can they use regression as an efficient weapon for punishing their therapists or themselves. Only after they have shown considerable gains on several levels can they successfully trap us into confusing surface improvements with real change or taking their more pleasing behavior as a sign of advancement rather than of the resistance it really is. The "promise" to be good and the "threat" to regress—by word or deed—are new subjects at the strategy-discussion table during those phases in the children's clinical life.

ESTRANGEMENT FROM PEER GROUP AND PEER CULTURE

This phenomenon is most visible, of course, when some of the children move "faster" than do others in the same subgroup or when an individual's move out from under pathology happens more rapidly than the behavioral code of the peer group can keep step with. As the latter situation is the more frequent anyway, we shall describe briefly the problems of the "improving" child under these conditions.

First, behavior that is rated as "improved" in the world of the therapy-success eager adult may have the opposite rating on the peer-code scale, which still has strong natural power in the children's lives and must be retained for quite a while to come. For instance, the ability "to ask for help rather than to lash out in wild destructive despair" is a clear-cut improvement item on anybody's scale. For the kid who produces such behavior, it easily contains the flavor of "sissiness," of "giving into" or "playing up to" adults, of being a "teacher's pet."

Second, improvements in basic health issues invariably also are accompanied by changes in taste. Accepting sublimated gratifications for more primitive ones obviously creates a gap between the child now and the child before and therefore between him and his less advanced playmates. We find two phenomena in the wake of such moves: Our improved youngster may become contemptuous of or hostile to those who still linger in their old rough, obviously "crazy," and uncomfortable pleasures and behavior, or he may become envious of them, developing nostalgic yearnings for the more simple life of yore. These experiences, by the way, are some that he may not yet be able to cope with, even when his improvement in sublimation of his taste buds has already taken place.

Third, there are the problems of exposure to additional dares and group-loyalty tests and of ambivalence toward this new self-image. Groups don't like to let people go. In the organized adult crime gang, the punishment for estrangement is death. In children's groups it is ostracism or an endless chain of "loyalty tests." The changing child in the not-yet changing group finds himself suspected of being a "fifth columnist" in the battle against adults because of the very "improvements" he has not yet learned how to savor. He is exposed to a constant flow of "dares" to show that he is still okay, in spite of that suddenly discovered eagerness to hold up his hand in class or to finish products adults are proud of or of his obviously gratifying use of his relationship with a therapist. Our changing individual thus undergoes a new phase of group conflict at the very time when his first improvements need a chance to emerge.

THE TURMOIL OF CHOICE

Improved personalities need wider scopes to operate in. The nourishment of improvement potentials invariably implies the increase of free choice. The very children who, during their sicknesses have to be protected by the adults from exposure to too exciting choice-making, because their egos could never bear such loads, now have to emerge into choice-making on a stepped-up scale. Rather than having behind them adults who can hold them when they make the wrong decisions, they have to be kept in a program that gives them a chance to be on their own, to make their own decisions whether to behave or to misbehave, so that the consequences of such decisions can then be picked up in therapy or life-space interview work. No matter how closely supervised their over-all life frames may remain, this withdrawal of the adults in tactful awe of the importance of an autonomous decision-making process is the core of all treatment into health.

The result of this change for the internal households of our children is obvious: Wrong decisions have to be made. Their egos are then tempted to use the old alibi and projection techniques to ward off the conclusions that might have to be drawn from wrong decisions. Our life-space interview records are bursting with colorful illustrations of this very thing. It is the clinical exploitation of life events that are allowed to occur—that marks this phase of therapy, in contrast to the protection from stress that marked the previous one. Although this is the only safe way back to health, it isn't an easy one, and the casualties on this path are no less numerous than are those on the previous treatment stretches.

All in all it should be clear by now that we are deeply impressed with the fact that real improvements—on any one of the counts mentioned—make additional demands on the child. This is especially true in settings in which the children under treatment live in groups with other child patients while simultaneously branching out into widened areas of school and community life. Although the "group" may, under some circumstances, support the way to health, it is also quite likely to block it. In either case, the "improving child" will be faced with frustrations and failures that are the results of the widened horizons of his experience and to which he would not have been exposed to begin with had he not improved. The child's ego also assumes with each "improvement" step the challenge of managing more complex life situations and a new batch of frustrations, anxieties, confusions, and fears. It has quite a job to perform until digested experiences of this sort can be entered, by the child, into a renewed concept of his self.

IMPROVEMENT—THE COST TO THE CLINICAL OR EDUCATIONAL ADULT

To lump both kinds of adult together isn't really quite fair, for obviously the problems we have to face vis-à-vis the improvement issue vary considerably in terms of the specific functions we are expected to fulfill in the youngsters' over-all treatment scheme and the specific roles we have to play in their daily lives. However, let us oversimplify and abbreviate without too much apology and guilt.

COPING WITH TEMPTATIONS TO "OVER EXPECT" AND EXPLOIT

Frankly, not all the resistance of youngsters against our therapeutic wiles is simply a function of their pathologies. Even without such distorting influence, I can't blame some of them for being leery of freedom to improve, for there is one instinct most powerful in all adults in this professional game—a terrific drive to hang onto whatever changes we finally seem to notice and when hardly a finger of improvement is showing, to grab the whole hand and try to pull the child into a level of health he is far from ready for.

We all know that, but we haven't spent as much time learning to recognize our secret wishes in that direction as we have spent learning to know when we are liable to get angry, frustrated, or hostile so that we can take professional action against such feelings flooding our clinical gates.

The more skill-oriented professions have a natural tendency in that direction by the very nature of their jobs. But the therapist, in the stricter meaning of the term, isn't free of it either. It only shows in different ways. In fact, I have seen Bobby's therapist mad at his group worker for expecting the child to enjoy games or experiences still much too frightening to him simply because he had improved some; yet I have found the same therapist disappointed an hour later that a youngster who had been so capable of insight-style therapy should suddenly return to a phase of nonverbal resistance to any and all interview work and wondering what mistakes he had made. In short, one of the greatest internal problems of staff is that, once members have sniffed a few moments of success, have felt the relief of seeing irrational kids respond normally, they are liable to forget all they have learned through the years of severe pathology onslaught. In fact, they are likely to throw it out the window as if the millennium had arrived.

BARGAIN-BASEMENT DEALS WITH THE PSEUDONORMAL CHILD

Worse than the temptation to expect too much and to exploit improvement potentials is the temptation to fall into the trap of using children's promises, "good behavior," or verbal threats of regression to make deals that are clinically as destructive as anything could be. To make this point, which I consider the most important of all, safe from misinterpretation, a slight detour back into our pre-improvement policies seems justified.

The specific type of child patient on whose backs, so to say, we discuss the whole improvement issue today requires, during the first years of therapy, avoidance of all punishment in the usual sense of the term. I cannot re-argue the reasons here.[1] Rather, I refer to the summary of our in-service training notes on staff strategy with this issue at the beginning of therapy, when the children were still in the full grip of the ego pathologies for which we had brought them to the hospital. Here is an excerpt from the "policy directions about the handling of

---

1. For further details, see Fritz Redl and David Wineman, *The Aggressive Child* (New York: The Free Press, 1957), pp. 472–487.

surface behavior" that I expected staff to follow during this phase of therapy:

a. Punishment, though deserved or reasonable, at this stage would have no other effect than to feed their already considerable hostile misinterpretations of the world around them.

b. Punishment remains meaningless unless a child can tie it up with the past, with his own contribution to the trouble, and make constructive use of such experience for a future moment of behavioral temptation. By the very definition of the type of ego disturbances these youngsters suffer from, this is a function much too complex for them to perform.

c. On the other hand, the youngsters must not consider us indifferent to what they do. In fact, often the only reason we interfere in their behavior, even when it is harmless, is in order to be sure that such misinterpretation does not occur.

d. They must never consider our termination of holding them while in tantrums as a "reward" for "good behavior" and must not be lured into too rash promises of "being good." Their return to a game from which they have been bounced is something we are as eager for as they would be if they weren't off the rocker at the moment, and our intervention is only an attempt to get them ready for just that.

e. The over-all attitude conveyed in all interference situations would read somewhat as follows:

We love you. We want you to have fun and participate in everything that's going on. If we stop (or hold) you now, it is only because you are doing something that we cannot and will not let you do. And this we shall guarantee: We shall protect you against your own impulse-flooding. That is all that is involved, nothing else. The fact that you "had to be stopped or held" is no point against you; that's what we are here for until the time when you won't need that anymore. We are happy when you are back to your reasonable self again; that's all there is to it. If in doubt that you are okay again, we shall use our own judgment. You don't need to "promise" anything. If you really are in good shape again you wouldn't even *want* to act as silly as you do when you blow your top, anyway.

Whether you agree with our clinical policy or not, it constitutes the line we pursued fairly successfully in our daily dealings with the child patients. To its interpretation and implementation we had dedicated a major portion of our staff training effort and clinical discussions, as well as our supervisory interviews. From our point of view, this policy stood us in pretty good stead throughout. Somehow, these guidelines seemed to help to regulate child-adult interactions in certain crises and to help the adults in their efforts to keep personal feelings and concerns separated from the clinical issues at stake.

End of Detour: The point of my rehashing all this is that the appearance of marked "improvements" seemed to confront us with the need to plan as carefully for our anxieties about optimism and hope as we had had to plan for the dangers of hostility and despair. It is my impression that there was no automatic transfer of the principles that had guided us against the wrong reactions to the youngsters' "bad" behavior to the avoidance of the wrong handling of their promises to be "good." From this struggle, these directives resulted as additions to our original batch of training policies:

Directives for the Handling of "Improvement"

Whenever we are confronted with it, we cannot afford to make them feel our widening of their leeway for autonomy and expressional scope is "reward" or "privilege."

a. If we did, it would only stir up their "make-a-deal" philosophy of life and seduce them into exploitational pseudopromises and adjustments, and they would escape the real issue again.

b. They could not tie up the experience of reward and promise with either their own past behavior or their future predicaments anyway, so these rewards and privileges would only be considered premiums for symptom disguise.

c. However, we must not be considered indifferent to their improved behavior and attitudes. It is important to show them that we are happy about them, but not to the degree that the loss of such recognition would become something to be constantly afraid of.

d. Whenever we have to terminate temporarily a new scope in their autonomy and mobility, we must make sure they do not experience this as punishment. This must be interpreted quite similarly to our previous intervention policy: "We just think you can't make it yet; that's all there is to it." Not whether they have been good or bad, but whether or not we know they are ready for an experience is the criterion for them to have it. We must also protect them from their own illusionary needs to produce phony or rash promises. We have to protect them against unrealistic self-expectations just as we used to protect them against unrealistic feelings of defeat.

e. The attitude to be conveyed: We love you anyway. We shall do everything to help you "make it" whenever you enter a new area of widened autonomous decision making, or experiential tryout of new situations. However, we shall also protect you from trying more than we know you can handle, even if you get mad at us at the time. We are happy about every step forward you can make, but we don't want you to feel you have to produce "improved behavior" as a prize. We shall help you move at your own rate. On the other hand, the production of "improved behavior" as a coin for special privileges is out, in this outfit, too. It isn't necessary. What you get, you get because you need it; it is good for you and you are ready for it. These are the only basic criteria on which the granting of special extensions in autonomy of decision-making and of experiential expansion depends.

To convey such an attitude in the turmoil of daily events is not an easy task, but neither is the handling of the negatively experienced interventions mentioned. But staff is usually caught unaware by the latter, and the very fact that these kids begin to look and act in many moments of their lives so much like ordinary normal kids easily fools us into the same type of "deals" or of institutionalized punishments or rewards that, with normal children, are known to work so well. In fact, the healthier these kids get, the harder it is to remain aware of the amount of clinical caution and clinical tact that still have to remain part of our treatment policy. In all those cases in which we made bad mistakes along that line and tried to rely on promises, threats, rewards, or punishments, no matter how mild and wise, we were soon forced to regret it. And even then it was hard for us to realize that the only people we could afford to get mad at for such mistakes were ourselves, and not the kids who "disappointed" our fond hopes.

IMPROVEMENT MUTENESS BECAUSE OF REPRESSED DESIRE TO CROW

After so many months and years of hard labor without any reliable signs of success that could be trusted, it is hard to avoid a strong wish to brag about real improvement or to overestimate it in case conferences or in luncheon gossip with the rest of the clinical crowd. Afraid that we might do so and realizing that it would be misinterpreted by the rest of the gang as a rather "prima donna-ish" and conceited act, we often defended ourselves against our own narcissistic hopes by not admitting or noting actual improvements to begin with. One often sees children handled with much too little improvement leeway, thereby slowing up the possible clinical pace. And recording, just when improvements of all sorts actually set in, becomes quite unreliable, a not inconsiderable deficit for an operation that is geared toward research.

RENEWED COMPETITIVENESS AMONG TEAM MEMBERS AND DISTORTED RELATIONSHIPS WITH "THE OTHER FIELD"

When the first "improvements" finally become undeniable, a new wave of competitiveness is likely to hit an otherwise quite team-oriented staff. It seems easier to love one another and to respect the other guy's discipline while we are all in the same boat, struggling with little visible success against overwhelming odds. Once improvement occurs, our narcissistic investments are re-inflamed. This may happen on a personal level—why should Bobby do this (showing reliable behavior when trusted with keys) for counselor X when I know he would never have done it for me? It may also happen on the level of displacement onto interdisciplinary issues: Sure that teacher thinks she got Bobby to read. Little does she know that he would never have allowed himself to want to if I had not opened it all up for him in that therapy hour the other day. To bring this new wave of potential staff conflict under control seems to be a more arduous task for all involved than to become aware of and cope with our feelings of frustration, aggression, and fear.

In summary, there seem to be considerable implications for the task of preservice and in-service training of staff and for the continuing supervisory process on all levels. Without going into any of these details, we may state that the clinical morale and astuteness of a given residential staff, well developed for the original onslaught of pathology in the raw, may need considerable restructuring, to be equally foolproof against the terrific onslaught of the first improvement wave.

IMPROVEMENT—WHAT IS THE COST TO THE INSTITUTION?

When child patients are treated in an institutional setting of any kind—and some of the following observations hold even in less enduring settings like out-patient therapy clubs—the phenomenon of improvement creates new tasks and new problems, which seem to me to deserve much more recognition than they have gained in the past. All too often we design our institutional frameworks primarily for the "treatment" of given disease entities or disturbances of some kind. Somehow we hope that within them the patients will "get better" and finally be ready for discharge. Not often enough do we realize how the step-by-step impact of improvements that have already taken place may change the whole treatment needs of individuals or group to the point at which co-existence with the originally clinically correct pathology-service design becomes a problem of the first order. I shall mention only a few of the most obvious observations to the point.

DANGER OF A RELAPSE INTO PRECLINICAL NAIVETÉ

The danger I mean here arises from a system of institutionalized penalties and rewards or of assessments of partial achievements. In a place where most kids have shed their worst primitiveness, it is quite possible to make demands and set standards that give a smooth image of a well-run place, with the kids closest to health more or less setting the tone and representing the place to the world outside. As soon as this happens, regression becomes a luxury hard to afford, and conformity to standardized expectations becomes a real issue with the group of kids, even if the adults retain clinical flexibility in their thoughts. Individualization and respect for special anxieties, oddities, and pathological blowups become things the institution is increasingly ashamed of. It's staff members blush if they occur instead of taking pride in how wisely they handle them. Even a clinically highly sophisticated setting may temporarily suffer such a relapse into preclinical naïveté at the very moment when the first successes become clear to all. In our own experience, for instance, I had little trouble convincing even clinically not very sophisticated or highly trained staff of the impossibility of punishing kids who obviously had no sense of future or past. When the children began to improve, I found myself forced to write long essays to reassure even the treatment staff of the difference between intervention and punishment, between normal children at home and child patients on a still-closed or just-opened ward.

THE EMERGENCE OF A SYSTEM OF "CASTE" AND "OUTCAST"

The adults may "understand" why Bobby is ready for more leeway and less tight supervision, more trust with gadgets, and less fussiness, and even Bobby may. But how will this understanding affect the other children? For *them*, what I and the child know is simply a concession to his greater self-control looks like rank favoritism of the worst kind. Also, if the group "improves" at too uneven rates, it is unavoidable that some will consider themselves excluded from "privileges" that the others seem to enjoy, and the concept of the "privileged character" can be as destructive in a treatment setting as in a detention home. And under presssure the system of "privileges one enjoys after one has improved" and "absence of rights one is doomed to because one isn't trusted enough" becomes more or less institutionalized; it develops a suction power of its own with disastrous effects all around.

Only the constant vigilance of staff over their own motives and the careful interpretation—by word or deed—of all events that might give rise to such suspicions to all children involved (including the group of "onlookers") can safeguard an institution against this trap.

PROGRAM DISTORTION FOR THE REST OF THE GROUP

Aside from these interpretational pitfalls, it also easily happens that the program diet of the less improved children actually changes way beyond what is clinically wise. This change may occur in two directions: It may lead to pauperization of the program for those who don't quite seem to be up to it yet. Staff may betray its annoyance with the level of operation of the less improved and may too openly display understandable gratification with the program for those who are more advanced and therefore more gratifying to work with. Or the change may lead to stepped-up demands for all, with disastrous results for those who simply cannot yet make it. In both cases, institutions lose their clinical value for some of the children, while increasing their value for those on top.

DIFFERENTIATION BETWEEN "REGRESSION" AND LEGITIMATE "IMPROVEMENT MESS"

One of the hardest issues to interpret to outsiders and occasionally to oneself is the fact that improvement in growing kids does not, of course, mean the termination of problems or even of problem behavior. An adolescent, for instance, who has spent his preadolescent years on a closed ward with a small group of also disturbed peers and who is really "coming along well" should be expected to have to live through all the usual turmoil of awakening adolescent sexuality, of concern about peer status, of battle with home personnel about his newly discovered status of emancipated young man. Life with teen-agers alone, no matter how normal, can be full of problems and of problem behavior of considerable proportions. Why should "our kids" be an exception? Yet we were very tempted to interpret their first steps into adolescent rebellion as "regression to their old ways," to react to their normal adolescent overestimation of anything outside and devaluation of what they have at home as though it simply meant "we never got anywhere; they are as hostile and hard to please as they were when they came." In fact, if your youngsters enter their adolescent phases just at the time when improvements set in and when their scope of activities is branching out into the community more and more, staff is likely to develop some sort of envy toward people outside, who seem to have an easier time with them than do the home-base personnel. Yet any parent of any normal child is quite used to just that. The real problem, however, lies in the difficulty of *assessing* correctly, even in our own domain, just what we have before us: regression or problem behavior that accompanies coping with a new part of life. Research in this direction is practically non-existent; its expansion way beyond its present state is devoutly to be wished.

ACCEPTING THE CHALLENGE OF THE CALCULATED RISK—AND THE PUBLIC HATRED IN ITS WAKE

It is hard but safe to run a place for the extremely sick. Nobody expects any better from you, as long as you keep the patients out of his hair. You yourself have a constant alibi in your vest pocket—in view of the enormous pathology that stares you in the face, even superhuman effort can't well be blamed for failing.

Once the children "improve," doubt rises about whether or not we couldn't do "more" for them, and indeed, ever more seems to be needed. To cater to the needs of "improved" personalities on the way back to health, however, is quite a different task from treating a bunch of incurables humanely and with some clinical hope. It involves an increased demand for calculated risk. For some institutions, mental hospitals for instance, this task even constitutes a legal and administrative problem of considerable scope.

To use two illustrations for many: At a certain state in his development, Bobby can be trusted with the ward keys for a short trip down to the coke machine. In fact, he needs such trust experiences when half-way ready for them, for how can anybody develop autonomy on a leash? On the other hand, in a mental hospital such practice is strictly against the rules, and lower-status staff can well be fired for such a breach of rules. Or Johnny and Max are now in need of partial independence from the group and of experiences of behaving well, out of decency to the counselor who is "on." The result is that the counselor gives in to their request to "go on up the creek a little for some more crabs while you are packing up—we will be back in five minutes, honest." If the counselor knows his children, their moods, and the clinical phase they are in, such permission is a clinical must. But he had better not record the incident, for it is against all laws of the land. And, of course, we don't even insist that his judgment be entirely right. We even hope the risk will misfire from time to time, for only such misfiring gives us the chance for the "clinical exploitation of dramatic life events," which may shorten a child's treatment by months.

In the transition from a closed unit to open life in the community, the cost of the improvement of our children became even more pain-fully visible. For the public in general has little tolerance for a risk that misfires, no matter how well it has been calculated or how wisely ex-ploited for the therapy of the child. In fact, this intolerance may well be one of the reasons why we still have so many closed wards or highly restrictive institutions and so many fewer places where the "last stretch from sickness to health" can be covered. For, our societal hatred of those who deal with the dangerous and the mentally sick being what it is known to be, who could take the risk of supporting that last stretch toward mental health without losing his own?

Improvement of What, and How Do You Know?

After all this discussion of "improvement" and its implications, we can hardly dodge one of the most urgent staff questions that arises whenever this concept is mentioned: Just *what* is it, specifically, that you expect to improve, and how do you know if you've succeeded? It is obvious that this question is also of such scope that trying to cover it even once over lightly at the end of this discussion is a hopeless task. We shall have to reserve such discussions for a future opportunity. Instead, it seems advisable to mention briefly the most urgent area of research in which the issue of the improvement concept becomes hot-test, in the very nature of things.

If we take seriously even part of the clinical complexities that we have raised around the concept of "improvement," several implications for follow-up studies come to mind.

First, it is no longer enough to measure improvements by simple paper-and-pencil intensity scales on items of skills or traits willfully selected. I mean instruments of the type that should have gone out with the bombers of World War I. No increase in quantity of such data can substitute for the clinical sophistication of the premises on which the countable items are selected to begin with.

Second, any analysis of "items improved" remains clinically im-potent, unless we also learn how to catch the peculiar set of circum-stances in all the subtleties under which improvement takes place, holds up, or collapses.

Third, the real test of the pudding, however, depends on our ability to learn to *describe* not only child behavior and attitudes but also the full situations within which they take place. At this writing, we have a better vocabulary available for the description of behaviors and states of mind in children than for the psychological ingredients of the "settings" and situational stimuli by which they are evoked. The question whether a given behavior really is or is not "improvement," indeed, seems to me to depend on our chance to develop such a science of "micro-ecological diagnosis," but of course in clinical terms. Only with the achievement of such a feat will we have any chance to arrive at "follow-up studies" and at appraisals of "mental health" that combine statistical respectability with real clinical meat.

Ego Disturbances and Ego Support

The concept of the "ego" and the functions it has to perform has grown in complexity over the years—so much so that nothing but a book in its own right could do justice to all that has been described, postulated, and said about it. The complexity of the job of the adult who meets the child in the role of therapist, nurse, teacher, or parent has grown proportionally too. Yet—and this is a most deplorable state of affairs —the specificity with which we can advise that adult on what to do has in no way kept pace with the increase in complexity of the concept itself. In short, I can give long lectures on the concept of ego and impress my psychiatric trainees no end with the wisdom packed into them. But when they ask me, "Listen, you said we were supposed to give 'ego support' at times—*just what are we supposed to do?*" they catch me with my consultative pants down.

In the books *Children Who Hate* and *Controls from Within*, David Wineman and I tried to be somewhat more specific about this issue. But these are voluminous tomes, and even they fall short of the goal. For a preliminary taste of what an attempt to come at least closer to the task of more "specific" suggestions for giving "ego support" might look like, this combination of two papers may serve well.

*I*T IS HOPELESS to try to find a short definition of the term "ego" with which a whole roomful of people would easily agree and that would, at the same time, be precise enough for theoretical speculation. Nor would it be feasible to try to follow the development that this concept has undergone since its earliest formulations by Sigmund Freud. For the sake of creating some kind of starting point for discussion, however, I shall at least try to suggest what I mean by

"Ego Disturbances and Ego Support" is based on "The Concept of Ego Disturbances and Ego Support," *The American Journal of Orthopsychiatry* (April 1951), copyright 1951 the American Orthopsychiatric Association; and on "New Ways of Ego Support in Residential Treatment of Disturbed Children," reprinted with permission from the *Bulletin of the Menninger Clinic*, Vol. 13, pp. 60–66, copyright 1949 by the Menninger Foundation.

"ego." By "ego," I refer to that part of our personalities that has primarily two duties to fulfill: to establish a relationship with the world in which we live; and to see to it that we behave reasonably in line with it without too serious inner conflict.

This rather crude "job analysis" of the ego obviously suggests that it has a variety of functions available by which to do these jobs. The first basic function seems to be of a cognitive nature. As the "research arm" of the personality, it seems to be the ego's task to perceive, assess, predict, and so forth what social and physical reality will do to us "if." However, it is not only the "outside world" that must be brought into the realm of ego awareness. If it is to do its other job, the ego's research department must also supply it with adequate data about the dictates of the conscience and about the nature and intensity of strivings, in short, of the "inner reality." At least it seems always tacitly assumed that impulses or superego particles that would not be accessible to the self-perceptive department of the ego would also be outside the reach of its power.

This "research arm" of the ego seems to be coordinated to some sort of "executive branch," which has the task of exerting force, in order to keep impulses and behavior in line. Just where it derives the energies to do this still perplexes us.

The importance of the ego, and with it the focal role of ego psychology, has increased tremendously since its early "part-time employment" as a guardian on the borderline between inside and outside reality, and the details of this development, as well as the most recent speculations about it, are a most fascinating story indeed.

This short paper, however, sets itself a limited task: to lure the practitioner into becoming much more impressed with the need to be very specific in the use of the term "ego disturbance" and to stimulate the clinician to seek a much wider repertoire of techniques whenever he is confronted with the task of "ego support."

Deficiencies of the Current Concept of Ego Disturbance

No matter how elaborate the speculations of the theoretician about ego functions may be, it seems to me that the concept of "ego disturbances," when used in connection with actual clinical material, shrivels up into a rather oversimplified little gadget, hardly able to do the job we expect of it. My main criticisms of the current use of the term in connection with case material are three.

First, the term "ego disturbance" frequently confuses qualitative and quantitative aspects and lumps them together as though they were the same, so much so that the terms "ego weakness" and "ego disturbance" are often used synonymously. It is obvious that this mixture must lead to a great deal of diagnostic and prognostic confusion. If Johnny, for instance, attacks me in a prepsychotic temper tantrum, his attack can be blamed on disturbance of his ego functions. For the clinician, however, it would be of paramount importance to know more specifically just where the disturbance lies. Johnny might, for instance, perceive me correctly as the person I am and the role I play in his life, but his ego may not have "strength" enough to hold his terrific impulse upsurgence or frustration onrush in check. The same behavior may result with a youngster whose ego is perfectly able to cope with an onrush of impulsivity but who is so "confused" about the difference between present and past that the mere role similarity between me, Johnny's camp director, and his foster father of earlier childhood years stirs up old images instead of a correct reality appraisal. In both cases, the behavioral results will be highly similar. Clinically, however, the two are very different.

Second, the most frequent breakdown of the concept of "ego disturbances" parallels our concept of "ego functions," of course. However, most of these "functions of the ego" have been derived from the psychoanalysis of the neuroses of children from the middle or upper classes. In order to be amenable even to the very basic requirements of analytic therapy, most egos have to be intact, and their functioning can be described in terms of the usual list of "ego-defense mechanisms," which become disturbances primarily if they get out of hand. The kind of children I refer to seem to have a variety of seriously disturbed functions that obviously belong to the realm of the "ego," but we would never arrive at them from the study of the ego of the neurotic, which is still more or less intact. I think there are many more "ego functions" than we have assumed in the past, which we simply take for granted and which may be separately disturbed. I shall try to describe a few of them shortly.

Third, in blaming symptomatology on "ego disturbances" we usually automatically assume that things go wrong only if an ego or part of it does not function or is too weak to assert its role. We seem to forget a wide variety of behavioral disturbances that seem to me to arise from overfunctioning of ego activities, at least in certain areas. For example, I would call it a job of the normal ego to be aware of large parts of the id. The unusual self-perception that we find in certain types of schizophrenic stages has puzzled us for a long time. For, although obviously part of a pathological state, it seems a hypertrophic development rather than a "disturbance." Similarly, we find that certain egos that are totally in the service of delinquent superegos have terrifically overdeveloped skills of appraisal of the world as far as delinquent enterprises are concerned. Some of my toughest customers, for instance, have skills in "casing the joint," acuities of observation of job-relevant facts, that are certainly overdevelopments rather than disturbances or underdevelopments of ego functions. The fact that the subsequent behavior can be called "disturbed" has misled us into assuming that these children suffer from "ego disturbances," whereas partial "ego hypertrophy" would be a more correct term. Not all disturbances that happen to be connected with "poor adjustment to reality" are by that very fact also real "ego disturbances," and before the term "ego disturbance" assumes any practical sense, a much more specific description of symptomatology as well as causality is indicated.

Ego Disturbance—Just Where?

It would not do simply to mention obvious and understandable weaknesses of our present conceptualizations. The job to be done is really to work on a much more specific psychology of ego disturbances than we have yet attained. To arrive at it, we have to extend our studies much beyond the usual classical psychoanalytic interview or play situation, and we have to create settings in which we can see ego functions and their disturbances in operation, even when conscious or unconscious expression of them within regular treatment channels is practically not to be had.

We have tried to do just this in various projects. The observations presented in this paper were all made in the framework of the following three projects: the Detroit Group Project, an agency for group therapy with children on a small-club basis; the Detroit Group Project Summer Camp; and Pioneer House, a residential treatment home for ego-disturbed children. I must forfeit the fascination of dwelling either on the treatment designs or on the intakes and other details of these projects and can, of course, not even try to list some of the findings. In a nutshell, I think we can describe about thirty very distinct forms of "disturbance" of ego functions, all of which may be independently observed in varying degrees. For illustration, I shall select only a few.

INABILITY TO COPE WITH FRUSTRATION AGGRESSION

We frequently, and rightly, consider the inability of a child to "hold his own" under the impact of impulse onrushes an "ego disturbance." The healthy ego is supposed to have considerable energy and to be able to use it at times of emergency.

What I want to imply here is that some of our children are able to maintain reasonable ego intactness in the face of certain rather heavy impulse doses but still lose all control in the face of typical "frustration aggression." For instance, Johnny may successfully cope with the temptation to yield to an urge for the possession of somebody else's toy; he may be able to hold his own under the impact of quite sizable doses of temptation in this realm. However, when confronted with the slightest "frustration," like simple interruption of a game for a meal, his ego reacts with total loss of control. This seems to suggest that the ability to cope with frustration-produced aggression may be a separate function of the ego and may be disturbed by itself, even though in other areas more complex ego functions are quite intact.

LOSS OF EGO CONTROL THROUGH GROUP-PSYCHOLOGICAL INTOXICATION

We usually assume that the amount of "ego control" that a child has achieved in a certain area remains reasonably constant for the time being. This is an illusion indeed. We have all the evidence to support a theory to the contrary. It is clearly visible that, under certain group-atmospheric conditions, some of our children suffer total losses of ego control even in areas in which their egos otherwise seem to be intact. For example, a youngster with a considerable desire to "behave reasonably in line with dining-table expectations," especially in the presence of certain staff members, may be thrown totally out of control the moment the "group mood" has reached a certain level of hilarity, especially if, for a variety of other reasons, the "contagion index" for the whole group has gone up for the time being. In short, Johnny, who ordinarily wouldn't think of taking a chance by breaking a rule of table behavior that has just been reinforced, suddenly goes haywire under the impact of that element of "group-psychological intoxication," which is so familiar to the practitioner and yet so hard to describe.

This item has an importance far beyond the situational implication in each case. In fact, we have arrived at a desire to define something like the "group-intoxicational breaking point" of every child's usual ego control and thus could arrive at the following rather puzzling fact: A child with a relatively low level of ego control sometimes has a rather high melting point at whatever level he has achieved; that is, although he has lower ego control than his neighbor, whatever ego control he has is group psychologically more indestructible than is the other fellow's. Another child with a very high level of ego control but a very low melting point under group-atmospheric conditions is more of a risk to the practitioner than is the first child. Instead of talking about ego strength and ego weakness even in specific areas, we should therefore introduce as a further variable the concept of "group-psychological melting point" of whatever ego-function levels are otherwise in action. In short, the highness or lowness of the group-psychological melting point of existing ego functions is in itself as important an item clinically as the functioning or disturbance itself.

APPERCEPTION OF THE INHERENT STRUCTURE OF SITUATIONS AND THINGS

Most anybody, if overwhelmed by a sudden onrush of aggressive impulsivity, may suffer a temporary loss of control. In such a state of mind he is likely to use anything at hand as a weapon against his opponent. Such a situation seems so simple because whatever contribution the ego may have tried to make is flooded by the obvious impulse intensity with which he deals, so that it looks as if all that has happened is an overpowering of the ego through impulsivity onrush. It becomes easy, however, to see how much more complex the situation really is if we vary the intensity of the impulsive side of the picture so that the cognitive signal functions of the ego can more clearly emerge. The following illustration may clarify what I have in mind: In the early months at Pioneer House, the children, entering their toy room even in a mild state of restlessness or hilarity far removed from their usual more dangerous aggressive moods, would have reacted to practically any toy in the same way. A piece of wood, as well as a typewriter, would have suffered the same fate as a piece of clay: It would have been joyously thrown around, banged up, and finally trampled under. In a later development, with increased specification of ego function, the same medium degree of restless hilarity would not have led to the same scene. One of them would have perceived immediately the potential of the typewriter for typing a "dirty" insult to an opponent or an adult; another the uses of the piece of wood as a source of fun, first cutting a gun out of it, and then throwing the scraps at the people around. In short, in the second case, the youngsters would have been able to show more "civilized" reactions to the inherent structures of the toys they were confronted with, not because their impulsivity had been reduced, but because the ego function of perceiving the inherent structures of situations and things had improved. It can well be seen of what tremendous importance for the whole problem of sublimation and socialization this very special ability of the ego may become, and it can easily be seen how an attack upon this type of ego disturbance would require entirely different strategy and techniques from those for any one of the others.

REMAINING "REASONABLE" UNDER THE IMPACT OF UNEXPECTED CHANCE

Very often the concept of "ego control" is narrowly identified with the task of the ego to visualize the limitations that the "reality principle" sets and to enforce the limitations of reality against a recalcitrant id. This definition of task seems to me much too narrow. What if the ego is suddenly in the embarrassing position of having to set limitations when reality does not set any? Many an ego I know, which does a reasonably good job of "reality-limitation enforcement," would miserably flunk this other task. In the children I am thinking of, this other disturbance usually did not become visible until we had exposed them to the treatment process itself. Briefly, this is what we saw: Some of our children were reasonably able to take some reality limitations in some areas of their lives. The deficiencies of their egos suddenly became overt when limitations were taken away. In that case, their egos proved entirely unable to cope with the task presented to them. The result was that the offering of freedom, presents, or love would, in many of them, produce terrific amounts of anxiety. The old, well-known "fear of one's own impulses" would emerge, and reckless, aggressive demands would result.

Example 1. A child who manages well to keep his hostile impulses against other children subdued in the face of a sharp disciplinary regime may become entirely reckless the moment organizational pressures are removed. It would not do to call this youngster simply "ego-disturbed." His ego is good enough to signal clearly and demand submission sharply in the face of direct reality limitations. What it lacks is the resourcefulness to substitute for the sudden disappearance of outside reality limitations a limitational system of its own.

Example 2. Some children have been deeply deprived in terms of love from adults and of possessions and toys. When given what they have long needed, they may go through periods of partial regression and exaggerated dependency, but on the whole that is all. Under the impact of the diet they need, their egos soon gain strength and are able to unfold in many ways.

Not so the "toughies" I am thinking of at the moment. They have been equally deprived in terms of adult love, possessions, and toys. Of course, because of their very disturbances, they also have developed strong defenses against open acceptance of what they originally needed. So we know it will take quite some time until we can get them to accept our offerings. But that is not the problem I want to concentrate on here. The trouble I want to talk about begins after we succeed in breaking down their defenses. At the very point at which they openly and greedily accept the fact that old reality frustrations have ceased and at which they begin to "take" to our affectionate and giving attitudes toward them, we suddenly see their egos in further fits of despair. They have learned how to deal with some reality limitations, though not too well. They seem entirely at a loss, however, in dealing with sudden disappearances of limitations. The demands of these children for love and total possession of adults, for gifts and permissiveness, assume such terrific and absolute proportions that nobody can or should try to fulfill them. In short, these children, when getting what they obviously need, may suddenly be found lacking in ego functions that are necessary for the new, therapeutically created situation. We could not have seen before that these ego functions are disturbed. The ability of the ego to set self-demand limitations when reality is unexpectedly granting seems to be as essential a function of the ego as is the old stand-by of signaling barriers from the outside.

I can hardly exaggerate the impact that the functioning or non-functioning of this phase of ego effectiveness must have on the clinician's strategy and especially on the problem of permissiveness versus interference, as well as total treatment design. If this item is not calculated accurately, the basically best treatment design may easily leave the child's ego in a panic that is more than it can handle.

What Do We Mean by Ego Support?

If we are in dire need of a richer and more specific symptomatology and etiology of ego disturbances, we can certainly do with more knowledge about possible techniques of "ego support." An attempt to demand more precision in the use of the term itself might be a good beginning.

The importance of giving at least partial ego support even in the most orthodox form of treatment of the most classical anxiety neuroses in children is, fortunately, a demand that can be taken for granted today. But popularized distortions of psychoanalysis and, unfortunately, some of the earlier theories in group therapy are regressing still to the old model of pre-ego-conscious therapy. We know now that we do not treat just by cathartic opportunity lure, interpretation-happy id analysis, or a "do-nothing, see-nothing, say-nothing" style of group leadership. In any serious treatment of a child's problem, whatever it may be, we have to take into account the state his ego is in at the time of the treatment, the added strain upon the ego during and in spite of our special treatment goal, and the special problem his ego may be confronted with by the very impact of treatment itself.

Ever since Anna Freud first clearly delineated this issue, some respect for the shenanigans of the ego has been insisted upon even in cases in which the ego itself is not the primary object of treatment. However, I wonder how far we have moved from that point. The following seem to me to be the present limitations on our current concept of "ego support."

First, when we talk about ego support, we usually think of something the therapist says by way of interpretation to a child in interview or play situations or by way of argument in favor of reality issues that the child might tend to ignore or deny. In short, ego-supportive help is often considered the domain of the verbal medium.

Second, when we talk about "ego support," we usually assume by implication that the person who gives it has been able to establish a certain type of "positive rapport," whatever we may consider its nature to be, with the child. Ego support thus requires a high level of child-adult relatedness in order to be possible at all.

Third, when we talk about giving "ego support," we sometimes think of indirect measures like, for instance, our influence on parental behavior, the manipulation of school situations, the exposure to "supportive" recreational and other experiences. It is easy to see that such manipulation in a life-space interview with the child is of a much more complex nature and that, in this instance, "ego support" means primarily a partial and chance use of the relationships of other people with the child, rather than what is indicated by the term "ego support" in the two instances already cited.

The insufficiency of this concept of ego support for our child population at large is easy to see. Let me simply raise a few questions to the point: What about children who do not talk, cannot relate to people, are so restless they will not stay put long enough to be given ego support on a rapport-interpretive basis? What about children who not only need ego support while we treat something else but who also need ego repair before they can even be treated by the usual channels at all? Is it sufficient to consider such children "not amenable to psychotherapy" and to keep complaining that we cannot do anything with them and that they clog up the channels of detention home, foster-home referral, and institutional intake?

None of the children we started with at Pioneer House was amenable to the usual forms of "ego support," because something else had to be done to their egos first to make them amenable to the usual channels of therapy. And I could point to hundreds like them. What about them? Are there other forms of relationship or activity that could be used with these cases?

At this point I am afraid we may fall into a grave error that has led us to drift from a fair and realistic appraisal of our ignorance into a sudden and hardly pardonable naïveté. Because we, as therapists, feel at a loss about nonverbal, action-close, toughness-proof, transference-exempt techniques of ego support, we readily think that maybe others know and can do what we are so desperately groping for. It is along this line of naïve illusion that I see many of us impressed by the most unwarranted, foggy, and unsubstantiated claims. If therapy hasn't produced much in the way of ego-treatment techniques, how about education, institutional work, recreation, group work? And here we are in-variably engulfed by the most reckless confusion about what really constitutes "character training," "reality support," "ego support through authority," and so on and are in danger of two extremes. One is to fall into the trap of the old educational confusion between en-forcement of reality-geared behavior and real treatment. The other is to adopt one or another of the most unsubstantiated claims of those who recommend them as marginal "ego-supportive" measures. I am ashamed to admit that the statements that have been made recently even by psychiatrists on issues like physical punishment and child-rearing or the confused claims of many trends in group therapy itself bear ample witness to the danger I am trying to describe.

The real way out lies, of course, only in a frank admission of our ignorance, a proudly maintained awareness of the complexity of the issues at hand, and a patient attempt to get research results in specially designed frameworks over the year to come. The difficulty of having to create special—and I might add extremely costly—designs in which to gain data about ego-treatment techniques may hold us up for a few decades, but this is still the only way out.

Some Illustrations of Ego-Supportive Techniques

In organizing materials gained in the projects mentioned previ-ously, and especially in the Pioneer House experiment, we can at this time differentiate among about forty techniques, each one of which bears upon the attempt to give ego support or more directly to con-tribute to ego repair. Needless to say, the number is somewhat arbitrary and may vary, depending on later and more adequate chances for subcategorization. These various techniques are obviously on very dif-ferent levels and are meaningless alone, that is, unless they are pre-sented in a total treatment design. I shall mention only a few for the purpose of illustration.

MANIPULATION OF "HANG-OVER" EFFECTS

When children are engaged in intense activity, it is not simply that much "liveliness is drained off so they don't get into trouble else-where." It invariably makes certain very specific demands on their con-trol systems, as it also offers very specific chances for certain impulse gratifications. In short, it creates a quite unique pattern of internal distribution of impulse-control constellations, and this specific distribution usually does not stop with the discontinuation of the structure itself. It seems to "swing over" into the next phase and, depending on its nature, may create problems and confusion. An illustration may help make this situation clearer. Cabin 7 has just had a lively game of capture-the-flag, which, however, has left a number of emotionally charged issues dangling in mid-air, such as whether or not the umpire had rightly declared Johnny tagged. Assuming that this activity had to be interrupted prematurely and had to be followed by exposure to a story within a larger group setting, which required passive listening, we can anticipate some trouble. Some of the youngsters seem to have special difficulties coping with "hang-overs" from previous patterns when the new situation demands an entirely different state of mind. Some youngsters have good ego control over mild impulse quantities as such, but their egos are overwhelmed whenever they are confronted with transitional jobs. The result is that, if the daily-life program contains too many special, difficult, transitional situations, breakdowns of ego functions can be observed. If the daily diet of schedule and program is wisely planned, with "transition hygiene" in mind, the sum total of intolerable ego problems will be reduced, which empirically seems to lead indirectly to a total increase in ego resilience. For instance, it was very important in the treatment of the Pioneer House children to plan careful activity diets for every hour of the children's day, with special attention to the *sequence* of events. Confronting them in the early afternoon, after a tense school period, with another competition-loaded situation would have led to ego breakdowns, whereas wiser program planning did not exhaust the sum total of available emergency resilience of their ego strengths.

PREVENTIVE SIGNAL INTERFERENCE

The trouble with some children's egos is not so much inability to cope with ordinary situations. It is that they get themselves, under the impact of momentary excitement or group contagion, into behavior far beyond the levels that their own superegos will allow to go fear- and guilt-free. As a result they are suddenly flooded with upsurgences of guilt feelings. However, this is where their ego disturbances hit them heavily. Although they are able to cope with many of the usual ego tasks, the manipulation of guilt feelings is one of the disturbed areas.

Therefore, laden with their feelings of guilt, they produce aggression, hostility, anxiety, or whatever and from there go into increased stages of disorganization. In those cases it is important to avoid too many serious guilt-charged situations for a while. In short, interference when Johnny starts getting himself into a stage he will later not be able to control prevents the production of so much excess guilt that new hatred against the adult who left him helpless through his hyper-permissive ways results. Therefore, we planfully save them for a while from the production of too-heavy guilt situations so that their egos are not exposed to having to handle such guilt until they are strengthened all around and we can concentrate on that specific repair task.

INTERPRETATION THROUGH RESHUFFLED REALITY

Some things can be talked down. Others can be listened down. There are a few that have to be lived down, or they will not budge. We have the impression that the last is true of some of the more serious forms of pathological response, at times when rapport or verbal interpretation is still out of the question. For example, Johnny forces us into separating him from the group through skillfully produced behavior that makes his temporary removal from the dinner table essential to the morale of the rest of the group. His real design is, of course, to produce a situation in which the adult is pushed into the role of hostile bouncer, depriver of food, loveless frustrater of little children. Needless to say, we can easily avoid falling into the well-devised trap Johnny hoped to lure us into, but the basic issue of having to go to the other room with him for a while, away from the other children and their contagion-loaded build-up, cannot be avoided. Johnny now sits there, exploiting the rest of his delusions. He daydreams that we hate him, want to starve him, would like to poison him anyway, and so on. At this time, interview rapport and organized verbal interpretation are months away. Falling into Johnny's various delusional traps, on the other hand, would make treatment impossible. The answer is what we might loosely call "interpretation through reshuffled reality." It prescribes:

(a) avoidance during this time, by careful program diet, impulse drainage, and so forth of as many run-ins or potential frustration situations in other areas as possible;

(b) keeping the crisis situation in which Johnny has embroiled us entirely free of counteraggressions, side issues, and so forth;

(c) offering him visibly, with calm reassurance, the very food he claims we want to withhold from him and avoiding being drawn into an argument by his delusional accusations;

(d) creating ample opportunities to demonstrate evidence of affection from the same person during the same day around other life issues.

If carefully planned, this type of policy has an amazing cumulative effect. Even though Johnny's delusional desires far outbalance his reality insight at the time, the concrete offer of a three-decker sandwhich has a chance to sink in when verbal acrobatics would have made no impression. Johnny's ego is being strengthened in its attempt to establish some kind of control over delusional patterns by being offered tangible counterevidence at the right time and in the right amount. It is strong enough to use it when it gets it but not developed enough to produce it out of its own data regarding human beings. Needless to say, such a technique is meant only as one among a variety of others and is tied to elaborate conditions without which it would remain an empty and ill-applied "trick."

EXPLOITATION OF GROUP-PSYCHOLOGICAL SECURITIES

One of the greatest strategic advantages of the group situation, especially the residential one, is the possibility of inserting a variety of direct ego supports into the child's life that are relatively independent of individual rapport and of verbal communication at the time. We had ample chance, for instance, to be impressed by the great ego-supportive power of traditionalized routine—once we got that far. In the beginning, each evening seemed to offer new confrontations of their egos with a new accumulation of crises and became an endless sequence of breakdowns in their attempts to control frustration, aggression, time confusion, transitional anxieties, and adult-role hostilities all at once. With the establishment of some sort of regime around bedtime—which had to be tailored to fit the situation in all its details—it became quite clear that, through the emergence of a "group-habitual pattern," their egos had a load taken off their tasks. The ego seems, then, to have to function only as a signaler of what is proper time and proper avenue of behavior, instead of having to try and produce the whole creative chain of ideas of how to behave while being confronted with frustration aggression. In the same way, it was easy to see that a skillful exploitation of the native group code could, temporarily at least, relieve the ego's task. At a time, for instance, when reality insight would not have stood a chance of dealing with the excitement of a fight starting in the middle of a boat ride, the group-code propaganda for an attitude that "we Pioneers wouldn't want to act that way in a boat" could carry the burden of impulse management for the time being. In short, group-code value tie-ups made it possible to put issues for which actual ego insight could not yet be expected temporarily under the control of another department. This technique, too, makes sense only as a partial step and in close connection with a total policy of strategic handling.

In summary, I think that the concept of "ego disturbances" needs much more specified study; that some of its ramifications become observable especially under group situational conditions; that organized research into all forms of ego function, beyond those customarily summarized under the title of "mechanisms" and the like, is sorely needed.

I am also convinced that the whole problem of "ego support and ego repair" needs study far beyond the scope available to us in verbal or play-interview situations; that some new techniques especially needed for nonverbal, severely ego-disturbed, and hyperaggressive children could be obtained by the planful use of group therapy and especially the planful design of residential settings, with their opportunities for the exploitation of group-psychological securities, as well as the strategic advantage of action proximity and total milieu manipulation.

Special Implications for "Giving Ego Support" in Residential Treatment

If you choose as victims of your therapeutic ambitions hyperaggressive delinquents from tough slum neighborhoods, you soon find yourself in a situation of most fascinating technical embarrassments. For it is obvious and has long been conceded that these children cannot be approached by the same techniques as can neurotics from middle-class neighborhoods. It seems that these children need strengthening of their control functions before you can even survive with them, and, although you reel under the first impact of life with them, you are easily convinced that their problems are quite different from those for which our classical techniques have been designed. You are reluctant to try to undo more repressions—it doesn't seem they need encouragement along that line—and before you risk further id analysis, even if you know how, you certainly want to have some guarantee of what they will do with newly released id contents. It seems that the views of previous researchers have been corroborated: These children need synthetic help up to a certain point before you can aim at them the analytic guns of the more traditional approach.

This statement, however, confronts us with a most embarrassing discovery. We seem to know little yet about the specific functions of the ego, and the techniques of "ego support" about which we talk in our traditional analytic work with middle-class neurotics, do not seem to apply here. Whatever mild forms of "ego support" we use in a classical analysis, the techniques all presuppose the very functions that seem to be disturbed in the group I am talking about. We can not "point out reality limitations" to these children. They don't like to talk, and they can't listen (certainly not to us, the symbols of a world of hostile adults they have learned to.fight with the ruses and devotion of a political underground), and the use of traditional techniques of ego support already presupposes the existence of processes of transference, identification, and so forth for the very establishment of which we have a long way to go. The result of this technical problem is obvious: Child analysis does not find many children of this description among its clients. Even treatment institutions in mental hospitals have excluded them from their clienteles, sticking rather to the more manageable "delinquents on a neurotic basis." However, evasion, no matter how realistically understandable, has never solved a research problem yet. And, frankly, our own deep desires to avoid the unpleasant implications of lack of success with this type of child became the main motivation for concentrating a special experimental study on just this phase of the problem. This is how Pioneer House became a reality.

PIONEER HOUSE, AN EXPERIMENT IN RESIDENTIAL GROUP THERAPY

The Children. Five toughies between eight and twelve years of age were picked because their disturbance patterns fitted the preceding description and combined the usual array of "delinquent" behavior with serious ego disturbances along prepsychotic lines.

The Staff. Caseworkers and group workers, a whole flock of them, lived with the children and worked with them under my direction in a carefully planned design of "total group therapy in a residential home."

Duration of the Experiment. The experiment lasted about two years. In the most successful phase of its development professionally, the house had to be closed for the simple lack of finances. However, a follow-up budget was made available for casework, foster-home care, and a club program for these children for another year. The project was financed entirely by the Junior League of Detroit. Although it is impossible to describe more of its design here or even to hint at the most fruitful observations and results along many lines, I shall make a few remarks on the nature of our work.

RESIDENTIAL TREATMENT MEANS GROUP THERAPY

For a long time, residential or institutional treatment has been accepted as a half-hearted use of "environment" and "recreational group life" in a "supportive" way. This is usually done on the assumption that it can be handled by minor and badly paid manipulative apprentices, as long as they abstain from at least the most lurid cruelties to children. It is usually taken for granted, however, that the "real" treatment happens during the few hours the child spends in play or verbal interview with the psychiatrist, who does the "therapy" and benignly keeps the neck-washing personnel from making too many mistakes and obstructing his success.

We do not doubt that there is a place for institutions of just this type. Children who need individual therapy as the main vehicle of their recovery will benefit from it greatly. However, this is not what we mean by "residential treatment." We think we have materials to prove that residential treatment of ego-disturbed children has possibilities far beyond this. In our experimentation in the Detroit Group Project and in its summer camp, we had developed a design of "total group therapy," which seemed to imply that the group situation as such, with its implied dynamics, can be used as a direct therapeutic agent, beyond the individual therapy that may have to be included in such a framework. Pioneer House was an attempt to apply these findings on the basis of a year-round residential pattern. Although we were not forgetful of the importance of the "marginal use" of individual and group-interview situations, ours was basically an attempt to show that

action-group life offers a marvelous chance for therapy in itself;

group dynamics produce emotional "currents" that can be switched on and off for therapeutic purposes, beyond individual relationships between children and their therapists;

the most important persons in the process are those who live in daily contact with the children;

most of the therapy takes place in real-life situations, eating, getting up, going to bed, playing, working, and every other phase of daily life, rather than in selected individual or group-interview situations;

the impact of the total residential group atmosphere and organizational structure is as much a part of the actual therapeutic process as is what goes on between child and adult in the more classical form of play interviews.

I think we have enough evidence in our extensive recordings over the two years to demonstrate the possibility and clinical validity of such a design and to show the difference between a "home for children in which treatment is being done" and a "residential treatment home on a group-therapy basis." I also think that we can solve a large number of the obvious technical problems arising out of such a reversal of the usual therapeutic design. For presentation here, however, we shall have to limit ourselves to just one aspect of the total job: our experimentation with new techniques of "ego support" that this concept of residential group therapy seemed to offer us.

Since all this material is quite deviant from the traditional design of psychiatric treatment and involves the introduction of new and more differentiated concepts of the problems of "ego support," a short summary cannot be attempted. Instead, I shall substitute a mere outline.

"Ego Support" Techniques

A "weak ego" often means the existence of more impulse tension than the ego can cope with. Technical conclusion: The total life program of the children has to be designed so that adequate impulse drainage avoids overstimulation, pathological impulse pile-up, and so forth.

Disturbed egos usually are unable to handle frustrations adequately. In order to strengthen ego functions, we have tried to use a variety of techniques that we summarize under headings like "antiseptic programing," "in-conflict aid," "hypodermic affection support," and so forth.

Ego weakness and disturbance usually also involve inability to grasp or accept the "reality pattern" in which children live, especially its rules, routines, and time and space arrangements. Studying the various disturbances of our children along these lines led us to a variety of procedures in which we think every institutional worker will be interested. We talk, in this connection, about concepts like "avoidance of managerial-comfort rules," the use of "protective routine," and "organizational crutches" and have found the manipulation of rules, routine, and time arrangements to be one of the most crucial factors in our successes, as well as in our failures.

Disturbed egos seem to have special problems in meeting the onrushes of their own impulsivity: Anxiety blocks in moments of impulse danger, as well as absolute lack of control in moments of seductive overstimulation, seem to be the major risks. We are used to discussing under the heading "protective interference," techniques designed to help weak egos against the onrushes of unmanageable impulse-ego conflicts. We have developed a host of criteria for protective interference and are fascinated by the possibilities of "antiseptic grouping" and of "subgroup insulation" against the danger of "group-psychological intoxication." Out of our frantic efforts to cope with these factors we have started a special study on group contagion and shock effect under the auspices of the United States Health Service.[1]

Another handicap of "disturbed egos" seems to be their inability to maintain anticipatory images of previous structured satisfactions, which would help them to find acceptable resources in moments of boredom or crises later on. We have experimented with ways of creating well-structured game situations and special rub-in techniques to make their images last, so that children suddenly hit by moments of impulse surplus or ego weakness or both can still retain enough imagination to use such structural images as guides.

1. See "The Phenomena of Contagion and 'Shock Effect,' " p. 197.

The greatest problem of our children seems to be their heavy resistance to any and all adult interference, which it takes many months to break down. During this time the heavy use of patterns of depersonalized control seems to be the only way out. We found that many neighborhood games have such high levels of native group-code acceptance that their structures offer ego-control patterns that can be accepted without loss of face or surrender to adult leadership, at least on a temporary basis.

By "interpretive decontamination of experience" we mean the tremendous importance of using "hot life conflicts" for "reality rub-ins" in life with the children, but we also use this term for the host of technical cautions that such a concept implies. We are, however, deeply impressed with the great opportunities that the closeness to daily life, daily conflicts, and mistakes offers the clinician, in contrast to the traditional seclusion of the action-remote interview technique.

Through build-up of realistic role expectations we hope to counteract the peculiar difficulties of "weak and disturbed egos" in differentiating between real behavior of people they live with and hang-overs from those who peopled their earlier lives. This effort implies great care in role consistency of all staff members who meet the child and ways of continual role interpretation whenever role confusions arise. Our attempt to meet the dangers of multiple treatment personnel with already reality-confused children will fascinate all those who work in treatment homes.

By "action interpretation" we mean a process intended to make up for the impossibility of using verbal interview work, especially in the initial treatment phase. We have materials to prove that occasionally the mere consistency of handling case-history-determined tantrums in a clinically strategic way has the same effect, after several months of reality clarification, as verbal interpretations in the classical interview technique would have, if it were usable. The impact of such themes for work with hyperaggressive and nonverbal types seems to us rather heavy.

By "group-psychological impregnation of adult personnel" we mean the one and so far only way we have found with children whose defenses against adult interference are supported by identification with heavily delinquent, tough-neighborhood group codes. Such children may establish "friendly" relationships with isolated therapists, but they do not allow those relationships to enter the stage of real identification. We noticed, however, that the insertion of the therapeutic personnel into the group climate of their daily lives offers possibilities for "treatment rapport" undreamed of previously. Possibilities and limitations of this sort constitute some of the most fascinating experiences of our work in the group projects at camp and at Pioneer House.[2]

By "group-code insertion of un-explainable reality factors" we mean something so complex that it defies short-sentence description. Maybe an illustration can do the trick: At a certain level of development, our Pioneers (children) were ready for much more "outside-the-house programing" and were in need of less protective reality contacts. However, they were not yet ready to have enough imagination about reality dangers like, for instance, the consequences in heavy traffic of reckless station-wagon behavior (jumping out in the middle of traffic, climbing out of windows onto the roof, wild fighting, and so forth). "Reality" interpretation of such behavior was impossible at the time; actual suppressive attitudes by the adults would have defeated the very program opportunities for which we had taken them out. We managed to circumvent this problem by a planned propaganda effort to make misbehavior in the station wagon as group-rejected an item as tattling on a pal or "acting like a sissy." With this temporary support, we could enable a reality-blind ego to be exposed to the very experiences by which we hoped to strengthen it, without having to wait for full recovery to handle the total job.

"Provision of satisfaction guarantees and security symbols" through total residential life exposure is the phrase we use to allude to the many "little ways" in which a confused ego is helped to relax its impulse fears. Under this item fall concepts like group-atmospheric support, provision of selected symbols for total life security ("our club," planned propaganda for the concept of "we, the Pioneers"), and a lot of indirectly supportive policies (for instance, the chance for a lot of waste in arts and crafts to convey our real acceptance of imaginative experimentation and our real wish for them to have fun, which for these children could not be conveyed in words but only by our real reactions to their provocative challenges in wasting materials for a long time).

The discussion of the implications of this item for every phase of residential life, from the cook who must cook with libido (beside her

2. See "The Psychology of Gang Formation and the Treatment of Juvenile Delinquents," p. 224.

other ingredients) to the problems of pocket money, candy, chewing gum, smoking policies, bedtime routines, washroom policies, table serving, and so forth, would most interest institutional practitioners.

The following statements are meant to safeguard this highly condensed report from misunderstandings.

Residential group therapy is *not* meant to be a substitute for individual therapy. It is applicable only to certain types of ego and character disturbances that are so far not reachable through classical channels of child therapy. For many other disturbance types the already developed techniques are quite sufficient. For cases of mixture of neurotic disturbances and more serious ego disturbances, the residential group-therapy treatment outlined here is meant as a preparation, rather than as a substitute, for individual treatment. After bringing the egos of some of our children to a point at which they can survive with others' egos and with the therapist, remainders of more clearly neurotic phases in their problem development must be picked up by traditional child-therapy techniques.

Group therapy is neither shorter nor cheaper than individual therapy. On the contrary, for the children I am talking about, I am convinced that during the next thirty years it will be longer and more expensive. I seriously object to the "quacky" way in which group therapy is currently sold to the public by otherwise serious and reliable therapists. As far as we are concerned, we do not look for ways to make the treatment of what we already know shorter or cheaper. We are trying to develop ways of treatment for what we do not yet know how to treat. And, as you can see, we should rather stop what we are doing successfully and hope for future opportunities than to surrender to the shortsightedness of the money-holding public or of foundations' managers by compromises on a qualitative level or by compromises with the "numerical naïveté" so current in our civilization.

Psychoanalysis and Education

Rocco Motto and Rudolph Ekstein have started on a most important and very badly needed enterprise: namely, to open up all over again the issue of psychoanalysis and what it may mean for the educator. They describe it to perfection in the publication for which the subsequent pages were originally prepared as a foreword. The fact is that this issue, so hot in the early days of child analysis, seems to have been dormant —or nearly so—since psychoanalysis's immigration to the United States. With the penetration of many psychoanalytic concepts into the general educator's vocabulary and with increased interest among psychoanalysts in the educational life of their patients, a renewed appraisal of this relationship between two disciplines is devoutly to be wished. But it does not do to stay with a historical review—we also need to carve out the new issues as close to reality as we can. The following pages aim to supply guideposts that should not be ignored along the road.

*I*T'S ABOUT TIME we recovered from the sins of the past. Motto and Ekstein's description is a classic: Nowhere else have I found such a lucid and realistic history of the efforts of psychoanalysis and education to come to grips with each other. As I was part of the historical epoch that they describe and analyze, I may be allowed to summarize and be less polite about it. Here are some of the sins of the past, on the side of psychoanalysis, that it seems to me we ought to junk for good, never mind how understandable or even important it was to have committed them in the first place.

Escape into Delusional Thought

This phase, by the way, was actually of very short duration. The idea that "the liberation of the child" from adult pressures was all that

"Psychoanalysis and Education" is based on the Foreword to the *Reiss-Davis Clinic Bulletin* (Spring 1964).

was needed was a delusion hung onto only before analysts started taking work with children seriously. It was punctured for good when child analysis came to grips with the real lives of children, rather than with reconstructions from couch fantasies of neurotic adults. By the way, we were punished for this sin more than we deserved. For, although we abandoned it quickly and remorsefully, the "general public" picked it up, is still cultivating it, or fights it as though it were still our theory now. I suggest we bury this silly issue for good: Permitting and setting limits are not controversial theories. They are both realistic issues that have to be integrated in varying patterns in the life of each child.

Throwing Crumbs from the Tables of the Rich

This one I remember more vividly, though the mere thought of it makes me blush. It is understandable enough: Impressed with the rich findings brought up from the depths where they had been hidden from view for centuries, one was easily misled into a somewhat condescending and utterly phony missionary zeal. If those poor teachers only "knew more" about what goes on in the "unconscious" of their charges, what a real and beneficial job they could do! Our schools and homes would stop producing the neuroses we struggled with if only the other adults who dealt with children knew what we knew. By the way, by this purposely overdrawn statement I do not want to imply that there aren't some crumbs that would be good to have for all involved or that the spread of knowledge isn't a worthwhile task. What bothers me about that phase we went through "way back when" is, rather, the incredible naïveté with which we indulged in such gestures.

Let's Pick a Few Indians and Make Good House Indians of Them

Having been lucky enough to be picked as a "good Indian," I can attest to the enormous value of such an approach—provided you also permit me to criticize the shortsightedness that came with it. For, obviously, teachers who have been analyzed and then, to boot, trained in whatever might be useful to them or might make them good helpers on cases in analysis are a commodity devoutly to be wished. But this method is as far from solving the problems of education and schools as the giving of Christmas baskets is from solving the problems of social welfare. By the way, there was another hitch that came as something of a surprise. For many a good "house Indian" developed a strong knack for continuing life in that comfortable house, and few wanted to go back to rough life on the reservation or in the sticks.

Setting Up a New Partnership— Psychoanalysis and Co.

In this new enterprise, educators were to be partners in the treatment of the sick. As long as we look at the partnership as an outfit created for the treatment of the sick, this approach is no sin. On the contrary, it probably constitutes the most important and beneficial gain in the field of child therapy this century can be proud of. However, if you look at it in terms of bringing psychoanalysis and education closer together, it is obviously bound to fail. Although it admits educators to new roles as partners in therapy and prevention, it does not come to grips with the issues of teaching and education per se. In fact, because it has been such a successful and important therapeutic development, it has contributed to our blindness to the real problems still untouched.

As far as the interrelationship of psychoanalysis and education is concerned, the real issues are still before us. It seems to me that the Reiss-Davis Seminars and Institutes constitute one of the most effective efforts toward burying the mistakes of the past—after learning from them.

However, recovering from the sins of the past is not enough. It is also time to renew our efforts to take stock of the unfinished business, the challenges of the present and the future. It is a great temptation to try to begin spelling them out right now, at least as far as their visibility has increased under the impact of previous study and research. But this paper is meant as a foreword, not as the story itself. This much, however, should be said, even within such a modest framework: Aside from what we have learned about "content" from the analysis of adults and children and from the joint experiences of therapists and educators in our present-day clinical designs, great challenge seems to lie in four directions.

First, teachers, as well as parents, do not deal with individuals in one-to-one relationships only. Many of their efforts are attempts to reach individuals while they are embedded in the psychological matrix of the group. Much educational leadership is also group leadership. The management of group behavior and the cultivation of group atmospheres that are supportive of, rather than detrimental to, the tasks of learning and growing constitute special areas in their own right. It seems that the analytically oriented teacher in a classroom has a unique chance to contribute to the study of group processes and what they do to individuals, especially if his eye is sharpened to those "inner events" that psychoanalysis has done so much to make visible to us.

Second, the process of learning weaves cognitive, instinctual, and affective events into an impenetrable design. Although the preponderance or dominance of one or the other of these factors has fascinated us in the past, much is yet to be learned about their unique interweaving and about the optimum givens if constructive learning is to take place in the classroom group.

Third, whether invited or not, all parts of a child's—or an adult's—psychology "sit in on" the classroom scene. And, although our deeper zeal may be geared toward the "underlying" processes of growth and character formation, the classroom, as well as the family room, invariably abounds with the noise of overt behavior. Far from being "superficial," the task of managing the behavior of learners in groups or growers in the family setting remains a nearly unattempted challenge of enormous complexity. Only recently have we become more aware of the need to inspect techniques of educational behavioral intervention with as depth-oriented an eye as we are used to viewing the child's personality as such. The search for a psychoanalytically oriented pharmacopoeia of "behavioral-management techniques" has moved from a vaguely perceived fantasy into the realm of attainable goals. It is obvious that the educator in the trenches of daily child life is as important a partner in such an undertaking as are the psychoanalyst and his clinical colleagues.

Fourth, what Anna Freud taught us about the necessity, in child analysis, of remaining aware of the effects of the child's natural habitat, as well as of parent and teacher behavior, on the course of a neurosis or its cure has opened our eyes to the importance not only of taking the children's "defenses" and ego functions more seriously but also of increasing our push for knowledge about which of the "environmental givens" do what to the child. Thus, from a statement of respect for environmental factors as they impinge on the treatment of neurotics, we have long since come to wish for a very specific psychoanalytically oriented analysis, not of the child or his parents alone, but also of the very milieu factors with which both have to cope.

Any one of these aspects, even though only modestly approached, requires, of course, the teamwork of clinical and educational personnel, and such undertakings must be greeted as the most promising framework for renewed exploration of the old puzzle: What about psychoanalysis and education? Where does each belong, and what can it do for the other—and for the child?

Part Three

And What
About Groups?

Group Emotion and Leadership

Rereading this article makes me feel "funny" inside, and it does so for two reasons. For one, the illustrations used in this article bear the obvious stamp of their origin: I developed these concepts and dug up my "type" examples from my own experience as a classroom teacher and from my "camp-like" experiences way back in Vienna several years before my arrival in the United States in 1936. Thus the "group situations" quoted as paradigms still exude that peculiar aroma of life among European kids and in Vienna classrooms, which English syntax has not quite been capable of suppressing. Besides, the "ten types" have since been reprinted several times.

Yet it is not only the reawakened personal narcissism clinging to my pre-American life that motivates me to include this article here. I have two really good reasons for doing so.

First, it is still all true. By "still" I mean in spite of the differences between Vienna and the United States and the passage of time. Just which of the issues involved in the group-formational types listed here become visible in just which combinations certainly constitutes a considerable difference between the two places and times. The basic issues of group-formational process that I tried to unfold, however, seem to me to remain with us, not only in clinical group work with children, but even in youth groups in the community's political life, as I have been able to study them since.

Second, only the nude form of the "ten types" has won the favor of reprinters in symposia. The rest of my speculations have rarely appeared in print and have not been lucky enough to find ample professional discussion. In other words, the wide range of actual problems that these observations seem to me to open up for us has as yet not been taken care of. Among psychoanalysts, by the way, it was Otto Fenichel who was first to respond to the challenge involved in my concepts of "exculpation magics" and "spatial repetition compulsion."

Beside the strictly metapsychological theories involved, though, it seems to me that the very practical problems with which the youth of our

"Group Emotion and Leadership" is based on the article of the same title that appeared in *Psychiatry*, 4 (November 1942), 573–596, copyright 1942 by the William Alanson White Psychiatric Foundation.

time confronts us force us back into that very same pair of auxiliary concepts. For how, other than with the "magics" theory, can we conceptualize what happens when otherwise well-put-together youngsters find themselves so helpless under the impact of group-psychological dares or suffer the severe "shock effects" that any educator or clinician can observe in daily life?

Thus the problems of research posed by my ten types and the challenges they contain for the practitioner seem to me as lively as they were the day they appeared or even when they were first observed way back when.

$\mathcal{F}$REUD'S ARTICLE on mass psychology and the psychoanalysis of the ego has influenced psychoanalytic literature since 1921, mainly in two directions. A series of valuable attempts has been made to expand psychoanalytic explorations through the application of sociological, anthropological, and socioeconomic theory. Then, in the field of education some of the later publications in *Zeitschrift für Psychoanalytische Pädagogik* clearly recognize the growing importance of group psychology, especially for educational practice. Strictly speaking, however, Freud's article has not found supplementation on the same level at which the author started his investigation of the problem.

This lack is all the more surprising because people during the last decade have been more interested in these problems. They clearly understand how futile it is to attempt to interpret events in the world at large without more thorough group-psychological consideration. In addition, there is no doubt that Freud's article is incomplete and that it does invite more supplementation than do any of his other writings. His paper is chiefly limited to the methodological equipment used and the material to which it is being applied.

The methodological equipment is markedly different from the one he would have used had he written the article after his concepts and fundamental theories had undergone their later changes, especially in light of the following points.

His concept of the ego ideal—frequently called "ideal ego"—was not yet differentiated between the two components that he later distinguished as elements derived through incorporation of parental threats (conscience) and the residues of narcissistic cathexis of personality traits (ego ideal) in the later meaning of the term. He used the term "ego ideal" in a way that comprised both functions indiscriminately.

In his use of the term "identification" Freud changed his meaning several times during the course of the article. In some places, he distinguished between the "establishment of an object in the ego ideal," on the one hand, and the "identification of the group members 'in their ego,'" on the other hand. Elsewhere, he used the term in its later meaning.

Freud's article appeared shortly before he developed his theory of the differentiation of love drives and aggressive drives. There is no doubt that the application of these concepts would have made a considerable difference. It seems especially promising to apply this differentiation to the chapter on group-psychological explanations of the army.

The material Freud used for his discussion is also responsible for some of the peculiarities of his publication. He applied the insights gained out of rich experience in handling individual patients and used them to draw analogies with situations in "the church," "the army," and other group-psychological phenomena. The generality of some of his formulations is clearly due to the fact that he did not compare concrete personal experience with equally direct group-psychological experience, which is why his formula reads, "Such a (primary) mass is a number of individuals, who have put one and the same individual in the place of their ego-ideal and have, through doing so, identified with each other in their ego."

In general, there can be little doubt of the validity of this formula, but there is serious doubt of its adequacy for every group formation found in practice. Of course, Freud purposely excluded from his investigation those group formations that occur without the influence of "leaders." Even if one follows him in this limitation of the problem, it seems highly probable that the formula needs modification and supplementation. It must, perhaps, be partly replaced by other formulas, if it is to cover the rich field of practical group formation around a central person of some kind.

This investigation tries to supplement Freud's study in the points just mentioned. It attempts to utilize the methodological equipment developed after 1921; it applies this equipment to such group-psychological observations as could be gained from practical work with groups of children and adolescents in school and camp situations. Nevertheless, the fundamental object of investigation remains strictly the same: to examine the intra psychic emotional and instinctual events in the members of a group, especially those that happen "around" a central person and are constituent factors in group formative processes.

Psychoanalytic Exploration and Sociology

The final word about the relationship between the two fields has not been written—nor should this study be weighted with such an attempt. However, methodological considerations of this sort are sufficiently vital that a clear statement of the author's position might well help to avoid a number of possible misunderstandings. This statement can easily be given.

A psychoanalytic study of group emotion is not identical with a psychoanalytic study of "the group" or "groups." It is only the first that is being attempted here. To try the second seems nonsensical. "Groups" are phenomena containing so many different ingredients that the attempt to bring them into any one formula by the technique of psychoanalytic exploration must remain futile. Indeed, an attempt to do so seems analogous to the idea that any one person could be understood by psychoanalytic methods exclusively, eliminating all the data about this person's organic structure, for example. The importance of understanding the manifold factors constituting group life—psychological, socioeconomic, and all others—is therefore fully recognized, but this paper does not attempt to deal with all of them. It purposely singles out only one of the aspects of group life, the emotional and instinctual relationships among persons who constitute a group. This paper is, therefore, an attempt to supplement, not to substitute for, work on other or wider aspects of the problem.

Nor is this paper an attempt to mix psychoanalytic with "sociological" points of view. Such mixtures are frequently offered as an advanced development. Attempts at keeping the psychoanalytic technique in its "pure" form are threatened with the stigma of narrowmindedness and lack of "sociological sensitivity." Yet this study obviously confines its scope to the merely psychoanalytic sphere for the following reasons.

It is hoped that some blend between psychoanalytic and sociological insights may eventually be created. However, it is definitely felt that the time is not yet ripe. One cannot mix two things before one has them. Today, there is a sociology of the group, on the one hand, and a psychoanalytical psychology of the person, on the other. These two elements do not blend. The product of such mixing is either sociology with a certain number of friendly compliments to the contribution of psychoanalytic thought or psychoanalytic study with more or less eager recognition of the importance of sociological research. The desirable blend would first require a psychoanalytic psychology of the group. To develop this psychology, following the steps made in that direction by Freud's article, seems to be the first task. Only after exhaustive studies will there be some meaningful integration between sociology and psychoanalysis.

Definitions and Basic Assumptions

GROUP EMOTION

The term "emotion" is used here with the same broad meaning that is implied in phrases like "the emotional development of children," for example. In all these cases, emotion "proper" alone is not intended; drives are included as well. As the word "drive" does not have an adequate adjective, a further complication has been introduced into these formulations. The term "instinctual" will be used as an adjective for drive. The summarizing of emotions and drives under the same phrase is a deplorable shortcoming, but it corresponds to a widespread scientific habit based on terminological tradition and convenience.

When "group emotions" are discussed, it is realized that they do not occur in a vacuum but are events that take place within and among the persons who constitute a group. In all probability they are composed of the same ingredients found in any "emotions," although they occasionally seem to obey their own special laws. The term "group" in this context does not designate some special quality but rather the "conditions for the arousal of emotions." Thus "group emotions" refer to instinctual and emotional events taking place within persons under the pressure of group-formative processes.

From this definition, it is obvious that further distinctions should be made. Not all the emotions people have while they are in a group are really "group" emotions. For example, a pair of lovers holding hands at a political-propaganda meeting might justly refuse to have the love emotion in which they participate considered under the category of group emotion. When it seems necessary, this difference can be taken care of by calling emotions that are not the results or causes of the concurrent group-formative processes simply "individual emotions"—although it is recognized that this term is misleading to the extent that any emotion is basically a process occuring within a personal situation. Furthermore, not all group emotions are equally basic to the process of group formation. Some, for example, are sources of group formation. The adoration 100 people have for one and the same person may make this person their leader. It is basic to the formation of the group. On the other hand, through this group formation, a number of other emotional relationships may develop among these people that might not otherwise have been experienced. Such emotions are the results of, rather than the causes for, group-formative processes. For example, A may begin to distrust B, without any highly "personal" hate against him, merely on the basis of a general group aversion that has developed because of the role B has played within his group. In that case A's feeling toward B is the product of a special group-emotional constellation. The following distinction will therefore be made:

Constituent group emotions are instinctual and emotional events in the potential members of a group that are basic to the group-formative processes: secondary group emotions are such instinctual and emotional procedures within and among the members of a group that have developed on the basis of group-formative processes.

Of course, any emotion may be constituent in one situation and secondary in another. The diagnosis is not always easy, although it is vital to the judgment and influence of group-formative processes.

The Central Person

Freud called the person around whom the group-formative process crystallizes the "leader," following a well-rooted linguistic habit. However, since 1921, quite a few things have happened that make us all more sensitive to the tremendous differences of meaning that this word takes on under certain circumstances. This investigation, especially, led to the discovery of a number of types of group formation that do occur "around a central person" but to the designation of which the word "leader" simply does not lend itself. It is therefore necessary to begin with a terminological correction, reserving the word "leader" for only one type of role of the person central for group formation and relationships with members, giving different names to the other forms.

By "central person" is meant the person "around whom" group-formative processes take place, the "crystallization point" of the whole affair. The word "central" is simply willful and should not be taken literally. "Focal" might be better for logical reasons, but for linguistic purposes it is unsatisfactory.

The term "central person" designates the one through emotional relationship to whom the group-formative processes are evoked in the potential group members.

Ten types of "leadership"—ten different roles that this central person may play in group formation—can easily be distinguished.

The object of this investigation must be recognized as the study of drive relationships and emotional procedures within each member of a group, on the basis of which group-formative processes are evoked.

Freud's limitation of the topic to those types of group formation that occur "around some person," is followed, excluding other mass-psychological investigations from this study.

The weight of the study is on the constituent group emotions; the secondary consequences of group formation on the emotional relationships among the members are only alluded to occasionally for the purpose of illustration. The interpersonal relations should provide the basis for another study, equally important for the purpose of education.[1]

The methodological equipment developed by Freud is used in this study. Two further assumptions are suggested, both of a metapsychological character. They are the assumption of the guilt-and-fear-assuaging effect of the initiatory act and the assumption of the infectiousness of the unconflicted on the conflicted personality constellation, that is, of the spatial repetition compulsion. These two assumptions will be explained in detail; a partial attempt at their justification will be made in this study.

1. Studies made by Kurt Lewin and Ronald Lippitt furnish data on this topic.

Ten Types of Group Formation

All ten types presented deal with group formation "around" a central person. The differences among the ten types lie in the different roles of the central person for the basic processes of group formation. The method used to present these ten types is somewhat involved. Its peculiarity for the whole problem will become a topic of discussion later. Let it suffice at this point to say that an attempt has been made to present each type by describing one or more "illustrative examples." The explanation and formula that differentiate each type from others is then given. This presentation summarizes the nature of the constituent group-formative processes at work.

The "examples" are not necessarily identical with clinical material, nor are they to be used as "proof" for the formula that follow them. The examples are intended as illustrations for the purpose of introduction and explanation of each type. In condensing many observations into a composite picture, a host of practically irrelevant items was discarded in order to isolate one process. These illustrative examples are best understood if they are taken as graphic slides. They all claim to be based on concrete reality experiences, but none pretends to be a photograph. Problems of frequency and actuality, for example, will be taken up in "discussion" of the ten types immediately following their presentation.

TYPE 1: THE PATRIARCHAL SOVEREIGN

Example. This group is composed of approximately ten-year-old children, most of whom are at that point in their development at which they most fully represent the end state of "childhood" immediately before the outbreak of preadolescent symptoms. In charge of them is a teacher who fits the following description: He is an elderly gentleman of stern but not unfriendly exterior, decided but fundamentally mild in his manner. He stands for "order and discipline," but they are values so deeply ingrained in him that he hardly thinks of them explicitly, nor does it occur to anyone to doubt them in his presence. He believes in good and thorough work, knows very clearly what he expects, and leaves no doubt about it in the minds of his students. The atmosphere of the classroom may be easily described. The children accept his values without question. Their emotions about him are mixtures of love and adoration, with elements of anxiety in all those instances in which they are not quite sure of his approval. As long as they behave according to his code, they feel happily secure—sheltered. Thoughts and imaginations that do not comply with his code are suppressed in his presence. The jokes he makes or acknowledges are funny. If one youngster is not quite so ready as are the others to concentrate his filial adoration upon this type of teacher, makes unfitting remarks and unruly gestures, or shows lack of submission, the others experience deep feelings of moral indignation—even though they may have enjoyed this youngster's jokes a few minutes previously during the recreation period. They all love their teacher and trust him infinitely, but certain thoughts must never enter their minds in his presence. When they are questioned or doubted by this teacher, tears come more easily than words; behind the happy security felt in his presence, there is a nagging fear of its loss, which streams into awareness every once in a while without apparent cause.

Explanation. These youngsters love their teacher, but that is not all that occurs. Their love is of a type that leads to "identification." It would be absurd to say that they want to be like their teacher, but they want to behave so that their teacher will approve of them.

Formula. These children become a group because they incorporate the "superego"—conscience—of the central person into their own. On the basis of this similarity among them, they develop group emotions toward one another.

TYPE 2: THE LEADER

Example. This group of boys is between fifteen and seventeen years of age. Most of them are far beyond their preadolescence—at the verge of transition from earlier adolescence into later adolescence. The teacher in charge of them is, or has the appearance of being, very young. He has an attractive exterior. He is somewhat juvenile in his views and behavior but not too unpleasantly so. He also stands for "work and discipline" and gets his youngsters to comply without much outward pressure. However, the basis on which he gets them to accept his authority is a little different. He differs from the patriarch mainly in that he strongly sympathizes with the drives of the children. They are clearly aware of it. He plays a dual role in his teaching. In his own superego, he is identified with the order and the demands of the school he represents, but he is keenly aware of the instinctual demands of the youngsters. In order to combine both, he has to display considerable technical skill. If he succeeds, he makes his class feel secure and happy; if he fails, the boys are frightened either of him or of their own drives. The boys adore him, but they also accept what he stands for without much question. The boy who misbehaves is not the greatest danger to the emotional equilibrium of the group. He elicits moral pity rather than indignation from the others. The danger is the boy who tries to elicit a more intensive emotional response from the teacher than do the others, while being less ready to pay for it with conscientious output of work. He is hated and despised by them. A single youngster in that group, feeling negatively viewed by the teacher, is unhappy rather than frightened. Undesirable thoughts and actions still remain confessable. To be "understood"—accepted—is the minimum requirement for group happiness in this class.

Explanation. A central person of this kind appeals to the love emotions, as well as to the narcissistic tendencies in the children. However, it would be difficult to say that they put the teacher in the place of their "consciences." Rather they place him in the other part of their superegos, in what is usually called their "ego ideals," which means that they start wishing to become the type of person he is.

Formula. The children become a group because they incorporate the teacher's personality into their ego ideals. On the basis of this similarity they develop group emotions toward one another. This formula coincides most closely with that of Freud in *Group Psychology and the Analysis of the Ego.*

TYPE 3: THE TYRANT

Example. This class consists of children approximately ten years old, near the verge of preadolescence. In charge of them is an elderly or middle-aged teacher, among whose motives for teaching are one or both of the following: He is compulsively bound to repeat a certain pattern of "discipline" against the children because it is the only way he can prove late obedience to some of the demands of his own parents, or his most intensive drive satisfactions lie in the direction of sadism, and he has to use the children as objects for that purpose. This teacher will not "stand for" anything but has to "impose" some kind of capricious "order" or "discipline" all the time. Nor will he be satisfied to do so quietly. He will require a noisy machinery of special tricks, rules, and revenge techniques. His concept of discipline, too, will be of the most compulsive, unrealistic sort, and the way he works it out will be as "unchild-minded" as possible. In short, there is a "regular tyrant" in charge of this class. Everyday psychology might tempt one to expect children to hate the teacher and fight him as much as they dare. Indeed, this reaction does occur in a few examples, which I shall describe later. The entirely different reaction of most of the youngsters is surprising. These children submit easily. They rebel against the silly pedantry of this tyrant less vehemently than other groups do against the reasonable demands of their beloved leaders. Nor do they submit only temporarily. What they show is genuine "identification." How strong is this identification? The strength is illustrated by their reactions to the youngster who does dare to rebel in such a class. He has a difficult time. He has everyone against him, the teacher, the other youngsters, and himself. The others show intensive signs of moral indignation and eventually become afraid of the child.

However, one difference seems obvious. The emotional relations these youngsters develop among themselves seem less intensive than in the other illustrations. Children in such classes develop little "comradeship"—unlike those who simply hate their teachers without identifying with them—and they seem to be afraid of one another and distrustful. They seem to fear that too much intimacy might endanger the successful repression of their hostility and might force them to realize what cowards they are.

Explanation. Doubtless, the identification of these children with their tyrant is genuine. He is the central person for the group. Unlike those in the two previous illustrations, this identification occurs from a different motive. It is not love that causes the children to identify but fear. Of course, not all fear leads to identification, but it does in the type just described.

Formula. These children incorporate the superego of the central person into their own by way of identification, the outgrowth of fear of the aggressor, and on this basis establish group emotions among one another.

TYPE 4: LOVE OBJECT

Freud mentioned an example of group formation that he exempted from the leadership type. It fits into the pattern according to the broadened concept of the central person I have introduced.

Imagine a number of women who are in love with a singer or pianist and crowd around him after his performance. Certainly each of them would prefer to be jealous of all the others. However, considering their large number and how impossible it is for them to reach the aim of their infatuation, they resign, and, instead of pulling one another's hair, they act as a group in a uniform way. They bring ovations to their idol in common actions and would be glad to divide his locks among themselves.[2]

Life in the school class furnishes two similar examples for illlustration.

Example 1. There is a group of sixteen-year-old girls in a class in a girls' high school. In charge of them is a male teacher—young, attractive, but narcissistic enough so that they are not too greatly frightened sexually from the outset. It is known that in some such cases "the whole class falls in love with him." From that moment on, the girls will act as a group in many ways, along the line of Freud's example. Despite their infatuation for him, it would not be surprising if the teacher complained that he had trouble with discipline—that these girls did not obey him or follow his wishes without pressure. It seems that this kind of "being in love" with the central person does not make for the "identification" described in the example of the leader.

Example 2. In a coeducational class of approximately sixteen-year-old children, there is one especially pretty girl, rather narcissistic. In similar situations one frequently finds a whole cluster of boys loving and adoring her in various ways but equally unsuccessful insofar as their wishes for exclusive possession go. The girl is equipped with special skill for keeping them all equidistant yet equally near. Symptoms of dense group formation may sometimes be observed among these boys. They seem very close to one another, yet their relationships are not genuine friendships. They are based on group emotion. This fact becomes evident when the girl ultimately decides in favor of one of her suitors. The other boys then begin to hate him as their rival, with the exception perhaps of the one or two who may move even closer to the successful colleague and thus enjoy some of the satisfaction otherwise denied to them via the mechanism of altruistic concessions.[3]

Explanation. There is no doubt that the group emotional symptoms are genuine and that the teacher in Example 1 and the girls in Example 2 are playing the role of the central person without whose presence this

2. Sigmund Freud, *Group Psychology and the Analysis of the Ego* (London: Hogarth Press, Ltd., 1922).
3. Anna Freud, *The Ego and the Mechanisms of Defense* (London: Hogarth Press, Ltd., 1922).

type of group-formative process would not have been evoked. However, it is also evident that these central persons could not be called "leaders" by any interpretation of the term—that the other children do not "identify" with them. Nor do they incorporate their central persons' standards. The central persons remain "outside" but do call out displays of group-emotional symptoms in these children.

Formula. The children choose one and the same person as an object of their love, and on the basis of this similarity they develop group emotions among one another.

TYPE 5: THE CENTRAL PERSON AS OBJECT OF AGGRESSIVE DRIVES

Example 1. A type of teacher similar to the one described under the heading of "tyrant" is less intensive in his sadism, less superior in the rest of his personality traits. He is in charge of a group of rather problematic adolescents in a school setup that is so well regimented through an established system of suppressive rules that no one dares to rebel because it would be too futile. These children obey their teacher under the constant application of pressure. They behave sufficiently well to keep out of trouble, but they do so grudgingly. They identify neither with the teacher nor with what he represents. Their relationship with him—with the possible exception of a "sissy" in the class—is one of intensive hatred, of piled-up aggression that is kept from exploding only by their insights into reality. Yet, although they do not identify with the teacher, the emotions they develop toward one another are truly positive and strong. The amount of "comradeship" these children display is enormous—greater than in any of the other groups. He who dares to identify with the hated oppressor is an outcast—arouses a lynching attitude in the rest of the class. Its members' feeling toward him is one of moral indignation, but its content is different from the other examples. It is moral indignation "from beneath," to use one of Nietzsche's terms.

Example 2. Here is a group of children who have developed no special group structure. There is no person in charge of them with a sufficiently outspoken personality to encourage any of the previously mentioned types of group formation. A new youngster suddenly enters the class who differs from the others in that he is of a very outspoken type. This new youngster is especially narcissistic, defiant, lofty, and unskilled in handling other people's weaknesses. If he is intellectually superior, he need not even be of a different ethnic group. Everyone's aggression is immediately turned against him. At the same time one may observe that his entrance into the class has indirectly influenced group-formative processes. Its members move closer together; their common aggression against him seems to "bind" them, and they become more of a "group" than they were before.

Explanation. This new youngster cannot be called a "leader." The others neither like him nor "identify" with him. They do quite the contrary; yet he does apparently become the focal point of their group-formative procedures, much as the teacher did in Example 1.

Formula. The children chose one and the same person as an object of their aggressive drives and through this similarity develop group emotions toward one another.

TYPE 6: THE ORGANIZER

Example. In a class of approximately thirteen-year-old boys, there are five who find clandestine enjoyment of the cigarette as a symbol of adulthood. Yet all five are of the type that has decided worries about how it can obtain cigarettes. They have neither the money to buy them, the courage to do so, nor the impudence to steal them from their fathers. Preadolescent revolt against adult concepts of what a good child should be has not progressed far enough. A new boy, for whom smoking is no great problem, enters the class. He neither invites, instigates, nor encourages the others in this enterprise. They all know that he can get the desired cigarettes for them if they but ask. I have seen cases in which hardly any other factor was involved. The boys neither loved nor admired this youngster; on the contrary, he was rather looked down upon as socially inferior. They did not fear him, nor did he use any direct or indirect pressure upon them. Yet, by the mere fact of his getting them the cigarettes, they suddenly emerged as a regular "group," held together by their participation in the same forbidden pleasure.

Explanation. Perhaps this example seems more complicated—less credible—than the others, as we are unaccustomed to finding this function of the organizer isolated. Usually, it is coupled with other roles that the central person assumes for the potential group members. Although there are not many clear examples of this type, they cannot be reduced to any of the other types because neither love, hatred, nor identification is involved.

Formula. The central person renders an important service to the egos of the potential group members. He does so by providing the means for the satisfaction of common undesirable drives and thus prevents guilt feelings, anxieties, and conflicts that otherwise would be involved in that process for them. On the basis of this service, the latent undesirable drives of these youngsters can be manifested openly. Through this common conflict solution, group emotions develop in the interpersonal situation.

TYPE 7: THE SEDUCER

Example 1. In a group of thirteen-year-old boys, six involved in "group masturbation" are apprehended. The first superficial examination by school authorities reveals apparent unequal participation. Some are onlookers; none is mutually active; all agree that one of them is the "leader" of the gang. After thorough investigation the following situation is revealed. The obvious "culprit" is most "actively" engaged in masturbation. He is the "first to start it." However, he is not at all active in encouraging the others to join or to perform. He is a little more developed than any of them; he masturbates freely at home without special guilt feelings. Masturbation means something entirely different to him than to the others, nor does he need the group from the point of view of sex satisfaction. He gains nothing from the group situation except prestige. He is not homosexual in the usual sense of the term; more surprising, perhaps, is the fact that the others neither especially love nor fear him. They are more infantile than he. They have sufficiently conquered their anxieties about sex curiosity to take the first step in active experimentation on a highly pregenital level. However, they might not have done so alone, as that would have made them feel guilty about it. Actually, they use this boy for the purpose of "seduction." They need him, and the group situation allows them to overcome their restrictions. Only after he is the "first one to do it" are they ready and able to join.

Example 2. A class of fifteen-year-old children, in high spirits toward the end of their morning sessions, waits for the teacher to arrive. He is somewhat late. He is the "leader" type, with a slight patriarchial tendency. Recently, at an examination period, a considerable amount of tension and dissatisfaction was extant. The relationship between the children and their teacher was rather strained. He now enters the room. They stand at attention as is expected. Suddenly, one youngster, neither much liked, respected, nor feared by the others, starts yelling aggressively in a much more rebellious manner than anyone would have expected, especially toward this teacher. There is a moment of surprise. Before the teacher can react manifestly, they all join in. The whole class is in an uproar, more intensely so than any can afterwards "understand."

Explanation. Both examples beyond doubt represent group formation through the existence of a central person. In both cases, the potential group members have much in common before the group-formative processes begin. It is also evident that a group does not start before the central person commits the "first act." Apparently what evokes the group-emotional reactions is the fact that the central person commits an "initiatory" act. Through this act, the satisfaction of undesirable drives becomes possible for others, who would otherwise not openly express them. This concept of the "initiatory act" is not an invention but the description of a procedure observed so frequently in school and adult life that it does not require proof. It needs, however, to be explained. Thus far, I do not attempt to show why the "first act" may have such magical power over other people's suppressed drives. I simply allude to the fact here and keep its explanation for a later presentation.

What occurs in these children is here described. There is a strong increase in the intensity of undesirable drives—sex in Example 1, aggressions in Example 2. The personal superegos of these children remain strong enough to suppress any possibility of the drives becoming overt. The egos of these children are in predicaments. Pressed with equal strength from oppressed drives and superego demands, they know not what to do. Anxiety and uneasiness are the usual emotional accompaniments of such disturbances to balance. It is on the basis of such a situation that the effects of an "initiatory act" seem to occur.

Formula. The central person renders a service to the egos of the potential group members. He does so by committing the "initiatory act" and thus prevents guilt feelings, anxieties, and conflicts. On the basis of this service, the latent drives of these children are manifested openly. Through this common conflict solution, they develop group emotions.

TYPE 8: THE HERO

Example. This group is the same as that described for the tyrant—in which all the children are fully identified with their oppressor—at a later interval. These children have developed further into preadolescent rebelliousness. The reality insight begins to fade on important issues: Yet, sufficiently frightened, they keep their defensive identifications against rebellious wishes. The tyrant now begins to make deplorable mistakes. He chooses, for example, one child as the preferred object of his sadism and persecutes him more and more persistently. The others almost pity the child, but pity would imply criticism of their tyrant, and that would tend to revive their own dangerously rebellious feelings against him. So they hold as tightly to their protective identification with the oppressor as they can. However, one of them has more courage. Something in his history makes him less able to endure this situation—or perhaps his insight into the real dangers implied by rebellion dwindles more rapidly. In any event, he is one day unable to tolerate the teacher's attack upon his victim. This boy defends his colleague and is considered "fresh" and reckless. The whole class gasps with surprise. Its members expect something fearful to happen. Surely the teacher will kill that child, or lightning will strike out of the clear sky. But no avenging stroke of lightning descends to quell the rebellion. The teacher is evidently too surprised or frightened momentarily to know what to do. When he demonstrates his fury, it is too late. The "hero" has worked his miracle. All the youngsters have altered their sentiments, at least secretly. Now they adore him and even start identifying with him. He takes his punishment but remains victorious.

Explanation. The situation is similar to the one previously described, but events now move in the opposite direction. These youngsters suffer similarly from a number of suppressed tendencies—like just rebellion in favor of a suffering colleague, however, they are too fearful of the realistic consequences of such feelings. Their personal cowardice hinders them from doing what they feel is right but would have awful consequences for them. Again the hero commits the "initiatory act." Through his demonstration of courage, the others suddenly discard anxieties and dare, if not to act then at least to feel what their own standard of justice has long wanted them to experience.

Formula. The central person renders a service to the ego of the potential group members. He does so by committing the "initiatory act" and thus saves them anxieties and conflicts. The "initiatory act," however, leads in the direction of moral values versus cowardly self-protection this time. On the basis of this service, the undesirable tendencies toward cowardly submission in these children are conquered.

Through this common conflict solution group psychological emotions are evoked.

TYPE 9: THE BAD INFLUENCE

There are children in many classes who are constantly accused of being "undesirable elements" by teachers, parents, and the other children too. Yet they can scarcely be accused of "having an evil" influence. Usually what they are accused of is unclear, but it is assumed that their mere presence in the classroom affects the others badly—"brings out the worst in them." Yet it would be embarrassing to say how they do so. Accusations against them often have to be withdrawn, because no definite bases exist in fact. Nothing can be proved. Sometimes, admittedly, these children are not so difficult to manage; they are better than the influence they are accused of having on the others. Fundamentally, the accusation of being an "undesirable element" is an accusation of seduction through magic. Apparently belief in the infectiousness of something within these children seems absurd, yet it is not. The background upon which the accusations are made is usually real. These children do affect the others, not overtly—in contrast to the "seducer type"—but by their presence in the same room something happens to all the youngsters that makes them unruly, full of "dirty" ideas, or just difficult to manage. What supports this reaction?

Example. In a botany class of eleven-year-old children, a word is mentioned that reminds those who "know" of a sex situation. About a dozen are preoccupied with associations of this sort. When the word is mentioned, they all look at one boy, then at each other. They grin. He grins back. The whole room, at this moment, is divided in two. The threads of this little clique are spread like a net over it. Next day a nearly identical situation recurs. However, that boy happens to be absent from class. Nothing happens. The children fail to make the same association that they did the day before. Their little "gang" remains submerged in the group without interruption.

Explanation. This type again is very similar to that of the "seducer"; the difference, however, rests in the technique used for "seduction." Nothing like the "initiatory act" is implied here. The explanation has to be reduced to a more descriptive statement to show how the "bad influence" works. The dynamic explanation must be considered later.

With the inner constellations of the potential group members similar to that described in the seduction type, it can apparently be said that they possess a number of undesirable drives that seek expression; their superegos are in command, so that satisfaction of these undesirable drives is impossible without the penalties of remorse and anxiety. And the ego is in a "bad jam," squeezed between the urges of their drives and the demands of a strong superego.

The inner constellation of the "bad influence" type of central person is different from those of the group members. In him there is no conflict. His drives in the same direction do not set loose conflicts and problems for him. He faces them and does not care. Alertness on the part of the others to this state seems to be sufficient encouragement for the expression of what they have been trying to suppress. This alertness really means the assumption of a definite process that might best be described by saying that the "unconflicted" personality constellation has an infectious influence on the conflicted whenever they meet. This description again is of an easily observable fact, which by itself provides no understanding of the process. However, it is enough to explain the group-formative processes in these cases. It is important to realize that these examples of so-called "bad influence" are usually group-psychological procedures.

Formula. The central person renders a service to the ego of the potential group members. He does so by virtue of the "infectiousness of the unconflicted personality constellation upon the conflicted one." He thus saves the others the expense of guilt feelings, anxieties, and conflicts. On the basis of this service, the latent undesirable drives of these children can be manifested openly. Through this common conflict solution, these children develop group emotions in relationship with one another.

TYPE 10: THE GOOD EXAMPLE

Example. The same class as the one mentioned in the previous example contains another group of boys who "gang up" with one another even more intensively than do the undesirable ones. Nevertheless, the teacher would hesitate to call them a "gang" or even a group. They are simply a bunch of very good friends, he would say. However, one of them is the obvious center, and he "has a marvelous influence" upon the others. They are much nicer when he is around. If pressed, the teacher can hardly explain how that boy manages to influence them, for he obviously does nothing. In looking at this group more closely, the following situation is discovered. These children are not "friends" in the personal meaning of this term. All are at that stage at which they are full of new curiosities of which they are afraid because they would feel guilty in satisfying them. This one boy, however, is far removed from any undesirable thought or act.

Explanation. The inner constellations in the potential group members show a number of undesirable drives seeking expression, the super-ego is decidedly against them but scarcely able to maintain its position for long, and the ego is in "bad jam" about how to maintain balance in such a situation. The inner constellation of the central boy in this situation contains no conflict of this kind. The mere idea of expressing undesirable thoughts in his presence is impossible. So the group moves closer to him; in his presence its members feel secure. What they fear is their own drives; what they look for is some support for the endangered superego. The situation is the exact reverse of the "bad influence" example.

Formula. The central person renders a service to the ego of the potential group members. He does so by virtue of the "infectiousness of the unconflicted personality constellation upon the conflicted one." Through this service he saves them the necessity of facing their own drives, of which they are afraid, and all the resulting conflicts. This time, however, the solution leads in the direction of moral values instead of undesirable drives. On the basis of this service, the children can suppress their undesirable drives according to the commands of their own superegos. Through this common conflict solution, they develop group emotions in the relationships with one another.

Summary

For the purpose of rapid summary, these ten types can be grouped into three main categories and tabulated.

The Central Person as an Object of Identification
    On the Basis of Love

Incorporation into Conscience	Type 1
Incorporation into the "Ego Ideal"	Type 2

    On the Basis of Fear

Identification with the Aggressor	Type 3

The Central Person as an Object of Drives

As an Object of Love Drives	Type 4

As an Object of Aggressive Drives   Type 5
The Central Person as an Ego Support
  Providing Means for Drive Satisfaction   Type 6
  Dissolving Conflict Situations Through Guilt-Anxiety
    Assuagement
    Through the Technique of the Initiatory Act in the Service of
      Drive Satisfaction   Type 7
    In the Service of Drive Defense   Type 8
    Through the "Infectiousness of the Unconflicted Personality
      Constellation over the Conflicted One" in the Service of
      Drive Satisfaction   Type 9
    In the Service of Drive Defense   Type 10

Discussion of the Ten Types

GROUP-PSYCHOLOGICAL SPECULATIONS

The description of ten different group-psychological patterns under "type" headings does not effect a compulsively logical separation among them. In fact, they are not rigid "types" of groups so much as they are typical "trends" in group-formative processes. Simplification and abbreviation may have made the types seem much more final and exclusive than they are meant to be. The ten "types" are auxiliary concepts for exploratory purposes only. Testing them against practical life situations should help to show certain trends that might not otherwise have been discovered. That is all they are good for. Nothing could be more wrong than to extrapolate practical group experience from any one of these "types," as though any one real group situation would ever be a clear exemplification of any of them.

Example. The "organizer" of a group usually combines "leader" and "seducer" functions and vice versa—there is rarely a leader, tyrant, or seducer situation without some organizing activity linked up with it. Yet there are usually differences in the degrees to which one or the other type of relation of central person to group is basic or secondary to group formation. Also a person may start out as the "hero," "seducer," or what not, and on the basis of this group formation he may later enter leader-organizer and other relationships or even transform himself entirely from one to the other role. This case seems to be one in which a person suddenly becomes central as a "hero," then on that basis develops more pervasive leadership functions for his group.

In establishing the "ten types" as auxiliary concepts for exploration, the question of their application to historical, political, and educational reality was neglected. This question is certainly a big temptation. For, no doubt, it would be interesting to know which type of group formation—or which mixture of types—is most frequently represented in any one cultural situation, at any one time in history, or at any one socioeconomic, national or "racial" place.

However, I am convinced that it would be premature to attempt such speculations at the moment. There are two main handicaps. First, any decision about frequency and reality distribution of types or type mixtures can never be the result of speculation but only of very specific research. Such research, on the basis of the conceptual equipment suggested here, has not been undertaken yet. It might be interesting to play with analogies, but scientific statements on such questions would be definitely out of place. Second, the real psychoanalytic structure of any one group situation is very hard to ascertain. It definitely need not be identical with the terminology that the group chooses to express its allegiances. Nor can it always be guessed easily from a surface study of expressions of group life. In fact, the distance between the actual underlying group-emotional constellation and the surface manifestations of overt group verbiage and group behavior may be as great, at times, as the distance between the conscious dream content and the latent dream thoughts.

Examples. Many a so-called "gang" situation (the seducer) may, upon close study, turn out to be much more the leadership type. It may only have looked so undesirable because of the philosophy of the judging teacher. Many a group that proudly professes its belief in the "leader" ideal may, upon closer inspection, reveal itself as nothing but a bunch of delinquents indulging in reckless satisfaction of their destructive drives under the protection of a seducer who assumes the leader title for the purpose of disguise. Equally, it would be deceptive to judge educational groups by the names of the political systems in which they occur. For example, the idea that all school classes in a democratic state are free from the traits of "patriarchal"—or matriarchal—sovereign atmospheres would easily prove to be an illusion, if followed up by detailed research.

Mention of everything that happens in the groups illustrating the ten types is not even attempted. Only some of the constituent group-emotional factors are presented. There is another side to this problem, which deserves at least equal attention. What types of emotion are being evoked in the members of any of these types of group formation; and especially, what type of character traits is favored or inhibited under the pressure of any one of them? It seems that Freud purposely neglected this side of the picture. He describes what happens among the group members as "identification in their ego." However, there is no doubt that this term can refer only to the constituent situation. It is obvious that the group members, on the basis of those very identifications, also do develop new emotions in relationship with one another. What are they?

Example. The groups based on leadership have to handle the danger of jealousy among the members as one of their crucial problems. For, if every member loves the central person strongly enough to establish heavy identifications on the basis of that love, then it is apparent that the problems of demanded counterlove and rivalry among the group members must enter the picture. A tendency to envy and suspicion of other group members is one of the handicaps of this situation. The group centered on an object of aggression (Type 5) seems freer of this burden. Common hatred of the outside enemy engulfs all aggressiveness that might still exist among the single members of the group. Therefore, from the outside, such groups look so much more "comradely" than do those of the straight leadership type, so much more "united." This observation may even be suggestive of the idea that common hatred unites so much better than does common love. However, this conclusion would also be rash. For it would depend on what is meant by "uniting better." If the momentary intensity of positive feelings of unity in the members is meant, it is true. Any expectation, however, that such sudden unity guarantees lasting changes in their interpersonal relationships would be disappointed. The unification on the basis of common aggression against an outside enemy does not seem to bind much longer than the open outside aggression lasts. After the fight situation is broken up, such groups relapse into aggressive free-for-alls among all the members unless, in the meantime, group-psychological ties of a different nature have been built up.

Although a positive application of my typology to any actual political or historical situation seems premature, I believe that I am ready to make one negative suggestion: The picture I have portrayed makes one highly suspicious of all attempts at group-psychological mysticism, at a too naïve rationalism, and also warns against what could be called "psychiatric individualism."

Examples. The "strong-man theory," which is so frequently shared by even highly intelligent persons, aims at explaining the group-formative effects of any one political leader by emphasizing his "strong personality." On the basis of investigation I cannot see such a simple solution. On the contrary, I expect group-psychological flexibility to be more effective than the "one-sidedness" of the strong man. The aims of Hitler, for example, seem to be furthered by his ability to become the "central person" for many reasons in different types of groups. There are distinct signs that wide areas of the more reactionary bureaucracy make him their "patriarchal sovereign"—much to the disgust of the younger, adolescent, representatives of the Youth Movement. For some of the Youth Movement leaders he seems to assume the role of genuine leadership (Type 2), continuing the tradition of ascetic and idealistic glorification of the leader idea, which was so characteristic of the German Youth Movement long decades before the Hitler Youth Movement began and which was so strong that it even urged definitely anti-totalitarian movements, like those of socialists, into patterns of "leadership cult." To many of the more aggressive storm troopers, the *Führer,* or his representative, did not seem to play this idealistically glorified role but more that of the seducer who allows the aggressive and destructive act and the satisfaction of sadistic impulses through his skill at exculpation magics. No doubt, many women "adored" their *Führer* as a love object, his nondescript role to the other sex definitely aiding them in this activity. His most effective weapon seems to be illustrated by the case of the tyrant (Type 3). By willfully playing the role of persecutor to one part of the population, this type of leader becomes the "tyrant" to those who reject him and not simply the object of aggression, which means that he leads them into genuine identification with his basic goals. Those who remain on the level of Type 5— choosing the head of the state as their object of common aggression— and who are genuinely revolutionary enough not to be frightened into real identification remain the only "realistic" problem to be dealt with by factual suppression and supervisory control.

Of course, this illustration only alludes to the "type" of process I assume is going on. In what frequency distribution any one of these group-formative phenomena is taking place could not be reasoned by psychological speculation. One may be warned, of course, against the dangers of theorizing on the basis of superficial data—only the interpreted, not the overt, material could serve as a basis for such a study.

Attempts at analysis of the complex group-psychological pattern versus escape into theories of group-psychological mysticism seem to be one of the negative consequences my theories could have on political thought.

The other negative application lies in the destruction of a widespread tendency toward a "rationalism" of the most naïve sort. Deepseated powers of a group-psychological nature are at work. Neither the talks nor the acts of leaders of totalitarian—or any other—states should be interpreted on their surface values and judged in the light of their rationality or purposefulness alone. Critics of Hitler, for example, repeatedly ridicule the extent to which totalitarian leaders emphasize the fact that they are going to take "all responsibility upon themselves." These critics argue that it is absurd to "assume responsibility" when there is no one to challenge their statements claiming it. The arguments of these critics are only logically correct. Group-psychologically speaking, those leaders know the importance of the "magic of the initiatory act" and know, better than their critics, what dynamic power lies in it. A later section of this study will make this point clearer than it may now be.

The third theory that is frequently used by sociologically and group-psychologically oriented laymen is of special importance because it is shared by so many otherwise authoritative specialists in the fields of clinical psychiatry and psychoanalysis. These specialists try to explain what happens in the world by demanding clinical histories of the persons who are currently in the limelight. Thus, many are misled by the hope that, if they only had a complete case history of Adolf, they would understand what was happening in Europe.

Such naïveté cannot be condemned too strongly. A case history of Hitler could only explain why Hitler and not Schmidt or Huber is in his position and some of the symptomatic paraphernalia of the European scene. It would not be correct to try to dissolve European events into a one-person case history—or even the case histories of a whole inventory of persons. Such an attempt is blind to the socioeconomic as well as to the historical involvements, on the one hand, and—and this point is the one I want to emphasize—to the deeper group-psychological mechanisms at work, on the other hand. It is by the nature of these processes that any person or group of persons in power anywhere manages to gain and keep control. The understanding of group-psychological processes, therefore, is basic to any understanding of political events. This does not mean that I deny the highly stimulating value of clinical studies of leaders—only the idea that such studies suffice for understanding of group phenomena.

Which is first, the leader or the group, is a problem frequently raised in connection with discussions on leadership. Let me phrase it in a way that is less reminiscent of the futile hen-egg priority quarrel. Which is the more active factor in group formation, the influence of the leader or the readiness of the group?

From my way of centering the discussion around the role of the focal person, it might seem, at first glance, as though my types suggest that the group-formative power emanates more or less from the central person. I therefore cannot stress emphatically enough that no such implication is intended. The degree of "activeness" or "passivity"—in the role of the leader or in the members in group-formative processes is entirely a problem of its own. In fact, there is no general answer to that problem. My suggestion is that each practical group situation contains both possibilities in varying degrees, and there are some groups that approximate one or the other of the two extremes. In my experience with children I have found all these various situations.

Example. There obviously are situations in which members of a group who would otherwise not enter distinct stages of group formation are induced to do so by virtue of the special type of personality that becomes their central person. A highly active "bad example" or "seducer" type of child among a group of youngsters who are still strongly involved in their latency submissiveness may perform miracles of gang formation when other youngsters could not possibly attain the role of central person. However, I also have observed situations in which the central person was almost forced into his role by virtue of the intensity of drive quantities within the group members, which were ready to erupt at the first opportunity. Thus, many a youngster in the "seducer role" may have been seduced by the group into becoming its seducer. It is sometimes the central person who is practically more "passive" than is the group. This point is an important item for which teachers should be on the alert. Practical considerations should, therefore, never enter the cul-de-sac of either-or propositions; defining the degrees of activity and passivity on both sides should be the aim.

The question of the durability of group-psychological effects upon each member has been raised in many contexts. I am inclined to suggest that this problem is also very complex, and hesitate to ascribe it to any one factor in group formation—like the degree of organization or tradition—at first glance. I further suggest that the problem be divided into the question of intensity of group influence while the group is together and the question of postgroup-situational effects.

Example. Some teachers of the "patriarchal-sovereign type" (Type 1) have strong group-formational influences. While such a teacher is in charge of the classroom the children are under his silent influence to a nearly hypnotic extent. However, the moment they leave the classroom, the children divide into a number of more or less delinquent gang formations, which previously seemed to have been submerged beyond recognition. Again, a "leader" may sway his students to high degrees of moralistic drive control while he is with his "youth-movement" group. In their private lives, these youngsters may be capable of leading very different types of existence—the delinquent youngster with much "Boy Scout" enthusiasm.

Nevertheless, I know of group situations that carry over into one's personal life; have a part in reshaping an entire philosophy of life; or even interfere with a person's attitudes toward other group-formative units while he is among them—when the youngster with "youth movement" enthusiasm of Type A comes home to his family, which believes in a political system Non-A, for example. How strongly many seemingly "individual" reactions to situations and values are secretly colored by unspoken group-psychological loyalties has often been described by sociologists—the dependence of many personal ideas upon the silent submission to class prejudices and national and "racial" ideals. It is interesting to note how much repression is at work. Each social class, for example, seems as defensive against the possibility of having its values recognized as exponent of class affiliations as it is keen in spotting such dependencies in other classes. The studies of Warner, Dollard, and Davis contain ample evidence in this connection.

Whether group influence is limited physically to group members and central person or is capable of trespassing these limitations is a problem of psychoanalytic interest.

It seems that this problem is somewhat analogous to another with which the psychoanalyst is more familiar. To what extent are the actions of a child to be understood as reactions to the "real" persons around him, and to what degree are they the results of previously incorporated images of these persons? One might inquire about the weight of manifest libidinal and aggressive relations in contradistinction to the effects of previous libidinal-aggressive relationships already established for good or ill in the form of durable character traits and the results of identification.

This question is one I am not ready to answer here. I hope that it may be kept in mind, for it promises new material from everyday work situations in schools and camp setting. Only one trend seems fairly obvious.

Whenever more lasting personality changes are wrought within the members of a group, there is a tendency to have an "idea" or "ideal" beside, sometimes instead of, the "central person." In rare cases this ideal may assume the durable power of a guiding agency even without physical representatives. Experts in mass leadership usually do not rely on the group-formative and character-changing powers of the "idea"; they would rather maintain security by constantly reinforcing the central persons installed. The theoreticians may eventually learn from this fact.

What is group libido? By "group libido" I mean libido aroused under group-formational conditions. It is sometimes astounding what people can do on the strength of libido evoked in group configurations. Some persons will exhibit degrees of sublimation they would never manage alone. Others will show libidinous intensities under group-emotional conditions exclusively. For others the barriers of individual differences disappear. Although most discriminating in their person-to-person relationships, they are suddenly able and eager to love anyone who meets them in certain group-psychological situations. Others see their libidinal scopes shrink to minimums in the same configurations: Capable of a relatively choiceless distribution of libidinal quantities in their personal lives, they are approachable only in one type of leader-member-relationship when group-emotional affairs are concerned. Briefly, if group libido means something entirely separate from what was originally intended, then I advise against its use as misleading. If one agrees to think of it in terms of "conditions" under which libidinal quantities become usable or blocked, then it might as well be used as a linguistic short form for what is quite a complex affair.

The problem of first interest to the analyst, as well as to the educator, seems to be the widespread assumption shared by many analysts that all group libido is homosexual. I do not have enough available clinical material to contest it, but I should like to present a few arguments against it.

The general statement about the homosexual nature of all group libido has developed from the fact that homosexual libido most apparently needs and finds outlets in group-emotional forms. It is questionable, however, whether or not that statement can be so easily reversed. My argument assumes that group libido develops on the basis of identifications. At least one type of identification is the simple transformation of originally libidinous quantities. These libidinous quantities are "reduced to" identifications if there are strong reasons why they should not come out in their original forms. Such reasons exist if there is no chance for a libidinous countercathexis by the loved object or if the libidinous quantities engaged are under the pressure of strong taboos and are therefore exposed to repression. Rather than erupt through the repressive lines, the libidinous quantities seem to seek satisfaction on the level of oral—incorporative—identifications.

It is obvious that those two conditions are most frequently present in connection with libidinous urges of the homosexual type, that they may even be the one way out for a certain surplus of unconscious homosexual tendencies in the overtly normal person; and that such drive elements are then used for the creation of social ties and group loyalties. However, it is probably not necessary that this fate occur only to the homosexual components of libidinal demands. Although probably less often present, the situations for the repression of libidinal demands of the heterosexual type may occur in much the same manner, the incestuous for example. It ought to be an interesting challenge to the clinician to try and find clear traces of these manifestations in his detailed material.

Beyond this point, I should like only to draw attention to another tendency to generalize that seems premature: The statement that group libido is originally of a homosexual nature is often made with that sweeping finality that puts an end to argument. I suggest using such a statement rather as a starting than as the final point of an investigation. The problem is which libido remains homosexual, and how much— and under what conditions—can it be used for the development of group-emotional ties? For, although homosexual in origin, the libido does not necessarily remain close to homosexual satisfaction. Much of the group libido can be translated into further sublimative procedures

—into the service of work for and enthusiasm about the group—whereas only some of it finds relatively direct satisfaction in personal contact and oral-symbolic ceremonies. The further destiny of the desexualized and depersonalized libido should become an object of much more intensive research. The educator is especially interested in this point, as it is his task to invent new channels for the otherwise unusable libidinous quantities and to discover the conditions under which energies become amenable to influence.

Applications to Education

The tremendous importance of group-psychological investigations for the practice of education can best be suggested by the statement that schoolteachers never deal with persons as if they were "individuals" but always as they are embedded in particular group situations. Even more radically, it may be said that much of what they have to do does not primarily concern the group members but definitely consists of tasks of handling the groups; although they may want to influence members, they really act in and toward the groups.

This is why so many teachers complain that many of the insights gained into the development of the child seem difficult to "apply." Too long have such arguments been handled as though they were nothing but stubborn "resistance." They are more than that, in many cases. They are well-justified complaints about the lack of advice on one of the most tangible tasks of teaching—the task of establishing group-psychological rapport with classes and of creating the group-psychological atmospheres most favorable to the educational process. There is also the necessity of reconciling guidance of the particular child with the definite demands of group leadership.

It is no wonder that innumerable group-psychological problems are suggested the moment one begins to think of the teaching situation. Each one seems to be more urgent than the other. Although this study cannot list each one, a few may be noted for the purpose of illustration.

The most obvious implication of my "types" for teaching purposes is the fact that they do not all lend themselves equally well to the various educational objectives. The most apparent difference evolves from the fact that the role of the central person as a leader or patriarchal sovereign is very different from that as object of love. When neglected, this difference makes for educational trouble and disappointment.

Example. Only that kind of love that can eventually be translated into identification is of value for more lasting, educational changes. Teachers who are "liked" only, without inspiring even temporary or partial identifications by their children with them, do not greatly extend their educational effects. How to elicit love that can be organized into identification, rather than merely responding to the children's appeals with too much direct countercathexis of a libidinous nature, is one of the most vital problems of education.

The educational value of a group-emotional atmosphere resides not only in the density and the nature of the relationship between member and central person but also in the type of secondary emotion this group situation is liable to create.

Example. Cynicism against Johnny may increase the group density of the rest of the class, which may thus be seduced into identifying with the punitive teacher out of "fear of the aggressor." On that basis, it may be easy to unify the members. One may also force more academic achievement and more admirable "goose-step" discipline. However, educationally, a very high price is paid. At the same time that the group is made more efficient, its opportunities for character development are distorted. Its members become more snobbish, and outcast-lynching mob psychology is encouraged. Most group situations have a few advantages and a few disadvantages for certain educational objectives that I have in mind. Careful appraisal of all the items, pro and con, seems a highly desirable improvement in educational planning.

At first glance, the educator will look with more favor upon the patriarchal sovereign (Type 1) and the leader (Type 2). Some will enjoy the comfort of the tyrant (Type 3). Others will mistake the chances of the central person as object of love (Type 4) for genuine educational influence. The organizer (Type 6) seems to be involved in most educational activities. The hero and the good example (Types 8 and 10) may seem desirable or at least tolerable at times. Preferences or rejections of any of these types will most strongly depend on the educator's philosophy of life, his personality type, and a few other conditions. Still most educators would prefer any of these types to the object of aggression (Type 5). They would consider all attempts of children to assume the roles of seducer (Type 7) and bad example

(Type 9) as forthright challenges. This reaction is natural, as patriarchal sovereign and tyrant (Types 1 and 3) suggest suppression of undesirable drives in favor of moral values, whereas the object of aggression (Type 5) is useless from the beginning, as he destroys educational influence. The seducer and the bad example (Types 7 and 9) seem evil in that they protect drive interests from sublimation processes favoring maturity.

Many educators, therefore, have a tendency to designate all the types except the object of aggression (Type 5) by the term "group" and to classify the seducer and the bad example (Types 7 and 9) under the pejorative term "gang."

In fact, for purposes of quick demonstration we might agree with this terminology, stating that "groups" aim at the suppression of drives and the protection of cultural aims, whereas "gangs" seem to serve undesirable drives in contradistinction to the development of moral standards and values.

However, such terminology is grossly oversimplified, for the phenomenon called "gang" is usually much more complex than any one of the types I have enumerated. I therefore prefer a classification of types of group formation that are basically friendly to the educative process and those that have a tendency to become hostile to it.

In dealing with group or gang situations, educators have a tendency to behave unwisely. They consider the creation of the right kind of group atmosphere much too simple a task. They believe that they can destroy gang formations by simply fighting them or their symptomatic expressions. More detailed studies of the question to which educational task any one of these group patterns lends itself are highly desirable.

Developmentally, children do not seem ready for all these types of group formation at any one time during their growth. A very crude analysis leads me to suggest the following developmental parallel.

In earlier childhood, they seem to function naturally and fairly well in more or less patriarchal- or matriarchal-sovereign types group pattern. This observation is also psychologically true for democratic political systems, according to the natural role of the adult, especially the parent, for the child, although extremes in this line are avoided in such patterns. During preadolescence, it seems normal for youngsters to be intensively attracted by the "gang" type of group relationship, a mixture of organizer, seducer, and bad example (Types 6, 7, and 9). This age is the one at which, in the language of some research experts, "peer culture" dominates the previous tendency toward submissiveness to adults. Even a very egotistical and spoiled person may go through a phase of intense loyalty to a gang. It brings prestige. Acts of definite self-sacrifice for the "pal in danger" are the rule. A considerable degree of security is derived from this type of group relationship. Such children are desperately in need of expressing suppressed drives and urges. Many need drive protection more than drive sublimation. The adult is often quite upset about this phenomenon. The overt picture of gang life is anything but pleasing to aesthetic and moral hypersensitivities. However, it is important to recognize that normal tendencies toward participation in some degree of gang formation must be protected; that suppression of normal developmental needs will be paid for dearly in later difficulties.

The adolescent exhibits a growing preference for a more sublimated group formation, especially based on the leader (Type 2), as characteristic of most adolescent youth movements. The needs of youths seek outlet in the group, which also protects them from guilt feelings and anxieties and leads into more mature patterns of life. The youth movement constitutes one of the most interesting problems and offers the richest materials for studies of group formation in the adolescent age. The delinquent youngster, however, retains his need for preadolescent drive protection against the educational process, which is why all so-called "criminal" gangs are obviously fixed at the preadolescent level of gang formation. An analysis of gang daydreams, which the movie and gangster fantasy offers, would corroborate this analogy in more detail than can be done here. This fact seems so clear that the preferences of adolescents for more gang-like or more group-like affiliations might be used for diagnosis. They would show up the more genuinely delinquent type versus the youngster with simple growth problems. Which of the group-formative types is more normal for the "adult" definitely depends on the philosophy of life that the adult population of a certain age and place has developed. According to the "democratic ideals" of life, the following description seems appropriate.

The potential group members have enough in common to evoke group-emotional relationships toward one another without the decided functioning of any one "central person." On the basis of this "brotherhood" type of group formation, central persons may secondarily assume the roles of organizers or may begin to serve some of the emotional needs of the group members, as leaders and as patriarchal symbols for example. The difference between genuine and pseudodemocratic patterns, however, is one between a situation in which the central person is the basis of group formation and one in which he is only allowed an organizing or secondary function in the system.

This description of what might be considered the "idea" of an adult group-formation type should, of course, not be mistaken for an attempt at describing the real structure of present-day adult society.

The educational problems that are raised by these developmental considerations are numerous. The most vital seems to be the recognition of the law of healthy growth. The value of a group formation for a certain phase of development should not be judged on the "idealistic" desirability of that type of group formation but on the basis of its fitness for the immediate task of growth. Thus even the basically anti-educational gang-seducer type of group formation must find its place in the form of a protective, hygienic institution to secure drive growth and expression during preadolescence.

The clinical importance of certain types of group formation, or of mixtures of such types, deserves as serious consideration as does the strictly educational one. By this statement I mean that certain persons may have more difficulty than others in adapting to any one existing pattern of group formation and that this difficulty may constitute a problem in itself. Parenthetically, many so-called "adjustment" problems are the results of attempts to fit persons into patterns of group formation that are developmentally not adequate for them.

For example, many school problems in preadolescence—sixth, seventh, and eighth grades—arise from the fact that these children undergo periods of rapid preadolescent development while they are expected to fit into earlier or later stages of group life. However, the clinical problem also comprises those cases in which the lack of group adaptation arises from basic deficiencies in drive organization or personality constellation. For example, some types of personality will always have trouble in transforming any libidinous relationship into identification. They will obstinately insist on "loving" their leaders and demand libidinous countercathexis with little concession to processes of sublimation. Others will grasp the opportunity to transform any libidinous impulse into identification processes, so that they seem more able to incorporate than to love and to incorporate through identification without critical selection. Others react against certain group-psychological conditions for identification and refuse to make any group-psychological adaptations unless these conditions are given. They refuse, for example, to identify with anyone but the tyrant type they had to identify with in early childhood. Briefly, there is a plethora of possible and practical complications.

I believe that I am justified in stating that too little attention has been given such goup-psychological data in clinical work. People who handle group situations seem unaware of the fact that many children who have trouble in making group adjustments need changes in their personal drive patterns before they can adapt effectively, although it is equally true that many children are only assisted in effecting personality developments under certain group-psychological conditions. This fact has impressed itself upon me most clearly in three fields: first, the development of the normal preadolescent, who is frequently mishandled unless in a group-psychological situation suitable to his developmental structure, which unfortunately is one that most schools and all parents are especially loath to consider; second, clinical work with delinquent adolescents who are capable of making certain identifications but only under particular group conditions and never with adults in group-psychological vacuums (the failure of many otherwise excellently handled therapeutic interviews seems to fall into this category); and third, the utilization of observations of a youngster in different types of group-psychological medium for the purpose of diagnosing the degree of his delinquency or disturbance or the state of his growth at various points in his development.

The fact that schools and especially institutions for difficult or delinquent children know or are aware of little about the essential group-psychological elements and their effects upon character growth and libidinal development is probably the one item on the list of desirable educational improvements that most needs attention.

One last item that the educator should be taught is that a group may consist of only two people. These two-person configurations may seem strange, but they are frequent. There is a tendency to mistake the prevailing affect in such groups for genuine love, friendship, or lust—the homosexual type of relationship, in particular. Nevertheless the differentiation is vital. Attempts at dealing with such groups have to be modified accordingly. Anna Freud complains in *The Ego and Its Mechanisms of Defense* that adolescent love relationships seem astoundingly changeable, inconsistent, and short-lived—adolescents are faithless in their loves and friendships. This observation can easily be corroborated. Most publications stress the sudden intimate friendships that endure intensively for but a few weeks, to terminate with apparent forgetfulness shortly thereafter.

I have often been puzzled by this phenomenon. However, upon closer investigation of a few such groups, the suspicion has grown that such short-lived intimacies are not genuine love-friendship relationships. Some seem to fulfill the requirements for durable interpersonal relations, whereas others are revealed as groups, each consisting of the "good" example and his pal who seeks protection from temptations and desires or of the "bad" example and his pal who seeks opportunities to utter thoughts his parent-ridden superego would never permit. Briefly, these groups are formed for mutual—or one-sided—protection rather than for interpersonal love or friendship. It becomes important for the teacher to recognize the two- or three-person types of group relations because the children who need this kind of security for their growth are not helped by being "guided into more social contacts with more people." Nor is it true that frequent homosexual pairing means a definite increase in homosexual versus heterosexual attachments. Quite a large number of heterosexually inclined youngsters may be found in "homosexually" paired group relations for mutual support in drive-superego conflicts.

Exculpation Magics Through the Initiatory Act

I have mentioned, without explanation, the guilt- and fear-assuaging effects of the initiatory act. This concept was used to explain the fundamental group-formative power of the seducer or hero as central person. Seriously, I mean that this same process is basic to gang formation and also that other group-formative types make ample use of it.

I have admitted that this investigation postulates this process as an auxiliary assumption without which one obviously traceable fact of group life could not be understood. No completely exhaustive explanation of this mechanism will be advanced, inasmuch as it involves problems far beyond the scope of this paper. I should, however, like to inquire if there is any other evidence supporting this assumption. There are three speculations that I believe may eventually indicate somewhat more clearly where the data may be found.

All children up to a certain age have a tendency to use the initiatory acts of other children as adequate excuses for what they have done. This tendency is strongest in the years of preadolescence. Even very conscientious and intelligent youngsters will feel justified if only they can argue afterward, "But *he* did it first." Here their reasoning stops.

Most people think that this exculpation habit is easy to understand because they are so used to it, although, on second thought, they may find it rather difficult to explain. The naïveté of the argument is frequently quite incompatible with the sensibility, intelligence, or moral uprightness that the same person exhibits in other situations. Another more startling point is the frequency with which adults fall victim to this projection technique of their children. Parents seem invariably to believe in the magical exculpating effects of another's deed. If their offspring can only demonstrate clearly that another's child "did it first," the one who "did it first," was, of course, the real culprit.

If parents think that way, should one be surprised if teachers start their investigations with the question: "Who began?" or "Who was first to do that?" If the investigation threatens to become involved, they prefer to interrupt it. The "culprit" bears the full brunt of their punitive actions, meanwhile nothing is done about the latent instincts of the other children, which may have been basic to the results effected by the seducer.

This situation is more ridiculous than is at first realized. It seems that adults definitely do believe in magical exculpation through the initiatory act when it fits their plans. The same is true for other superstitions that people believe only when they want to. There are potential superstitions for all. Remnants of these superstitions have survived in this culture from primitive times.

Language has similarly developed its more logical form of expression from naïvely magical roots. Most of the causal elements originally had but "temporal" meanings. Primitive thinking had no place for "cause"; the first thing was the cause. This naïveté has been nearly eliminated in science. Only in the political field and in education do otherwise highly educated persons indulge in "logical primitivism" without concern.

In the Middle Ages people clung more frankly to superstitions. In medieval "gang" situations, thoughts comparable to my illustration about the children were openly expressed. When the ringleader was caught, he was decapitated—sometimes he was the only one to be punished, or the others merely had fingers or hands chopped off. If men were needed, the others were set free or even selected for the army. Thus it seems that some such "superstitious expectations" were actually borne out in the social and legal customs of the specific historical period. The leader of the gang did take the punishment—all the "responsibility"—for the others. He had the main share not only of profits but also of the danger and the actual consequences of vengeance. He was truly exculpating the members of the gang.

What was an overt exculpation in the Middle Ages seems to have been based on an inner process of guilt assuagement. Even now, both seem to be coexistent. The unconscious still reacts parallel to primitive thinking in that the one "who did it first" also has all the "responsibility and guilt." Could not one also fall victim to this trick, as has been seen to happen in children and parents, *their* parents at least? Could some of the surprising declarations of political leaders that they take "all the responsibility upon them"—even when there is apparently nobody ever to make such suggestions stick—be understood as remainders of the magical-exculpation beliefs released by group or mob-psychological conditions?

The primitive process of taking temporal priority for causation is reminiscent of another odd coincidence. The Latin *princeps* like the German *fürst* were called the "first people" and also *were* the "first." However, being the "first" of an aggressive warrior group has not always been connected with the privilege of staying at home in the event of war. The original situation was exactly reversed. These people became the "first" because they happened to be the first to charge into battle. Whether they continued marching into battle first or not determined the durability of their emotional relationships with other soldiers. What is so significant about being first? Some of the reasons are clear. Being first exposes one to the greatest danger threatening the group. This exposure assuages feelings of envy among the group for various other privileges one may have enjoyed in peacetime. However, it is doubtful if this rationalization explains the whole problem. There is another type of "risk" that the "leader" assumes. The one who commits the first aggressive deed is the murderer. All others are followers. Murder has now been transformed into holy aggression for them. For the first one it was not. Someone killed the father in the primal horde. Although the others identified with him—probably helped—one initiated the act and took risk *and* guilt upon himself by means of priority magics.

It seems that all the license and romance about aggression and killing cannot render the unconscious at peace with the fact that it is murder. Hence the institution of exculpation magics. The exculpation act is not repeated fully each time; no temporal priority is necessary in more highly organized groups. The temporary priority is replaced by seniority of rank. The official state of authority ranks someone superior to others, and through this rank he receives the magic power to sanctify killing, into making it a holy act. However, the yearning for the more primitive forms still lingers. Soldiers like to see the real sanctification of murder re-enacted. That is why they still like their officers to be the first ones into battle, even though there may no longer be much "reason" for it. It is this thought that led me to suggest a thorough revision of Freud's theory on the group-psychological nature of the army and to discover trends that seem to suggest an entirely new theory of the nature of discipline. I intend to preserve these items for separate presentation.

My concept of magical exculpation through the initiatory act is parallel with these speculations. What makes the youngster feel better when someone else has "done it first" is the same old superstition that functioned in medieval law and still operates in many situations. True, it is "only" superstition. What I wish is to establish that it *is* superstition. If anyone, the psychoanalyst should be most ready to see how *real* an explanation through the magic of superstition can be when the unconscious is concerned. The seducer renders the potential group a service: He does first what the others hardly dare to think. If my speculations are correct, this service explains what happens in group formation. The leader really does render a service merely through doing it "first": He destroys the magic expectation of punishment— through a magical act.

Spatial Repetition Compulsion: A Metapsychological Speculation

The other auxiliary assumption that I introduced in this paper needs justification even more than does the theory of "exculpation magics through the initiatory act"—and I am even less able to present it. I refer to the concept of an original infectiousness of the unconflicted personality constellation on the conflicted one of the same drive pattern.

I used this principle as an explanation for two types, the bad example (Type 9) and the good influence, (Type 10). The power of this principle is easily documented. Johnny, who is afraid he might want to know about sex, is made happy when Jimmy is around because the latent goodness of the latter precludes such a wish. Or Mary feels at ease in Joan's presence because she knows one does not have to feel badly if one thinks about sex. Joan has sex curiosities, and they do not cause her any guilt or fear.

The child is confronted with a dilemma in the field of the ego whenever the id demands something its superego decidedly rejects. The solution is determined by the type of support that the ego is able to obtain in its conflict. If this support tends to be in line with superego wishes, it will successfully manage the unruly drives. If the type of support it is given encourages the satisfaction of the drives, the decision will be in their favor. Of course, whichever way the ego decides depends on various factors in the situation. A transition from one type of solution to another is not only frequent but also normal in special phases of growth and development. The trouble experienced by the ego in making a transition from superego support to drive support has been described by Anna Freud as one of the basic difficulties in early adolescence. I have noticed that children are obviously helped in their decisions, in favor of either the drives or the superego demands, by association with other children who definitely represent the one or the other solution. It seems that the ego insecurity of the conflicted child is somehow "magnetically" influenced by the already fulfilled solution in another person. I found, as a condition for this effect, that the first person must be on the verge of having to make either the one or the other decision. Furthermore, the influential person must have definitely resolved his own conflict. It is upon this basis that I assumed there is a certain infectiousness of the unconflicted "personality constellation" on the "conflicted one" of the same drive-conflict pattern. By "personality constellation" I mean here the relationship among the id, ego, and superego.

Without such an assumption there is no rational explanation for the reality demonstrated. The phenomena I describe are facts of group life. The assumption is therefore a group-psychological postulate. But is it a new assumption? I believe that this "infectiousness of the unconflicted personality constellation on the conflicted one"—which can be seen functioning so clearly in group life—is but another manifestation of Freud's famous assumption regarding the repetition compulsion.

Freud distinguished between two different types of identification in his paper on group psychology. The usual type (in which identification is the result of what was object libido before it underwent repression) may be formulated: The children "love" their teacher. Part of this "love" is homosexual—never fully desexualized. It is therefore exposed to the forces of repression, and, because this love must be partly frustrated by the demands of so many, these children transform their love into identification. Freud also mentions another type of identification, which, he says, is even more primitive. He calls it "primary identification." He says that it happens without a libidinous relationship having first been established—a process more primitive than has been ascribed to the libido. Methodologically considered, my assumption differs only in that I extend this primary principle of influence from the field of identification into the field of infectious influence in interpersonal relations.

Another speculation may fortify my assumption. Freud's assumption of a repetition compulsion really means there is a basic principle that what was once shall be again in all living substance. The mere fact that certain events once led to the solution of a conflict is supposed to release a strong urge to return to this experience, to revitalize it, even at the expense of realistic considerations—including the pleasure principle. This word "repeat" is captivating. It has a double meaning. Something is repeated if it is revived in time. The word also allows a spatial interpretation. One might also say that an ornament "repeats itself" or that nature repeats itself if the same species is discovered on different planets. Time alone is not implied. The repetition also becomes one of space. Various events are *coexistent*—not after one another but next to one another. Repetition takes place in space, as well as in time. If the repetition compulsion is basic, why not extend the concept? A nice parallel may be offered.

A conflict solution that has once been effected by the ego tends to be repeated—a temporal repetition compulsion. A conflict solution that definitely exists in one person tends to be "repeated" in another person in whom it does not yet exist—a spatial repetition compulsion.

The precondition for this second repetition effect is that the situation in both persons be strikingly similar, that the solution for the one really is a solution of approximately the same conflict, similarly organized, in the other. This theory would also explain why only certain children have such influential effects on certain others.

My theoretical problem would be simplified if there were but one basic auxiliary assumption instead of two. It would explain Freud's assumption of a primary identification as well as my theory of infectiousness.

A child may select an object for identification because the economic pattern of this other person represents what exists merely as a trend in himself—primary identification.

A child may effect a conflict solution because he notices it as a *fait accompli* in the other what has been a strong trend in himself—infectiousness of the unconflicted over the conflicted personality constellation.

Both are manifestations of the same urge—the power of the existing solution over the one that is "not just yet" accomplished. There is no need to remind the reader how close these speculations are to Plato's assumption of the power of "ideas" over "reality," a resemblance already noted in Freud's other theoretical speculations.

$\mathcal{T}$*he Phenomena of Contagion and "Shock Effect"*

The establishment of the concept of "behavioral contagion" pushed me into a whole sequence of exciting events. On the one hand, it took a long time until I was able to convince my psychoanalytic friends and colleagues that I was not simply regressing to the pre-Freudian, over-simplified, LeBon type of theory of imitative behavior and that the exploration of either the initiator's or the recipient's unconscious alone would not suffice to clarify the whole phenomenon.

With the increasing frequency with which well-trained psychoanalysts began to expose themselves to group-therapy experiences, their interest in what I was talking about increased, and their sympathy with my puzzlement about the phenomenon rose. By the way, there was also concern about the sheer use of the term "contagion." Franz Alexander, for instance, one of the first prominent theoreticians of psychoanalysis to become favorably excited about this specific paper, made me quite aware of the importance of making clear to the reader that the analogy between the term "contagion" as used here and as used in physical medicine is limited indeed.

On the sociological and group-psychological side of the fence, I had little trouble with having the concept of contagion itself accepted and sympathetically too. Rather, it suffered from overacceptance: Scientists in those fields seemed quite uninterested and even puzzled by the complicated speculations I tried to foist on them and considered it a somewhat unfortunate whim of mine to muddy an interesting but otherwise quite uncomplicated issue that could so much more easily be caught by simple factor analysis.

The biggest problem, however, came from my own research project, conducted in cooperation with Ronald Lippitt, Norman Polansky, and their staff, with funds supplied by the Research Grant Division of the National Institute of Mental Health. The study itself was exciting and

"The Phenomena of Contagion and Shock Effect" is based on "The Phenomenon of Contagion and 'Shock Effect,'" from Kurt Eissler, ed., *Searchlights on Delinquency* (New York: International Universities Press, Inc., 1956).

provided wide ranges of respectable and quantifiable data; my colleagues and staff proved enormously imaginative in catching variables, through tests and research techniques, that otherwise seemed to elude such efforts. But, although we learned a lot more about the specifics and the range of the phenomenon and about variables that we had previously missed, real understanding of the issues that seemed most crucial to me kept eluding us to the end. It remains my conviction that this issue of the "contagiousness of the unconflicted over the conflicted personality constellation" is an unexplained residue of our speculations. It probably won't be caught in experimental designs until such time as we have the courage to revise our theory of personality to a greater degree than we have done in the past, to get rid of its somewhat two-dimensional flavor, and to bring the concept of personality closer to the level of sophistication that the concept of the atom has long since achieved in physics.

THE PHENOMENON of contagion is not new to the social psychologist. In fact, the "spread" of behavior from one person to another or to a whole group has been described in connection with studies of "mass behavior" in most textbooks and publications on social psychology. Riots, panic situations, and incidents of "mass hysteria" furnish good illustrations for this purpose.

However, group psychologists, as well as students of individual behavior, have so far neglected this phenomenon when it occurs in small face-to-face groups or even in larger groups with well-structured organizations. The practitioners of group leadership, teachers, recreation leaders, and others are familiar with the event, but are ill at ease when challenged to explain it. The educator has been inclined to a general theory of "germophobia"—the idea that one bad apple may make the whole classroom rotten has deterred many a principal or teacher from trying his hand with Johnny or Mary when they are suggested as additions to his group. The psychiatrist has neglected the phenomenon for other reasons, mainly because to him it seems obvious that the real reason contagion can take place at all is to be found in latent trends within the individual.

If Johnny begins to steal under the contagious influence of Bobby in the same group, there must have been something in Johnny to respond to Bobby's seductive wiles. As, before the recent development of group therapy, psychiatrists were mainly limited to operation in two-person consultation situations, the actual domestication of contagion behavior was no problem to them.

With the development of group therapy the picture has changed, and the phenomenon of contagion deserves to be, to my mind, in the foreground of our practical as well as theoretical interests. For no matter what the basic explanation may be, the following phenomena can be established beyond doubt.

First, sometimes the behavior of one group member is "picked up" nearly "automatically" by other members of the same group or by the majority of that group. This "pickup" takes place through rather mysterious channels; it is not even necessary that conscious or unconscious intent be present in the person who commits the "initiatory act."

Example. Eighty rather disturbed children between the ages of eight and fourteen are in a large camp mess hall. Johnny, in a fit of temper against one person at his table, throws a plate at him. A minute later, plates fly all through the air, and the place is in an uproar, even though Johnny neither contemplated nor planned such an effect and is otherwise a rather inconspicuous figure at the camp, without any leadership role.

Second, sometimes there is an equally puzzling absence of such an expected contagion effect of one group member upon another or on a larger part of the group, even though previous experiences with the same group might suggest that it would occur.

Example. In the same camp mess-hall situation, a child throws a plate; nothing happens; it remains an entirely isolated incident without any relevance to the wider group situation.

Third, sometimes the addition of one child with an openly expressed area of clear-cut problem behavior to a smaller group of others who had never previously shown this behavior may make overt in all of them what previously had only been present as dormant possibilities or as trends on the fantasy level.

Example. George is added to a group of children, who are all hesitant to form positive relationships with adults in general but who have begun to form positive attachments to their specific group leader.

Upon George's arrival, his open defiance and hateful sneers against everything the adult suggests or does are immediately "picked up," and the other children show similar behavior, to the leader's and their own surprise.

Fourth, sometimes, again, the addition of a child with an openly expressed area of specific problem behavior has no direct effect at all on the behavioral trends of the others as far as imitation goes.

Example. Mary is added to a group of preadolescent girls who have a wide assortment of behavior problems from sex delinquency to stealing and so forth. Mary's open display of wild, close-to-paranoiac fantasy life, including mainly accusations against adults, remains ineffective upon the otherwise not easily manageable group. The other children do not use her "example" to pick up similar behavior; in fact, they run to the adult for protection and develop a scapegoat formation against the newcomer.

With these phenomena in mind, it seems highly relevant to find out just what determines whether such "contagious" influence from one group member on others or on the whole group takes place or not. The psychiatric explanation that contagion presupposes the existence of similar trends within the imitator seems acceptable but inadequate. For practical purposes, it makes quite a difference whether your group member only daydreams about stealing or actually begins to steal after the advent of that other child.

We do not know the answers. The United States Health Service gave us a grant[1] for a two-year study of these phenomena, considering such study essential to more effective work in therapy groups. However, on the basis of rich if not systematic observations in our previous work, we should like to set forth a number of tentative hypotheses, which suggest themselves from what we have seen.

It seems to us that the factors that decisively determine whether or not contagion takes place can be divided into two categories: those of the psychology of the group and those of the psychology of the individual. Needless to say, we assume that most incidents of contagion are the result of a cooperation between both types on a sliding scale.

1. Research Project on "The Use of the Group Medium for Clinical Work with Disturbed Children." Two-year grant by the United States Health Service, Division for Mental Hygiene, Washington, D.C. Principal Investigators: Fritz Redl, Wayne State University, and Dr. Ronald Lippitt, Research Center for Group Dynamics, Massachusetts Institute of Technology. Director of Research: Mr. Norman Polansky, research center, Wayne State University.

Group-Psychological Factors Determining Contagion

THE GROUP STATUS OF THE INITIATOR

If we mean by "initiator" the person whose behavior is being imitated, then it seems to us that, other things being equal, the trend toward contagion is greater if the initiator enjoys high status in his group, whereas it is less likely to occur if the initiatory act comes from an individual of low status.

Example. In a group of toughies who hated adults, the obvious and recognized ringleader, the toughest of them all, was the first to make open advances of friendship toward the adult leader. His behavior worked like a charm (positive contagion). From then on the other youngsters gave way to their own beginning desires for leader acceptance, which they previously had not dared to express for fear of being considered "sissies." Whenever another child in the same group tried similar advances toward adult affection before, he was exposed to ridicule and contempt.

THE AFFINITY OF THE BEHAVIORAL AREA TO THE GROUP CODE

Other things being equal, it seems that behavior that is related to items with high value rating in the group code is more easily contagious than are other acts by the same individual.

Example. Jack's attempts at getting other members into sex play are warded off effectively by everybody in the group. On the other hand, whenever Jack becomes tumultuous in a situation in which the whole group is supposed to be quiet and listen to somebody else's announcements, his behavior has immediate contagious effect. Needless to say, the group is one of preadolescent boys with not too strong a trend toward sexual precocity but with a high degree of pride in mischievous pranks. The thing that "counts" in this group is whether or not one is openly daring against adults. Sexual precocity is left to individual differences and carries less weight in determination of group status.

THE COMMUNALITY OF BASIC EXPRESSIONAL TRENDS

Other things being equal, behavior that is liable to give vent to the suppressed needs of the largest number of group members with high group status will be the most sweeping in its contagious effect.

Example. On the day when one child's plate-throwing found such promiscuous imitation there was a suppressed mobility and wildness present in practically every member of the group, because of a series of rainy days and the nature of the preceding program, which had involved passivity and listening.

It seems to us that this item of communality of basic expressional trends determines spread rather than the actual occurrence of contagious effect.

SIZE, STRUCTURE, ORGANIZATIONAL PATTERN, AND NATURE OF THE PROGRAM OF THE GROUP

When we lump these factors together under one heading we do so under the pressure of space limitations. We realize that each constitutes an item independent from all others and of great variability. But this paper must limit itself for the present purpose to a summary of the following observations.

It seems that the factor of the size of the group has some bearing on the occurrence of contagious events. We are not prepared to say, however, that large groups automatically make contagion easier. Depending on the behavioral item in question and other factors, we found that sometimes the larger and sometimes the smaller group size was favorable to contagion. For instance, the spread of a group mood of a ritualistic nature around a campfire seems easier in larger than in smaller groups. The spread of a group reaction against the adult seemed more effective in the smaller group, provided, of course, that the structure in both cases remained the same. In other cases, the structure of the group certainly makes a considerable difference. For instance, if a group is clearly substructured into well-defined units, the spread of contagion is minimized, as compared to a group without subgroup formation. Strong *organizational* dependence on an adult "leader from above" seems to favor contagion in certain areas, as compared to democratic group organization. The degree of *program absorption,* too, functions as an insulational layer against contagious effects of the negative type, whereas it fosters the effect of "positive contagion" in terms of "enthusiasm spread."

The most obvious fact we could notice is a peculiar reaction of groups to certain combinations of structural and organizational factors. For instance, contagion of one clown's behavior in a huge dormitory (organizational regimentation in a large group, with its substructures submerged through routine pressures) is much greater than the spread of mischief or noise from one four-kid room to another. Or the discipline problems resulting from contagion on "tense" days are much greater in a detention home with a chow line and long-table-and-bench arrangements than when children and (group-related) adults are seated at smaller tables in a skillful distribution based on natural sub-group formations.

GROUP ATMOSPHERE

The "sum total of the feeling tone prevailing among the group members, among the members toward their leader, toward the things they do, and toward the image of their own group" constitutes another variable in this problem of contagious effect. By and large it seems to us that behavioral incidents that have a high affinity to the present "group mood" have more contagious possibilities than do others. In an "atmosphere" of happy, mutual acceptance and cheerfulness of all members toward one another, including the leader, even a recognized toughie's rebellious pranks may be ignored. In an atmosphere of "resentment of punitive pressure," even the chance clowning of an otherwise inconspicuous group member will be "picked up."

Personality Factors Determining Contagion

Important as they are as variables in determining contagious effect, the previous group-psychological factors alone seem to us insufficient to explain the phenomenon as such. In fact, we have a strong suspicion that they determine more the "when" and "how far" than the "why" of the contagious effect. However that may be, the clue to the basic process of contagious effect seems to us to lie in the same principle we have described in "Group Emotion and Leadership." Instead of referring to that paper, however, I should rather modify the formulation on the basis of more recently observed examples.

Example. In a cabin of six preadolescent boys with quite strong trends toward destructiveness, there had been a considerable number of incidents of window-breaking. For a while a good tie between the children and their adult group leader had been developed, and the incidents had been well handled both individually and in group discussions. Nothing further had happened for some time. One morning, however, one of the youngsters who was sweeping the floor picked up the broomstick and with a war whoop charged against the windows full force. In a flood everyone else's destructiveness was set loose, and an orgy of destruction followed.

The mere mention of what the instigator did is not enough to explain the event. More detailed knowledge of everybody involved and of previous events suggests the following analysis.

Five of the children were filled with suppressed destructive desires. Their newly developed "group conscience" forbade destructive acts within their own group, which they would have to pay for by guilt feelings. The instigator, in this case, was a clearly psychopathic youngster, a type for whom even the controls defined by the group code have little meaning and even that for only a short time. What really set loose the wild imitation pattern was not his pattern of destruction by itself.

If another child had done the same thing, the others would have jumped on him for breaking their promise and "getting them all in trouble." The instigator in question, however, did more than just start it off. His mannerisms when charging at that window, as described by the children and as subsequently acted out by himself, were most intensely suggestive of a reckless, devil-may-care mood. His whole pattern of gestures, as well as that gleam in his eye, suggested that he was entirely free of fear or guilt while doing it. It seems to us from this and innumerable other similar incidents that this mood of his is one of the conditions for contagious effect.

Because of our space limitation, we shall try to condense into a list the steps that we think are involved in the production of contagious events, as far as "personality factors" are concerned.

1. The existence of an acute conflict area within the imitators: strong impulses toward fulfillment of vehment needs on one hand; on the other, sufficient pressure from ego or superego forces keep them down;

2. The high degree of lability of this "personality balance" in the area concerned: impulses strong enough to press for release, controls strong enough only to prevent that release (if the latter were somewhat stronger, no contagion would occur; if impulses were stronger or controls a little weaker, the children would not have to wait for somebody else's "initiatory act").

3. The existence of a similar type of strong urge toward impulse expression along the same line in the initiator (his urge must lie in the same direction as those of his imitators, destruction in this case).

4. Open acting out in favor of impulse satisfaction by the initiator, with equally open display of an entire lack of fear or guilt.

In short, what the initiator really does is to show the fulfillment of the others' desires and also to show that it can happen without fear or guilt. What happens inside the imitators can be formulated as follows: The sudden observation of fearless and guiltless enjoyment of what they really want to do sways their own labile balance between desire and control in favor of the former. Their own potential conflict is being resolved into open action along the lines suggested by the visualized behavior of the initiator.

It seems to us that sometimes it is not even necessary for the initiator to go the whole way: Strong and open gestural and physiognomic expression of his own lack of guilt and his fearlessness about impulse gratification may be enough to sway the rest ("the bad example"). In other cases, *direct visibility of the* initiatory act is essential for the effect ("the seducer").

Needless to say, contagion can also take effect in the opposite direction, in which case we might call it "positive contagion."

Example. In a cabin of delinquent thieves who took great pride in their code, using rough language and swearing, one of the youngsters suddenly knelt down when the bugle sounded taps, pulled out his rosary, and started his evening prayers. Amazement temporarily paralyzed the rest of the group. As our religious hero also happened to be one of the most openly delinquent representatives of toughness and the delinquent philosophy of life, he was suddenly joined by three others, who also knelt down by their bunks, while the rest simply stared in open-mouthed surprise.

Analysis. Open religious devotion is considered sissy stuff in the group code of these children. Yet they are all labile about this code and really feel somewhat guilty after their blasphemous orgies. The clear-cut "solution" that their pal presented them by throwing his fear of ridicule aside and openly obeying the religious dictum of his superego suddenly made it possible for the others to overcome their shame

at letting their consciences openly triumph, and they abandoned all
further urges to ridicule or blasphemy.

Indirect Contagion and Shock Effect

In the previous illustrations, "contagion" always leads to imitation
of the behavior of the initiator. We think we should pay attention to
two other phenomena, which seem to us to be based on the same principle, even though direct imitation is not involved. By "indirect contagion," we mean a process that occurs in situations like the following
one.

Example. The "spitfires" were a group of eleven-to-thirteen-year-
old boys who had had about a year of intensive club work with an
adult leader who had unusual skill in developing a style of "democratic" group leadership and a pattern of "group expression" of feelings
and thoughts related to their group life. When faced with conflicts or
problems, these youngsters would have "gripe sessions," bring their
complaints against one another or the leader herself into the open, and
show remarkable group pride in an attitude of frankness and an ability
to "take it without offense." I have to describe this pattern in such detail
to show how the subsequent events were typical for this group. It was
into this very "friendly" group that Al was placed when the whole
gang came to camp. Al's insertion into the group had been well prepared; the camp director and group leader had explained to the youngsters why an addition of another member was necessary and had handled the youngsters' feelings about it extensively. The stage for Al's
entry was as carefully prepared as could be; the group attitude toward
him was one of most favorable cooperation.

It didn't last long. We knew that Al had considerable tendencies
toward masochism. That was exactly why we tried placement in a group
so cooperative with its leader and so self-expressive in cases of conflict.
After a few days, the group was in an uproar. Al's bids to be chased,
wrestled with, and pushed had been so strong that the other youngsters
had lost all self-control. They would begin in a spirit of fun, but Al
would invariably coax them into more sadistic satisfactions than they
could foresee. After about a week, the group could hardly be recognized; it was like a bunch of sadistic bullies, had become defensive and

"alibi-wise" in its group discussions, had started to bicker and fight within itself, and had become aggressive and restless in its relationships to the adult.

From a great "gripe session" about all this change and from individual interviews, the basic structure of the event became unequivocally clear. The children complained that they knew they shouldn't give in, but "he just does something to us"—"he always makes us chase and hit him, and then complains." They had no comment when asked just how he "made them hit him" and admitted that this statement was, taken literally, incorrect. It was obvious, however, what they were trying to say. Al's mere display of extreme masochistic desires "stirred up" within them more sadistic pleasure temptations than they could cope with. Needless to say, the wrath over their own lack of controls finally accumulated as an additional cloud of rejection over Al's head, and the "intangibility" of the whole process blocked their former skills in free group expression. The guilt over their own behavior into which they were lured became a collective motivation for real scapegoat formation against the "source" of all the trouble, and they finally wanted Al "out."

What we want to show by this example is that something like "contagion" was happening here. But "contagion" does not mean that the other children began to "imitate" Al. It means that they were stirred into falling into the reverse side of his satisfaction pattern (sado-masochistic temptations). The basic principles seem to me clinically the same, even though no "imitation of behavior" was present. We might, for lack of a better name, call this phenomenon "indirect contagion" until we learn enough about it to give it a name of its own.

The phenomenon of "shock effect" is of even more concern to the clinician. An illustration may show what we have in mind.

Example. The "puppeteers" were a group of eight-year-old boys and girls, all referred because of their basic fears of self-expression. They were all "shy and withdrawn," "afraid to express themselves," and so scared they could not even use finger paint or other materials that are messy. A few weeks later, the leader's efforts had taken effect, but by that time it had become obvious that these children were alike in symptoms only and not in the levels of repression of their forbidden urges. For by then all but one not only used finger paint freely but also produced drawings with the most fantastic content and indulged openly in Oedipal and other fantasies and games while they did so. This behavior was too much for one of the girls. Janie dropped out. Her caseworker reported that she was quite upset, and a closer examination of the total situation showed clearly what had happened. The open visualization of so much material that for Janie was "repressed" more severely than for the others had thrown her into an anxiety phase. Instead of "imitating" the more open expressiveness of the rest of the children it merely caused her to reinforce her own reaction formation against self-expression.

Analysis. We can briefly compare this case with the analysis of contagious behavior in the previous pages.

1. Some desire for self-expression in Janie but also a very heavy reaction-formational taboo against it; balance less than labile, rather in favor of repressional taboos.

2. Open visualization of "conflict solution" in the other children, who express wildly and freely (and with leader approval) without guilt or fear what Janie does not dare to accept.

3. Discrepancy between Janie's range of self-acceptance and that of the other children much too great for imitative enjoyment.

4. Failure of visualization of the others' self-expression to solve the problem along the line of impulse expression; rather forcing Janie into greater efforts at reaction formation or at least threatening her original conflict solution and producing anxiety.

Not always is the result the production of fear or increased reaction formation; sometimes it goes much further than that and has quite serious group-psychological consequences.

Example. The intensity of Aileen's hatred for Martha assumed proportions that were hard to comprehend. Not only did she go out of her way to hurt, tease, offend, embarrass, and torment her cabin mate, but she also went to great pains to circulate vicious propaganda among Martha's boy as well as girl friends. And there seemed little on Martha's side to account for this reaction. Martha kept out of Aileen's way whenever she could and was unusually decent and tolerant of the leader's effort to help Aileen rather than to punish her for some of her quite outrageous exploits. Things came to a point at which Aileen had set every girl in the group against Martha and had made her into a real "scapegoat."

Analysis. Aileen is big for her age (thirteen) and physically over-developed, but the caseworker and the school have assured us that she is really not yet interested in boys and that we need not be worried about having her in a coeducational camp. She lives in a slum neighborhood where most girls of her age openly brag about their promiscuity and where sex and boyfriends are the constant topics of discussion and gossip. She lives with her aunt, a most virtuous woman, who wants to make sure that Aileen does not become "the kind of woman her mother was." To make a long story short, Aileen is threatened by the open talk and braggadocio that go on in her group at camp, and Martha is the greatest threat to her. For Martha has no conflict about her interest in one of the boys and enjoys the courtship in such a way that Aileen cannot simply "despise her" as a "bad girl." To express one's erotic wishes and have no guilt feelings about them and also to have success in accepting sexuality without conflict threatens to weaken her own tremendous task of repression.

Her "balance" is threatened, and it is not enough to increase her own reaction formations against her sexual wishes. She has to destroy or eliminate the person who causes it all, in the good old style of the witch hunt.

We may briefly summarize these two and other forms of "shock effect" in the following list.

1. *Diffuse anxiety.* Children having to live in the same group with one who is threatening to their id-ego-superego balances have often shown nightmares, fear of a particular child without actual threat, and displaced anxieties like fear of the woods or snakes, psychosomatic symptoms, and homesickness.

2. *Temper tantrums.* Children thus threatened in their personality balance through the visualization of unacceptable behavior have sometimes had sudden increases in their temper outbursts or have shown fits of rage that can clearly be traced to anxiety attacks.

3. *Increase in "goodness."* Sometimes they have to become temporarily "good" because of these shock reactions, and such changes may easily be confused with real improvement. Actually this transient effort to accept group values is only a counteragent to threats to their inner balances. They are threatened by observing the fearless and guiltless enjoyment of others, and this observation necessitates intensified reaction formations.

4. *Avoidance and withdrawal.* Some children, under the impact of "shock effect," begin to "avoid" certain other children, want to be regrouped or sent home, run away, drop out of activities they previously enjoyed, or take refuge in daydreaming and reading instead of play action.

5. *Hostility and scapegoat propaganda.* If pushed too far, they have to go further, to the lengths to which Aileen had to go. Only the exclusion or destruction of those who threaten their precarious personality balances can

solve their problems. You may thus find them engaged in real political machinations against this or that child or leader or in attempts to get the group to establish punitive rules against certain offenders or offenses; or they may turn themselves into gossip mills, solely in order to eliminate the threats to their virtuous but unstable equilibriums between strong urges and implacable superegos.

The question of what determines in a similar situation whether the reaction is contagion or shock effect is a fascinating one, and I wish I knew the answers. Tentatively, I can only venture the following suggestions.

Contagion will take place if (other things being equal).

1. the "balance" within the recipient is strongly loaded in favor of impulse expression to begin with;

2. the degree of freedom from fear and guilt shown by the initiator is just strong enough to relax the imitator but not so extreme that it drives him to fear of loss of all control;

3. the area in which contagion takes place is relatively free of other problems.

Shock effect will take place if (other things being equal)

1. the "balance" in the recipient is strongly in favor of a solution in terms of superego triumph, especially if the suppressed urges are threateningly strong, so that even temporary enjoyment would involve risk;

2. the initiator's freedom from fear and guilt is so great as to threaten the recipient beyond the momentary issue by jeopardizing his basic principles and superego control;

3. if the area in which contagion might take place is in itself much too conflict- and taboo-ridden, so that much too heavy counterforces would be set in motion for even a little bit of "sin."

Practical Implications

No less interesting than the question of when and why contagion or shock effect takes place is the problem of determining why they fail to work when we might otherwise have expected them. The group leader especially needs this knowledge, for it is obviously of greatest importance to be able to control these phenomena. Specific technical suggestions must be left to future research. On the basis of our previous observations, we can venture the following tentative clues.

THE IMPORTANCE OF GROUP COMPOSITION

It obviously is not feasible to group people together on the basis of such simple criteria as age, "interest," I.Q., or the like. Somewhere, sooner or later, other factors come into play that may decide whether the group atmosphere developed in a certain mixture of individuals will be favorable or unfavorable and who will influence whom in which way.

We have been increasingly impressed with the multitude of criteria that has been offered for "hygienic grouping." But this issue is too elaborate to be dealt with here. Suffice it to say that it is through methods of grouping that we can sometimes prevent Johnny or Mary from exerting either an excess of contagion or shock effect on the rest of the group.

GROUP-PSYCHOLOGICAL INSULATION

As subgroup formations, group structure, and factors of organizational control seem to play important parts in the process described, the following observations may offer leads for further investigation.

Example. Sometimes contagion or shock effect can be limited by placing children in different cohesive subgroups while they still live in the same overgroup. For instance, Cabin 7 was composed of youngsters whose wildness and delinquent leanings could not be compared with the elaborate and near to professional toughness of those in Cabin 4. Johnny, who was somewhat less delinquent than the rest, could live happily with them. What he knew about the behavior and goings-on in Cabin 4 excited him somewhat, but, as he is embedded in the emotional ties of his own group, it had little meaning beyond that. He, together with his pals, occasionally gave vent to his indignation at those "awfully tough kids over there" and questioned my wisdom in letting such youngsters come to camp at all, but he had neither to imitate them nor to develop exaggerated shock reactions. This attitude would have been different had we made the mistake of putting him into Cabin 4. Exposed to the same group code and group-emotional relationship pattern as were those youngsters, he would either have had to imitate in order to attain prestige, or he would have been thrown into an emotional tailspin out of fear of loss of self-control. Also he could hardly have forgiven his group leader for showing the same acceptance to the "bad" youngsters as to him and would have developed a diversified hysterical display.

Example. Children who come to a large group entertainment with their counselors and come in by cabin groups are usually much easier, even when exposed to the program pressure of sitting still, than if they all crowd in topsy-turvy as they happen to arrive. Among other reasons behavior (clowning) visualized by somebody who is not a direct member of the subgroup that surrounds him is not half so contagious as it is otherwise.

SPECIALIZED HANDLING BY THE LEADER

Contagion and shock effect are really unavoidable in the life of any group. The problem is not completely to avoid them but to handle incidents wisely, so that their effects can be counteracted. Knowing the "contagion potential" and the "contagion area" of Johnny and his group greatly helps a leader to anticipate and handle group developments and individual incidents. Shock effect, too, can be dealt with up to a certain point by increasing the direct and indirect support the adult leader gives the child. Individual interviews, group discussions of the expressional type, and other techniques can be used additionally.

IMPLICATIONS FOR INTAKE

Many previously rather "mysterious" phenomena like increased irritability of whole wards or groups because of the addition of new members or restored manageability and relief after the expulsion of certain old ones begin to assume new meanings. It also seems obvious that both the addition and elimination of group members have strategic implications far beyond the consideration they are usually given.

Theoretical Implications

These phenomena raise anew the question of what processes are going on in the kind of groups we have been observing. Even though we hope we have adequately delineated for the purpose of this study what we mean by "contagion" and "shock effect," we are far from knowing what they are. The following seem to be the most urgent speculations that force themselves upon the theorist's mind.

What are the differences between these and other forms of member-member influence?

Does contagion take place only among group members, or is the same principle at work when a leader really "sways" the group or individuals? The same question applies to shock effect.

By what subtle means do people communicate such things? How does Johnny know that Bob is really guiltless and fearless, whereas I have read his whole case history and still am not sure? How does Aileen know the depth of Martha's sexual-acceptance? How does a whole roomful of people sense the implication of one gestural act (plate throwing) as a potential for impulse release, when other opportunities are passed by? The intuitive precision with which group members seem to "convey" meaning way beyond the reach of ordinary language and signs baffles us.

What gives an act such "signal function"? Would any behavior along the same line have similar contagious or shock effect, or is there something specific in the way or in the intensity with which Bob acts that effects the results?

Does the same principle hold for situations of intentional influence? Can it be learned and taught, and does it perhaps underlie many other influence situations that we have so far too glibly interpreted as being entirely based on direct verbal or gestural connotations?

How is it possible that the mere "visualization" of an "unconflicted superego situation" has such an effect on somebody else's "conflicted one"?

How can we translate such phenomena into measurable units so that they may be scientifically investigated and perhaps taken from the realm of intuitions based on observation and hunches based on experiences?

Well, the purpose of this little study is not to solve this problem but only to raise it. More people working with groups in which more is known about both the constituent group members and other backgrounds, as well as about the dynamics that actuate the groups, may finally answer these questions. For the present, we conclude with a strong plea in favor of research into group dynamics that combines the disciplines of psychoanalysis and sociology.

$\mathcal{R}$esistance in Therapy Groups

The times when group therapists could lull themselves into the illusion that the "group medium" was much better and easier and would allow us to get rid of the perplexing phenomena of resistance are long gone psychoanalytically. With more and more sophisticated therapists entering the group-therapy field, awareness of and interest in the complexities that enmesh all serious attempts to cure major afflictions have gone way up. In fact, if pleading for respect for the phenomena of resistance, even those of patients in groups, were necessary, this article would be out of place.

But there remains a difference between the kinds of resistance patients develop in the course of treatment "anyway," so to speak, and the specific forms of resistance that the group process seems to offer the patient as an additional bonus. Also the group-psychological implications of an individual patient's resistances constitute a challenge in their own right, beyond the rest.

The following pages describe some of the group-psychological angles of the resistance phenomenon as they were observed in work with children with specific disturbance syndromes. They are meant to stimulate speculations about other groups and other patients and much more research into problems of form and technique.

TOO OFTEN the term "group therapy" seems to be used glibly with an astounding lack of precision. The difficulties in use of the term seem to be classifiable according to two major confusions.

Neglect of the Importance of Group Dynamics

I often hear the term used to describe situations and techniques in ways that seem to ignore the existence of a psychology of group life.

"Resistance in Therapy Groups" is based on "The Phenomenon of Resistance in Therapy Groups," *Human Relations*, Vol. I, No. 3 (1948).

There seems to be an assumption that group therapy is simply a matter of applying what we otherwise would do to one person in a room with us to twenty-five in the room at the same time. Fortunately I think the workers in this field are slowly but surely recovering from this mistake. There is an increasing recognition of, and respect for, the tremendous impacts of factors like group composition, contagion and aggravation, special and spontaneous group processes like scapegoat and subgroup formation, and the conditions under which these processes occur—in short, the whole gamut of group-psychological phenomena.

Reckless Use of the Term "Therapy"

This confusion is most clearly expressed in a tendency to call "therapy" anything that is done in groups and is considered better and fancier than other people's work, even though no attempt at repair jobs is being made. I think we are about to recover from this confusion too. We are becoming more interested in the analogies between real "treatment" in a group situation and the basic processes of all "treatment" in individual therapy.

The overcoming of these immaturities in the field of group therapy will not be securely achieved, however, until we get over both confusions at the same time, rather than becoming clearheaded and sophisticated about one as an excuse for heavy indulgence in the other. Let us now look at one aspect of the group-therapy situation with these confusions in mind.

The Role of Resistance in Therapy

This brief article focuses on only one phase of the complex problem of resistance. If it seems that we ignore or minimize other aspects, it is because of our feeling the need for a selected demonstration. It will be clear that we are hitting mainly at confusion number two, attempting to show that in group therapy, as in all therapy, resistance is one of the crucial phenomena that has been relatively neglected for too long. In the selection of our illustrations, we are also trying to hit at confusion number one, for we want to make the point that not only is there resistance in therapy groups, but also there are very special "group-psychological expressions" of resistance.

We do not need to give much space to the well-known, though sometimes still-neglected, fact that resistance is the core of individual treatment. Just to remind ourselves of what we have all learned to accept during the last decade we might summarize briefly.

Resistance is an unavoidable process in every effective treatment, for that part of the personality that has an interest in the survival of the pathology actively protests each time therapy comes close to inducing a successful change.

Far from being a sign of inefficiency of the therapist, real resistance to change is one of the most important handles by which he can seize disease. Diagnostically it reveals the real forces that he fights, and therapeutically its removal is the only guarantee for lasting success.

The diagnosis of which behavior is really resistance in its therapeutic meaning and which behavior is not cannot be made glibly. In most cases, a lot of individual work has to be done before this issue can be defined. However, we do know that certain forms of behavior are especially often used as expressions of resistance.

We expect that the moment we begin to carry out treatment in group situations we shall get as rich a display of forces of resistance by each individual as we would get in individual therapy. It is too bad that we have not paid enough attention to this fact. We had better get much busier studying the ways in which individual resistance shows itself and can be handled in group situations. The emphasis in this article, however, turns on a second thought—that maybe there is even something that should be called "group resistance." It is our experience that there are group-psychological defenses against change and treatment reaching far beyond the scope of individual-member behavior. I now want to offer a few illustrations relevant to this hypothesis concerning "group resistance." These illustrations come from a very specific observational and treatment framework—our work with "delinquent children" in three different settings:

the Detroit Group Project club program (a once-a-week club-meeting program);

the Detroit Group Project summer camp (six weeks of intensive work with children who were all referred by clinics and courts because of their need for diagnostic and pretherapeutic work); and

Pioneer House, a group-therapy home for delinquent boys where children were studied and treated on a year-round basis with twenty-four-hour-a-day boarding-home care.

It should be emphasized that the illustrations used in the rest of this paper are naturally very specially related to the natures of the particular children being worked with and to the settings in which they were observed. No direct conclusions should be drawn about other forms of resistance in other frameworks and with other children or adults. I am also very insistent that we must not forget for a single moment when reading these illustrations that they are meant only as one-way streets and are not reversible. That is, the phenomena described were found in our study to be expressions of "resistance," but that does not mean that all forms of resistance must look the same, nor does it mean that these same forms of behavior must always indicate resistance. The fact that one form of behavior may indicate resistance in one case, whereas it may have an entirely different meaning in another, is as true of group therapy as of individual work.

Some Forms of Group Resistance

ESCAPE INTO LOVE

In group therapy as in individual treatment, real character changes are not elicited by the leaders' simply being "loved" by their children. As in individual treatment, the step from an affectionate tie to real "identification" must be made before actual changes can occur. In both situations, the libidinous desires of the children for love possession of the therapist must be surrendered in favor of wishes to "identify with" him or her. After this process has taken place, a child does not want to "have" the group leader for himself but "to be like him or her" or at least to be the type of person who would fall within the confines of his value system. The stepladder to successful characterological change is the same as in individual education and treatment: love-identification-partial incorporation of traits and value patterns.

This whole process of "treatment" of characterological deficiencies may be hard to describe. It is amazing, however, how fast the delinquents themselves catch on to it. They develop a skillful counter-technique against our therapeutic plans. All they have to do to avoid the necessity for real change is to lure the group leader into a continuous "love" relationship, and they are safe. They even seem to know that this technique is better in many cases than is outright rebellion. They "accept" the leader; in fact they seem to be especially "good" with him or her around. They crave very intensive "friendships" with him or her. If they get them, they modify their behavior enough to sustain this happy state of affairs. But that is about as far as they will go. They do not budge an inch in their basic "delinquent philosophy" of life. Many a therapist or group leader has been fooled by this trick. The voluptuous surrender of a little "toughy" to an ardent love and friendship cult around a glorified adult looks good on the surface, but for the therapist it constitutes a most ticklish dilemma. If he rejects this love appeal too vehemently or too soon, the youngster withdraws entirely and has an easy alibi for a disappointed return to his previous rejection of any and all adults. If the therapist falls into the trap and gives too full a response to the love wish displayed by the previous rebel, he loses the chance to arrive at identification, and the child uses his personal relationship with his leader as a defense against real change. To teach group leaders the difference between educationally and clinically valid rapport and the forms of love that hinder rather than promote final identifications is one of the most difficult training jobs I know.

Protective Provocation

When the danger of developing a good rapport with the group leader and therefore of softening up toward his demands becomes too strongly felt by our toughies, they sometimes try another way out. If a kid can only get that fellow mad at him and if he can get him to repeat what other really hateful people have done to him previously in his life, then he can safely say to himself: "See? I knew it wouldn't last. Adults are all the same." The delinquent therapy group will therefore often begin to provoke the leader all the more intensively, the closer it comes to real surrender to identification. This period is the most fascinating and the hardest in a group therapist's life. All previous semblance of "improvement," so carefully built up and so proudly maintained, seems to be gone suddenly when he least expects it. The youngsters get worse than ever before. They really seem to "ask for it." And that is exactly what they do. They search for an opportunity to put their leader into any one of the categories of their traumatic life histories, in order to get rid of this dangerous enemy of their delinquent fun. This trap is one into which punitive educators invariably fall. The youngsters do literally "ask" for punishment. However, they ask for it not because they want to atone and become "good." They ask for it because they can use it as their most efficient defense against surrender to identification. Unfortunately, this technique of resistance is very hard to combat even for skillful group leaders and educators. The youngsters, if they really want to, can think up so many more forms of irritation so much faster than the adult can catch on to and cope with therapeutically. Only persistent ability to resist irritation and fear of one's own failure, coupled with equally persistent use of reality interpretation through individual and group interviews whenever actual interference becomes unavoidable, so that the danger of delinquent misinterpretation of that interference can be avoided, can do the trick.

ESCAPE FROM GUILT THROUGH DISPLACED CONFLICT

The most upsetting period in the treatment of a delinquent is the phase in which he develops incipient traces of guilt feelings toward his group leader for some of the things he does. He has tried to hate him first—that didn't work; he couldn't keep it up under the impact of group atmosphere and skillful leader behavior. He then tried to develop that ardent love relationship of the "little boy-older friend" variety, but this technique too could not remain successful because the leader was skillful enough to handle it well. So now Johnny is really in the process of accepting not only the leader but also some of his values. Before he knows it he is in a state in which he can't do all the things he did before without feeling badly about some of them. From now on certain forms of delinquent behavior are not tax free any more. When afforded, they have to be paid for by guilt feelings.

As yet, however, these guilt feelings are only centered around the person of the accepted leader of one's own therapy group. Displacement is still possible and remains a lot of fun. So this is what happens: The youngsters stop affording some of their delinquent behavior within the framework of the therapy group. They really become "better" there. However, they shift their problem behavior into areas that are, as yet, not directly loaded with guilt obligations. It is always at this stage of the game that a cabin group seems to "improve" miraculously at camp and becomes so "reasonable and decent" in the reactions it shows whenever its leader talks over some problems with it. At the same time, its members seem to develop uncanny skill and frequency in getting themselves into trouble with the world outside. They offend innocent bystanders at the public bathing beach; they throw stones at motorists who pass them on a hike; they chase the farmer's bull (it nearly always is really a cow but assumes paternal-substitution roles in the tall stories they tell about it afterward) and get themselves into trouble with the farmer. The leader's own cash and trinkets are suddenly safe from them, but he had better watch the loot he can get from their pockets when they come home from a trip to town.

What they really are trying to do is to resist the total surrender of guilt-exempt delinquent fun. Because they have already made serious surrenders in areas covered by the leader and the therapy group, they try to rescue the rest of their lives from being engulfed in the process of domestication. Troublesome and hard to handle though this phase is, it really is a good sign when it happens. It is one of the last-ditch resistance forms, which usually are not used until the youngsters already have made a lot of moral commitments in many other respects. It is important, however, to recognize this process for what it is—still a sign of resistance against what we are really trying to achieve. I have found that many therapists or group leaders have trouble resisting the temptation to be too narcissistically triumphant during this phase. The leader is often secretly flattered by the fact that his children have made such a visible surrender to him and all the life that happens under his jurisdiction, while they obviously still hate and attack "the outside world" or people who do not "handle them right." We must never forget that this resistance technique, although indicating a lot of previous success with a group, is still resistance against *us* in what we are finally trying to do.

ROLE CONFUSION

For the adult leader of a delinquent group, the establishment of realistic role awareness in the group members is one of the most difficult but also one of the most important tasks. He has to worm his way from role expectations, which push him into the category of "enemies not to be trusted," through moments of closeness to the role of "good sport who really makes you forget he is not one of the kids," into his real role of group leader and group therapist. It is amazing how well youngsters often can be made to "understand." After the first confusions about leader function have been overcome, they know pretty well what they can and what they cannot expect. They will, for example, expect the leader to "be a good sport" and not to get too angry at minor mischief when some windows get broken, but they will not expect him to lie for them, to cover up for them, or to pretend he likes every phase of the misdeeds they enjoy. Just because of this differentiation, role confusion with a vengeance seems to offer itself as a good form of resistance when the danger of total surrender to the therapist comes too close. Sometimes this technique is used purposefully by some more consistently delinquent group members against their more leader-amenable pals. We found a group of boys developing the trick of invariably accusing their therapist leader of being a "squealer" whenever he would so much as consult with other adult personnel, even about issues not related at all to discipline. What the youngsters were trying to do was obvious. By throwing adjectives out of the inventory of words used for people in the role of group member at the very person who was in the group-leader role, they got away with quite a lot of subversive antileader propaganda before the other kids even recognized it. These other children would become as angry at their leader for simply talking with somebody from the overgroup hierarchy, without checking what he was talking about, as they might justifiably have been if another group member had been found in a situation suspicious of "tattling." Sometimes this technique has no purposefully subversive trend to it but is unconsciously chosen by the whole group in the members' fight against their own acceptance of the adult. Needless to say, skillful and continual clarification of role functions through a variety of techniques can be used to deal with this form of resistance.

ESCAPE INTO VIRTUE

A child's dropping symptoms for which he has been sent into treatment, at the very moment when treatment seems to come close to the real thing, is a well known defense against the continuation of therapy in individual cases. Only very naïve beginners or quacks rely too much on the miracle of sudden "improvements." The experienced clinician knows what many of those cases really stand for. It is interesting to see that sometimes, when we enter a new field of application, we repeat some of the old naïveté that we had already abandoned in our original field. It can be understood why even group therapists with good backgrounds of psychiatric experience in individual treatment are often found to be naïve in their evaluations of therapeutic group-reactions. Too often I hear them brag about the "quick responses" they get from this group or that or about the "excellent spirit" that a group shows over this issue or that. Many of the early and premature illusions about group therapy as a time-saving device arise from this easy self-deception. Actually, we must face the fact that reality is no less harsh in group treatment than it has been in any other form. Therefore "escape into virtue" is often used by whole groups of delinquents as an effective defense against the real impact of educational or therapeutic efforts. I have had many a delinquent gang in the therapy project who, after an amazingly short time, would develop most laudable improvements in the management of their affairs, astonishing accessibility to reasoning, and astounding reductions in their open delinquent exploits with us. Follow-up studies of those same children show that this display of virtue is nothing but a smokescreen. Through it they can like us, be liked by us, and, as a vacation experience, enjoy the happy group life of the nonproblematic boy, simply reserving their delinquent exploits for more opportune and tax-free moments. It is important to be realistic about this phenomenon in both directions though. It is just as bad to suspect that every improvement of symptom expression is another form of "resistance" as it is to fall into the trap of this resistance device.

Summary and Implications for Practice

In group therapy, as in individual therapy, the phenomenon of "resistance" calls for careful attention and study and often becomes the core around which treatment must focus.

Whole groups may, if their group codes and outlooks on life are threatened, develop one or another form of group resistance under all sorts of disguise. It seems probable that such group-wide forms of resistance are especially welcomed by the most resistant members of a group, because in this way they can cover up their own individual resistances without being driven so close to discovering their meanings. Individually established resistance behavior shown only by themselves would be more difficult to sustain.

It seems that the same cautions that we know are essential in individual therapy must also be applied to group treatment. There must be a careful investigation into each specific situation before we arrive at the conclusion that a certain form of behavior really indicates "resistance." There is the same need for very specific planning about the ways in which each type and phase of resistance should be handled.

The question of just what are the most efficient ways of dealing with resistances of different types is obviously the first one we should ask after observing and diagnosing phenomena of this sort. In our projects we are very impressed by the multiplicity of possibilities here. A discussion of even some of our tentative findings to date goes beyond the framework of this paper.

The phenomenon of group resistance that we are dealing with here is not limited in its importance to the clinical scene. It seems to us, on the contrary, that clinical resistance is merely a special edition of a much larger area of phenomena, the total area of "resistance to change." It seems reasonable, therefore, to expect that some of the experience from the clinical field, with proper cautions and modifications, will be useful whenever we approach individuals or groups with the purpose of change in mind. The analysis of resistance should therefore have an important place in education, teaching, leader training, and attempts to change the performance of management and labor, as well as in attempts to combat prejudice, long-ingrained habits of autocratic submission, problems of group-rut formation under the impact of bureaucratic pressure, and many more. It can also be hoped that learning more about the phenomenon of resistance in these many types of situation will throw considerable light back onto the clinical field. There is certainly need for such help from other fields of endeavor beyond what we have been able so haltingly and slowly to discover through direct work in individual and group therapy.

The Psychology of Gang Formation and the Treatment of Juvenile Delinquents

This is not a clinical study of delinquent juveniles exposed to psychoanalytic treatment. On the other hand, it is not a sociological essay on "society and the individual" either. It might best be described as an attempt to make an analysis of the group-psychological conditions under which delinquent traits are reinforced or counteracted, as the case may be. It is the assumption of the author that such a study, although it assumes its final meaning only after it is connected with specific clinical material, may be of stimulation value for the psychiatrist on his job.

Which Delinquents Are We Talking About?

*A*LTHOUGH IT IS IMPOSSIBLE to load this little paper with the task of establishing and defending a categorization of delinquent cases or a definition of delinquency, we should like to clarify the way in which the word is being used here, just to avoid major terminological misunderstandings. We think we can distinguish four fundamentally different types of delinquency among juveniles. They are

Type 1. that of basically healthy individuals whose delinquent behavior is a natural defense against wrong handling, wrong settings in which they live, or traumatic experiences of certain types;

Type 2. that of basically nondelinquent youngsters who are drifting into delinquent behavior through some acute adolescent growth confusion;

"The Psychology of Gang Formation and the Treatment of Juvenile Delinquents" is based on the article of the same title that appeared in *The Psychoanalytic Study of the Child*, Vol. I, published by International Universities Press.

Type 3. delinquencies that are really "on a neurotic basis," by which we mean that the delinquent behavior in itself is part of a neurosis or that it was developed in order to disguise one;

Type 4. "genuine Delinquency," by which we mean certain disturbances in the impulse system of the individual or malformations of ego, superego, and ego ideal in intensity or content.

It seems to me that Type 3 has so far been the most successful domain of psychoanalytic treatment: When the delinquency of a juvenile is really only part of or a superstructure over a neurosis, it is logical to expect that it will clear up soon after the neurosis in itself has been removed. However, Type 4 seems to puzzle the psychoanalyst no end. Treatment often seems to go through phases encouraging good prognoses, in order to end up in sudden and unexpected relapses all along the line, in spite of an obviously positive transference to the analyst. It is this type I shall select for exclusive discussion today—needless to say I refer to these types not in strict isolation from one another but mainly in terms of emphasis and preponderance.

Group-Psychological Support of Delinquent Traits

Too long have we indulged in stereotyping the "delinquent" along the lines of psychiatric romanticism. According to these theories the genuine delinquent is the "asocial" or "antisocial" individual, too egotistic and narcissistic to submit to the demands of "society" and bent on gratifying his impulses against the limitations of society. The "lone wolf against the world" idea is still clearly traceable even in clinical descriptions of our time. There is no doubt that representatives of such types do exist, and this is not an attempt to deny them or to wave away their importance. However, at least as far as delinquent juveniles go, it seems to us that an entirely different type is much more frequent and less studied. This type comes closer to what Topping, Hewitt, and Jenkins[1] used to call the "pseudosocial"—though "pseudo-antisocial" is probably a better term.

The confusion about this type rises out of a stereotyped use of the term "society"—using the term as if it were a unified code of ethics to

1. Ruth Topping, "The Treatment of the Pseudosocial Boy," *American Journal of Orthopsychiatry*, April, 1943; Richard L. Jenkins and Lester Hewitt, "Types of Personality Structure Encountered in Child Guidance Clinics," *American Journal of Orthopsychiatry*, January, 1944.

which "everybody adheres," whereas only the mean and befuddled delinquent doesn't see the light. Well, there is no such thing. Our delinquent youngsters do not live in a group-psychological vacuum against "society." Society itself is not a simple and unified structure but is highly substratified into thousands of little subcultures, all of them vitally different from one another in essential items.

What really happens with our delinquent juveniles could more adequately be described this way: They refuse to identify with exactly that substratification of society that the parents or the law-enforcing middle class represent. They rather identify with one or another subgroup, the group code of which is not so prohibitive of some of their vital gratifications as the other seems to be. This subgroup identification may happen in three ways:

On a Class Basis. The delinquent juvenile in some cases makes an enthusiastic identification with "the tough way of life" versus the "sissy stuff" that school teachers and middle-class church boards represent to him in the name of "the law."

On a Development Basis. This delinquent juvenile identifies heavily with the unwritten code of his peer culture versus the code of behavior represented by "the adult"—which includes the adult of his own social stratum. As many laws forbid the juvenile the same gratifications that are not only permissible but openly bragged about by the adults of his own subcultural pattern, this disparity in itself constitutes a simple source for "juvenile delinquency."

On a Neighborhood-Gang Basis. The third possibility is not only not contradictory to the first two, but it is also often nothing but a more concrete expression of either or both. In fact, sometimes this small "neighborhood gang" is nothing but the concrete way in which the youngster meets his "class culture" or his "adolescent peer code." In other cases, however, it must be admitted that some such "gangs" add their own quirks of code deviation and assume more specialized contents.

It is true that conventionally the word "gang" is usually limited to these smaller neighborhood groups. For the purpose of this study, however, we shall ignore this fact and talk about "gang psychology" whenever either of the three group-psychological ties is referred to. Without having a chance to justify such terminological deviation at this point, we can venture the following statement.

The larger number of the "genuine delinquent" type does not comprise "individuals against the group" but "members of one group against another group." In fact, we are ready to go even so far as to say: Far from being the "strong personality that defies law and order," the genuine delinquent is deeply dependent upon group-psychological support to be able to "defy law and order" and to "afford" his delinquency at all. The resistance we meet in our attempts to "treat" this delinquent, then, not only arises from the personal resistance any individual develops in the course of a therapeutic procedure, the laws of which we know so well from the clinical picture of the neurotic. The forces that resist our efforts in the case of delinquent juveniles are even richer: Beside his "personal resistance," a delinquent juvenile is equipped with excellent "group-psychological defenses," which he plays against our therapeutic attempts with tremendous force.

Needless to say the nature of just these group-psychological defenses must be of great interest to the therapist.

Just How Does "Gang Psychology" Do It?

The intricacies of the ways in which group-psychological elements hit the organism of the individual, the process of group formation, and leadership effect have been explored in earlier papers. I have discussed ten different bases for group-psychological effects on individuals, and I should like to summarize here some of the suggestions directly related to the topic before us.

It seems to me that the operation of "gang psychology" supports the individual's delinquent trends especially in three basic ways.

THE PROCESS OF "MAGICAL SEDUCTION"

By "magical seduction" we mean that whatever delinquency-directed impulses are active within the individual member, they are "reinforced"—made more intensive and more daring—within the gang climate in two different ways.

First, they are reinforced through the mere *visualization* of guiltless and fearless drive satisfaction by other members of the group. The infectious value of the "bad example," which is hard to demonstrate in a few words, can best be remembered if we think of the increase in anxieties compulsive children experience when exposed to the display of reckless behavior in their less inhibited pals. The "increase" in defenses in such a moment is direct proof of an underlying increase in drive upsurge.

Second, they are reinforced through the "exculpation magic of the initiatory act." We mean the ability of the group leader or comember to put existing inhibitions out of force by simply "doing things first" and thus bringing about unconscious exculpation.

In both cases the individual has his "seduction" guaranteed, which is one direct service the gang renders to delinquency aspirants.

Ego Support Through Organization of Ways and Means

Our formulation of the organizing function of the central person in gang-formational processes reads: "The central person renders an important service to the ego of the potential group members. He does so by providing the means for the satisfaction of common undesirable drives and thus prevents guilt feelings, anxieties and conflicts which otherwise would be involved in that process for them." In other words, Johnny is ready to participate guiltlessly in a raid on a boxcar or candy store. However, he feels too guilty to *plan* such a thing, too scared that something might go wrong. He can afford his delinquency if somebody else does the planning for him and if somebody else will shoot the guard, if it should come to that.

Through this mechanism, a wider range of delinquent satisfactions becomes possible than the individual superego of the delinquent could otherwise afford.

Guilt Insurance Through Coverage by the Group Code

It cannot be expected that a delinquent juvenile will have no trace of ego criticisms or conscience left. Therefore at least one or another of his delinquent gratifications has to be bought at superego expense. Those who are not only interested in occasional illegal satisfactions but are also bent on developing good and thorough delinquent character traits in order to be morally tax exempt ever after need the group-psychological support especially badly. Gang psychology operates for them on the following basis: Through their emotional ties to the group, they eventually identify with the "group code"—which corresponds to what we could call "superego" in an individual. It is the residue of all values the group "stands for." This group code supplants the individual superego and puts it out of business—temporarily at first, on a retirement basis later on. It is not true that delinquent youngsters do "not have any superego." They may have very finicky ones indeed—but their contents are the group code that may be very different from or even contradictory to the societal demands on the basis of which laws are written. Their consciences as well as their ego ideals are still in operation—but they function only within the confines of the "group code."

Through these three mechanisms, "gang psychology" enables the youngster to enjoy otherwise guilt-loaded or dangerous gratifications without the expense of guilt feelings and fear. It even offers him all the gratifications of "morality" at the same time: pride, moral indignation, the feeling of "being in the right" are still maintained, but they are carefully defined in terms of group-code criteria.

Group-Code Defenses

However, the production of identifications with the group code would not be enough. There is no doubt that it works very visibly as long as the group is "together." The question is what happens to all these group-code identifications as soon as the individual steps out into "private life" or even into "group affiliations" of a different nature? Can a group take a chance and just expect that the individual's group loyalty will be so strong that nobody else's value system will ever make a dent on him?

The fact is groups do not take such chances. On the contrary, they all seem to be very highly concerned with this problem; their greatest danger is that the group-code identification of individuals may be successfully attacked or may peter out in nongroup life. This danger is present for all groups, no matter what type. Thus the greatest fear of the "educator" is that the children so obediently identified with the good and the beautiful might be impressed by some dirty ragamuffin who does not believe in Emily Post and succeeds in undermining Johnny's virtue in no time. In the same way, however, the "tough" organizer of a delinquent gang takes good care that his clientele is imbued with thorough contempt for "sissy stuff teachers want you to believe in," lest they admire the "wrong" guy and fall in love with virtue overnight.

Therefore, groups have developed special mechanisms by which they inoculate their members against this danger. These mechanisms are not visible while the group is together. They can easily be studied, however, in retrospect, when we watch clashes between a group member and outgroup standards of a different code content. To make it possible to describe these mechanisms of "group-code defense" in short space, we shall introduce a few auxiliary concepts here.

We shall use the term "outgroup" for any other group but the one whose code we are talking about. We shall call "overgroup" the larger organization of which the group we are talking about is a part. We shall call "code-dangerous outgroups" such groups whose codes are basically hostile to the code of the group we are talking about.

The following seem to be the mechanisms of defense by which groups secure the postgroup loyalty of their members against outside attack.

SEGREGATION AND INDIVIDUAL HATRED

Some groups demand of their members that they avoid people who are not members of the same group-psychological unit or that they hate those who belong to groups of different kinds. Such segregation demands and individual hatred are carefully practiced and prepared when the group is together and reinforced through the application of well-known devices long studied and well described by the scientists who do research on propaganda. It is this mechanism through which even large group-psychological units operate—political parties, religious bodies, racial and class structures. The success with which racial-superiority theories can be maintained in a large part of the population on the basis of such devices is so well known through contemporary history that we can save ourselves details here.

It should be added, though, that this technique is extreme, applicable only under certain very specific conditions. Besides, only basically very insecure groups usually have to stoop to such primitive mechanisms.

DEPERSONALIZING SYMBOLIZATION

By this artificially introduced term we refer to a rather complex process. Some groups do not insist that their members keep away from nonmembers or from members of other groups. They do not need to be so fussy—they do a better job of inoculating their code loyalties to begin with. They allow their members to associate freely with anybody, to like or dislike people as they wish. However, the moment a person belongs to a code-dangerous outgroup, things are different: In that moment a beautifully prepared mechanism goes into action. People who belong to a code-dangerous outgroup are not to be considered "people" any more but only symbols of the value system of this outgroup, which is to be rejected and fought. The group robs these people of their weight as "persons" and demands that the group member consider them simply as representatives of the hostile unit.

This defense seems to be a very efficient device—people can afford to stick to their race prejudices, for example, and brag that "some of their best friends are Jews." They can do so without feeling disloyal to their anti-Semitic cause—for in items that matter they know that these "friends" will certainly lose their quality of personal relationship and will be treated by them as just so many representatives of the "code-dangerous outgroups." With this safety device in their pockets, they can be allowed to associate freely with whom they like, without any basic danger to the code of their groups.

TABOOS AGAINST CODE-DANGEROUS IDENTIFICATION

The two previous mechanisms are not applicable universally enough either; therefore groups have developed a third one for last-ditch defense: Their members can have all the freedom of even entering libidinous ties with nongroup members or even outgroup members, as long as they remember that they may *love* members of outgroups but they must never *identify* with them, especially not when code-dangerous items are involved. This mechanism insures the tough businessman from allowing his socially inclined and beloved wife to have too much "influence" on his loyalty to his business associates. It also enables the member of a delinquent gang to become an efficient member of many other groups without really jeopardizing the code of his own. This mechanism can be studied beautifully by watching the behavior of some delinquency-identified youngsters in a camp situation. Their development looks somewhat like this: They start with avoidance and suspicion of the adult group leader, as she is definitely an "adult" and an outsider on that basis. After the adult is able to crash through this barrier, they enter strong personal affectionate relationships with her. But the moment this adult acts as a "representative of the outgroup" (the world of adults), she is "depersonalized" and becomes nothing but a symbolic representative of the hostile code. Thus youngsters who have obviously "loved and adored" their counselor will turn rudely against her whenever she meets them in a role of outgroup representation. In cases in which reaction can be broken down, the youngster is pushed to this last ditch stand: He accepts the adult as a friend; he also accepts her leadership and discipline. But the moment it comes to criticisms or discussions of certain code-dangerous items, like the matter of "stealing" or "delinquency," the youngster withdraws from any relationship he has previously developed, closes up like a clam, and refuses to identify with what the adult stands for.

In a nutshell, what we want to point out is that, through the inoculative mechanism of gang psychology, delinquent juveniles act under the influence of their gang loyalties even when they operate in other groups or are in consultative isolation with an adult psychiatrist. They protect their own identifications with the delinquent group code by either avoiding or hating us as persons, by treating us as if we represent a code-hostile outgroup, or by feeling safe in going far in love as well as identification with us except in code-dangerous items.

Implications for Psychotherapy

If some of the previous observations are true, then it is obvious that they must have important bearings upon limitations as well as chances of psychiatric therapy with delinquent juveniles.

The prognosis for treatment of delinquents has been a hesitant one to begin with, and the odds against which the psychiatrist works have been expounded at great length and are so well known that we shall not endeavor to list them here again. There are, however, additions to which our group-psychological observations challenge us.

GROUP-PSYCHOLOGICAL BARRIERS TO TREATMENT

The psychiatrist who sees his patient in his private consultation room or at a guidance clinic—which means in group-psychological isolation—is still "marked" by the fact that he is an obvious representative of an "outgroup." He finds that his client, beside whatever resistances he would have developed anyway on the basis of his case history or through the treatment process, is constantly being furnished with group-psychologically produced defenses. This observation is not only true of youngsters who are actually members of delinquent gangs. For the mobilization of defenses mentioned above, it is sufficient that the youngster be identified with what is commonly referred to as a "tough-guy philosophy" of life. These "group-psychologically produced" defenses are not traceable without thorough insight into the nature of the group climate of which the patient feels himself a part, and they offer strong resistance against techniques that are otherwise effective with the neurotic client.

The psychiatrist who works on the staff of an institution or of an agency that is closely identified with one is marked to begin with as a member not only of an outgroup but also of *the* hostile overgroup against which most of the gang code is directed in its most vicious heat. This situation is most glaringly exemplified in the grotesque situations we find in many court clinics or guidance clinics that try to serve detention homes or punitive institutions for juvenile delinquents. In those cases, youngsters are stored for weeks and months in group-psychological climates well known to be the most delinquency-productive of all and even more vicious in the defenses with which they furnish participants than is the delinquent gang itself. Several times a week the youngster is taken out of this climate for an hour or a half, is exposed to the influence of a psychiatrist in interview contact, and is sent back to a place where every wall oozes gang-psychological defenses.

The situation, although nearly universal, is about as grotesque as if a hospital were to offer pharmacological treatment to pneumonia cases but took good care that the air they breathed between these applications was carefully emptied of oxygen.

GROUP-PSYCHOLOGICAL CHANCES

If the group medium has such powers over individual resistance even beyond the immediate presence of the group, then it should encourage us in an attempt to harness those same powers in the service of therapy. The following opportunities seem to offer themselves as possibilities at this stage of the game.

THE SUPPORTIVE GROUP CLIMATE

Instead of working in group-psychological mid-air, the psychiatrist and his helpers might create or initiate special types of group climate that would counteract the original "delinquent defenses" and at the same time provide for the normal group-psychological needs growing youngsters have anyway. We mean more, of course, than general advice to send youngsters to the Boy Scouts or the Y because "groups are good for them." We are thinking of an elaborate, near-to-pharmacologically precise prescription of just the type of group organization, climate, and leadership that would fit treatment needs exactly. Our experiences in the Detroit Group Project—an agency created by the School for Social Work and Public Affairs for just such type of research—encourage us to think that such group-psychological prescriptions can be worked out with some degree of accuracy right now.

GROUP-CLIMATE PARTICIPATION BY THE THERAPIST

In some cases, we have been able to watch the disappearance of even heavy defenses of the group-psychologically produced type, as soon as the psychiatrist ceased to operate in group-psychological mid-air and became part of the group life of the delinquent juvenile himself. We do not mean that he should join a delinquent gang, nor is it sufficient for him to be administratively on the "staff" of a group-work agency or institution. We mean, however, that he should live in or close to the group-psychological facilities created for the youngster's therapy and that he should be considered as "belonging" in terms of the member psychology of the youngsters themselves. Especially in camp settings—preferably of the all-year-round type—it can easily be observed that some youngsters are ready to surrender group-psychological resistances to the person who is part of their group life. The defenses the therapist has to work with are thus reduced to the individual minimum he would meet anyway. Whether or not the psychiatrist himself should be part of this group setting and to what degree and to what extent cooperation with a group therapist can be worked out successfully are not to be decided at this point.

Conclusions

Psychotherapy with delinquent juveniles, even on the traditional interview basis, must not operate entirely in "group-psychological mid-air."

It is essential for the individual therapist to have as thorough a diagnostic picture of the group-psychological characteristics of the climate the youngster lives in as of the individual dynamics of the case.

For certain types of case—especially those with highly developed "taboos against code-dangerous identifications," it is advisable to undertake treatment in a setting that combines group therapy with the individual approach and in which the psychiatrist or his group-therapeutic helper is part of the group in which the youngster lives.

It is desirable that group-psychologically correct prescriptions be worked out by which supportive treatment in and through the group can be added to the work of the psychiatrist within or outside institutional situations. Places where youngsters are stored must not only comply with the best that is known in practice educationally and clinically, but also they must absolutely obey the laws of group-psychological antisepsis. At this moment there is hardly a handful of such places in existence in the whole United States.

The Art of Group Composition

The question "Just who would do well with whom else in the same group?" might well be listed as the most vexing one for all those who have to make such decisions and who have to live with their consequences. At the same time, the old illusion that group composition is either of no importance at all (the proud "the more, the merrier" theory) or that absolute "homogeneity" in grouping guarantees success is fortunately on the way out. Alas, the type of research that we really need in order to handle our practical problems in classrooms, children's institutions, psychiatric hospitals, and so forth more appropriately is not yet in sight.

On the other hand, it is my firm conviction that this issue of group composition will assume enormous degrees of heat in the near future. For, as a nation, we are happily engaged in ditching some of the old and rotten practices of grouping, which were based on racial or other forms of discrimination, and this is only as it should be, and indeed it is about time! Still the professional question of what makes for a good group in a specific situation remains as compelling as ever. For instance, you may want to make sure that the hospital in your neighborhood does not discriminate against Negroes, whites, or what not. Does that mean, though, that you want to stuff Ward A for communicable diseases with a few cases waiting for spinal surgery, simply to keep the numbers of Negroes and whites in both wards constant? Now, in this case, the answer is probably clear enough, and doctors who insist on having their professional criteria for grouping heard and respected won't have too hard a time.

In the psychiatric and educational fields, however, we can hardly hope for that much clarity or even for that much community trust, for that matter. This, in my estimate, makes it all the more important that we develop clear enough professional criteria for us to demonstrate and for all to see. For how can the professional worker be exempt from the accusation of unfair discrimination, even when he is only interested in efficient group composition, if such clear criteria are not yet formulated?

"The Art of Group Composition" is based on the article of the same title that appeared in Susanne Shulze, ed., *Creative Group Living in Children's Institutions*, published by Association Press.

It is with the thought of stimulating further research on this crucial problem of group composition and its various meanings in diverse professional settings that I include this description of the problem as it
appears in children's groups in institutional settings.

*L*ET'S BEGIN the discussion of the art of group composition with the story of Johnny.[1]

Johnny is a restless lad of thirteen and lives in a small cottage with
eleven other boys, most of them somewhat under his own age but not
too much. None of the children, including Johnny, is unusually disturbed, though all are "live wires" with quite emphatic needs for motion, noise, and activity.

The housemother is an elderly woman with a cordial and motherly
atmosphere around her but quite capable of holding her own and
skilled in firm but not unkind interference when the waves of juvenile
excitement rise a little too high. She runs her cottage extremely well,
has few cases of more "extreme" behavior to handle, and does not lose
her sense of humor under the impact of boyhood mischief. But Johnny
has her stumped. His behavior is getting worse; he seems to be on a
constant binge of triumphant clowning, has to giggle and act silly all the
time, is very mean and exploitative of the younger and weaker members
of the group, seems to be asking for more emphatic forms of punishment than she is willing to use, and if he gets them seems triumphantly
proud. In fact, he seems to bask in the reputation of the "bad boy" and
"toughie," and reasoning has no effect. Even more than about Johnny's
behavior, the housemother begins to get frantic about Johnny's decidedly "bad influence" on the rest of the group. For a while she doesn't
want to see it that way, for she feels that maybe she just gets irritable
and is now ready to blame things on Johnny that he can't really be held
responsible for.

However, the other day it became quite clear what was really
going on. Johnny happened to be sick in the infirmary when the housemother had one of her "let's talk it over sessions" with the group
around some incident or other. The previous weeks such sessions had
become nightmares. Johnny had led in clowning, and even those chil-

1 All names are fictitious.

dren who obviously liked their housemother and were otherwise quite well behaved had become so wild and silly in those "talks" that she already had considered the possibility of having to drop them altogether. But the other day things went well. Nobody even thought of any mischief. The youngsters were frank and serious as they used to be long ago, and even when somebody spilled the inkwell they entirely ignored a marvelous chance for mischievous uproar.

It was clear what had happened: Johnny's behavior did have an extremely "contagious" influence on the rest of the group, even though he never really tried to influence them and even though they themselves didn't know it. The housemother felt bad about this discovery. Did this mean you can't have a child like that in a group? What then is going to become of John, who obviously needs help just as much as the other children do?

A careful investigation of Johnny and his life and of the group and their individual peculiarities, shows that Johnny is not actually a "bad egg" but that most of his behavior in this group is produced by the very fact that he is in it. Johnny is similar to the other children in I.Q., in general school ability, and interest. However, this is where the difference comes in: Johnny comes from a much tougher background than do the rest of his pals, has had little chance for intimate relationships with any adults in his life, and on top of that has just gone through a phase of quite vehement body development into a more adolescent way of feeling and acting. In fact, even though chronologically not too badly placed, he is more advanced in terms of "adolescent emancipation from adults" than are any of the other children. The group, on the other hand, although still much more "childhood close" to its housemother, is just entering that stage in which the seemingly daring behavior of the older boy becomes a fascinating source of boundless admiration. The two facts together furnish Johnny with his seductive charm. Whatever he does seems so "emancipated" to the younger ones that imitation seems the only way of salvaging their own prestige as "big boys," and the chronic admiration of his daring acts of course overstimulates Johnny into bigger and better performances. He feels bad about this at times, for he likes the housemother too and knows that he is unfair to her. But he has now a role to maintain, a role desirable for his adolescent pride as well as his envied position with the rest of the group.

Johnny is moved, after careful preparation of him as well as the old and the new groups, into a group of older, more typically adolescent boys. He doesn't like the new cottage parent as well as the old one, but his "messy" behavior soon clears up. His adolescent pranks do not stick out so sharply as they did in the group of more childlike youngsters; some of his desire to be considered more emancipated is automatically satisfied by his inclusion in the "older boy" cottage and its different style of life. For a while he tries, as was anticipated, to outdo the older boys at their own adolescent game, but that is handled fast and efficiently. The group and the adult leader see to it that he gets plenty of chance for ordinary "prestige" in his group and little support by the rest of the group for silly antics of the old type.

Johnny's main problem to himself and the housemother, as well as to the other group members in his old cottage, is mainly a product of mistaken grouping. It therefore disappears when this source of trouble is removed.

Not always can a way out be found as easily as in Johnny's case, for often the trouble is not due to wrong grouping alone. Other factors, like really serious disturbances within the troublesome child, a bad group atmosphere in the rest of the cottage, and hysterical or thoughtless handling by the adult, may combine to produce a situation similar to the one we have described. In those cases grouping is only one among a larger number of other factors, all of which have to be handled in getting rid of the problem. However, the example of Johnny may help us to see the impact of a factor in group life that we have all too long ignored. To state it bluntly: The very fact of group mixture in itself may sometimes play a great part in what happens in a group, even when the best of conditions and the best and most skillful adult leadership are taken for granted.

If that is true, doesn't it become worth while to ask just how children should be put together in groups so that the best chance for the development of the most favorable "group climate" is guaranteed? Which are those factors? Are they simply age, I.Q., interest in sports or the lack of it, physical prowess or disability, and so forth? And, even more important, what are the basic laws of human nature underlying this business of group composition? Do they mean all youngsters have to be homogeneous in everything under the sun to make a good group? How can they? By the very fact that we mix them correctly on the basis of age, they may become heterogeneous in terms of I.Q., interests, or skills. In fact, there is no such thing as a totally "homogeneous group," for any one group can be homogeneous only in terms of one or, at most, a few specially selected criteria at a time.

What then is the answer? Can't we ever have a "well-composed" group? Or do we have to be so careful we never take any youngster into a group who might "deviate" too much from the pattern of the others?

Let's take a look at the situation of another child in a coeducational camp. The age range is from eight to fourteen; all children are referred by clinics and social agencies because they are hyperaggressive, disorganized, delinquent. Cabin 4 in the girls' village consists of five girls twelve and thirteen, all of whom are "wild numbers" and have records of stealing, truancy, and antisocial behavior. All have been pushed around a lot and have patterns of rejection and hostile handling by adults in their backgrounds. All, however, seem to be at the stage in which they really would like to be accepted by adults if they could only find adults who knew how to go about it and if they could show acceptance without losing face among themselves. We expect, of course, that we shall find the following behavior for the first two weeks: open defiance of adult leaders, provocation into punishment, and when they don't get the punishment they hope for (so as to hate adults some more) a phase of crude exploitation of our kindness because they confuse friendliness with weakness. After that come gradual clandestine gestures of reaching out for adult affection when nobody is looking and finally, if the first gestures are handled skillfully by the leader, surrender to leader-identified group formation.

We are asked by one agency to take Mary into our fold. This group is the only one Mary would fit into by developmental phase and a variety of other items. However, Mary's record has us scared. It is much worse than that of any of the others; there are repeated incidents of wild sex bravado, and, what bothers us most, Mary seems to hate any and all adults to such a degree that, not only does she seem to have no need for adult acceptance, but she has shown marked skill in inveigling groups of children into rebellion against the adults. In fact, she is something of a rumormonger and gang organizer, with some quite ingrained experience along that line. In accepting her, we feel we take a great risk. Our task already being as complicated as it is with the rest of the group, how can we survive if we put such an effective force against us right into its midst?

Well, we take a chance, as we all do sometimes. We are lucky. We have a heck of a time for a while, and there is no doubt that Mary's finagling slows up the process of adult acceptance in the other children. However, just because Mary is so extreme in her adult hatred, she really indirectly helps us in our job in the long run. Her stories against the leader, and her rebellion even against the most reasonable demands on the group and on individuals are so obviously screwy that even the other children, who at first exploit this chance for supported rebellion, begin to look up in amazement. The very extremity of Mary's reaction and paranoiac gossip against the leader makes the others see how silly it all is, and their sympathy swings in our direction with a bang just because of that. Needless to say, we pay a price in timing; it takes longer because of Mary's presence, and we have a lot of "incidents" to handle and anything but a smooth life. But it is worth it. And, as for Mary, when the other kids finally turn against her because of her exaggerated leader hatred, she is left high and dry and without her group support. This desertion gives us an in with her too, and for the first time she is able to enjoy some happy moments with her group and with the adult.

Of course, there were many factors involved that made the experiment work well in this case. One of them was the fact that the rest of the children were well matched, could really enjoy a number of common interests together, and felt quite congenial on the whole. Had we also loaded the group with great differences in recreational tastes, in developmental phases, in background sophistication, and so forth, it could not have worked out. It is also obvious that great flexibility in the program and plenty of time spent in well-handled individual and group interviews with the leader and others constituted the conditions under which this experiment could be tried. But it does show that there is nothing automatic in "contagion" and that under certain conditions even a very "bad egg" can be kept in a group and helped in it without ultimate detriment to the rest of the group.

There is another danger lurking behind the curtain of group composition, however, which we must not ignore. Sometimes it seems that some youngsters are so obviously "normal" and "all right" that we do not have to fear that they may imitate the behavior of more disturbed children at all. We can consider them safe against contagion. The wild behavior of others does not even seem desirable to them; they have no need for it. They are happy enough in their program and their relationships to us and secure enough within themselves to live their own lives. Such children are a great asset in any group. If you have many of them, you can take greater chances with the addition of some more difficult ones. However, there is a limit to this approach too. There is a point beyond which the exposure of "good" children to behavior that is too frighteningly extreme for them may do damage in a way that it took us a long time to see.

Richard was put into a cottage of very tough boys in a reformatory. The reason was that he seemed an unusually nice boy himself, who happened to land in the reformatory through some emergency home problem rather than because of his own real character deterioration. The referring department felt sure that if any boy could be trusted not to take on the bad behavior of the other "customers" in that cottage, it was Richard.

The referring department was right as far as the danger of "contagion" was concerned. Richard was a safe bet; he felt no need for the rebellious and mischievous behavior of the others and was no problem along that line. However, an entirely unexpected chain of problems soon began to present itself. Richard began to withdraw more and more into his shell, became morose and whiny, began to show lack of ability to sleep, was nervous and distractible in his school work, and finally had a whole sequence of very severe crying spells, which took on more and more obviously neurotic forms.

The adults, who liked Richard, were worried about him and at first began to suspect that some of the tougher boys in the group might have put pressure on Richard or might have threatened him. However, upon closer inspection, this suspicion proved incorrect. The other youngsters in this group were so involved in their own affairs that they paid little attention to Richard; in fact, some of the tougher ones had remarked that "this kid really shouldn't be in this place." When interviews with Richard finally took effect, here is what came out: Richard was not only a basically "good" boy, but he was deeply ambitious to work himself out of the reformatory and never to get into anything like it again. Also he had quite a deep concern with moral values. Living with a bunch of rather tough and oversophisticated "customers," he could not fail, however, to see what was going on. The crudeness of their talk, their openly guiltless bravado about their delinquencies, the brutalization of weaker children, including sexual abuse by older ones, upset Richard no end. Even though nobody bothered him directly, a whole wave of psychological fear was set loose in him by the mere knowledge of what was going on. The whole conflict of "good versus bad" was so constantly kept stirred up within this child that an anxiety neurosis with all the usual trimmings was the inevitable result.

We might call this effect of wrong grouping "shock effect," and we found it quite similar to the effect called "contagion," except that in this case we can be sure Richard would never have "imitated" the other boys. We were perfectly safe as far as that goes, but it would not be true to say that the other children had no "effect" on him. In fact, they threw him into a serious anxiety neurosis, which constituted plenty of effect, even though the manifestations of the damage were not so clearly and uncomfortably visible to the adult in charge of the group. Thus, sometimes the potentially damaging effect that placement in a group might have on an individual must be as seriously considered in group composition as must the opposite point.

Not always does the grouping problem become so acute as to raise the question of "danger." Sometimes wrong grouping doesn't exactly harm anybody involved, but it does mean we don't get far with what we are trying to do.

Alfred was sent for swimming instruction with a group of boys who were especially happy and proud water enthusiasts, were unusually well coordinated, and seemed to have natural affinities for this medium. The reason Alfred was put with this group was exactly this. Alfred himself was scared of water, afraid of most physical activities, and easily embarrassed about his ineptitude along those lines, and he derived no enjoyment whatever from such sports. It was felt, however, that he should acquire enthusiasm and skill in this direction because it would be "good for him" and that the company of the other water enthusiasts would draw him out of his shyness. The actual results in Alfred's case moved in exactly the opposite direction. Instead of being stimulated by the other boys' enthusiasm, he hated the very thought of having to try and keep up with them. Instead of losing his fear of water by the good example of fearlessness that the others set for him, his anxiety seemed to climb to new heights. And, even though the other youngsters were patronizingly tactful about his clumsiness and fear, Alfred suffered pangs of constant shame about the whole swimming situation.

Reason for failure: Although well matched otherwise, Alfred and the rest of the group were much too far apart in terms of water-sport enjoyment and readiness. The others were so happy and secure in this medium that Alfred was impressed with the unattainability of their skill and comfort rather than stimulated to renewed effort.

We could not say that, in this case, either Alfred or the other children were really "damaged" through the bad grouping, but it is also obvious that the bad grouping had a lot to do with the failure of the experiment of using this group placement to help Alfred.

The previous illustrations are meant to document a few very basic principles of group life:

First, the way a group is composed must not be left to chance; it may be of very great importance for the kind of group life that will develop and for the effects the group will have on some of its members.

Second, some of the most dangerous mistakes we can make in group composition lie in the direction of three group psychological principles:

We must not ignore the possibilities of contagion. Children put into a group in which they do not belong will either become serious disturbances to the group and to discipline, or they will suffer grave damage through exposure to the wrong group life.

We must not develop blind "germophobia." In other words, the fact that one youngster is "worse" than others in itself does not mean he will wreck the group or cannot be worked with. There are ways of combining his or her needs, under skilled group leadership, with the needs of the total group.

We should, however, watch out for the danger of "shock effect." If Richard is too far from the behavioral level of the rest of the group, serious neuroses may be developed through an intolerable conflict within him, constantly stirred up by wrong placement.

We suddenly realize then how worthwhile it is not only to know in what ways group composition may be important but also to be in on the secrets of specifics. Just what is it that makes one group "click" in spite of obvious heterogeneities in its composition, whereas the other one seems to go to pieces even though it looks on the surface well matched? What are the criteria on the basis of which groups should be matched to begin with?

Unfortunately, practically no research on an organized basis has yet been done to reveal the innermost mechanics of group life in this respect. Those experiences that have been accumulated, however, can yield very fascinating insights if properly exploited. Yet this theme is of such complexity that it far transcends the framework of this brief paper. As we are not able to deduce and prove some of the basic principles of group composition we are experimenting with, we shall simply limit ourselves to listing in rapid-fire succession a few of the things of which we are sure, even at the risk of being misunderstood.

First, there is no such thing as a homogeneous group. The moment a group is well matched according to one criterion, it is, of necessity, as different as can be in relationship to some others. But this doesn't matter too much, for the idea of finding *the* solution by just grouping children easily, by intelligence, age, physical size, or whatnot, is a naïve illusion. Life is more complex than that; solutions don't grow on one-criterion trees anyway. So why bother? The problem is not to get an absolutely homogeneous group but to find out which combination of criteria is most important for the job you are trying to do and then match your group members accordingly.

Second, this means that different institutions will have to use different criteria for grouping, and even within their institutional life they may have to do some thinking before they know how the various groups should be composed. For instance, if you have to teach mathematics three hours a week, you had better mix that group first of all so that its members are reasonably similar in their awareness of the fact that two times two are four. You would have a hard time teaching the members anything if half of them couldn't count and the other half were ready for some more Einstein. But that doesn't mean that I.Q. or mathematical ability is the criterion that counts in all your groups. If you ask which children you should have live together in a cottage, it would certainly be foolish to consider their math abilities first. Characteristics that are relevant to the skills of living together and "hitting it off" are far more important for composing that kind of a group.

Third, even so—assuming you have them well grouped for one purpose—don't forget about other issues involved. Your math class, for instance, even if mathematically well matched, will be poor if you put young and shy kids together with a bunch of hyperaggressive adolescent toughies. In that case, their discrepancies in "developmental phase" will be so disastrous that neither of the two parts of your group will be able to listen much to the mathematics they might theoretically be able to do; they will spend practically all their time either fighting or scaring or impressing or imitating one another.

This means that the "primary criteria" for grouping, if well applied, should not keep you from an inspection of some other criteria, which are not quite so important but which lead to disaster if you ignore them.

We sometimes formulate this idea as the "law of optimum distance," which says: If Johnny is well matched with the other kids in terms of intelligence, watch to see whether he isn't too far removed from them in terms of toughness, physical prowess, sex sophistication, or some other characteristic. In fact, the children do not have to be exactly alike in any criterion. But they ought not be more than about three inches apart in primary criteria (those that count most for the major objectives at which you are aiming) and not more than twelve inches apart in secondary criteria. If it's more than that in either, you have poor grouping for effective functioning.

How far are three or twelve inches? Nobody really knows. We are trying to find out in our research projects. But you don't have to wait until you know; almost any experienced practitioner develops a very efficient "hunch" skill at spotting extreme deviations along that line.

Fourth, taking life in children's institutions in an average way, what are the most frequent criteria that should be thought of in order to avoid a wider-than-twelve-inch range? We are listing only a few, each one of which may be irrelevant to your group, crucial in another. You can't tell without further study of your group. But here are those we found, more often than not, important.

Developmental Phase. Sometimes you can mix youngsters of very different age ranges. In any happy family you can do so quite well. In larger groups and in institutional life this mixture becomes complicated. Although you don't have to worry about exact chronological ages, you had better watch out that the children are in about the same developmental phase, or you can't possibly find any one program that fits them all and any one leadership style to which they all respond. The concept of developmental phase is more complex than can be discussed here in detail, but, in a nutshell, here is what we mean: Very young children have different needs from third- and fourth-graders. Most children around fifth- and sixth-grade age go through phases that are markedly different from what a fourth-grade child would experience. Your "young adolescents" again are really quite different human beings from those who are far into their pubescence, and many of those differences count. They count mainly in the following ways.

Program tastes. Younger children are frightened by some of the older ones' recreation; the older ones find many very happy childhood games just so much "sissy stuff" and can't possibly get anything out of them.

Adult relationships. Younger children are naturally happy if they fit into whatever pattern of life a reasonably decent adult deems fit. Preadolescents or adolescents deem it normally their aim in life to pretend to want none of that and to bask in the glory of "emancipative behavior." They would rather die or be beaten up by an adult than be called a "sissy" by another child their age.

Sex and language sophistication. The kind of joke that would make a younger child feel he is a bad boy or girl is normally for the younger adolescent the very source of pride in being grown up, without which life would indeed seem cowardly and dull.

Security appeal. Younger children get their security from the awareness that they are in line with the value system of family and educators' patterns. They may act contrarily, but security comes from dependence on affectionate adults. Preadolescents and older adolescents get their security elsewhere: the preadolescents in their "gang" affiliations, the older adolescents in submission to a general "adolescent style" of talking, walking, dressing, and so on.

In short, whatever style of life you develop in your cottage, it can fit only some of the normal growth patterns at a time. If the patterns of certain youngsters vary widely from your style of cottage life for one reason or another, such children will be misgrouped, even if their chronological ages correspond.

Organizational Maturity. This factor is another grouping criterion to consider. Some youngsters really function much better if there are not too visible signs of rules and regulations, if most of their behavior is stimulated by challenges to their feelings of decency, self-reliance, or group loyalty. Others, however, are very differently built. They are "scared stiff" if they ever have to make decisions; they lose all self-control unless they know what the given rules are; and they can't walk a step without the props of clear-cut policies and strong reminders of right and wrong. Different children achieve different stages at different times. Your cottage life can be designed to match some of these different degrees of need for organizational support or free-choice challenge, but it can't possibly run the whole gamut at once. Children who are way beyond the range of the particular organizational pattern that fits most of the rest of your group will have to become discipline problems, misfits, "pains in the neck" for you and for themselves. They should be placed in groups with organizational-pattern mixtures that fit them better. It wouldn't be fair to the rest of the group to try to adapt the style of organization that fits them to those who differ.

The Toughness-Shyness Line. This phrase represents a crude over-simplification. But, in rough outline, we can say that most youngsters have varying degrees of outgoing-aggressive-tough self-assertion versus easy yielding-withdrawing-even masochistic self-effacement. If youngsters go far off either end of the rather wide normal range, they will be a bother to the rest of the group or to themselves. The restless, hyper-aggressive, or even only hypermobile child in a group of normally quiet and self-sufficient youngsters will be a constant discipline problem or a "stirrer-upper" of trouble or an outcast in the group. The withdrawing or passive child, in a group of even normally hyperactive or aggressive children, will be the butt of all jokes, the exploited sucker, the teacher's pet, or the daydreaming isolate. Neither role is good for a child, who ought to have a chance to develop the life style that fits his personality pattern. Only in a reasonably congenial group can he do so.

In our clinical projects, we operate with a sum total of seventeen different criteria for grouping. Needless to say, enumerating all of them would trespass the framework of this paper. Therefore we shall end this listing of criteria with only this word of caution: You can't always group them ideally. But once you get extremes of deviation in any one item that counts in the life of this specific group, you must expect trouble with the group and the individuals involved, even though your group leader is a genius.

If They Are Not Well Matched, What Can You Do?

Most groups we get are too large to be well grouped to begin with; most institutions have wider ranges of intake than of facilities in terms of sufficient subgroups to take care of those ranges. Most workers in institutions operate in groups of poorly matched individuals. As long as this cannot be entirely avoided, we might at least look for ways to mitigate the damage to all involved.

Subgroup Insulation. The laws of group psychology offer a happy way out of some of these troubles. In the first place, the negative in-fluence of the fact that Johnny is not quite well matched with the rest of the whole institution can be counteracted by the way in which you subgroup him. It is a peculiar but very clear fact that some of the bad effects of contagion or shock do not jump subgroup lines. For example, one clown's wild behavior in a "chow line" with everybody standing in a regimented pattern is much more catching than if children are in the same room in different but well-contained game groups. Or a wild incident at a large mess-hall table with everybody uniformly embedded in a large mass as just another "number" will have ten times the disturbing effect of a similar incident at one of a number of small tables, each of which represents an "everyday living" group.

Sometimes, even within your cottage, you can take care of some of the unavoidable differences among youngsters by still further subgroup formation. To be sure, the youngsters may not all quite fit your cottage. But you can at least arrange that those who should be together can have subgroup experiences some of the time through hobby clubs, seating arrangements, bedroom distribution, committees, and so on. Most youngsters have an amazing amount of resilience: If they can just travel some of the time in the group composition that is congenial to them, they can take many experiences involving obviously "wrong" grouping without too much damage or trouble. The practical implications of this concept of subgroup insulation present a fascinating challenge to the practitioner.

Specialized Leader Handling. The fact that any one of our groups is not ideally grouped bothers us less if we know it in advance, because the most thoughtful and skillful leader can be assigned to it and given special leeway for the excruciating job. If you know your group is not well mixed, you have to know these things too:

Your group will show more problem behavior than other people's groups. This is natural and is no discredit to the person in charge.

More individuals in this group will need more specialized handling than in others, and this is no discredit to the individuals involved either.

The leader will have to take time and energy from other functions to "handle" many more incidents than have to be openly handled in better-mixed groups.

It should be obvious from the examples at the beginning of this paper that a lot of time spent on the special situations described carries a long way. This specialized leader handling will have to come out in the following forms:

leeway for more deviation from general practice and for making exceptions; more time spent in individual interview work to make the deviant or those irritated by him understand what really is going on;

more time spent in skillful "expressional" group interviews to ventilate surplus aggressions and to clear up misunderstandings among all of them, the leader included.

With the right leeway for specialized leader handling, even otherwise badly matched groups can still be used well, up to a certain point.

Exceptional Program Flexibility and Skill. If a group is badly matched, skillful programing can still go a long way to make up for it. The writer will never forget the arts-and-crafts teacher he visited a while ago who had fifty children in an inadequate room. They differed so widely in art interest, as well as in art skill, and presented such a wide mixture of different personality types and development stages that even a Leonardo da Vinci would have thrown up his hands in despair. Yet work went on with the most amazing enthusiasm and in relative order. The answer to the obvious question "Just how do you do it?" was simple. Instead of making those fifty children paint one vase or some other object, the art teacher had subgrouped them into ten groups of five each. On top of that, in subgrouping them she had not consulted the alphabet but had followed her "hunch insight" about the youngsters. She had put them into subgroups on two bases: first, according to interest and basic skill—so kids who were scared of brushes could use finger paint or clay and youngsters who loved wood didn't have to fuss with paint materials—and, second, to add a dash of salt, according to the idea of "personal compatibility." She had in each of those subgroups one who was much too restless to do much of anything by himself but was drawn into an enthusiastic, energetic subgroup in which he would have been the only visible loafer. She was careful to respect natural sympathies and group affinities, so that children who belonged to antagonistic cliques were not put into too embarrassing dependencies upon one another. Needless to say, this teacher could do it because she "understood" so much more about the basic laws of grouping than our scientific research so far "knows" about it. But if more practitioners will dare to follow their ingenuity, research will catch up after a while.

Concessions in Routine and Institutional Custom. Sometimes grouping has to be worse than we know it should be. But what can we do? They have dumped those four fourteen-year-olds on us, and we know we are really set up only for an age range from six to eleven. Or we have to move those two eight-year-old girls into the older ones' cottage—we just couldn't work it out any other way. Okay, let's assume we are stuck for this time at least. What can we do about it? Beside the previous suggestions, especially that of programing, we can at least recognize that we have created a wrong situation and then be ready to make up for it through concessions in routine and exceptional arrangements. To be sure, it is a policy that children should not go out by themselves. But now we have these much-too-old ones in with their much-too-young companions. Why not make an exception and see that this special trip to a friend or a movie makes up for much of the wrong grouping during the rest of the week? Or maybe this one is too young to be expected to benefit from the same routine that the older ones can very well take. You can make an exception. And don't say it will demoralize the others. You can always explain it to them if you only try. And if you can't, something else is wrong to begin with, and you had better find out what. There are so many policies that are made to fit a "general pattern," then become sanctified by sheer age and enslave the people they are supposed to help. For instance, there is a rule that "the children in each cottage should always play together." This was all right as long as developmental-phase distribution was such that you had better not have this older adolescents' cottage mix too much with that little kids' cottage over there. Now, however, there are wide deviations in age range in every cottage. So why not develop clubs that cut across cottage groups? To take another example, in a certain institution there are punishments meant for hardened toughies who can't be kept in line without them. Half of a cottage in this place is filled with younger first offenders sent by a rural judge who has no other facilities in his community. The other half consists of youngsters sent by urban judges who have tried everything else first and sent only the tougher ones as a last resort. How can the same play, punishment, or reward pattern fit them all?

The more deviant group composition becomes, the more flexible and open to revision must items of routine, discipline, and traditional procedures become. What would be "inconsistent" in a very congenial group becomes "normal adjustment to a variety of factors" in a poorly mixed group. The very concept of consistency itself must undergo a logical modification in that case.

Regrouping. Sometimes unfavorable grouping can be repaired by putting a youngster into a different group, provided there is one that really fits him better. However, even on such rare occasions, the recourse to regrouping should not be taken too lightly. Here are the things you want to think of before you take such a step.

First, sometimes regrouping would do away with a problem, but quite often it is better to work the problem out where the youngster is now than simply to get rid of the problem itself.

Second, often regrouping means cutting into already developed ties, and we confront a child with a very serious change. It must always be taken into consideration that the real adjustment after regrouping may involve a lot more than just moving the suitcase and bedding. Johnny or Mary may need help on that very problem of growing out of one group and into another.

Third, the group out of which Johnny is taken often needs some help if you want to be sure it doesn't misunderstand the move or consider it a triumphant victory spurring it on to greater intolerance when the next problem occurs.

Fourth, the group into which Johnny is put must be considered carefully; his entry into this group must be well prepared on all sides.

Fifth, temporary problem behavior of each group as well as of the regrouped individuals is to be expected and is no evidence against the wisdom of the move, but it requires special handling by a skillful adult.

Sixth, sometimes we may have a number of "misfits" and may feel we might put them together and start a new group for them. This plan may work out, provided we remember that the mere fact that they are all misfits in their respective groups does *not* make them similar. Only if the new group is also well grouped on other counts can the trick have the effect you expect.

Cautions in Intake and Institutional Self-Appraisal. Many bad groupings happen because the community that refers children or the institution that takes them is filled with naïve zeal to serve everybody under all conditions. Such zeal is laudable in motive but poor in results. It is comparable to a foot clinic that solicits tuberculosis cases, just because it can't see "people turned away who asked for help." In the long run it is wise to consider the following facts.

The best institution cannot be good for all. The very fact that it is well designed for some purposes and children makes it poisonous for others. It is no detraction from an effective drug against pneumonia that it doesn't pretend to do all the tricks of Alka-Seltzer.

Protective intake and awareness of one's own limitations of service are in the long run a wise protection of those who really need and benefit from this service, even though it may seem "exclusive" to whoever asks for admission right now and could not be served well.

Needless to say, such limitations of intake must be defined on the basis of real professional principles. There is no place for the idea of adult comfort or pride in a smoothly running program, which so often unjustifiably prevents institutions from helping those who need help most.

If there is an ambition to serve types or age ranges of children not served before, allowance must always be made for modification in subgroup possibilities, changes of policy, program flexibility, and other aspects. Widening intake without the resources to meet the needs of those you take in usually ends in discontent for all concerned.

Discipline in Classroom Practice

The word "discipline" has many connotations. Even linguistically it offers the temptation to use multiple meanings in the same discussions: "I had to discipline him," compared to "I don't think that teacher in the classroom next to mine has good discipline," compared to "Don't you think that discipline is one of the most important goals of character education?"

In this study, I was trying to be as one-sided as possible and to serve only one purpose: to *help the classroom teacher* with some of the baffling life situations he runs into under this label. If you are not a classroom teacher, skip this essay, unless, of course, you have to live with children and therefore simply have to understand what a classroom teacher is up against—or unless you have ever made the mistake of taking wonderful kids and their pals on a station-wagon trip, which turned out to be too long, and on top of that it started raining and turned cold.

ONE GREAT TASK of the teacher, apparently, is to understand and accept principles of democratic discipline and to defend himself against the demoralizing lure of long outgrown and primitive punitivism, which so successfully cloaks itself behind arguments of "toughness" and "realism." This is only one side of the picture, however. Let us not for a moment fall into the illusion that by understanding and accepting the principles of democratic discipline, we immediately move into a state of affairs in which all problems are solved or disappear. This is not so. On the contrary, administering constructive discipline is a more laborious task than is taking refuge in a few simple punitive tricks. It is just as much more laborious and challenging as is

"Discipline in Classroom Practice" is based on Fritz Redl, "Part II. Discipline in Classroom Practice" from George V. Sheviakov and Fritz Redl, *Discipline for Today's Children and Youth,* New Revision by Sybil K. Richardson, Washington, D.C.: Association for Supervision and Curriculum Development, NEA, 1944 and 1956, pp. 17–64. Reprinted by permission of the publisher. Copyright © 1944 and 1956 by the Association for Supervision and Curriculum Development, NEA.

modern medical thinking compared to the proud hocus-pocus of the primitive medicine man.

The other great task, therefore, that confronts the classroom teacher on his job is to translate the principles of democratic discipline into daily action in his classroom. It is with this idea in mind that the following pages have been written.

From Theory to Practice

THE TEACHER—AS AN EDUCATOR OF INDIVIDUALS

The responsibility of the teacher toward the "individual's" rights and developmental needs is inherent in the concept of democracy and does not need further elucidation here. It may be worthwhile, however, to remind ourselves in passing of the tremendous progress we have made along this line during the last four or five decades. In times of emergency and strain we are likely to get all excited about the problems we haven't solved and to forget about the things that have been achieved. So let us just point to a few facts.

Research in this country has dug up and compiled more knowledge of the individual and the ways he grows physically, mentally, and emotionally than has been available ever before in history in any other nation of this world. Much of this knowledge has not been sufficiently organized; we are also behind in our applications. But the fact that it exists is something not to forget.

Psychiatry, psychology, mental hygiene, and similar fields have helped us to develop ways and means of studying the children we deal with, of organizing this knowledge for the use of the educator on the job, of understanding and sizing up even such developmental needs of children as are not visible on the surface of classroom behavior. It is also true that not all these techniques have been worked out sufficiently to be used profitably in all situations. But many are there ready for use, and others are being prepared.

Teachers have become so interested in this singular chance to enrich their knowledge about the human beings they teach that even universities have had to modify some of their curricula and to allow practical courses and seminars on guidance and personnel work much larger space in their catalogues than their traditional fears of the untried sciences would otherwise have suggested to them. It is true, of course, that much remains to be done. But it cannot be denied that more specific concern about the human child and what makes him tick is here to stay.

Some may check my enthusiasm at this point and say, "But listen, isn't it also true that many teachers reject and despise the very achievements you seem so proud of here?" I thought so for a long time myself. After arguing with many of those who do, I have changed my mind. Yes, it is true that many teachers reject the improvements we have made in terms of individual child study as "sissy stuff" and "fads and frills." But do you know why they do? Not because they don't see the value of it all, but because they get discouraged if you open up vistas for them and then don't give them a chance to apply what they see. For at the same time that the teacher is invited to become psychological, he is still loaded with classes too large for their own good and with work too predefined for him to insert what he would like in terms of individual work, and it is the frustration of these factual limitations, rather than a lack of forward-mindedness, that causes most of the dissension.

On the whole, I think we have a right to be optimistic: We are far from having licked the problem of individualization, but as far as the American teacher's basic conviction goes we are on the road to making individualized understanding a real issue in our school system.

In fact, in this respect I think educators are even better off than is the army. For we are not so pressed for time—most of our children are known to us over periods of years. We do not meet the child in isolation from his natural life but pretty close to it, so we can see much about the way he acts and lives outside school and can "get a feel" as we go along of the community of which he is a part. We do not work in the close shadow of death and emergency. So we can often "study" for a while in order to act with more insight, whereas the army officer has to insist on some action at once.

In short, as a nation, we have advanced tremendously during the last five decades along the road to individual understanding of the human beings we teach, even though much is left to be done in closing the gap between knowledge and actual application.

THE TEACHER—AS A LEADER OF GROUPS

We have tolerated a blind spot in our vision, however, that causes us much concern. For while we were busy digging up knowledge about the "individual," we neglected an equally important phase of our professional task. I might try to put it this way:

All this knowledge about the individual is fine. But so what? We never work with the "individual" in mid-air; school classes are *groups*. The moments in a teacher's life when he has one child at a time in his room are rare. His daily role is that of a leader of groups. It is true that the teacher wants to reach each individual by what he does and by what he makes the individual do. But his direct action is in and through the group. He meets individuals mainly embedded in groups, that is, as parts of some group pattern or other.

For a long time we did not know what this idea meant. Even now many people seriously believe that a group is simply an arithmetical accumulation of so many individuals and that the whole problem is one of numbers.

That is where the army is way ahead of us. The army always has known that groups are organisms in themselves. Such groups consist of individuals, it is true, but they are more than simple collections of people. They develop something like personalities, "spirits" of their own; they develop some power within them, something upon which their functioning depends a great deal, something that goes beyond the individuals who constitute them. In a group whose spirit or morale is high, for instance, many an otherwise weak individual will be spurred on to better and more efficient performance. In a group whose morale breaks down, even individually well-meaning members will eventually become indifferent or ineffectual.

The army knows that the leadership of groups is a task in itself, following special laws and peculiarities, a science in itself. The schools have had a vague awareness of this fact for quite a while, but they have expressed it in the wrong way. They have either tried to imitate blindly leadership techniques that were developed under certain army conditions, no matter how different direct goals and special group psychologies may be, or they have conceived of the "group leadership" needed in schools merely as the managerial task of keeping a large mass of students subdued enough so they won't make life too uncomfortable for the adults.

There is no doubt that the managerial manipulation of group behavior remains one task basic to group life. This task, however, is only part of, but is not identical with, the task of educational group leadership. If we compare not only our tasks but also our chances for success with those of the army officer, we must admit that we have reasons to be envious. The army carefully selects those who are fit for its purposes, and it has elaborate machinery for this selection. The schoolteacher is destined to deal with whatever groups of individuals his community presents him.

The army has all the power to decide how large an effective group should be and who should be sent to which group (no matter in what town or part of the country), and it has a wide choice for referral. Comparatively, the teacher is a poor wretch. For decades he has tried to convince the tax-paying public of the professional inadvisability of having groups of certain sizes, only to meet with absolute rejection or the suspicion that he is too lazy to do the job. The army can even modify public opinion and its concepts about what the life of a young adult should be like, and it can successfully cross the sensitivities of individuals who are touchy about grammar, dice, or behavior that deviates from Emily Post. Have you ever tried to get your community to understand what the life style of a healthy growing adolescent should be, and did you get away with it?

In short, there is no doubt that the teacher works under tremendous handicaps when he gets really interested in the art of group leadership —but teachers are used to that; so I don't worry that this statement will scare them away.

It does imply, though, that teachers need as much help in their task of effective group leadership as in studying the individual child. We also have to admit that we know less about this phase than about the other. Research has let us down—it is only very recently that scientific studies of group psychology have increased. Psychiatry and psychology are getting interested but are as yet poorly equipped to meet the problems of group behavior. The teachers, who always wanted help on that, are still being fed with generalized statements instead of with specific aids for problem solution, and many have trouble seeing the problem beyond the point at which it disturbs their own comfort.

This is just the point, however. I seriously think that we are making one tremendous step. We are becoming aware of the task of group leadership more than we ever have before. Awareness of a newly discovered task is, of course, usually accompanied by a lot of dumb behavior, hysterical prejudice, futile controversialism. Some of us, for example, want to meet the challenge of group discipline by doubling the number of intelligence tests taken. Others want to have a "psychiatrist for every child," laboring under the illusion that problems of group behavior would disappear if every member of a group were "psychiatrized." Others use newly discovered awareness of the need for group leadership to sell their special brands of punitive trick to befuddled bystanders or cut out pages from the manual on "how to use night sticks on the beat" and glue them over the pages of *Education for Democracy*.

I for one, however, am happy and proud to declare that I am not bothered by any of this nonsense. Any period of great discoveries has always been accompanied by the tomfoolery of scared hysterics, greedy charlatans, and hypochondriac gripers. The very existence of this spectacle seems to me only a sure proof that something marvelous is happening—something that will wake us all from lethargic sleep.

GROUP DISCIPLINE—NOT A CONTROVERSIAL ISSUE

Progressives as well as fundamentalists were just about to go to sleep, only occasionally waking each other up by taking pokes at each other's ribs. Progressive education has not in the past given sufficiently detailed answers to the problems of the teacher who wants to achieve good group leadership in his classroom. Fundamentalist educators have been so preoccupied with fighting what the progressives say that they too have not produced any data-based insights on the basic mechanisms of group discipline. Both sides have pitched "belief" versus "belief," leaving the classroom teacher alone on the job in the process. Well, then, why the heck don't we forget about our theoretical disputes or convictional competitions and get together on the job? The job is simply to

find out what the most frequent practical problems of the classroom teacher are, in terms of group leadership;

find out the basic laws of group behavior, and I don't mean in general;

make specific studies of the way known group-leadership techniques affect certain types of group setting, by working with the teachers on their jobs.

develop a body of well-documented and really practice-based insights and criteria, not meant to make teachers conform to our personal convictions or creeds, but to serve as practical guides to problem solution within the group.

It is the conviction of the author that by getting together all of us could help produce something really applicable for the teacher on the job and that in the process of doing this we might forget rather than reinforce some of our outdated squabbles over stale controversies.

This paper is an attempt to do just that, though in a very limited fashion only.

Thinking Straight About "Discipline"

No matter how wide the variety of meanings of the word "discipline" may be in any given dictionary, teachers seem invariably to use it in their talks at the luncheon table or in the staff meeting in three different ways.

MEANING NUMBER 1

In this sense we mean by "discipline" the degree of order we have established in a group. We say, for example, "Miss X doesn't seem to have much discipline in her 7A." Or "Mr. Y doesn't seem to me to know so much about his field, but he sure has a lot of discipline in his classroom. I must say that for him." In both cases we usually use the verb "to have" in conjunction with "discipline." By the "discipline we have" we usually refer to the degree of organization we have achieved in a group. The question of just how we have arrived at this organized functioning of a group is left open in that case.

MEANING NUMBER 2

In this sense we mean by "discipline," not the order we have, but the trick by which we have established order. For instance, "Say, Miss Jones, what discipline do you use in your grade?" Or "She's got a good homeroom, but I don't quite like the discipline she uses." In both cases we usually find the word "use" in conjunction with the word "discipline." By the "discipline we use" we mean anything we do to establish, maintain, or repair order in our groups.

It must be obvious from the outset how confusing such double use of the word "discipline" can be. No wonder we get confused if at times we use the same word to point to the thing we want to establish that at other times we use to point to the technique by which we establish that thing. This confusion is why there is so much controversy among teachers over what is nothing but a problem of simple semantics.

In this sense, people often use the word—the verb especially—as a euphemism for "punishment." "I am sorry there wasn't anything I could do with him anymore. I simply had to discipline him." Or "Don't you think that children should be disciplined at times?" In such cases we do not talk about order but about a special way of enforcing it. And among the dozens of ways of encouraging the growth of order, we mean simply one, punishment, as though it were the only one.

There is no trouble in pointing out that this use of the term is, of course, fallacious. When it occurs along with other uses in one and the same discussion, we may easily see what confusions arise:

Mr. A. I don't agree with the way you disciplined Johnny the other day. I think this is only going to make him more stubborn than he already is.
Mr. B. What! Don't you believe in discipline?

The solution of such a misunderstanding is simple; there is no such alternative as Mr. B. suggests. Believing in discipline (order) does not mean that any type of punishment is the right way to get it, in spite of the identity of terms.

SUMMARY

Thinking straight about discipline requires that we know just which way we and other speakers use the term—or we shall never get beyond a Babylonian confusion in our discussions of the topic. For this little study, I suggest that we eliminate meaning number 3: When we mean punishment, we shall say "punishment," instead of hiding it under terminological disguises.

We shall, however, have to talk about both of the other meanings at different places. But we shall always add specific enough statements to make it clear just what we are talking about at the time—discipline as a certain type of order or as techniques to establish, maintain, and repair it. As long as we make this distinction clear in each instance, major misunderstandings can be easily avoided.

The Three Main Headaches

We are now talking about the problem of choosing the right disciplinary technique (Meaning Number 2), though some of what we want to say here also applies to planning the right type of order (Meaning Number 1).

From our work with practitioners on the job, it seems to us that the problem of group discipline with which they are faced constantly rotates around the following three thought complexes: the individual or the group? managerial manipulation or attitude change? how do we know whether or not "it works"?

THE INDIVIDUAL OR THE GROUP?

It is funny that, with two good things, our first thought should usually be just how we can sacrifice one in favor of the other. For that is certainly the way the problem is usually stated in relation to group discipline. In theoretical discussions, most teachers can easily be split on this issue.

On one hand, there are those who want to sacrifice the individual to the group. When any issue comes up, Johnny's got to be kicked out because "his presence disturbs the group," or he's got to be socked to "set an example" for the others (no matter what it does to him), or he must be rewarded as an "example" to the group—even if this reward does transform him into a conceited snob and makes the rest of the kids good and envious. The defenders of this attitude obviously have a point, but, when you ask them how far this approach solves Johnny's problems, they don't like the question and tell you to be realistic or go home.

On the other side of the fence we find those who don't care much for the group Johnny lives in. They insist that you pamper the most sadistic brat no matter how many kids he slices up in the process. They demand that you give Johnny all the praise he needs to get along better with his siblings at home, no matter how "unfair" you act toward the rest of the classroom. Or they insist that Johnny be given the classroom as a playground to become a little Hitler, just because it will make up for the frustrations of group participation he suffers at home. If you ask them "But what about my group?" they don't like the question and tell you to understand Johnny or go home.

The teacher with vision knows that both these attitudes are silly and that there is no way out but always to consider both issues at once.

The group leader's problem is always both to influence the behavior and growth of the individual and to influence the behavior and growth of the group. There are several complications he often finds himself confronted with.

First, in certain instances of everyday group life, one or the other issue may be in the foreground. Some events of group life are more "group relevant" than are others; others bear more meaning in terms of the "individual case."

Example 1. Johnny is just at the stage of development in which a lot of clowning is frequently used by children in order to gain group prestige. There is nothing really wrong with this clowning. In fact, knowing Johnny, we are glad it has happened "at last." It is also, however, usually unavoidable that children overdo this ambition for group effect at times and become so intense in their wishes for applause that they really disturb every serious teaching situation.

In this case it is not sufficient to know that Johnny's behavior is all right, normal, understandable, even desirable from the angle of his own development. The teacher is still confronted with the job of limiting it, or else his whole teaching situation goes to pot.

Example 2. The teacher notices that Mary is sitting back, obviously daydreaming. After a while he finds that the child is seriously disturbed about some family situation. Mary's behavior is restricted to her fantasy life, however. She does not act in any way that would disturb the group or the teacher on the job. Her behavior remains, from a group angle, innocuous, though it is alarming as far as her own case history goes.

In that case there is no disciplinary need for the teacher to interfere, but Mary's behavior is still an important educational challenge, for she needs help.

Second, the techniques that are good for one purpose (to help individuals) do not always coincide with the techniques that are effective for the other angle of the problem (to influence group behavior).

Example 1. George is the type of youngster who does not respond readily to any nonautocratic approach. Appeals to group spirit do not mean much in his life, for he doesn't care much what the rest of the children think about him. What he seems to need at this moment is close supervision plus a very cordial friendship with his teacher. As long as this technique is used he functions pretty well. There are many other children like him in the group; so the teacher decides he will work through this combination of dependence on the benevolent autocrat and personal love appeal. After a while the group members are exposed to situations in which they ought to run things on their own. They are entirely incapable of doing so. For none of them has learned to act under anything but benevolent adult pressure.

The technique of benevolent autocratic friendship is thus right in terms of some of the children involved, but it does not do the job of educating the group into a self-reliant unit.

Example 2. The teacher has discovered that his classroom has deteriorated somewhat, has gone into a phase of being rather too wild and woolly for its own good, and is getting quite out of control. Instead of giving the teacher time to find out just what happens and go at the solution of this problem gradually, the principal insists that something be done right away and no fooling.

The teacher therefore decides to clamp down on the group, sets up a few "examples," gets tough, and becomes very suppressive and threatening in his approach. This "works" as far as surface group behavior goes. The class has a better record, produces less noise, is more submissive during teaching hours.

At the same time, however, some children in the class lose interest in schoolwork, begin to be late and to truant, and neglect home tasks; some of them attach themselves to delinquent gangs outside the school, even though they do become more submissive to discipline in school.

The technique of the teacher does work in terms of influencing group behavior but not in terms of what these children as people need.

Third, in cases of conflict between the interests of the individuals involved and the challenge of group behavior, there is one basic law that may guide our disciplinary choices: *the law of marginal antisepsis.* A technique that is right in terms of Johnny's problems must be at least harmless in its effects upon the total group. A technique that is rightly chosen in terms of group effect must be at least harmless to the individuals involved.

Example 1. Let's remember Johnny's problem with clowning. It must be curtailed or the group goal will be too seriously hampered. Now, however, comes the question of just *how* to change Johnny's behavior so that what the teacher does is also at least harmless to Johnny.

Under ideal circumstances the teacher may plan to solve his group problem and Johnny's problem all in one big swoop, for instance, really using a lot of time on Johnny, fixing up his home problem, finding him a nice boys' club where he can do all the clowning he needs without upsetting other people's applecarts, or having him psychoanalyzed, whatever his special need may be. Rarely are the circumstances as ideal as that, however. Often the teacher does not have this choice, cannot use so much time on changing Johnny's behavior, yet must get results somehow.

What our law of marginal antisepsis demands is that the teacher act at least in such a way that Johnny is not damaged. For instance, simply punishing Johnny hard each time he clowns or kicking him out of school would solve the group problem easily. But what would it do to Johnny, who would then be not only without social approval but also more confused than before? Shaming him before the others might also do the trick as far as classroom behavior is concerned. But wouldn't it take away what little social adjustment he has made and drive him into bigger and worse bravado before less sympathetic groups?

Cooperation of other kids in the classroom in helping Johnny understand the limits to which he can go will do the trick of checking Johnny's clowning, without making his own adjustment problem more difficult.

Example 2. Ann is a youngster with a lot of inferiority feelings. The psychologist has advised the teacher that she needs a lot of approval and encouragement to regain confidence in herself. As a result the teacher goes out of his way to give Ann praise, more than she deserves and more loudly and obviously than he would ordinarily give it to other children. As a result, Ann simply blossoms for awhile. She is happy and proud in class, more self-confident. The teacher thinks he has been successful in solving the problem.

However, after a few days it transpires that the other children do not really understand or even know enough about Ann's special problem. They are therefore bound to misinterpret all the special attention she gets all of a sudden. They begin to distrust their teacher. They also begin to show him what they feel. They become sloppy in fulfillment of their tasks, gripey and grouchy about assignments. At last it all ends with some of the youngsters acting very fresh to the great satisfaction of the group.

The technique the teacher uses to handle Ann's behavior is right in terms of Ann's case history. However, it is bad from a group-psychological angle. Uninterpreted preference of one child's action before others may be misunderstood and may release group jealousy and destroy group morale. The technique is theoretically right for Ann's case but wrong because it is not "at least harmless" in its group effects.

This analysis does not mean that the teacher cannot do anything at all for Ann, in order to avoid hurting other children's feelings. It does mean, however, that he has to modify what he does and that he has to get the other children's understanding first—or that maybe he should work through the group to begin with.

Fourth, contradictions that are unavoidable in any one moment of group life can often be solved by additional planning for later situations.

Example 1. The teacher is taking the children on a trip that involves a boat ride. Naturally they are in high spirits. He knew they would be. That's why he took them on a trip to begin with. One among them, Bob, apparently is the type of child whose self-control is much lower than that of the other children. So the removal of usual behavioral inhibitions, although it makes the others only reasonably noisy and mischievous, has too much effect on Bob. He becomes entirely wild, unmanageable, and acts in such a way that he threatens to upset the boat.

Let us assume there is real danger involved. Then there is no doubt that the teacher simply has to act. He will, therefore, even though he does not believe in physical punishment or is not mad at Bob because he understands, restrict him by all means from upsetting the boat, even if he has to hold him or to have the other youngsters keep him in line. This method "works" to the extent that Bob does not upset the boat. We know that the emergency technique he has to apply is very bad, however, and must have ill effects on Bob and the other children.

The moral of the story is that the teacher can't avoid doing what he does and would have to do it again. But he can avoid going home and thinking everything is all right simply because the group effect he feared was avoided. He will

have a talk with Bob later to see whether or not he can help him to have more insight;

make Bob see by the way he acts afterward that he does not dislike Bob simply because he had to stop a silly act, even though Bob himself didn't see that difference at all;

arrange for all-round planning that may make a more reasonable being out of Bob and may involve home and other manipulation; or remove Bob to a group of children whose program does not include such advanced situations of free planning as does that of the first group, which may be socially too mature for Bob.

Which of these or which other measures might be right will all depend on Bob and his problem. What we want to point out here is that the necessity on the spur of the moment to do something that we know is wrong in some other way does not preclude our making up for such unavoidable mistakes by additional action later.

Example 2. Martha lives under most undesirable home circumstances. The teacher knows it and also knows the special strain the child is going through just now. Under its impact, the girl becomes overemotional and bursts into a temper tantrum in the schoolroom, using rather wild language and, if you please, even hurling insults at the teacher.

Ordinarily it is the practice of the school to bring such an incident before the principal, to punish or at least reprimand the girl very heavily, or to follow any one of the frequent practices of social ostracism or whatnot. The teacher realizes that the problem this child faces is so serious that it simply wouldn't do to use any of these techniques or to call in the parents or even to do anything that might make the child feel she has lost her last friend—the teacher. So he decides to make an exception. He does not react to Martha's insults at all, waits until the fit is over, then quietly goes over to the crying child and gives her all signs of undisturbed affection.

This behavior is just what Martha needs. Without it her case would have been unpredictably messed up. Yet the teacher also knows that this way of handling the case is not right in terms of the group as a whole. For he can not tolerate the same behavior by any child in the group just the same way, and as the other children know that they must begin to hate Martha and become jealous of her and thus produce another problem for her on top of the ones she already has.

Still, the teacher thinks he acted rightly and would do the same thing again. Yet he does not stop there. He realizes that something must be done to counteract the group-psychological mistake that was unavoidably involved in his behavior toward the individual case. So he has a talk with the class after school, gets the children's frank reactions to what happened, and lets them blow off steam against the bad behavior of Martha and come pretty close to criticizing him for too much leniency. Then he has a chat with all of them or a few—that all depends on details of the situation—and explains that he has special reasons why he acted as he did. This helps the group to understand and not to misinterpret his behavior toward Martha. He also leaves no doubt about his own criticism of Martha's behavior and thus makes it clear to the group that he does not mean to ignore or condone what Martha does but that he has other things in mind.

In summary, we want to assure the teacher that we do not pretend that the problem of "individual and group" is always soluble or always easy to solve. We do want to imply, however, that in many more cases than we might think at first an adequate solution can be found if we are only aware of the fact that good group leadership needs this double orientation all the time. Such an attitude helps to assure the fitness of what we do in terms of the individual involved as well as in terms of group-psychological effects. Many discussions that become controversial either-or fights could be much more constructively resolved into combinations of these points of view, as we have demonstrated. In all those cases, however, in which the teacher finds himself repeatedly faced with situations in which a combination of these two points of view seems impossible, we can safely say that something is wrong with the way the group was composed to begin with. About this item, we shall have more to say later.

MANAGERIAL MANIPULATION OR ATTITUDE CHANGE?

There is another problem that often confronts the teacher in his planning of group discipline. It is posed by the question "Just what am I trying to accomplish?" The purpose of any disciplinary measure can be geared in two directions, to influence surface behavior right then and there or to influence basic attitudes.

The alternatives offered here, by the way, may present themselves regardless of whether it is the individual or the whole group that we are trying to influence.

The following seem to us to be the basic principles underlying the "purpose" phase of group discipline.

First, sometimes it is really important to manipulate surface behavior here and now, by all means. Failure to do so would constitute a serious mistake.

Example 1. The teacher handles a class of rather disturbed children from a rough neighborhood in which vehement fighting does not belong to the socially rejected items of behavior. At the moment his efforts seem pretty successful. The group is going fine and is obviously interested in the way he explains things that these youngsters had never really quite grasped before. But the group is an odd mixture of shy, withdrawing children and wild, close-to-murderously aggressive youngsters with temper tantrums of long standing. While the teacher is busy doing his explaining, a little rumpus begins between two boys in the back row. In a group like this one it would not do to pay attention to every little rumpus that occurs, or the climate would have to be kept on such a punitive level that no wish for learning or school acceptance could develop. The teacher is used to ignoring little disturbances from time to time and has found that they usually peter out pretty well on their own. In this case, however, he is out of luck. One of the boys suddenly jumps up and pulls a knife on the other. In this case there is little doubt in his mind that the knifing should be stopped, no matter in what way he may have to interfere. Let us assume that the boy is so upset that no mild form of approach has any effect; so the teacher has to hold his arm, take the knife away from him, yell at him, or kick him out.

The importance of avoiding injury to the threatened child is sufficiently great to justify using the technique that is needed to bring about a surface change in behavior.

Failure to do so would be a serious mistake. It is needless to remind you that this technique constitutes only the first part of the real "handling" of this discipline case. Our examples in the previous section easily point the way to more complete action.

Example 2. The whole of 7B finds itself in assembly together with all the children of the elementary school. The 2A of this school has planned a performance into which it has put a lot of time and enthusiasm, and it has waited months for this chance to be applauded by the whole school. In this school 7B is the highest grade. It is spring; the end of the term is not far away and with it the end of all the 7B-ers' stay in this school building—or so they hope. An hour before the program there is a violent dispute about the outcome of a baseball game that has ended with a doubtful tie.

The 7B isn't a bad bunch, on the whole. Today, however, it is insufferable. The children behave so loudly and disturbingly in the assembly that the whole performance is threatened with disruption. Miss Jones has good rapport with her group, but today it seems to be in a mood in which gentle interference does not last long. The only way to stop the trouble is to kick out the worst mischief-maker; then the others will wake up to the fact that she does mean business and will be all right for the rest of the performance.

In spite of the fact that Miss Jones knows that the loudest disturber need not be the real cause, that throwing the youngster out will neither change him nor really produce a better morale in 7B, out goes Bob, who happens to be the first disturber after her last reprimand. The manipulation of surface behavior is her real task at this moment. Her technique is right and effective for her purpose.

Of course, we hope she realizes the limitations of such techniques and will plan for other ways to meet the real problem later.

Second, sometimes it is really more important to reach basic attitudes by what we do, even though surface behavior does not change right away. To use a technique that does reach surface behavior in such a case but at the same time counteracts our deeper plans for influencing basic attitudes would constitute a serious mistake.

Example 1. School system A establishes a "special class" for all those children who have become delinquent, especially those who hate school and who feel that no one cares what happens to them anyway.

It is obvious that the only reasonable purpose that such a special class can have is to change basic antischool attitudes. The "discipline" in such a class must be guided by this main goal all down the line, which means that the first task of the teacher is to show those school-suspicious children that she is "different" to stir up the wish in them to become identified with her and to accept her as "okay." Miss Evans is well on the way to succeeding in this respect. After weeks of careful study of those children and the way they are, she has figured out pretty well what behavior she must avoid so as not to be pigeonholed along with previous teachers who have marched past these children's souls without effect.

Last Monday two boys were caught smoking in the toilet. The teacher reprimanded them for their act in just the way she was expected to as warden of school rules. But she avoided carefully the display of any moral indignation in talking about the incident, nor did she make an undue fuss about it. Later discussions with the children prove how excellently she has succeeded in gaining their confidence through her handling of this little incident. Her technique was thus highly successful.

The rest of the staff however, does not look at it this way. Miss Evans is openly called down for undermining the "discipline" of the school; she is commanded to search each youngster for cigarettes before he enters the classroom and to set up rewards for those who squeal. For the reasoning goes that the repetition of smoking must be absolutely avoided.

As far as fitness for surface behavior goes, the rest of the staff is right. Miss Evans's technique does not promise the safest insurance against the danger that another cigarette might be smoked in that school. A system of surveillance and especially a system of Gestapo and in-group "quislingism" might reduce the number of cigarettes smoked more considerably than would Miss Evans's technique.

As far as the real purpose of the school goes, however, the staff is wrong. Ensuring cigarette avoidance demands techniques that directly counteract the basic educational goal the school system had in mind in establishing this special class to begin with, that is, the change of basic attitudes of the children toward the school. By searching the members of the class, by offering praise for squealing, and by making a moralistic fuss about an undesirable but neighborhood-accepted piece of behavior, Miss Evans would lose all chance of making any dent in the basic reactions of those children toward their teacher and what she stands for.

Example 2. Just to be sure we are not misunderstood to imply that such considerations count only when "abnormal" behavior is involved, let us think of an ordinary school for normal children where it has been decided to enter an experiment in self-government. Doubtless, such an experiment cannot be expected to add to the comfort of the adults in the building, but it has only one goal: to develop basic attitudes in the youngsters that will lead to a growing understanding of the democratic process, the responsibilities involved in it, and the learning that is necessary to make it work.

What we have in mind, then, is the gradual learning of living together under a pattern of self-government. We must realize at once that any technique that would promise 100 per cent "success"—meaning a frictionless life at the expense of this margin for learning from mistakes and developing self-reliance—would be obviously wrong. Entering upon such a project, we therefore understand to begin with that the first phenomenon will not be improvement but increased confusion as far as everyday routine goes; that this confusion must not be handled by autocratic interference but must be exploited for a process of learning from mistakes; and that techniques that promise smooth functioning are not "successful" in terms of the basic job undertaken in this case.

The success of the enterprise must be measured in terms of the learning that is derived from the experience, not by the extent to which trouble is avoided while we go through it. Not surface behavior, but long-range attitude change, is the goal in the light of which evaluation has to take place.

Third, most of the time we are really after both purposes: the manipulation of surface behavior and also the influencing of basic attitudes. The difficulty is that some techniques are better fitted to produce behavioral changes, others to bring about changes in basic attitudes over a longer stretch of time.

When confronted with this problem, we should again follow the law of marginal antisepsis, which in this application assumes the following form: Any technique used to bring about surface behavioral changes must be at least harmless as far as long-range attitude changes are concerned, and any technique used to invite basic attitude changes must at least be harmless in terms of the surface-behavior challenge we have to meet through reality pressures.

Example 1. Mr. Morris goes out and gets himself some disciplinary advice. Tomorrow morning he will start a new regime. He sets up a rigid system of well-defined rules and regulations, merits and demerits, rewards and punishments. The system is elaborate. It challenges some students by its lures and frightens others by its threats; the results are unbelievable. Shortly after it has been installed, everybody has learned his task; everybody gets books and papers and well-sharpened pencils. The actual work output has increased overnight.

We triumph too soon. We discover after a while that the basic attitude of those children toward subject or teacher not only has not changed but has deteriorated even further. They do not ask any more questions. They are not even confused any more about what Latin is good for—they have stopped caring. They do not fight their teacher's effort any more—they have come to despise him as pedantic, ridiculous, and "school masterish." They have no interest in the topic at all—they stall for time until the happy moment comes when they won't have to hear the word "Latin" any more. All that the new techniques have brought about is a skillful exploitation of the system so the youngsters will have less trouble as they go along. The real student motive is not to learn Latin but to know just how to avoid too much friction with something whose meaninglessness they have come to accept as inevitable.

In short, the advice Mr. Morris was given from his disciplinary wizards was foul. He substituted a lack of subject-related motivation through a candy-threat system for the manipulation of surface behavior, but he did not further—he even damaged—the real long-range objectives he was hoping to achieve, that of a group of children eager for the wisdom that he had to offer and for acceptance of him as a person.

Example 2. Miss Jones takes over 8B. This class has built up a bad reputation for itself. It harbors the worst hoodlums in the school. They and the less delinquent children in the room are going through a period of vehement body changes and are obviously out of bounds. Things have become so bad that the whole school is in trouble because of them. None of the daily routine, including attendance or any type of work output, is functioning any more.

Miss Jones has read a lot about "democratic procedures." So the first thing she does is establish a system of self-government. It has a few nice effects. The attitudes of some of these youngsters are better. They do not show so much obstinacy and spiteful rejection of school or teacher. But it is equally obvious that they cannot handle their affairs. Bullies develop who try to put their regime over on others but keep their own buddies exempt; rules are made and broken; beautiful examples of learning take place in the discussions they have about their affairs, but they still don't show any change in school attendance and work output, and they still get in everybody's hair.

The mistake is obvious. Miss Jones's idea was right as far as an experiment in self-government is the best way for youngsters to learn basic attitudes toward one another and their community. We also know, however, that such an experiment made with a group that is not ready for it will not affect daily behavior for quite a while. In a camp her technique might have worked. With the school demands remaining what they are, though, Miss Jones's technique requires a longer waiting time for some changes in surface behavior than she can possibly have anticipated. Therefore, the technique was right in terms of

basic attitudes but was harmful because it did not solve even the minimum of actual surface-behavior problems that *had* to be solved.

To be sure that we are not misunderstood, we'd better add that
there is no need in either of the two examples cited to swing to the
opposite extreme. In both examples we think workable systems of discipline that combine effectiveness in one area with antisepsis in the other
can easily be suggested.

In both examples, some of the work could have been planned by
teachers and students in such a way as to encourage increased participation and meaningfulness in order to prepare for basic attitude changes.
In each case some area of school life could have been left safely to
adult domination and interference without in the least jeopardizing
freedom and self-government in others.

In the example of the Latin class, for instance, the teacher could
have made changes in his teaching techniques that would have brought
Latin closer to the interest level and the momentary needs of that age
range and could have developed increased participation by each student
through adaptation in his technique of group discussion. At the same
time it would have been wise also to establish *some* well-thought-out
pressures and rewards to enforce certain work demands, without putting the whole weight of motivation upon these premiums and threats.

In the second example, on the other hand, Miss Jones could have
made a sharp demarcation line between two sets of problems: those
that the school would have to enforce, even though the children
weren't quite ready to see the light, and those that could be safely
opened up for free—*really* free—handling by the group itself. In this
way the youngsters would have had a chance to practice self-determina-
tion in an area in which they could afford to make some mistakes.

In summary we want to state again that we do not pretend that
there is anything like a ready-made recipe answering the question "Just
how much rope should be given for learning through mistakes, and
which things do we have to insist upon because we can't afford any
concession in surface functioning?" It is obvious that we usually tend
to err in either of the two directions. It seems to the author of this
paper, though, that a careful evaluation of this whole issue of surface
behavior versus basic attitude change would lead to many more satis-
factory solutions than we can hope for without such a comparative
study.

How Do We Know Whether or Not "It Works"?

When people start talking about problems of discipline, they have a habit of doing one of two things: They start a wild fight about "basic principles," pitching unsubstantiated belief against unsubstantiated belief, or they pretend to want to get together and become "practical" about it. With this statement they usually start on a binge of anecdotes. I have recently made a habit of analyzing such anecdotes about instances of good or bad discipline, about failure or success of punishments, about examples of how well physical punishment worked with John and how it wrecked his classmate.

There are two things all those anecdotes have in common. They all extol, with more or less attempt at disguise, the unique magical capacities of the personality of the speaker, and they are all on the level of primitive thinking as far as the criteria for evaluating why these tricks "worked" are concerned.

The following suggestions seem to me to offer themselves as guides for the practitioner on the job who wants to avoid being fooled by what other people pretend are their "experiences."

First, claims by even the most brilliant experts that their techniques "work" remain meaningless for you until you examine those incidents in the light of the individuals you have to deal with and the characteristics of your classroom as a group.

Example 1. Your classroom is a 9B in a highly conservative community with a lot of emphasis on Emily Post. The anecdotist encourages you to create as much "informality" as you possibly can so that "the youngsters feel at ease and let their hair down." Watch out for that one. It all depends on just what the speaker has in mind when he mentions "informality" and which clientele his own experiences are gathered from. Youngsters who are just moving into social strata a little higher than the ones their parents live in are often threatened by a return to the "informalities" of the groups they have left behind. (An example is the deep aversion among Negro youngsters of the middle classes—children of white-collar workers who hope to become college students some time—for their brothers under the skin who happen to display with naïve abandon the rough-and-tumble language and behavior of the slum neighborhoods from which their parents originally came.)

Example 2. Your principal has called you in to find some way in which the noise and disorder in the study hall, containing as many as 350 children, might be reduced. The speaker in a meeting that the principal has suggested you attend has just pointed out what a marvelous thing it is to abandon all rules, to let children learn from their mistakes, to develop a yearning for order out of chaos, gradually.

Unfortunately, he doesn't add that he is talking not about school but about a camp, not about keeping a study hall quiet but about keeping a camp-cabin floor clean, not about an assembly room of 350 students but about a club group of eight.

Example 3. Raymond behaved very badly in class today. He used a dirty swear word in front of you. You are uncertain how you should handle this behavior; so you ask the teacher with the greatest seniority to give you advice. This person knows the answer right away, and she speaks from long experience: "Let me tell you, my friend," she says, "you cannot afford to let this go unpunished. You must call the parents in. Then you must punish Raymond hard, or else all the other youngsters will start doing exactly the same thing."

While saying so, she remembers a scene with an overdeveloped bully of the knife-throwing variety in an assembly hall of sixty children, all on the verge of revolt, with the youngster's "gang" waiting to see just how the teacher would react. The situation for which the advice is given—*your* situation—is very different. Yet your "experienced" friend doesn't bother about such minor details as the fact that Raymond is a shy and weak youngster, intimidated at home, that he adores you and happened to have this fit of temper out of "hurt feelings"; that Raymond's parents are cruel bullies who have no sense of proportion and discipline, who would either laugh at you for worrying about bad language to begin with or would beat Raymond mercilessly, depending on how drunk they happened to be; that your classroom adores you, that they would "understand" if you wisely ignored the whole show, and that not a single one of them would ever dream of acting that way himself.

Example 4. The children in your lunchroom labor under too many restrictions on noise and activity. They must only whisper—not talk. They must not move around, may not play table games. Every rule limits expression, is devised to keep action down rather than up. At the same time, your principal is worried about too many "explosions" in class. The other teachers complain that the children are restless, hard to keep in their seats, and so forth.

You suggest that, if you could give them a chance for some reasonable social contact with one another during lunch period, they would not have to sneak in their chats with friends during class time, that, if you gave them a happy recreation period in between, pent-up energy would be released and they would be ready for quiet work in class.

One among your crowd jumps on you. "You are all wet," he argues, and he cites a case: "In the so-and-so school they tried it and it did not work. The kids just got rambunctious and went all over the place and could not be controlled any more."

This sounds like a "realistic" argument to begin with. But watch out for details. Upon closer analysis you will find out this about the fellow's "example": The X school children were of a different neighborhood altogether, bent on raising trouble, and of a hateful attitude toward their school to begin with—yours are not that way at all.

The X school experiment was not planned at all. It just happened that on the one day that the controlling teacher was not there things went wild—a situation very different from the one you meant.

The X schoolteacher, who complained that his kids went wild because of the freer lunch situation, didn't know how to control kids to begin with. They were always wild anyway, but this time he had a good chance to blame it on the lunchroom outfit.

In short, what we want to point out is that advice is often given from some situation that the speaker has in mind when he gives it. The suggestion that "it works" is meaningless, unless you know that the situation for which it is given is basically analogous in the most essential items with the one from which it is derived. Just such mistakes as this one are responsible for the millions of cases in which the "best of advice" does the "worst of harm."

Second, claims that certain techniques "work" remain meaningless until you have established just what the speaker is talking about: the effect of his technique on an individual child or on the group as a whole.

Example 1. You are worried about what you should do because Johnny seems to have become so spiteful and fresh recently and so obstinate in his behavior in class. Mr. Jenkins knows all the answers. He has it all worked out. He gives you a beautiful story of how he happened to be attacked by a kid once, how he simply took him by the scruff of his neck and threw him out of the room, and "you should have seen that classroom after that. None of these kids misbehaved ever again." He strongly recommends scruff-of-the-neck seizure as the remedy for obstinate youngsters.

He does not even notice that he is talking about the effect of a technique on a group, whereas you want to know how to help Johnny change.

Example 2. Dr. Adjust Themwell, psychiatrist at your school guidance clinic, has it all doped out just how children who are aggressive in class should be treated by the teacher. He still remembers the case of George. George was so aggressive he nearly murdered a kid once. Then he found a teacher who "accepted George," and from then on everything was hunky-dory.

You try it with Ned—only it doesn't work. First of all, Ned only gets more aggressive the more he feels backed up by your "understanding"—he happens to be a different type from George. Besides, the psychiatrist also forgot to check on another little matter. Even in George's case, which was supposedly such a success, something else happened that he himself didn't happen to be interested in but that you wouldn't want to miss for the world. The children in George's classroom happened to hate George. When the teacher began to be so upset about the way they fought him and began to defend him, they left George alone, but they picked on another youngster for a scapegoat. The technique suggested to handle the teacher's problem with Ned had implications far beyond its effect upon the individual in question. You want to help Ned without producing other scapegoats in class.

Third, claims that certain techniques "work" remain meaningless, until the speaker makes quite clear what he is talking about, whether he means by "work" a change in surface behavior or a change in basic attitudes.

Example 1. Miss Smith found a good trick for making her class "more peaceful." She simply told the children she would punish anybody hard who was caught in a fight with another child. She claims it worked beautifully and, with great gusto, recommends the technique to all less experienced colleagues.

The truth is that the children gave up open fights in class for realistic reasons. But they fought like cats and dogs outside school.

They simply kept a temporary truce for mutual protection while they were in danger. They were not "more peaceful" at all. So don't fall for this type of fraud.

Example 2. Miss Jones just got a letter from Chuck. This letter is a singular document, illustrating what a teacher can mean in the life of a child. Chuck is a soldier now, fighting in the front lines, and a hero. The principal says Miss Jones can be proud of this letter.

Miss Jones can barely suppress a smile, for the principal wasn't around when Chuck happened to be the little boy she saved from delinquency. Things were different then. What Miss Jones did for Chuck was not appreciated. It brought her the ill fame of being a sissy and a bad disciplinarian. The one outstanding thing in Chuck's life happened to be that Miss Jones was "different" from the teachers he had met before. He caught on to that once when he had been very mean to her in order to show off before the class and when she failed to punish him but called him in for a talk instead. This talk is what he remembers now in the foxholes. At the time, however, Miss Jones was nearly fired by the board because her "techniques didn't work."

Fourth, do not allow anybody to say whether his techniques "work" or not unless he is also ready to consider subsurface effects.

Example 1. In an institutional group, the counselor finds a beautiful way of "doing away with all swearing and bad language." He simply makes the children establish a rule that anybody who uses bad language is going to get a swat on his rear end. Bennie is appointed group executioner, and "he does a swell job." The technique "works" 100 per cent. A later study of the group reveals that

Bennie receives bribes from half the group, so that only a few incidents are reported.

Bennie beats up the rest mercilessly, so they have to do their swearing after they have locked themselves in the toilet.

everybody begins to hate everybody else after a while, and they pick on one another mercilessly.

it all ends in a revolt against Bennie, and the group simply doesn't want to hear of democratic self-government afterward, distrusting its first experience because of its mismanagement.

children in this group are found to be worse swearers than youngsters in other groups.

Still, while the subterraneous effects of these techniques were still un-x-rayed, their inventor could easily bask in the glory of having a "swell technique," the spread of which would solve "many problems of my colleagues."

Example 2. "I do not believe in physical punishment myself, but George is a boy who really needs it. And it works swell with him." An examination of this claim reveals that

George had been cruelly whipped by his father ever since he was a little child.

George was put into this teacher's group all of a sudden from a very suppressive schoolroom. He did not understand that these children—who also seemed to be from a more "refined neighborhood"—could submit to teachers without putting up a fight. So he began to brag how "he would show the teacher" and "he could take it." When he was not beaten to make his bravado true, he began to ask for it more and more.

when he got his beating he was satisfied for the moment—things were as he knew they were: Adults hated kids, and if he knew how to get them mad it was worthwhile to take a licking from time to time.

George had put this teacher on the already large list of people who were just "adults to be fought." The teacher had lost all educational power over him for good.

another teacher later met George and withstood his temptations to become provoked; after much trouble the youngster all of a sudden realized that here was somebody who was different, who did care who he was, not only what he did, and he then began to change.

Do you still agree that the first teacher's disciplinary trick "worked swell"?

Prevention of Discipline Problems

THREE TYPES OF "DISCIPLINE CASE"

The term "discipline case" is a beautiful example of a misnomer, for we obviously do not talk about a "discipline case" when we mean an example of especially well-functioning discipline but rather when the very thing called "discipline" ("order") long ago went out the window. Even so, the so-called discipline cases still fall, in their causal factors, into three categories.

TYPE I. CASE-HISTORY PRODUCED

By this willful term.we mean examples in which it is obviously the peculiar disturbance of one individual child that causes all the problems.

Example. The principal asks me to go into 5B to watch the teacher at work. He had thought she was a good teacher, but he had been forced to change his mind. He had sent Chuck, whom he knew was a difficult child, into her room because he had thought she might be good enough to handle him. But now he is disappointed and at the end of his rope.

Half an hour in 5B leaves no doubt about the nature of the situation. It is not true that the teacher has handled Chuck wrong. It is true, however, that her room has been deteriorating more from day to day, and the teacher is at the end of her rope too. The gist of the situation: Chuck is a seriously sick boy, to the point at which he should be institutionalized; there is no chance for repair short of extensive psychiatric treatment. For Chuck has lost all relation to anything that happens outside him. His sudden "singing" or swearing has nothing to do with anybody around him but pops up from inside fantasies, without any tie to outside stimuli.

The teacher is a swell teacher and would know how to handle a youngster who swore or sang from mischief or spite. But in this case anything she can do is bound to be wrong. If she puts on the pressure that would keep Chuck even temporarily in check, she has to put on so much of it that all the other children become afraid of her and mad at Chuck—the source of her punitiveness—and endless fights and squabbles are the result. If she ignores Chuck's behavior or approaches it by the technique of repetitive interpretation, the absolute failure of this approach and the tremendous patience squandered on Chuck are so obvious to the other children that they come to hate Chuck out of jealousy and belief that the teacher is silly to tolerate such acts.

In short, Chuck is prepsychotic, so far beyond the reach of the reality around him that he cannot be approached by any technique within the life of the group. He is the sole cause, not only of the discipline problems he produces himself, but also of the bickering, dissatisfaction, hysterical oversensitivity, and disorganization of the group. All the discipline problems with 5B were obviously produced by the peculiar case history of Chuck.

TYPE 2. GROUP-CONDITIONED

By this term we mean discipline problems that are not really caused by one or another disturbed child but by unfavorable elements in the group in which they occur.

Example 1. Roy was the most outstanding "discipline case" of the year, a case of "sex behavior." The teachers felt they had to "set up an example." They "eliminated" Roy from their school system, and obviously they "had done everything they could to keep their classrooms clean." The trouble was that, in a few weeks, another boy showed the same "sex behavior" in the same classrooms; the problem had stayed with them. Only the personnel had changed.

Invited to investigate the background factors in this situation, I was able to uncover this state of affairs:

Roy never had been a real "sex case" to begin with. On the contrary, among the youngsters in the classroom Roy was about the most normal, happily growing, and well-adjusted kid. It was true, though, that he was older than the others, was much more developed physically, and had gone through his first manifestations of sex curiosity a few years before.

The problem lay with the rest of the kids, or at least the majority of them. They all came from families with unreasonably strong taboos on the expression of any, even normal, sex curiosity in their children, and at the same time these youngsters were just about entering the stage of development in which an increase in sex investigation belongs to the normal, rather than to the abnormal, developmental characteristics.

Result: They were full of suppressed and overheated curiosity, searching frantically for someone to nourish it along. Roy, on his part, felt a little inferior to these children, for he did come from the "wrong side of the tracks," and his academic background wasn't anything to brag about either. He welcomed a chance to be "in with them" and to do some instructing as a recompense for all the help with his homework he received from his more successful pals. When some of them were not satisfied with the harmless stuff he told them, he drew them some pictures—the only thing he was pretty good at—and the pictures' success led him on to more and more daring productions.

Roy's problem behavior was not the result of anything wrong with his case history. It is true that the overt "discipline problem" was focused around the person of Roy, but the *actual* "discipline problem" emanated from the problem of the *group* with which he lived. Not Roy's elimination but a thorough and healthy approach to the group's sex curiosity by parents and school would have been the answer. As the latter was not sought, the group situation produced another problem of the same variety soon after.

Example 2. Miss Jones complained that "there is so much fighting" among her children that one teacher or another would invariably send in some complaint from the playground, the lunchroom, the gym, even the street—and it was always the children in Miss Jones's group who would be causing all the trouble. She added that her children were pretty good as long as she was in the classroom but that they were all "discipline problems" the moment she stepped out.

Miss Jones was smart—she did not try to pin blame on a boy with a bad reputation. She noticed to begin with that the trouble was more than that, that it had to do with group morale.

An investigation of the situation revealed that the children were lured into good performance in their work by attractive premiums for good behavior and by heavy punishments for even a whisper or a restless movement. After the hour was over, those whom she thought had sat still were highly extolled as pillars of virtue and offered to the others as worthy of imitation, whereas those who had not made the grade were exhibited as criminals, deserving of moral indignation and contempt by every righteous citizen in class. In fact, on several occasions, Miss Jones had dropped unmistakable hints that she would understand—though not approve—if the virtuous ones would put an end to the misuse of friendliness and freedom by the black sheep of the group.

The result was that all the suppressed body restlessness of Miss Jones's hours with the class had to come out some place. Besides, all the intermember furies and hatreds that piled up during those moralistic speeches by the teacher had to be translated into action at some time or other. In short, the undisciplined behavior of the various children sent in by other teachers in the school was not an outcropping of their delinquent case histories but was produced by the mistaken group climate and would not stop until that basic atmosphere was changed.

In summary, we might say that a large percentage of "discipline problems" in school classes are really of Type 2. I found those cases much more frequent than those of Type 1. They, of course, would not disappear even if we had "a psychiatrist for every child." For the trouble is not with the individual case histories of the children but with the psychological structure of the class as a group.

TYPE 3. A MIXTURE WITH DIFFERENT EMPHASES

This type seems to me to constitute about 70 per cent of all discipline cases in school life. The behavior situation that creates this type of problem centers around some individual child. This child, however, is not by himself a disturbed child of the extreme type; his behavior is produced by something in the group atmosphere in which he lives. Our problem is to define the emphases that must be put on individual as well as on group-psychological factors of causation, and the remedy must consider both angles to the same degree to which this emphasis is stressed.

Example. Don behaved so outrageously today that neither the teacher nor the other children in class can quite understand what happened. The teacher was investigating the alleged theft of a youngster's purse from one of the lockers. It so happened that Don was seen near the locker, and, in attempting to shed some light on the problem, the teacher first tried to identify those who were near. When she asked Don in the same quiet voice she used for the others whether or not he had been around, he jumped up wildly, protested at the top of his voice that nobody was going to call him a "thief" and get away with it, and left no doubt in anybody's mind that he questioned the legitimacy of the teacher's ancestral derivations. With this he ran out, tears bursting from his eyes, and slammed the door behind him.

As this behavior was quite unexpected by everybody in the room, it was easy for the teacher to keep her composure and to try and get at the source of Don's trouble right away. She turned her investigation of the theft into a discussion of Don's behavior with the class, had a talk with the culprit after school, and unearthed the following data about the case:

Don had had an unfortunate experience exactly a year ago. Some youngsters in the school that he had attended had tried to pin a case of stealing on him. His very strict, irascible, and opinionated father exposed Don to a severe beating without even investigating the truth of the accusation and did not even find it worthwhile to say something along the line of apology for his mistake when he later found that Don was innocent.

Don had not only a very strict and autocratic father at home but also the bad luck of running into opinionated autocrats in his school career too. Don's present teacher seemed like a miracle to him. He had met her with distrust but was now just at the point at which he was ready to admit that at last he had found a human being who was willing to stretch out her hand to him, no matter what people said. Then, all of a sudden, in hysterical overreaction to her question, he thought that maybe she was just like all the rest.

The group, too, had been nicer to him than had previous groups of children. He was eager to be accepted by the others and wanted to be "one of the family" as he had never wanted it before. The idea of being "suspected by the teacher in front of all the others" made him see red.

Needless to say, this teacher had an opportunity to solve the case without any fuss at all because her analysis had unearthed the most vital factors involved. Here is what she did: She explained to the group, in Don's absence, that she had talked with him and had found out what upset him so much, that she could not divulge the content of her conversation, of course, but that she knew the other kids would accept it if she told them she knew it was best to make no further issue of Don's behavior and that she would thrash it out between herself and him. She also had a talk with Don, showing him that she understood and preparing him to return to the class.

The analysis of the case shows that part of it was connected with Don's personal case history and could be understood only on that basis. However, it also shows that the other part was related to the group role that the teacher played in helping Don adjust himself to the other children and find his place in the group. The handling of the discipline case, therefore, demands an approach in the direction of both case-conditioned and group-conditioned elements.

According to our experience, we dare to make the following generalizations:

Only about 10 per cent of all cases of school discipline are simple cases of "individual disturbances" clear and proper. About 20 per cent of the cases at least are cases in which problem behavior is produced entirely by group-psychological inadequacies of school life. About 70 per cent of the cases seem to us to involve both personal case history of the individual and some deficiency in the psychological structure of the group. This means that at least 90 per cent of all discipline cases are in dire need of group-psychological analysis and consideration.

Prevention of discipline problems, then, must involve a quite extensive job of "group-psychological engineering."

GROUP-PSYCHOLOGICAL FACTORS IN DISCIPLINE PROBLEMS

At this point a thorough analysis of a wide variety of discipline cases should be presented. The group-psychological factors involved in them should be carefully isolated, and multiple choices for solutions should be suggested. However, such an approach—the only one that would be of real practical use for the teacher on the job—cannot be made in the limited space of this study. Nevertheless, we shall at least try to enumerate the most frequent types of group-psychological factor contributing to discipline problems. We have to leave all interpretations and applications to the reader's own imagination but hope that we may be able to follow this presentation with more concretely helpful illustrative materials at some later date.

Remember our thesis is that many discipline problems are not the results of things wrong with the individuals involved but are the outcroppings of factors in the structures of the groups in which the individuals live. When something is wrong with the group, even the most normal individual member is likely to produce confused action leading to problem behavior. What we are investigating now is just *what* it is that most frequently goes wrong with school groups and, therefore, constitutes the highest disciplinary risk. We think we can classify the results of our analysis under six main headings.

DISSATISFACTIONS IN THE WORK PROCESS

The fact that bad teaching or curriculum planning automatically increases the number of discipline problems we produce has long been known in a general way. In fact, for a while we placed so much emphasis on this factor that we regarded it as the only source of discipline problems. There are still some who adhere to this theory, by the way, loudly protesting that a teacher who knows how to teach won't have any discipline problems in his classroom. This is a wild exaggeration of an otherwise very worthwhile point. Exaggeration in the opposite direction can also be heard from time to time: that discipline is based only on "personality factors" and "mental disorders in the pupils" and that it has practically no relationship to the curriculum as such.

Rejecting both extremes and trying to salvage the morsel of truth contained in both, we should like to suggest that any disturbance in the satisfactions children get out of the work they do with their teachers is likely to reflect itself in the production of problem behavior. Here are some examples.

Subject Matter Much Too Easy. Too much of the work ability of the students remains unchallenged and has to search for other outlets.

Subject Matter Much Too Difficult. Frustration accompanies great stretches of the work. Research has proved beyond doubt that exposure to the frustration of not being able to do things well produces tremendous aggression or restlessness in normal children. The results are unavoidable diversions, taking pokes at one another, dropping and throwing things, irritability, and "I-don't-care" attitudes, which lower behavioral inhibitions all over the place.

Language of Teachers Too Remote. Language can be remote from the children's development level or from the native tongue ordinarily used on their social plane. If that is the case, the child feels out of place, not really wanted, or even looked down upon and begins to show signs of social-outcast reactions and protest.

Load of Assignments Too Heavy. In this case, the school hour is loaded with the emotional strain of guilt feelings, criticisms, and a general impression of not being up to what is expected, or an attempt is made to catch up on lost play time by having a good time during class.

Load of Assignments Too Light. Then the feeling of progress in learning is lacking, which again reflects itself in a growing unwillingness to do any work because the time spent on it does not seem profitable in the end.

Assignments Badly Planned, Poorly Explained, Unfairly Judged. The result is that typical "resentment behavior" pops out in little irritations all over the place.

Type of Work and Presentation Too Advanced. They do not click with the developmental needs of the children. For instance, lectures on nature in general should be given at an age when a strong curiosity about animals' bodies can easily be utilized for motivation.

Type of Work and Presentation Too Infantile. They are too infantile compared to the developmental level at which the children happen to be emotionally. For instance, talks about sex and the flowers are too childlike when youngsters are full of pride about their newly acquired preadolescent daring in sex exploration on a very different level indeed.

Activities Too Much on a Merely Verbal Level. Such activities leave the normal motor needs of growing children unchallenged for long stretches of time. We frequently find restlessness, noise, shuffling of feet, falling of chairs, and pushing when too much discussion or lecturing substitutes for real participation and manipulative activities.

Work Badly Scheduled. Scheduling can be bad in terms of sequences of different types or can be ill-timed in terms of exhaustion and fatigue. For instance, the English poetry class is at the end of a long day after a baseball game, at which moment it seems to be especially hard to excite manipulation-greedy sixth-graders about Shelley or Keats.

The examples could be multiplied by the hundreds. Suffice it to say in summary that any serious mistake in the planning or presentation of the curriculum in terms of the real growth needs of the children we teach produces an increase in discipline problems, even with the most normal and well-mannered groups of children. Boredom and fatigue are known to be the worst enemies of school morale. Only the moron doesn't care whether we bore him or not—he doesn't notice or care what happens around him anyway. The normal youngster instinctively searches for substitute satisfactions if taught the wrong way. This natural defense of the normal individual presents itself as a "discipline problem" at times.

EMOTIONAL UNREST IN INTERPERSONAL RELATIONS

The schools were originally designed as places in which to learn. Unfortunately, we do not invite only the various I.Q.'s of the children to come in. The youngsters bring, to our great discomfort, other parts of their personalities beside their intelligences. They bring perceptions, moral attitudes, and whatever else has to be taught. They bring their bodies—every part of them, no matter how disturbing or unnecessary for what we want to teach. And they bring the whole inventory of the emotions they use at home and on the playground, in addition to those that are relevant to the acquisition of wisdom and knowledge. No wonder they also "live" in our classrooms, whether we like it or not. This means that they form attachments and hatreds, cliques and subgroups; they hope, love, hate, and fear. They experiment with one another as potential friends, sweethearts, rivals, cooperators, bosses, even slaves.

They try to experience the whole scale of person-to-person relationships with which they have become acquainted in their private lives. In short, life goes on in spite of any curriculum plans we may have.

Conflicts arising from personal relations are reflected in the shape of "discipline problems." Such discipline problems are often not even directed at us at all, but they are there just the same.

Individual Friendships and Tensions. Strong, sudden friendships among youngsters sometimes produce stubbornness against the intrusion of the teacher through criticism or blame. Vehement antipathies, hatreds, and animosities among youngsters may encourage individual feelings to supersede reasonable adjustments to teacher demands or work interests. Sometimes even work and achievement become only a phase in this tension among individual children, instead of a serene process of intellectual growth achieved in emotional isolation.

Cliques and Subgroup Formations. These phenomena are often the backbone of group life, the greatest pillars of learner morale. Sometimes, though, they may confuse the school picture no end. You may get subgroups against one another, so that anything you say becomes unacceptable to group 1 simply because it is so enthusiastically received by group 2. Or you may find that various subgroups begin to impress one another by the degrees to which they submit to or rebel against your leadership.

Many fights and many instances of undesirable behavior are sidelines of such subgroup tensions, rather than direct attacks upon the order you represent. The basis on which such subgroup formation takes place may be developmental age, sex, degree of sophistication, social discrimination, racial or national difference, degree of academic interest, proximity to the teacher as a person, acceptance of the school code, and many others.

Disorganization in Group Roles. Every teacher knows what "group roles" are, even though he may not be familiar with the term. A few examples may suffice to show the phenomenon we refer to: Most any classroom has such typical functions filled by pupils as leader, second in command, organizer (with or against the teacher), janitorial assistant, teacher's pet, model boy, black sheep, scapegoat, bully, isolate, rejectee, group executioner, attorney-at-law, defender of the innocent, group clown (with or against the adult), hero in battle, fifth columnist (in terms of group interests), seducer and ringleader, trouble starter, rabble-rouser, appeaser, humorous rescuer of tense situations.

Whenever any one of these roles is badly filled or not needed in a group in which a lot of individuals strive to establish such roles for themselves or whenever many youngsters fight for the same group role in competition, you are likely to have a rise in your discipline problems, no matter how nice these youngsters or how smart you yourself may otherwise be.

Pupil-Teacher Frictions. The fact that strong frictions or emotional disturbances in the feelings of youngsters toward us are the source of many discipline problems has long been recognized in theory. Often, however, we are not quite aware of the degree to which pupil-teacher emotion enters the production line of discipline problems. For often these emotional elements are of low visibility, and sometimes even the youngsters themselves are unaware of their existence or deny them loudly to others and themselves. The most serious producer of discipline problems is the tendency in so many youngsters to project upon the teacher what are really basic attitudes developed in relation to the family at home. Strong feelings in youngsters of "not being liked or understood" or of "being discriminated against," for example, frequently may develop without any real mistake being committed in school.

Any tension, conscious or unconscious, among the youngsters is likely to color your classroom discipline. Especially in cases of general irritability and touchiness or widespread "uppitiness" and resistance on the part of whole classrooms, the suspicion that some of it goes back to disturbed interpersonal relationships is frequently justified.

DISTURBANCES IN GROUP CLIMATE

Without a chance really to define "group climate" adequately at this stage of the game, we still think we can put across what this peculiar term means by describing several instances. For teachers experience group climate all through their work, even though group-psychological discussions have been kept out of their teacher-training curricula. On the whole, we mean by this term the basic feeling tone that underlies the life of a group, the sum total of everybody's emotions toward one another, toward work and organization, toward the group as a unit, and toward things outside.

The Punitive Climate. The punitive climate is one of the most frequent distortions of climate in classrooms. A punitive climate is *not* identical with "a case of punishment." On the contrary, wise punishment usually does not at all imply the basic attitude of "punitiveness" of the teacher toward the child, whereas in a thoroughly punitive climate the pressure on children is often so high all the time that the teacher need make only sparse use of actual punishment as such.

However, the punitive climate is perhaps the most destructive of group morale and discipline of any classroom climate. It invariably produces these characterological side effects: The teacher shows little respect for the persons of the children in her room, being so sure he can manage their behavior by threat and fear anyway that he doesn't bother about them as human beings; the pupils usually expect absolute acceptance or rejection on the basis of the teacher's behavior code, and they usually fall into two groups—some rebel, hate, and fight back (the open "problem cases" in a punitive group), and others identify themselves with the teacher out of fear and, therefore, have to become moral hypocrites in their attitudes toward the other children. They are suspiciously submissive as long as the teacher is present, squeal on neighbors when they get a chance, and, in general, develop "holier than thou" attitudes toward their pals. The emotions of fear of reprisal and shame are in the air most of the time; the teacher, as well as the on-lookers, receives sadistic enjoyment of the chronic type.

It is this kind of climate that breeds sadists, bullies, and hypocrites. In this type of group it is a sign of character and courage to become a behavior problem. The morally healthy individual is the most frequent victim of the punitive climate.

The Emotional-Blackmail Climate. This climate is another distortion of healthy group living. It is a variation of the punitive climate but sails under a different disguise. In the emotional-blackmail climate the teacher "loves" all children and says so at the rate of three times a minute. He rubs it in about how nice and unaggressive he is—how he will never punish anybody for doing wrong—while he drips with enjoyment of the self-induced guilt feelings of his crew. In the emotional-blackmail climate, you don't get punished if you do wrong, but you know you have to feel like a heel for three weeks afterward. The teacher in this climate produces a tremendous emotional dependence on him, exploiting it as the only source of influence.

The results of this type of climate are surprising absence of physical or other obvious violence between teacher and children, often confused with understanding and progressiveness in technique; an extreme fear in the children of the disapproval of their teacher, resulting in extended orgies of self-accusation by the children and hurt feelings by the adult leader after each disciplinary breach; strong rivalries among some of the children who are the "good" ones against those of the children who are not so emotionally close to the teacher as they.

The discipline problems of this group are especially strong when its members move from younger childhood into early adolescence, when so much adult dependence is unnatural for them. The main casualties of this climate are those who want to grow up and become independent and would rather take the rap for mischievous acts than turn into self-deprecatory introverts at the teacher's command.

The Hostile-Competition Climate. The hostile-competition climate is a distortion of an otherwise healthy phenomenon in our society. Normally, a good deal of competitiveness is unavoidable, even liked, by children growing into a society in which there can be little doubt of the presence of competitiveness. However, there are two things that can go wrong with a normal competitive climate: One is that there may be more competitiveness than children need or can stand without developing negative character traits or defeatism; the other is that competitiveness may deteriorate into hatefulness.

The hostile-competition climate can be characterized as one in which everybody is whipped into aggressively competing with everybody else all the time. Reward is given to the child who proudly tramples under his feet whoever dares to compete with him. Shame falls upon the head of the child who would rather get a lower grade than feel "holier than thou" toward his best pal. This climate turns a classroom into a dog race. It is highly doubtful that mutual love and friendship are instigated in the participants while the race is going on.

The results are extreme uncooperativeness among group members (all organization has to be enforced by outside rules and pressures); the development of outcasts from those who happen to be last in the line of aggressive competition; and the development of snobs from those who happen to hold the front line easily and get more than ten times the amount of praise that their efforts deserve. The result is dependence of such groups on autocratic management, no real wish for democratic cooperation and self-management, enjoyment of punishment for discipline breaches as outlets for all the hostility and moral snobbishness fostered under cover.

The Group-Pride Climate. The group-pride climate has a very healthy counterpart. What we mean here is the distorted case in which the group leader tries to develop a strong emotional relationship of every group member with the total group and then overfosters feelings of vanity and conceit related to the group as such. Good "teams" sometimes allow their team spirit to disintegrate into the climate we refer to.

The group-pride climate usually involves a high degree of group consciousness among a classroom as a whole, with a variety of positive attributes connected with such development. At the same time it produces a whole host of potential group executioners who simply wait for moments when they can swoop down upon the unlucky devils who have stained group honor or rewards. On the other hand, it develops a certain set of chronic rejectees and releases wild mob-lynching psychology against them under cover of righteous group indignation. Violent fights and the chronic problem behavior of the constantly persecuted and despised rejectee are the main types of discipline problem engendered by a climate of this kind.

We could—and should—continue this analysis of typical classroom climates for quite a while. Suffice it to say here that the total climate that governs the social relationships among teacher, children, and total group has a tremendous influence upon the type of discipline problem that will be automatically avoided or automatically produced. We also admit, though, that this factor along the production line of discipline problems is still the most difficult to analyze without further group-psychological instrumentation.

MISTAKES IN ORGANIZATION AND GROUP LEADERSHIP

Many teachers do perfect jobs of teaching, as far as the presentation of subject matter and the organization of learning experiences go, and they also have fine teacher personalities and very fair approaches to "the child." Where they get into trouble is in the mechanics of group leadership. For the successful handling of groups of certain types is as complex a task as the organization of subject matter and is a chapter entirely of its own.

As teachers receive practically no organized training in group leadership, children are exposed to a hit-and-miss technique that causes many problems that could easily be eliminated. Again we shall have to select only a small fraction of the illustrations that offer themselves.

Too Much Autocratic Pressure. Too much autocratic pressure can be a problem, especially at age ranges in which gradual emancipation from adult leadership is a natural and important trend. Program and organization may be so adult-centered that there is little feeling of real and meaningful participation by the members of the group.

Too Little Security. Too little security given the group by the adult leader leaves the children constantly exposed to the strains of responsibility and moral guilt. Tossing all responsibilities over to the group with little reference to its members' developmental needs and emotional maturity is often mistaken for "self-government" and "education for democracy," which it certainly is not.

Too High or Too Low Standards for Group Behavior. Too high standards expose children to moral defeatism, with the result that irresponsible mischievousness becomes a way out. Too low standards give them no chance to satisfy normal amounts of "group pride." As a result they get disgusted and disgruntled and develop feelings that their group life is childish and not worthwhile; they produce reactions similar to those of boredom and fatigue.

Too Much Organization. When there is too much organization, life is regimented by a thousand silly little rules that you bump into wherever you turn, resulting in trouble-avoidance, taking the place of really serious group-mindedness.

Too Little Organization. With too little organization, all issues have to be decided on a moment-to-moment basis, and the children never quite know what to expect.

Out-of-Focus Group Organization. Organization can often be out of step with age, developmental maturity, special type, background and specific needs of the group. This is often especially true when schools change their clienteles, as, for example, when new boundaries are set up for the areas served by the schools and foreign relief clienteles replace hyperambitious, overprotected groups from "refined" neighborhoods, while teachers and school organization maintain the same basic disciplinary pattern. Constant revision of the organizational pattern to fit total school structure and needs is essential.

Lack of Tact. Lack of tact is especially frequent among highly ambitious and subject-matter-minded teachers who have little imagination about how children feel. It is especially frequent also in the transition from one developmental phase to another, when teachers often try to treat youngsters as though they were much younger than they feel.

Indulgence in Personal Sensitivities and Allergies. There is also danger of superimposing one's own personal behavior code on the children, regardless of whether or not it fits. It can take the form, for example, of tremendous sensitivity to language with preadolescents of a low-protection area or extreme touchiness in terms of personal vanity with children who have little school-mindedness or security with adults at home.

Overreaction to Dignity Violations. Many serious discipline problems have little to do with discipline at all. They are the hysterical overreactions of oversensitive adults to irritating child behavior, especially when differences of social background and manners are involved.

Plan for Revenge Instead of Educational Change. To "show them" or to "give them what they have coming" is often made the prime motivation for the way discipline problems are handled, whereas the chances for real changes of attitudes among the children involved should be the only thing that counts.

Inconsistency in Promise and Threat. If extreme in nature, inconsistency undermines group security and gives children feelings of unpredictability against which they rebel; or they become defeatist in their attitudes toward group issues.

Stupidity in Carrying Out Promises or Threats. The idea that consistency in itself is a virtue and that it is better to be consistent and do the wrong thing than ever to change one's decision is a serious mistake, too. Children watch the thoughtfulness with which you plan your action. Thoughtfully documented change of decision is more conducive to respect than is silly, stupid, or inconsiderate sticking to the wrong gun.

Wrong Use of Techniques. Wrong use of punishment and rewards, reasoning, interference, and "learn by mistake" techniques is included here. Obviously wrong applications of any set of educational techniques undermine group morale and develop a "try and don't get caught" psychology. What constitutes "wrong use" is, unfortunately, a chapter too involved to be opened up here.

Wrong Arguments about Educational Techniques. More children disobey because of the silly arguments on the basis of which obedience is sold to them than because of opposition to obedience itself. The same is true all through the line of educational techniques. Especially in talking to groups, teachers are likely to support the right things they do by the wrong arguments and thus to produce resistance where there wasn't any to begin with. This is especially true during early adolescence, when the group code changes so that the same argument that would have appealed to them a few years ago is just that much provocation now.

Mistakes in Emotional Distance and Proximity. Mistakes in emotional distance and proximity are so well known as a factor in undermining group morale that we can skip them after brief mention. We add only that such emotional preferences and rejections may be noticed by children even though we are not aware of them ourselves and that class- and race-based emotional reactions are special dynamite along that line.

It would be easy to continue this list for quite a while. Let us summarize briefly by repeating that, even with excellent teaching ability guaranteed, even with a fine attitude toward "the child" from the beginning, any one mistake in the organizational or personal management of the children and the group is likely to produce problem behavior. An inspection of the group-leadership techniques we use is essential from time to time, as children, as well as the world around them, change more rapidly than does our list of generally recommended, previously practiced educational tricks.

EMOTIONAL STRAIN AND SUDDEN CHANGE

Emotional strain, affecting a whole group, may in itself be sufficient to produce upsets and problem cases. We know this is true whenever the emotional strain on groups is easily recognizable as such.

Anxiety. The stage of anxiety in which many school groups find themselves for weeks during "examination period," and afterward waiting for the results, is a frequent type of group strain. In the same way, sudden affects that sweep classrooms at times are productive of problem behavior beyond expectation. Excitement about contemporary events (community riots), extreme fury, enthusiasm, unusual hilarity, and depression and fear are among the prime dangers to stable morale. Needless to say, the constantly whipped-up excitement and aggression in times of war work as chronic irritants to the discipline of many school groups and add unnoticeably but considerably to the problems of the teacher as group leader.

Boredom. One of the most deteriorating effects of emotions upon group morale, however, does not flow from wild acts and excitement but rather from the lack of it over too long a time. Boredom will always remain the greatest enemy of school discipline. If we remember that children are bored, not only when they don't happen to be interested in the subject or when the teacher doesn't make it interesting, but also when certain working conditions are out of focus with their basic needs, then we can realize what a great contributor to discipline problems boredom really is.

In classes too large, a number of the children will of necessity be bored, while the others enjoy what goes on, for rarely can any one teaching procedure be exactly on the right level for everybody involved. Another form of boredom in classrooms comes from overemphasis on verbalization, while the manipulative needs of children are left unattended. The same thing in reverse—prolonged manipulative activity leaving the imagination no chance to come in—may also bring on boredom.

Research has shown that boredom is closely related to frustration and that the effect of too much frustration is invariably irritability, withdrawal, rebellious opposition, or aggressive rejection of the whole show.

Reaction to Change. Reaction to change is perhaps the most frequent and, as yet, unrecognized factor in discipline difficulties. Of course we expect such bad effects from changes for the worse. It is important to keep in mind, though, that such a limitation of the problem is not realistic. Any change, even for the better, tends to upset group organization temporarily and to lead to a phase of increased problem production.

Many teachers will remember how even their "nice" classrooms are sometimes hard to manage when the usually light room is darkened, when the lecture setting changes to a discussion, a subcommittee arrangement, or a picture-slide demonstration. They know how much noise and confusion often accompany changes from one room to another, from class to luncheon and the other way around and how otherwise very studious children may all of a sudden act very foolishly in the museum they wanted for so long to visit.

A change in group leadership also weighs heavily as a factor in reaction to change. Much of the trouble substitute teachers have with classes has little to do with the real quality of those classes or with the teachers' real ability for group leadership. For, when you meet a class in which someone else is substituting for the permanent leader, it automatically has already deteriorated into something more akin to a mob than a group, and the task of leadership is very different from the task under normal conditions.

Changes in program affect groups the same way and especially changes in leadership technique. The most frequent example of this kind of change is the attempt to spring self-government on a school. What you find during the first few months has nothing to do with the children's reactions to self-government. It is only their reactions to the fact of change itself. Only after a few months do their real reactions to self-government, their ability to take it, and their immaturity toward it become visible at all.

The answer, of course, is not that change should be avoided at all costs. It is that the knowledge of this law of group psychology should guide us in our evaluation of what happens and that we sometimes can meet confusion caused by too-sudden change through planning for it by means of "transition techniques."

THE COMPOSITION OF THE GROUP

The problem of "grouping" has never been satisfactorily discussed —to say nothing of being solved. The most frequent controversial disputes are concerned with "intelligence" versus "maturity" grouping. Unfortunately, neither of the two is a way out. The real picture is much too complex for that.

Without entering this very important and devious problem here, we can generalize safely to the extent that, whenever something is very wrong in the composition of a group, discipline problems are the natural and unavoidable result.

If this is true, then the discovery of what constitutes healthy divergencies, as distinct from serious mistakes, in group composition must become of prime importance.

The following principles can be suggested without too much risk:

First, it isn't a question of whether or not groups are heterogeneous but of whether or not the criteria according to which they are heterogeneous are relevant to group life or not.

Example 1. The 10A is well matched in interest in and ability for Latin. At the same time it is rather divergent in terms of developmental age. Some of the students are wildly adolescent; others have left their adolescence behind them in many ways; still others are just in the transition from delayed childhood.

As they have all been picked because of their interest in and ability for Latin and as the Latin teacher does a superb job of teaching and group leadership, they are a happy group for the Latin hour for which they are together once a week.

They would be a mess and in chaos if they were expected to live as the group they are for even a day in camp.

Example 2. The children in Cabin 8 are of widely varying I.Q.s. Yet they are well matched in terms of camp interest, degree of sophistication, and developmental maturity. So they make a superb cabin group, in spite of the fact that it would be near to impossible to teach them any one academic thing the way they are.

Second, as every group is always badly matched in some criteria, even though it has been well matched in others, the real problem is to avoid extremes in those criteria that are "marginal" to the main purpose of group life.

Example. The 10A Latin class already discussed has one mistake in it. There are only three children who are very immature in their outlooks on life and sex. The more sophisticated ones are so far in the majority that these three are pretty much out of place. In such a case we will observe that after a few weeks of concentration upon Latin, the three Benjamins will become problems to the teacher. They will be either especially fearful of expressing themselves, or they will become especially clownish and wild in their attempts to impress their otherwise more sophisticated companions. Too-great heterogeneity in a secondary criterion of grouping will still encourage discipline problems.

Just how far apart the extremes between group members in one criterion can be without disturbing the group balance is a question still unsolved. Right now the situation has to be studied anew from case to case. Research efforts to develop generally applicable standards are under way.

Third, although practically any criterion may be relevant for grouping in one case and highly unimportant in another, we find that the following are often the most important criteria to be considered in analyzing the causes of discipline problems.

Age and development. Age and development, especially in terms of physical and social maturity, are a major criterion.

Socioeconomic backgrounds, racial elements, and so forth. Especially the various differences arising from the substratification in our society are central here: for instance, the difference in codes between youngsters who are highly "manner-minded" and those who are proudly unconventional. This factor should be considered more often than it usually is.

Home acceptance or emancipation. Differences in home dependence often count heavily during the late grade-school and junior high-school years, when children make the transition from strong home identifications to greed for emancipation at varying rates.

Shyness-toughness. Some shy children together with a few more expressive ones make a good mixture. If the distance becomes too great the opposite end is achieved: The shy youngster gets more scared than he was before and becomes a problem through his withdrawal. The wild one gets more "show-offish" through the cheap admiration he gets from his more retiring colleagues.

Intelligence and knowledge. This topic is so well known that commentary is not needed.

Interest and work acceptance. Especially vital in terms of learning morale.

Physical coordination. Extreme differences tend to encourage sharp subgrouping within a group.

Leader acceptance. From open defiance to strong need for childish dependence, two tastes hard to satisfy in the same group.

Organizational maturity. When two-thirds of your group can easily be expected to be self-governing, whereas one-third is on such a different level of organizational dependence that it cannot function without the pressure of outside lures and controls, behavior problems arise.

Enjoyment of group life. The factor of enjoyment separates the happily "group-eager" youngster from his more isolationist pal.

All in all, what we want to point out is that the mere mixture of your group out of too heterogeneous elements in highly group-relevant items may in itself constitute a constant producer of discipline problem behavior without anything else being wrong. Discovery and repair of such factors in time save you much undeserved criticism and much self-accusation, so that a psychological analysis of your group composition is a job well worth undertaking from time to time.

Needless to say, any one of the six group-psychological factors in discipline problems may co-exist with any other. The task for the practitioner boils down to three major parts.

First, don't allow yourself to be fooled by the surface appearance of a discipline problem. What youngsters do contains no indication of what the real source of your discipline problem is.

Second, you can find the trouble, though, by analyzing your discipline problems in terms of the following questions.

What did the behavior observed really mean?

To what extent was it produced by the peculiar case history of the individual involved? To what extent did it also (or even mainly) contain elements of a group-psychological nature?

Which of the most frequent group-psychological factors producing problem behavior in school classes are involved and to what degree?

Third, on this basis you will want to add these further questions, growing out of a previous chapter of our little study, to your calculations.

As I want to do something about it, do I plan mainly for effect on the individual or effect on the group, and how can I be sure to respect the law of "marginal antisepsis"?

In which direction do I have to aim most, toward change of surface behavior or modification of basic attitudes, and how can I be sure to respect the law of marginal antisepsis with regard to this problem?

How can I possibly evaluate whether or not what I want to do will "work" without being fooled by false analogies or by the cheap sellers of "bags full of tricks" and without neglecting the less visible subsurface effects of what I do over the more visible and tangible results?

None of this is meant to substitute for the personal analysis of each case, of each situation, by the teacher who is in it. It is meant to encourage that teacher to think through his problem instead of applying otherwise recommended techniques without critical examination.

The author is convinced that the good disciplinarian, though al-

ways retaining some of the qualities of a good artist, is still closer to
the modern physician than to the performer of magical tricks at a
county fair.

Discipline and Teacher Personality

Among the futile controversies that block progress at teachers'
conventions and in college courses is the well-known set of alternatives: What makes you a good disciplinarian—your personality or
your technical skill?

The frequency with which this question is asked, as well as the
dignified facial expressions of those who ask it, is likely to fool the
practitioner. The truth is that the whole question is silly. There are no
such alternatives. The formulation is nothing but a magician's stunt
invented to prolong discussion and to throw sand in the teacher's eyes
so that she doesn't find out how little we really know about the field.
The facts behind the problem can simply be summarized in a few
points.

First, "personality" and "technical skill" are never in conflict with
each other. Instead, they are complementary. One is meaningless without the other. There is no either-or situation involved.

Second, confusion about this item is mainly nourished by a widespread abuse of the term "technical skill." Some people mean by "technical skill" the possession of a bagful of little "tricks" and "devices"
that they think are "right" in themselves and the application of which
they recommend for any discipline problem. If this abuse of the word
"technical skill" is meant, then we have to admit that teacher personality can do very well without it. Many teachers who do not worry
or even try to accumulate these little tricks and have the stuff it takes
to meet children are doing very well.

However, the situation is different if we give the term "technical
skill" a more precise meaning. We mean the following:

knowledge of the human child in his developmental states and of the basic
laws of his behavior individually and in groups;

ability to size up and analyze the situation in which the teacher finds himself for its individual and group-psychological involvements;

knowledge of the most basic techniques of human influence and their rela-
t onships with certain developmental ages and personality types;

ability to figure out which of these influencing techniques fit which situations and to make fair estimates of possible subsurface effects that have to be
considered.

Referring to "technical skill" as defined here, we seriously maintain
that it is highly essential, that not even a genius or the most perfect
teacher personality can ever do without it.

Third, what do we mean by "teacher personality" anyway? This is
not the place to arrive at a solution of the most tangled problem of
what constitutes the best teacher personality. The author, however,
does believe that the problem is not so "intangible" as it is often made
out to be and that a list of about two dozen of the most vital traits for
the successful and hygienic disciplinarian could well be compiled.
However, such an endeavor must be left for another opportunity.

Only one remark about teacher personality seems so essential here
that we cannot make up our minds to postpone mentioning it. A *sense
of humor* is so obviously the most vital characteristic of the skillful
handler of discipline problems or tough group situations that its possession must be among the prime requisites for the job. If we had to
list along with it the one personality trait most injurious to successful
discipline, we would pick *false dignity* for first choice. We know of
no other single personality trait that causes so much confusion, uproar,
and mismanagement as this one. Unfortunately, we have to leave it to
the imagination of the reader to figure out just how we do and how we
do not mean this statement.

Fourth, just where the ideal balance between "teacher personality"
and "technical skill" should be is hard to state. It seems obvious,
though, that certain jobs in this discipline business need different emphases from certain others. Here are our hunches on the point.

For the job of establishing good discipline and maintaining it (by
discipline we mean here "order"), it seems to us that the personality of
the teacher is the most essential factor. Under ordinary circumstances, a
teacher can get along well with few technical considerations if this one
factor is strongly represented.

For the job of discovering sources of discipline problems and of
doing repair jobs in "discipline cases," we doubt that even the most
ideal personality equipment suffices. These jobs are closer to the work

of the surgeon than to that of the artist, and special knowledge and technical skill weigh very heavily indeed.

Fifth, the forces beyond should be considered. One of the most serious impediments to the development of disciplinary skills among teachers seems to be a peculiar disuse of "evaluation." We find that the evaluation of the disciplinary skills of teachers is more often off the beam than is the evaluation of any other of their skills.

The most frequent mistakes in the evaluation of teachers' real disciplinary skills are the following.

We confuse a teacher's skill in teaching and establishing order with his skill in handling cases of conflict and disturbance. And so we often load good practitioners of one skill with the task of counseling in the other type of situation, to the disadvantage of all involved. Or, the other way around, we confuse good psychological analysis of other people's discipline problems with the skill to establish good organization in one's own group and end up with great surprises all around.

We blame a teacher for the problem cases that turn up or praise him for the lack of them. Yet we know that the teacher's own behavior is only one of the manifold factors in the production of problem behavior in children, all the others being entirely out of his reach.

We praise or blame the teacher in terms of the "success" he has in handling his problem cases, yet we know equally well that the teacher's own activity is only one among a wide variety of factors on which "success or failure" depends, most of which are way beyond his reach.

We evaluate a teacher's handling of his discipline situation on the basis of criteria that have nothing to do with his own goals and the special conditions under which he works and thus badly misinterpret the real situation.

On the positive side we can say the following about evaluation of disciplinary skills.

The occurrence or nonoccurrence of discipline problems need not be under the control of the teacher at all. Whether it is or not must be carefully studied before any evaluation is made.

Example. The teacher with a few especially disturbed children in his class must have more blowups than the one without. The teacher in a school where community strife is vehement will not be able to avoid group conflict, no matter how well he plans his discipline. And so forth.

Success or failure in meeting the disciplinary challenge need not be in the power of the teacher at all. Evaluations should not be made before this point is clearly determined.

Example. Everything Miss Jones did for Johnny was right. But the home situation was so messed up that it was not possible for her to repair the youngster. At the same time Miss Smith worked with a youngster and did most of it wrong, but parental cooperation was so excellent that the case turned into a complete "success."

Only criteria inherent in the situations we talk about should be used for evaluation of skillful or wrong handling.

Example. Miss White built her discipline on the plan of developing attitude changes in her school-hostile clientele. Her discipline should not be evaluated on the question of how well she subdued the children.

Only the intellectual and emotional levels on which a teacher approaches a discipline case can be used as criteria for his abilities, for they are the parts that are really in his power—or are they?

Example. Miss Mills simply blew up at George's behavior, without thinking at all. This reaction did not constitute wise disciplinary planning. Miss Roberts had an elaborate plan for getting at the problem of the 7A. The plan was thoughtful and well founded. It did happen that her plan was opposed by the principal or by an incident that she could not have foreseen. Evaluation of her work should be based on the first, not the second, criterion.

Administratively, an open and clear policy of evaluation of teacher behavior along the lines mentioned would do a lot to help teachers *want* to become better disciplinarians. Too often they are told to do what is right by the principles of education in a democracy but are really evaluated along the lines of surface effects, administrative tastes, community opposition, or superficial comfort for the administrative machinery. The real hinge is in the principal's office. No teacher can afford to be more than 10 per cent wiser in her disciplinary planning than he, or she gets fired, because in that case she is necessarily misinterpreted and misunderstood.

This last statement is perhaps the most hopeful of all. For it may be hard to reach all teachers in a country as vast as this one. The number of principals in the United States is tremendous too, but it approaches a size that can be reached, and the channels are better paved because of the nature of administrative jobs.

Before You Go Back to Your Classroom— Remember This

We do not believe that the tremendous issue of "discipline" can be taught in a few sententious words. However, we know that an occasional guidepost is often a help to the hurried practitioner. We should therefore like to end this rather detailed discussion in a somewhat untraditional way by suggesting the following thoughts for the teacher who will step into his class after he has read this paper.

First, routine tricks aren't the whole show. You can't sew discipline together out of rags. Often, especially when we get jittery or when "ununderstanding" superiors or colleagues put the thumb screws on us for the wrong things—often, in such cases, we develop undue admiration for organizational "gadgets." We develop the illusion that they can do the trick for us, will save us thinking, planning, loving, and understanding. Well, they won't. If you overload your group atmosphere with the rattle of organizational machinery—try to have a "rule" for everything under the sun and a policy of revenge, if that rule is broken, for everything under the moon—you are just going to thwart your best efforts in the long run. Don't think you have to run around with your belt stuck full of guns and lollipops all the time either. Rely a little more on yourself, your "person," and your sense of humor. It saves you lots of headaches and a load of disciplinary noise.

Second, the "mystery of personality" is good when it works. But it is a poor excuse for failure. This statement is supposed to keep you from falling into the opposite extreme after reading the first. For, although our personalities—and the way we get them across to children —are the bases of most of what we usually call "respect" and "leadership," there is no doubt that there is such a thing as the "everyday trifle," which is more easily settled through a rule or common agreement than through your magic gaze. Children have—sometimes quite unconsciously—considerable need for regularity and predictability in their expectations. If their whole lives are dependent on the whims of your genius, you won't make them happy, and little frictions will begin to increase. So don't extend your contempt of the idea of using routine tricks instead of personality into mistaken contempt for *any* planning and organization as such.

Third, don't try to wash all your laundry with the same cake of soap. Sometimes we discover two or three nice little tricks that work. Then we develop the delusion that, if we just keep on sticking to those tricks, the rest of the problems of life will dissolve themselves kindly into so much smoke. Well, it won't wash. Don't expect tricks to work under all circumstances, and don't blame yourself or the children if they don't, but blame the tricks or, better, the way you translated them without enough planning. Watch out when you begin to tell "anecdotes" about how this or that "always works"—those are the moments when mental putrefaction begins.

Fourth, children are at least as complicated as pieces of wood. So you had better find out about their texture, elasticity, and so forth before you apply your various tools and machinery to them. Sometimes we want to get places fast, and then we bust the whole show by using too coarse an instrument. If you do that, don't blame it on the instrument.

Fifth, if you make a fool of yourself, why not be the first one to find out and have a good laugh about it? This is the worst superstition about discipline: that "respect" and "leadership" melt as easily as a chocolate bar. It is not true. If they do, they never were "real" respect and leadership to begin with. So don't be jittery for fear that you will "jeopardize" your dignity in the eyes of your kids if they find out you aren't the Archangel Michael after all. The fear of exposure to ridicule has caused more intangible discipline problems than anything else I know. There is a difference between the laughter you start and ridicule. Real, especially self-directed, humor is the most disarming thing that you can find in work with children.

Sixth, don't develop suicidal fantasies just because you aren't almighty after all. There are limits to the power of the greatest magician among us, as well as to the omnipotence of the most conscientious scientist. Every once in a while we run up against those discoveries. If you do, don't blame your kids because they can't be cured by you, and don't blame yourself. The biggest hurdle in our work is the time element. It deserves all due respect. It takes at least as many months of planful work to undo a wrong trait in a child as it took years of planful mishandling to build it up. But don't forget that many things can be started on the right track through long-range planning, though those same things can't be followed through to their final development. Don't be afraid of making mistakes. It isn't the mistake that produces distorted children, it is the wrong way of reacting to the mistakes after we make them. And that is entirely in your power.

Finally, what do you want to be anyway, an educator or an angel with a flaming sword?

It is upon your answer to this question that your decision about discipline techniques will finally depend. For it requires one type of person to be the proud avenger of infantile wrongs and sins against defied "rules and regulations" and another to be the guide of human beings through the turmoil of growth. You have to make up your mind.

Psychoanalysis and Group Therapy: A Developmental Point of View

This paper was originally presented as the "Leo Berman Memorial Lecture" before the Boston Psychoanalytic Society. I should like the reader to be quite aware of this point, for to Leo Berman psychoanalysts owe more than they know for opening their eyes to theoretical, clinical, and educational possibilities that might otherwise not have become so visible to us all. Also, some of the tasks in concept formation and the adaptation of a personality theory that was originally designed to hit the individual "from within," so to speak, badly need modification and adaptation to the full range of "group-psychological phenomena." Only a few of those "phenomena" that seem to me to fall beyond the pale of easily explainable processes are, of course, alluded to here, but the issue needs to be declared with force, even though the terrain is still rather uncharted.

IT SEEMS TO ME that newly emerging scientific disciplines go through a sequence of peculiar developmental phases, just as children do in the process of growing up. Some of them may have prolonged infancies and stormy adolescences and then either go to pieces or settle down to mature adulthood. Others may proceed more smoothly but from time to time show what is comparable to the measles or whooping cough, which they get over better at certain ages, hopefully with no serious detriment to their later health. Others again —but enough of this, the analogy is too obvious to need elaboration.

To map out the developmental cramps of such an emerging scientific discipline as group therapy in the clinical field would be a fascinating job in its own right, and I am sure most of us could think of a few vivid illustrations of its growing pains.

"Psychoanalysis and Group Therapy" is based on the article of the same title that appeared in *The American Journal of Orthopsychiatry* (January 1963), © 1963 by the American Orthopsychiatric Association.

What excites me more at the moment is a supplementary fact in child development, one that has not received so much attention, namely, that the *parents* of children also seem to go through amazing stretches of phase-typical behavior, depending on the specific developmental phases their children happen to be in. For too long we have tried to explain this phenomenon away by simply ascribing all parental reactions to specific growth problems in the youngsters or to the parents' individual neuroses, characterological peculiarities, or case histories. I think it is time—and efforts in this direction have emerged more clearly recently in psychoanalytic literature—that we stopped matching a developmental process in the child, on the one hand, with the individual neurosis of the parent, on the other.

We know now that, under certain circumstances, the mere fact of Johnny's adolescence or of his Oedipal contortions will produce in the parent certain techniques for coping with the behavioral output of his offspring—and the parental feelings about it, which go beyond the mere scope of Mama's personal neurosis. I really think there is something like a developmental, phase-conditioned parental reaction pattern, which cannot entirely be dissolved into the usual category of personal neurosis of the parent but more closely resembles a developmental process that the parent goes through as a phenomenon in its own right.

As we are comparing newly emerging scientific disciplines with the developmental phases children go through, we may as well take the next step: If any of the previous description holds water, we can expect that the parent discipline of a newly developing scientific endeavor will also have some ready-made patterns at its disposal for coping with the new phenomenon. It may be worthwhile to have a look at them.

Now, of course, the specific, newly emerging scientific discipline I have in mind on this occasion is that of group therapy, and one of its parent disciplines—certainly for analytically oriented group therapy—is obviously psychoanalysis. Here, by the way, the analogy had better end, for, unlike the usual form of procreation, procreation of scientific disciplines may take place with more than two parent disciplines, and the whole analogy with the parental situation must not be stretched too far. In fact, I want to make sure I am understood correctly—I mean this analogy only as a partial one and introduce it only as a heuristic principle to shake us into awareness of phenomena we might otherwise overlook. No real claim for full analogy between parents and children, on the one hand, and parent disciplines and scientific movements, on the other, is intended.

However, slippery analogies like this one have proved valuable as thought stimulants before, so let us indulge in it for a while.

If we may hypothesize such a thing as an "attitude of psychoanalysis toward group therapy," it seems to me it has gone through four stages of development. By the way, just as in all other speculations about developmental phases, it is obvious that I am not talking about a strict sequence here. Rather, as with children and their parents' reactions to them, historically speaking, several of these stages may coexist and one is rarely entirely gone even when the next one seems to have begun, so individual representatives of psychoanalysis at any given historical time may be found in any one of these stages, which should make it all the more fun to speculate about.

Phase 1: Suspicion and Contempt

That suspicion and contempt are all too frequently the first attitudes of a parent discipline to its newly arrived—and not appropriately anticipated—offspring has been well documented even in the development of psychoanalysis itself. I am referring to the emergence of child analysis, for what it claimed to do must have sounded simply crazy and revolting to the first generation of adult analysts. In fact, I have no doubt that, if anybody but Freud's own daughter had taken such a radical, revolutionary step, the mere cheek of using the name "analysis" would have been rejected—and no holds barred. For how could one, at a time when the question of whether or not the prone position of the patient made the difference between analysis and other forms of therapy was still a focal one, allow anything as crazy as what child analysts did to be called by the same name? To wit: no couch, no free association, no positional ritual; no guarantee that the therapist's aloof attitude could be maintained for more than a few minutes at a time; no guilt about association with family members or about turning up in the natural habitat of the child patient at times; no contempt of the "ego" as merely a "superficial" part of the personality; no attempt to withhold value judgments entirely; no hesitation at interfering, at times, in the patient's life-space arrangements; no guarantee against physical contact during the time therapist and patient spend together in their "pressurized treatment cabin"; and worse—not even a transference neurosis!

How could such things be called "analysis"?

The answers are simple, of course, from the vantage point of hindsight, but they weren't easy then.

First, all this crazy deviation from basic rules isn't just because somebody wants to lop off uncomfortable rigmarole but is clearly a technical necessity. How else could anybody but Anna Freud herself suggest it?

Second, all this deviation stems from the fact that we are dealing with different patients, that is, with children.

Third, also we are, in our work with children, operating in a somewhat different medium: the more life-space-soaked atmosphere of an adult participating in the play life of a young child while keeping one hand on the switchboard of behavioral controls by parents and teachers.

One condition on which all this deviation was allowed to call itself "psychoanalysis" remained constant, by the way, for a long time: We had to promise to deal only with that type of disease entity acceptable to the psychoanalyst of adults, that is, the same type of "classical" neurosis.

Well, if child analysis was to go through all this and come out of it as a respectable—though vanishing—scientific branch, a lot had to happen between then and the present. And it has.

Group therapy had no Anna Freud to blaze its trail. It didn't fare so well. The phase during which the parent discipline's reaction dallied in the attitude of suspicion and contempt lasted an extremely long time. Needless to say, whenever one thinks of those who had the most to do with a change in this attitude, Leo Berman first comes to mind.

Phase 2: Surprise—and Acceptance—of Some Facts of Group Life, Provided They Come from Enemy Territory

Psychoanalysts for a long time did not really expose themselves personally to experiences of group leadership in a clinical professional role. Even Freud's paper was not—nor were his other clinical writings

—based on clinical work within a group setting; it was speculative in nature. At the same time, however, the psychoanalyst could not keep from being exposed to all the writings from other professions; he soon had to take time out to come to grips with the challenges some of them threw at him. Furthermore, with controversies getting hotter, it would not be long before he was interested in what his enemies in the fields of sociology, anthropology, social psychology, and so forth were claiming as results of their research. In sort, it wasn't too long before his own trainees were not only allowed but also expected to familiarize themselves with what the sister sciences were saying about the nature of social organizations and groups. It seems to me that readiness to learn from another discipline is directly proportionate to the distance of that sister science from one's own professional domain. This reaction seems to occur in any group with a cause, be it scientific, political, or religious: One is allowed to learn from an outside enemy what would put a member under the suspicion of heresy if he should utter it. The term "enemy" is of course not to be taken too literally, although I do think the penetration of ideas and facts from outside is facilitated when they come from speakers hostile to the group they are meant to penetrate. And, although psychoanalysts have long since surrendered initial reservations against such disciplines as sociology and anthropology, there is no doubt about the hostility with which the representatives of these sciences have (and often still do) considered psychoanalysis enemy territory.

Anyway, the original suspicion that work with groups was nothing but a watering-down or distortion of intensive individual work was to give way to a strong interest in the phenomena these sciences were describing with respect to behavior of the human animal in groups. Even those who still rejected group therapy as clinical nonsense no longer minded listening to interesting tidbits about the behavior of individuals when exposed to group currents. It then became legitimate to speculate on such reported group-psychological facts and their relationships to psychoanalytic knowledge, provided one used such insights to understand, rather than to deal with, the behavior of the sick. For example, note the early papers on group observations written by "teachers-turned-lay-analysts" and accepted for publication in such media as *Psychoanalytische Pädagogik* or *The Psychoanalytic Study of the Child* or Kris's speculation, "Covenant of the Gangsters," and the like.

Phase 3: The Extramarital Slumming Party

Some feudal societies have managed to harbor enormous contradictions in the ethics of sexual behavior within their systems, letting them
coexist amazingly well. They have set their demands for respectability
and dignity of the legitimate spouse and of a man's relationship with
her so high that they have increased the honor, but reduced some of the
fun, of living with her. Consequently, it is the mistress or the concubine
who provides gratification for the less respected forms of sexual relationship or for the irreducible minimum of downright perverse needs. The
interesting thing is that, instead of threatening the existence of such a
system of marital ethics, this custom seems to be the very foundation for
its continuance. Actually, in such a system, the fact that you promise to
gratify your less acceptable sexual needs in extramarital relationships
with less respectable partners is even considered evidence of your loyalty
to the high level of the official marital code. This, of course, is well
known, and psychoanalytic literature is rich with examples of it.

My analogy is this: During a certain phase of psychoanalytic reaction to group therapy, a similar sanction seems to have entered the
arena. It seems to me that, during the last decade or so, an increasing
number of young psychoanalytic trainees, although in training with the
most high-minded analysts (who are anything but friendly to group
therapy), have been, if not encouraged, then certainly allowed, to play
around with therapy groups on the side—provided, of course, that they
don't take such activity too seriously, that they do it only for fun or perhaps for research. It is my impression that such young trainees really
have been getting a lot of fun out of this playing around, and that it
hasn't hurt the legitimacy of their official training at all. They certainly
seem to revel in opportunities to do all the things their supervisors in
analysis would never let them do, to work with patients their training
institutes would never select for their analytic experience, and, for
once, to enjoy the chance to forget about most of the hard-to-follow
issues of their official training and to live in a clinical free-for-all with
the security that no training analyst is going to breathe down their
necks while they are at it. In fact, for once they can ignore all they
have learned in their official sessions: They are happy to forget about
the hard facts of such phenomena as resistance, transference, and

countertransference, and they can let go with premature interpretations or downright moralizing (under the disguise of "ego support"); they can throw aside all the technical restrictions that otherwise plague their consciences and can enjoy with happy abandon their extracurricular affairs, without real censorship from their professional elders.

This phase in the reaction of psychoanalysis to group therapy, by the way, has, as far as the latter is concerned, a positive and a negative impact. In a way it is deplorable, for it has slowed group therapy's natural development. For, after decades of wild playing around by therapists otherwise highly devoted to technique, we must rediscover what we should have known all along, that the issues basic to all thorough clinical work—transference, resistance, and the like—turn up in therapy groups too, although perhaps sometimes in new and hard-to-recognize forms. If psychoanalytic people didn't scream about the importance of transference and resistance in group therapy, who else should? On the other hand, this practice has also proved a blessing to group therapy, for at last the very people being trained in psychoanalysis were free to expose themselves without guilt to actual clinical work in face-to-face groups. In my estimation, this advantage outweighs by far the unavoidable delay in rapprochement between the two fields.

Phase 4: Official Sanction for a Few

It is not enough for a young scientific discipline that the parent discipline allows its deviants, its students, or at best its "marginal men" to expose themselves to the specific experience it has to offer. On the other hand, by the time the more established discipline gets around to taking the newcomer seriously, much too long a chain of unfortunate encounters with quackery, confusion, or downright hostility have occurred to make the final relationship easy. Also, the younger field has, in the meantime, grown enormously in the bulk of material it presents to be examined and in the techniques and theories tentatively worked out. This makes it less attractive to the "old-timer," who is less willing to expose himself seriously to the new field just to see what is in it. Yet who but that "very-old-timer" in the parent discipline could afford to do just that without loss to his professional prestige, and who could better give the new discipline what it so desperately needs, the best theoretical brains available to work in it? Consequently the first real coming to grips with a new science usually takes place by official sanction for a few to do so. It seems to me that psychoanalysis has now reached this stage in its relationship with group therapy. Of course, even such sanctions are not absolute—they remain tied to four conditions: first, that the respected explorers of the domains of group therapy pick atypical cases, which smartly avoid any possible threat to the major domain of the older science; second, that they operate in nonprivate settings like mental hospitals, veterans hospitals, and the like; third, that when major claims for the new medium are made they be restricted to issues of low emphasis like guidance work, educational rehabilitation, symptom relief, preparation for real therapy, and—the safest—just work with children; fourth, that, whatever the findings, they be presented in such a way that the original priority of the whole enterprise is not to cure but to contribute to research.

The result of allowing only a few to expose themselves to group-therapy experiences without threat to their professional standing in the parent discipline is most auspicious, indeed. It is on this basis that the literature has grown in clinical relevance, as well as in thoughtfulness and depth. The usual early childhood squabbles of a new discipline about who can do it better has been replaced by a far more cautious comparison of similarities and differences between the group medium and individual therapy and a franker appraisal of the need to differentiate the relevance of techniques in relation to the specific disease entity one deals with. A discovery of the new hurdles and problems the group medium brings with it has replaced the silly old braggadocio and the claims and counterclaims of financial savings, ease of effect, and numerical reach.

In fact, it has been gradually conceded that clinical work in groups, if done well and by appropriately trained therapists, can at least take over what the analyst isn't too eager to deal with anyway, and group therapy has come a little closer to the position psychotherapy is allowed to hold in relation to "analysis proper."

Let me emphasize again that these four phases in the development of the attitude of psychoanalysis to group therapy are not presented as outcomes of anything like research. They are meant only as thoughts that come to mind now. Why now? That should be obvious, for nobody

I know has worked harder, more enthusiastically, more devotedly and effectively to bring about the basic changes implied in my story than Leo Berman. I shall never forget a meeting many years ago at which Elvin Semrad, Leo Berman, and I worried over the chances of getting group therapy the help it sorely needed from psychoanalysis and, as a first step to such a blessing, tried to get a meeting on group therapy accepted as part of a regular psychoanalytic conference. Ever since then, the number of colleagues who have joined him in his effort has increased. That helped, but what really contributed most to a development of the new field as well as of psychoanalysis's reaction to it was the very work of Leo Berman.

What I should like to memorialize Leo for, beside his actual contributions to scientific knowledge, theory, and technical skill, is this task of educating both a new scientific branch and its parent discipline toward a more mature relationship with each other. To achieve a job of this sort it took, not only the brilliance of a mind and the therapeutic astuteness of an eye like Leo Berman's, but also the incredible patience and, above all, the unmatched freedom from hostility and rancor that we all know Leo possessed. In fact, I have never met anybody else with such a combination of skill, brilliance, and devotion, on the one hand, and total absence of hostility, on the other, for this sort of task. In reference to such a task, I don't consider it out of place to celebrate and memorialize Leo's character as emphatically as the more traditionally acceptable contribution through therapy and through the printed word.

The Challenge Before Us

Personally, I consider Phase 4 in the attitude of psychoanalysis to group therapy, on which Leo Berman worked so devotedly a *fait accompli*. This does not mean that it is the dominant phase—the coexistence of several developmental phases on different levels is a thought not strange to this audience. Also it is quite obvious that not all representatives of a parent discipline at a given time will have gone through—or will even be interested in entering—the previously described developmental phases. It may take years before a given developmental phase that a given scientific discipline has reached penetrates to all its members and representatives. In principle, however, the existence of even one paper on the level of Phase 4—and any one of Leo Berman's would amply fill the bill—is enough to put up the developmental flag on the peak that has been reached.

However, Leo Berman's interest did not stop with the task just described. Beside his work on and his contribution to the question of just what psychoanalysis does to and with group therapy, he was equally concerned with the supplementary question: What are the implications of some of the by-now-undeniable facts of group life—especially of life in therapy groups—for psychoanalytic theory? If even a few of the observations made by psychoanalysts who have exposed themselves to group therapy hold up, don't they constitute a challenge to our customary theoretical formulations and especially to the model of personality that has proved so adequate for our work in the individual therapy situation? Don't some of the data thus discovered constitute, if not a threat, then at least a demand for reformulation? Should we expect all the group-psychological phenomena we run into to be explained with the same set of metapsychological assumptions used to explain the individual-therapy process?

A challenge to our theory should be a wonderful and welcome event for anybody who follows in the footsteps of Sigmund Freud. For, you may remember, he operated on the very same principle. If, in the course of clinical work, phenomena appear to be undeniable—however crazy or amazing they may seem—for which our present theoretical constructs have no appropriate places, well then, let those theoretical formulations go. They had better be discarded, modified, or supplemented to cope with the new facts. There is no need to remind this audience of what this basic principle of scientific thought did to Freud —and what he did with it. We ought to be proud that right now we are allowed to face a situation similar to those he faced several times. Coping with the impact of new group-psychological data of clinical relevance to our theoretical constructs was another one of Leo's life ambitions. Within the limits of this occasion, of course, I must confine myself to just putting on the table, so to speak, a few of the items of concern. I shall leave it to you to carry on from there.

In a nutshell, it seems to me that the following four phenomena constitute the "facts of group life" that emerge clearly in therapy groups but that our present model of personality is not flexible enough to explain: first, the phenomenon of "contagion and shock effect"; second, the power of "group-psychological role suction"; third, the tax-imposition and tax-exemption powers of group structure and group code; and fourth, the action-threshold impact of spatial designs and of things.

It will not be easy to present enough of a description of what I refer to as "group-psychological facts" to convince you that I am not talking about what we already know anyway, that the phenomena I have in mind really contain some core as yet hard to explain. It fills me with horror that my short and colorful illustrations may be interpreted as if they were meant to be adequate evidence for what I am trying to prove. So let me make sure it is understood that what I say from here on in only illustrates a special angle I am trying to convey. I think I have some proof for it, but I cannot, of course, unpack anything as complex as "evidence" in the few pages that remain.

THE PHENOMENA OF CONTAGION AND SHOCK EFFECT

This concept poses the following challenge to our psychoanalytic theory: Freud rightly opposed Le Bon's explanation of some group phenomena on the basis of his concept of "imitation" and showed, as we all know, how much more complex what looks like simple imitation really is, when viewed in the light of such concepts as identification. On the other hand, Freud directed his remarks primarily at "imitation" events as they were expected to occur in specific types of leader-related group. He left untouched a wide range of group situations we have since run into. I too am well aware that much "imitative" behavior in groups follows exactly Freud's formula. Yet under certain circumstances, one individual may "pick up" behavioral cues from other individuals in the group in a situation lacking any of the conditions Freud postulates—when there is neither libidinous nor any other type of dependency of the acting individual on the one whose behavior he seems to "imitate" and when nevertheless the impact of this other individual seems "coercive" to the "actor" in question. This goes beyond what we can easily explain.

Example. In a mess hall in a camp for delinquency-prone children, a boring performance on the violin is being given by an otherwise group-acceptable staff member. Most of the "tougher kids" try hard to remain still because they want to play fair with the guy who is playing the fiddle way over the heads of everybody. Suddenly, a little kid—the low man on the totem pole, with obviously no status in anybody's book—can't take it any longer. Out of the sheer desperation of his boredom he climbs up the fireplace bricks and swings head down from the rafters above. Two minutes later half the crowd is up there too. How did he do it? I don't mean scaling the wall; I mean the incredible feat of an otherwise powerless individual to sway the whole group into behavior its members really tried hard to avoid.

Example. In an early session of a relatively new therapy group, most group members are resisting the therapist's frantic attempts to "pull them in" and are reacting to everything that is said with nearly tangible emanations of a deeply hostile silence. Suddenly one group member—and, in this case again, one without any traceable sign of status or role in the group—"warms up" naïvely, without being aware of the chance he really takes, and starts to talk and to react cooperatively to the therapist's attempts at discussion. All of a sudden the "ice" seems to be broken, and the whole group is coming through with the goods. What gave this person the power to force them to drop their resistance and "do as he did"? What made it possible for the others to drop their resistance just because they saw somebody else act that way?

Example. A therapy group of adults is well under way, and a pretty good over-all atmosphere has developed by now. The group has been well at work on whatever the theme of its major discussion happens to be. Suddenly, one group member, through undeniable evidence of her deep-seated resistance and defense against anything the group or the therapist may be doing, spreads such an aura of "hostile silence" around that everybody else dries up in the process. What is the source of the power of that person to reinforce the otherwise well-relating group members' defenses and resistances by merely oozing hostility and defense? She is not admired or loved; she has no other status or power weapons at her disposal. Why should the other group members freeze up just because of the hostility from that one unimportant corner of the room?

The phenomenon of "shock effect" is equally hard to explain. In this specific instance, I mean by it the impact of one member of a group that forces new intensities of defense on another group member against the very impulsivity he allows himself to indulge in.

Example. The setting is a cabin of primarily delinquency-oriented thieves. Grouped with them by mistake is a child with a long history of stealing, which was more on a neurotic basis and which this child, as a result of previous therapy, had already tried hard to conquer in himself. Is the delinquency of the rest going to make him steal again? Guaranteedly not. However, the contrary pathology is going to emerge: Our youngster will be severely threatened, his only partially overcome internal conflict will be revived, and he will have to produce a double dose of "reaction formation" against his previous symptom trend. He will become a goody-goody or tattler, or he will be so plagued by newly evoked neurotic symptoms like anxiety, sleep disturbances, and whatnot that his stay in the group will be inadvisable. How is it that the overtly visible behavior of the other kids, whom our youngster neither loved nor liked nor selected as "identification objects" could throw him into such an internal revival of his conflict and that the mere visualization of their behavior started all this off in him?

In short, under certain conditions the very visualization of behavior by others is enough to start off either a chain of the same behavior or a heavy load of "defenses against it" in the individual who perceives it—all without the specific libidinous and identification-related processes we usually assume.

Question. How is it that others can have such influence on behavioral production in a child, and, even worse, how does that child perceive the precise basis for the behavior of the others?

THE POWER OF "GROUP-PSYCHOLOGICAL ROLE SUCTION"

Here I limit the term "role" to those situations in which certain performances basic to the need gratifications of a group are demanded by someone in it. Please let me get away with this heuristic oversimplification of the role concept, for it is all too obvious that any fertile discussion of a concept as involved as that of group roles cannot be attempted now.

Most teachers with some experience have observed that sometimes the nicest kids, who are quite friendly and pleasant in individual interaction, become a pain in the neck when they hit the group. They may turn into clowns, little rebels, rabble-rousers, or the ones who "tattle" on others' mischief. Sometimes a teacher remarks that, in this special group, an otherwise wild and unruly kid seems eager for chores and jobs, accumulating with glee before the teacher knows it all the janitorial chores classroom life has to give away. Or he may say that, whenever things get tight, you can "bet" on Johnny to come through with a good and appropriate joke that makes everybody laugh and relax or express his relief that Mary invariably yells "shut up" to the rest of the noisy crowd just a moment before he, the teacher, would have to do it. Group therapists, in recent years, have also produced ample evidence for the analogous trend among adults. Terms like "therapist's little helper," "group scapegoat, self-appointed," "isolate," "underdog," "defender of the underdog," "group admonisher," and "umpire" have recently entered the standard vocabulary of this field.

Most of this poses no special problem. In fact, psychoanalysts, more than most other people, find it easy to discover just why such individuals play such roles in groups. I have no quarrel with this. My only request is let's not stop there: It is not enough. Our usual explanation fits a large number of cases, but it does not hold true all along the line. We usually assume that the given individual has strong conscious or unconscious needs in that direction and has finally either forced them on this group or has used the group's inability to defend itself against him to allow himself behavior he otherwise might not have enough opportunity for.

Two facts seem to puncture this otherwise quite plausible explanation: First, some people do not use groups indiscriminately to live out their individual pathologies or personality needs. They seem to reserve some role acting for some groups only and do not show much of it in the rest of their lives. If that is so, I should like to know just what it is in that group that seems to bring out "the worst" or "the best" in them. Assuming the real cause is a basic need to act that way anyway, just what sets it off—or pushes it back—in specific group situations? Obviously, it must be a property of the group they are in, regardless of their own motivations. If so, what is it?

The second challenge is this: Although many a "clown" or "therapist's little helper" may be sufficiently explained on the basis of his personal pathology, I don't think this is true for all. Granted that nobody would do anything that he lacks the latent capacity to do, the push from within by no means always explains precisely what evokes the behavior. I think I have seen situations in which Johnny's need to tattle was among the least vehement forces in the child, when, in fact, it belonged to trends heavily opposed by his own superego. Only in certain group situations, for instance, when panicked by a too frightening lack of control within the group, would be assume the "tattler's role." Far from using the group to satisfy his tattling greed, he actually, with great disgust within himself, performed the salutary task for the sake of the group, for otherwise the group would soon have gone to pieces or things would have gotten out of hand. And not every kid who yells "shut up" when the group gets too noisy is a conceited egotist or a namby-pamby teacher's pet. Some really yell "shut up" just in time and in just the right way, because their own perceptions of group processes show them that the group is helpless, that some behavior has to be terminated, that nobody else seems ready to do it, so maybe they had better, for somebody must.

In all these cases—and I wouldn't care if you could convince me that they are few compared with the other type, for even one would be enough to get my theoretical visor up—it seems to me that something like "role suction" emanating from the dynamic events within the group itself is just as relevant in explaining behavior as is whatever we know about inner needs. If so, what is it, how can I nail it down, and what theoretical constructs do I need to explain the fact that the transition of a mild wish into open behavior can be influenced by something as "superficial" and intangible as a dimly perceived group need? A tracing, no matter how thorough, of the history of the youngster's individual readiness for such action certainly would not suffice.

THE TAX-IMPOSITION AND TAX-EXEMPTION POWERS OF GROUP STRUCTURE AND GROUP CODE

We know what a superego is made of and the source of its value content. We also know that, by the time kids reach their postlatency years or become adults, most of that process has long been under way, and the basic structure of the various individual superegos must be well established, on whatever level.

If any changes are to be made, we know they will require new libidinous relationships toward important "parent surrogate" figures in a person's life, which he will then ward off because of his fear of resexualization of the original wishes and so forth and that, on the basis of such renunciation of original drive wishes, he will incorporate ego ideals or superego content into his own superego. It takes all that to bring about a modification in superego content.

How does it happen, then, that under certain circumstances a group of youngsters suddenly lives way above or way below their usual level of operation? And I mean it does so without any of the basic, analytically assumed conditions but by the sheer force of situations that are difficult to assume to be powerful enough to account for all that.

Example. Delinquent gang, moved into the camp setting and kept together. No need to describe what it takes to survive with them and to make them survive with one another and with the rest of the camp. Suddenly, somebody thinks of some especially well-advised "project," which happens to catch the fancy of the kids. For about a week, with no other personal changes having occurred in the individuals, this group abandons its collective warfare against society and operates on a high level of reliability and work orientation, and its members even develop temporary changes in their superego functions. Individuals feel guilty if they do anything that endangers their project; they feel ashamed if caught slacking behind the effort expected; they stop stealing, raiding, destroying—their normal side enterprises; they live as though they have changed. The termination of the project, of course, terminates this whole episode, and concomitant work with the individuals makes it clear that no lasting changes in their superegos have yet occurred. Yet what is the source of the power of the group atmosphere created by that specific project to influence their superegos even to the point of production of appropriate guilt feelings, and how is it that something like group organization around a program is able to produce such atmospheric changes to begin with?

Example. A group of otherwise respectable adults, well oriented in their values, find themselves at a convention in a hotel in somebody else's town. How is it that a wide range of behavior suddenly becomes "tax exempt from guilt feelings" for the duration, while their individual superegos apparently emerge undamaged after their return home? How can solid agents like superegos and basic processes like appropriate guilt feelings be modified by changes as seemingly simple as geography and group-organizational pattern?

By the way, the very power of therapy groups to bring about some changes in individuals at times when their individual readiness for such changes is seriously in doubt has impressed us in many a case. Those of us with longer experience with many groups will also remember that we must keep in mind how many changes that turn up within the confines of a patient's group life may be limited to the very condition of his being immersed in the over-all value pattern of that specific group and that we must question whether we have a group-psychological process on our hands or a real personality change before we let him out as cured.

By the way, what constitutes a real change anyway, and, come to think of it, is some of this perhaps also at work when we predict what will happen when a patient leaves the two-person group of the individual therapy room?

THE ACTION-THRESHOLD IMPACT OF SPATIAL DESIGNS AND THINGS

This issue seems to be a new one, not faced either by psychoanalysis in general or by group therapy, although both have pointed to it with ample illustrations. After we have said all there is to say in our capacity of analytically oriented group therapists on the basis of such concepts as transference, countertransference, and libidinal cathexis, we are sometimes astounded by the incredible impact "simple facts" can have on the behavior of people in a group. We know now, for instance—as nursery-school teachers have always known—that occasionally the simple geography of a seating order may make or break a group session or may actually be a decisive factor in the formation of or failure to form a subgroup or in what shading the member-leader relationship will assume. We have also developed, without theoretical astonishment and sheerly for our survival as practitioners, a holy respect for issues as "superficial" as the size of the room in which we hold our sessions, the presence or absence of water faucets, the privacy or the heavy traffic of the terrain, or whether or not a recorder—although visibly unused—stands around on the table. Anyone who tries group therapy with body-restless adolescents or children will willingly add to this inventory a variety of "gadgets" that had better be left out, or else. That baseball bat, for instance, is okay when we take them out for a game, but, leave it around on the table or a chair while the group is supposed to sit down for a serious discussion of an incident its members are all really eager for, and you know what will happen in spite of their "readiness" for the discussion.

In short, it seems that a variety of properties of space, timing, and equipment or anything that can be used as a prop for anything else has a latent power over the behavior of people, which our psychoanalytic theory does not seem to me to explain sufficiently. Only those who deal with the borderline cases of psychotics and delinquent "actor-outers" have, even in their individual therapy, conceded that power, although conceding it is a far cry from being able to explain it. All of us seem to have forgotten what Freud had to say in his initial insistence on the conditions for analytic therapy. If the emotional interaction between therapist and patient by means of words, thoughts, and emotions is the main current through which treatment takes place, why should such little issues as a prone or upright position, a couch versus a chair, an exit or an entrance or the soundproofness of a room be deemed so important?

I think we were able to neglect all this for so long because we had learned how to control such factors efficiently in individual therapy with certain types of neurosis. In individual therapy with children, it was already harder, and, the moment we invited other patients into the room—individuals who might become live props for one another—the impact of spatial arrangements, gadgets, and props could no longer be ignored.

My question is how do we know just which spatial arrangements, time sequences, and physical properties of the therapy environment will assume such dramatic importance, and why? How can a silly thing like a baseball bat lying in the wrong place elicit open behavior that might otherwise have been fantasied but not acted out?

This, by the way, seems to me to be the crucial challenge to our over-all theoretical design: We have paid ample respect to the ego's role as a watchdog on the threshold between the conscious and the unconscious. I don't think we have studied thoroughly enough another function that certainly belongs in the description of a well-functioning ego, its power to decide which fantasy, emotion, urge, should remain just that and which should be allowed access to the muscular machinery and therefore find entrance into the realm of behavior that can be called "acted out."

I have no answers for all these questions. Whatever thought crowds itself into my mind pretending to be an answer soon turns out to be premature and oversimplified. But I know that Leo Berman was as seriously concerned with issues like these as I am. I also know that we shared the conviction that answers to them are as important to psychoanalysis as they are to group therapy. Furthermore, it is obvious that the task of building some of the previously mentioned "facts of group life"—and many others—into our psychoanalytic models of the personality and of the world requires the most experienced and the sharpest theoretical minds. I, for one, do not feel well enough equipped for the task. One of those who would have been we have lost. It may not be inappropriate to close this memorial to a man of Leo Berman's stature with the hope that the psychoanalytic community may pick up and continue the task in which we were so rudely interrupted by his untimely death.

Part Four

Talking It Over with My Staff

It is one thing to write a paper for a scientific periodical or to address an audience at a professional meeting. It is another to lecture to students, to address a group of parents, to argue points at teachers' gatherings, and then again—to discuss "clinical cases."

There are lots of good published materials related to any one of these levels of communication. Some of them, hopefully deserving of this description, are even included in this book.

There is an additional kind of experience, which is totally different from these but which is much less accessible—if ever—in published form. That is the kind of talking that goes on among people relevant to their immediate problems of survival on a team working with a bunch of kids or in professional roles of some sort or in a whole cluster of professional roles.

Such materials are hard to find, for some very simple reasons. First, taped directly, they turn out to be much too cumbersome and much too studded with side issues and undecipherable part-data for anybody to plough through. Second, if abstracted without detailed descriptions of the specific situations out of which they have arisen and to which the remarks are addressed, they lose all meaning for the reader who wasn't there. Besides, such publications wouldn't "look good"—or not good enough to print. The customary criteria by which a given society at a given point in time decides the "right way" in which respectable knowledge ought to be conveyed are all against them.

Yet I think there is one "in-between layer" of acceptability for such materials, which might be tried. That is the attempt to condense and summarize the over-all issues that a group of professionals working together will have to look at—before or after the event. In that case, the reader does have a chance to glean some sort of sense from the whole procedure, to leave out what doesn't apply to him, and to pull out what he may consider useful, and he may even catch the flavor of immediacy that real life with real children, sick or healthy, so uniquely exudes.

The following papers are such materials. They were prepared for use in camp situations, in treatment settings for disturbed children, in staff sessions on group-therapy problems, in school situations—in a variety of locales and projects. The last form to which I adapted these themes was designed for my staff at the Child Research Branch, which I headed between 1953 and 1959, at the Clinical Center in Bethesda, Maryland. The form of the materials printed here comes closest to that last version. To make it easier for the reader, I decided to stick to one

version only and to leave it to his discretion to make the necessary
selection of what happens to fit his set-up and what doesn't.

The following basic data about the framework within which these materials
were last used need to be known, though, in order to make it easier
for the reader to make the proper modifications himself:

> *The staff.* It included psychiatrists, nurses (both regular and psy-
> chiatric), teachers, caseworkers, group workers, clinical psycholo-
> gists, research psychologists, child-care workers with a variety of
> backgrounds and in a variety of roles (including "attendants"),
> researchers, and nurses in administrative roles.
>
> *The children.* We worked with small groups of youngsters at a
> time, youngsters whose disturbances lay somewhere between pre-
> psychotic and delinquent—some of them just plain "borderline"
> —all of them with extreme forms of "aggressive acting out" as
> the bases of their behavioral trends. Their ages ranged between
> eight and fifteen, and we worked with both boys and girls, de-
> pending on the "part project" at any given time.
>
> *The setting.* We worked in a closed children's psychiatric ward
> (research operation), supplemented by a wide-open cottage on
> the same grounds. We conducted a rich activity and recreation
> program and our own school, and some children attended public
> school regularly. Individual psychiatric treatment through regular
> "therapy hours" with each child was combined with a heavy dose
> of "life-space" interviews and the usual accouterments of psy-
> choanalytically oriented residential group therapy of a kind not
> too different from that discussed elsewhere in this book.

It is this kind of staff living with this kind of youngster in this kind of
setting that should be kept in mind in reading and understanding the
"linguistic shorthand" I use in the subsequent stories.

It is unavoidable that, at points, the reader may strongly disagree with
what we did or recommended, but we hope that he gives us the benefit
of the doubt and, especially, that he recognizes that some things had
to be the way they were because of specific situations and specific kids.

Much of this material, I hope, may convey enough of the special flavor of
the context to which it was all meant to apply to help the reader in
making allowances without damaging his understanding of the issues
at stake. For in spite of the unavoidable limitations of a "here and
now" operation, what is basic in the handling of kids and their lives
ought to come through.

Just What Am I Supposed to Observe?

$\mathcal{W}$HEN YOU ASK US this question, we are tempted to answer it by saying: Anything and everything. For, you know, sometimes the 'littlest' things, which seem quite unimportant or silly when they happen, turn out to be important clues to our understanding of a youngster later. And, more often than not, a lot of 'small,' seemingly unrelated observations, when put together with others, suddenly begin to make sense—but we could not have known that at the time when we made them."

You are right, though, when you object that this is a big order. You'd feel much better if we at least steered your observations in a few directions or if we at least would let on to just what *might* be the type of thing that is visible and also important in the lives of our youngsters. Therefore, we submit to you here a list of items that may be worth keeping track of. But don't let it overpower you. Before you even look at this list, read the following suggestions carefully.

Suggestions for Keeping a Behavior Log

Try to remember the various incidents that happened during the time you were on duty, and think of each child involved in them. Then put down those that seem revealing to you in terms of any one of the things mentioned in the list below.

Try to put your observations down as much as you can in the form of "anecdotal incidents." Only specific and concrete descriptions will help you later in your planning. General phrases, swanky terminology, or all-comprising judgments leave you high and dry. (For example, note the differences between saying "Johnny got mad, his face got all puckered up, and he picked up a piece of clay with a threatening

[333]

gesture toward me but finally put it down and didn't really throw it"; and "Johnny had a sudden outburst of agression but controlled same"; and "Johnny seems to suffer from hyperagressive drives.") Try to put down your anecdotes in such a way that the "feeling tone" of an incident is preserved as much as possible.

Do not get panicky when reading the following list. It is not meant to be complete, and we are sure you can think of a number of things that aren't on it. On the other hand, many of the things listed will often not become visible with a particular child or may not fit him at all. This too is not your fault but is to be expected. This list is only meant to stimulate your imagination about what *might* be worth looking at if it happens. Whether these things do happen or not with the children in your group no printed list can predict.

Whenever in doubt about where any given observation belongs, put it down somewhere anyway, and worry later. Please raise questions that plague you any time they come up; the staff whose job this is will be all too eager to help you along.

The List of Things to Observe

Here is the list of things that may be worth putting down about each child.

ATTITUDES TOWARD ADULTS

What is his relationship to you as a person? How well does he accept you as a leader? Does he act toward you realistically, or do you have the feeling that he sometimes acts toward you as though you were somebody else: his own mother, father, teacher, and so forth? Under what circumstances is he smoother to handle? When does he become unmanageable? Does he feel sure of you or in constant fear of losing your affection or attention? Is he jealous and antagonistic toward others about his relationship with you? How does he react toward your praise, your criticism? How does he try to show you that he likes you, that he hates you? By what techniques does he try to "pull a fast one on you"? How does he try to atone if he feels he has acted wrongly? What does make him feel guilty toward you? What behavior on your side seems to make him feel guilt-exempt? How long does your influence over him last? Does he develop relationships with other adults on the ward? What are they?

ATTITUDES TOWARD OTHER KIDS

How well does he get along? What are most of his conflicts with other boys and girls about? Who are his pet friends and pet enemies and on what basis? How constant or changeable is he in his personal relationships? Does he enjoy being with others, or does he prefer hanging around alone? How do the others react to him? How popular, ignored, or rejected is he and in which respects? Who is he especially afraid of, keen to be admired or liked by, jealous of, and so forth? How defensive, ready to share, or suspicious is he in connection with his property and special privileges and so forth?

GROUP ROLE AND ATTITUDES TOWARD THE TOTAL GROUP

Is he liable to assume or desire any one of the following group roles: leader, second-in-command, clown, teacher's pet, bully, isolate, rejectee, scapegoat, ringleader, model boy, organizer, and so forth? How does he act in case of group pressure, group acceptance, or group rejection? How jealous is he of his place in the group, or does he care? How much does his room mean to him? Or the whole ward? Is it just a place with so many people milling around? Under what conditions does he develop more intensive group pride, ambition, or group feelings?

ATTITUDES TOWARD ROUTINE AND DISCIPLINE

Which part of the daily routine functions most smoothly with him? Which seems to bring about most friction and difficulty? How well does he function, on the surface at least, under more flexible or under more organized routines? How accessible is he to reasoning and in which areas? What in him would you appeal to, to be sure to get his cooperation? What types of punishment is he obviously afraid of? What types does he expect? What types would he suggest to inflict upon others? When proved wrong, does he take it or become morose, sulky, or try to pass it on by being mean to others? Whom does he accept corrections from with better grace—the adult leader, certain other children, or "the group"? About what does he get into "trouble" most easily?

INTERESTS AND AVERSIONS

What things does he say he likes best and least? How do they compare with actual attitudes you have seen? On what levels does he satisfy the various interests he mentions in his questionnaire? What are his main aversions and areas of avoidance? How long or short are his interest and activity spans? How constant or changeable are they and how persistent or influenced by others?

SPECIAL STRONG POINTS

What would you consider his finest traits and his biggest assets? What special skills does he have? What characteristics has he that would make his company pleasant to others—adults, children? What are the things within him that you feel you can rely upon and build on in your own work or in a future educational program? Mention knowledge, skills, intellectual qualities as well as social charm, emotional characteristics, and personality traits. In which areas of his life does he function most "normally" and healthily, at least if given a chance?

PROBLEM TRENDS REVEALED

What do you consider his main difficulties, the weak points in his organization, his areas of greatest confusion and most inadequate functioning? Under what conditions are these weaknesses more emphasized or more in the background? Which of them can be modified by outside influences at least temporarily? Which of them seem to resist all interference and to retain their original strengths in most any situation? Give anecdotal illustrations of behavioral incidents, exemplifying the traits you mean.

THOUGHTS, FANTASIES, FEARS

What ideas, opinions, and attitudes has he verbalized at some time or other about himself, the world, God and religion, and so forth? Does he daydream a lot? Do you have a clue to the favorite contents of some of his daydreams? How realistic is he in the things he says and does? How far does fantasy seem to motivate him more than what actually happens around him—in which area? Does he show any special beliefs, superstitions, apprehensions, anxieties, or idiosyncrasies? Which are they? How persistent? How accessible to quiet reasoning? Does he show fear of the dark, of ghosts, of bigger children, or of fantastic dangers? Is he "anxious" in the presence of some adults, in small groups, in larger crowds, when summoned to perform even before friends and so forth?

HEALTH AND BODY ATTITUDES

What are the actual assets and handicaps of his body? In which respect is he underdeveloped, overdeveloped? Is he aware of either? Is he oversensitive about danger of certain illnesses? Is he lackadaisical about health habits or even reckless and contemptuous of them as so much "sissy stuff"? Does he show special embarrassment or fear about nakedness? Is he especially concerned about any part of his body or inner organs? Which minor or major ills does he try to hide, to lie about, or to exaggerate and brag about? How much does he know about body development, health, and sex? Does he talk about them? What are his main points of ignorance or distorted ideas?

BACKGROUND INFORMATION

What can you glean about his home, school, and neighborhood "background" from what he says or from the way he acts when visiting day comes along? What feelings does he express toward father, mother, siblings, teachers, "the school"? What life events does he talk about? What early childhood memories does he mention on occasion? Is he keen or indifferent to receiving mail? Does he get homesick easily? How does it show? What helps him get over it? Does he verbalize plans or ideas of what will happen when he gets back? What is the attitude of people toward him as guessed from the way he talks? Does he utter any strong attachments or enthusiasms that might be exploited in postward planning?

What Is There to "See" About a Group?

WE HAVE GONE over the categories of "things worth observing if they occur" as far as "individual behavior" goes. Now we ask you to pay some extra attention to "group-psychological observations." You are right if you ask how the heck is that different from the first list? What do you mean when you say "group" anyway? Does a "group" ever "behave"? Isn't it always one or three kids who do something, which would go on their individual behavior sheets? All these questions are perfectly justified. We shall deal with them in detail as we go along. It is too long a story for a short "memorandum." For the time being it is sufficient to remember these things about "groups":

It is true that it is always "individual kids" who do the "behaving" (or misbehaving). But some of what they do is just interesting for their own sakes—other things they do have terrific impacts on the rest of the gang. *Example.* Sometimes Johnny sits there and mumbles to himself, makes faces because he has a tic, and then starts doodling on his desk. As long as nobody much bothers about what he does, this behavior is interesting only for his own "behavior log." In contrast, remember the case in which Johnny starts clowning just at the moment when you want the whole group to quiet down and listen to an announcement you want to make. Remember what trouble you have if Johnny is a good clown and all the rest of the group "echoes" his silly antics? In the second case, you still have "individual behavior" on your hands, but this behavior is highly "group relevant." And that "echo effect," in which all the kids pick up something one of them has started, is definitely a "group-psychological observation."

Sometimes you get on that ward, and somehow or other the whole place feels "tense" or "resistive," even though you would be hard put to say just what it is that makes you sense it. It certainly isn't anything special that Johnny or Lily did. At other times the kids are much more "at ease"; they don't jump on one another for the slightest reason; in fact they are quite cheerful and were full of enjoyment in that game they played. It is hard to say just why. Now, we may not know why, but we certainly can sense and describe such "moods" of a whole group or such "group atmospheres." You couldn't possibly put it down on any one kid's behavior log, but it is there just the same. Here is another illustration of why sometimes we call things "group-psychological observations" and how they are different from what would go on the individual "behavior log."

The trouble is sometimes you won't know where it goes. In those cases, don't bother; just put it down anyway. It is more important to have an observation down than to be sure it is labeled correctly. In many cases, however, things are so clear you won't be in doubt.

The following is a list of things that might occur and would go into your group-psychological observation sheet. It is neither complete nor too well picked; it is only a start. Also, just as in the case of the "individual-behavior log," remember, this list is meant only to stimulate your imagination as to what might be worth looking at if it happened. Whether it happens or not in your particular group on a specific date is beyond this outline.

The Emergence of Group Roles and the Role Distribution on Your Ward

We have already mentioned such group roles on the individual-behavior log—we wanted you to see whether or not Johnny showed tendencies always to act as leader, organizer, second-in-command, scapegoat, rejectee, isolate, mascot, clown, leader's resource, leader, pet, idea man, tone-setter, ringleader, rebel, and so forth. Now we want you to forget about Johnny or Mary and to look at your "group" and ask yourself which of these roles are more or less represented, who is in them, and which are not there at all. Of course, these "roles" may not be clearly developed at all. Sometimes remember also that what you see during mealtime or bedtime may not be so at all on the playingfield or in the dayroom, so try to nail such roles down to the activities and times of the day when they become most visible. Warning: Don't put just anything a kid does down under "role"—he has to show such behavior consistently in the same situation for his role to deserve that label.

Group Mood and Group Atmosphere

This point has already been sketched in the previous illustration.

Try to watch "group moods," especially as they differ and vary around certain routine or program situations. A group often is quite different upon waking up or getting showered or at breakfast, lunch, dinner, or bedtime routines from when it is on the playground, in a council meeting, in the arts-and-crafts room, on an outside program, or in that station wagon. It is important to notice strong mood switches of this sort. Sentences that can be used to describe such group moods or "atmospheres" might sound like this: "The group became very disorganized, and a lot of senseless 'bickering' replaced its previous enjoyment of the game." "When I walked into that ward today the place seemed to seethe with some kind of tension, and it was to be expected that some excitement would 'blow' soon." "During this council meeting the youngsters seemed to be extremely punitive toward one another—the slightest disagreement immediately set off hostile remarks; whoever was even a little out of line was immediately jumped on by everybody." "After all that excitement the group was amazingly peaceful and quiet." "They rallied around the story reader right after putting on their pajamas, and, without much effort on the part of the adult, there was a feeling of peaceful 'kids around the fireplace' enjoyment of family atmosphere in the air." Such descriptions are anything but "scientific," but they will do for the time being. It is important that you try to catch this elusive item of "group mood" and "group atmosphere" as best you can, in the language that seems to convey it most adequately.

Group Code and Deviation Tolerance

The kids on a ward soon develop a sort of "behavior code" all their own. It may or may not coincide with what the adults think should happen, or it may even be in open conflict with our own standards of behavior. But it is a powerful agent in their lives and should be noted. This example may show what we have in mind: Take a classroom of normal and nice sixth-graders. They are reasonable enough to know they are in school to learn something, and they are decent enough to know that, after all, the teacher is only doing his job and helping them. They are also basically happy children who do not really want to be antisocial or delinquent. Yet even in such a group you will find that they often operate on the basis of a "double standard." The youngster who acts too "eager beaverish," even though he means well, will soon be jumped on for being a "teacher's pet" and ostracized. The youngster who is too sheepishly obedient to the teacher's command will be denounced as a "sissy," and the kid who may cooperate in the teacher's demand that the group admit who stole Mary's sandwich will be rejected as a "squealer" or "tattler." This means that behavior that is quite okay on a general basis of morality may still be obnoxious in terms of the "code" of the group.

In short, by "group code" we mean the question of just "what goes and what doesn't go" in a group, seen from the worm's prospective of the kids themselves, not by us adults. The best way to find what "code" is really in operation in a given group is to ask oneself the question: What does a kid earn prestige for with the other kids, and what, if he did it, would make him lose face or could induce them to call him a "sissy"? What, if he did it, would the other kids be really mad and indignant about? This also goes for some of the program activities. In some groups of kids it is perfectly okay for girls to rough-house and for boys to like to cook or sew. In other groups those very activities would be resented as severe breaches of the acceptable standards set for males and females in the eyes of the children. In some groups a bad pitcher is just a kid who is clumsy, but that is all there is to it. In other groups, a kid who doesn't know how to pitch loses so much face he becomes the butt of everybody's contempt in no time.

Beside an attempt to find out just what the code of a given group really is, it is important to gauge their "deviation tolerance." By this we mean the degree to which they allow other group members to be different or to which any deviation from their code makes an individual immediately an outcast. For instance, in some camp cabins a bedwetter is spared cruel razzing by others as long as he doesn't bother them too much. In other groups, the mere fact that one child has a problem the others don't immediately becomes a sore point and an excuse for scapegoat torment. By the same token, some groups pay no attention to the fact that one or two kids are somewhat late for breakfast or slow in packing up for the cook-out trip. In other groups the slightest negligence of a time routine immediately evokes group pressures for revenge, punishments, and fines or is followed by prolonged teasing, ridicule, and indignant reproval.

It is clear that the degree to which children are or are not tolerant of one another is quite highly dependent on the way the adults behave, and this will be an important item in our discussion of group leadership and treatment. However, regardless of our efforts, children frequently bring the group codes and intolerances of their native habitats with them. It is important to know what they are and how they manifest themselves, so we can plan what to do about them. By the way—most of this cannot be seen directly but "becomes transparent" from the way the children act over a stretch of time. Also most of this the children are not consciously aware of themselves, so they could nor "tell" you if you asked them about it. In fact, direct questions often evoke vehement denials rather than the real truth. Most of this, therefore, has to be "gleaned" from daily observation by us, the observers.

Group Tastes and Group Aversions

Different groups really often have their peculiar preferences, likes, dislikes, even "allergies" toward people, routines, and program activities. These tastes and aversions often become properties of a whole group and may be quite contradictory to the tastes and aversions of one or the other individual child in a group. It is important to get some picture of each group while they are with us, of what these tastes and aversions are. For instance, which phase of the program does it, as a group, really like best? Dislike most? (Watch the exclamations when you suggest a program activity at a council meeting or when the children read it on their schedule.) Which routine situations do the children seem to "take in their stride"? Which do they consider mean inventions of bossy adults? Which activity, no matter what they *say,* do they really get a lot of fun out of? Which activity, even though demanded by them, does fall flat very soon and does not really gratify their needs? Which toys and props are the most coveted, the most ignored, the most fought over?

Group Manageability

This is an item that, in conventional parlance, is often submerged in the term "discipline." What we have in mind is the fact that sometimes a given group really varies a lot in terms of the ease with which it can take a situation "in its stride" or the degree to which it needs constant interference by the adult to keep it going. This may be true for cleanup but may be just as true for a game. Questions to be raised in our minds pertaining to this item are "Which of the day's routines seem to go relatively smoothly—not counting, of course, Bobby, who is sicker than the others—and which other life situations or routines seem to call for constant interference or produce one blowup after another even in kids who are not supposed to have such tempers?"

"Which activities or routines can they plan independently or carry out with a minimum of supervision; which others find them soon helpless and in need of adult aid and support?"

"Which game leaves them reasonably happy and manageable afterward; which other game, although it goes swell as long as it lasts, leaves the group with a great amount of explosiveness, restlessness, or downright mischief on members' minds?"

"Which of the life situations seem to allow reasonably good feelings between me and the group—even though I did have to take that knife away from Tommy—and which other life situations seem to set the whole group against me no matter how reasonable or friendly I remain?"

"This specific group—just what do they think up and do if they get out of hand?" All groups have moments of "control breakdown" or "disorganization" or "resistance," but what they *do* when they break down or get disorganized or resistant, may vary quite a lot.

Subgroup Formation and Contagion Clusters

One group often breaks into smaller subgroups. Such subgroups may be openly hostile cliques that fight and exclude one another, or they may be quite peaceful toward one another; it just so happens that some of the kids hang around one another more than around others. Occasionally there is a "lone wolf" in the pack or some kids who don't really belong to a subgroup, but they are considered members of the group without question. It is important to know this and also to watch on what basis such subgroup formation occurs. It makes a difference whether Mary, Liz, and Ida are constantly found together because they like to play dolls together or because they feel that the whole group doesn't really like either of them and doesn't "let them in on things." It also makes a difference whether Bobby and Ted pal up to the exclusion of anyone else because they are really good friends, because they are hatching plans of domination over the rest of the gang, because they both think the adult is unfair to them, or because they think they are smarter or dumber than the rest. A more organized study of such "subgroup formation" is called a "sociometric." It is important to observe as much as you can without worrying too much how precise it is or how accurately worded.

Your Own Group-Gratification Chart

You are, of course, part of the group. As the adult, you are most frequently in somewhat of a leadership position—what that implies, we shall discuss later. In your role as group leader, it is important that you become more and more aware of what you are really doing and how you yourself feel about it. None of us can possibly really "like" all the things we do with the kids in a day's time, though, of course, we are good sports about it and don't let on most of the time that we aren't too happy about having to kiss Bobby's turtle goodnight. At the same time, we also find some phases of our work with a given group much more enjoyable and we look forward to them.

It is important to ask yourself questions like these: Which moments of life with this group do I feel most comfortable with? About which of them do I feel I don't really quite know how well I am doing? Which activities or routines do I really dread (but what can one do after all but go through them)? In which activities or routines do I feel most like constantly interfering "or things will go wrong"? About which of them do I have the confidence that things will go all right by themselves, as long as I just keep around? Which behavior of the group makes me cringe, even though I know it is "just one of those things"? Which moments in group life seem the most gratifying and sort of make me proud or pleased or just "tickled"? What strikes me as "funny" about this group? What as "cute"? What do I consider disgusting, impossible, and I wish they'd snap out of it? What really makes me angry so that I have trouble sticking to my "professional self"? And what makes me feel like hugging the whole bunch or buying the kids a candy store? Which of the program ideas I have can I really be enthusiastic about? Which of them do I dislike so much that the kids notice, and, of course, I have trouble then getting them enthused about them ever. If I had to do it all over again, which are the things I did or that happened that I would want repeated the same as they were; which would I want to handle differently or avoid altogether?

We do not mean that you should make a complete "self-analysis" of your own feelings about this group and your work in it each time you record. We do think it is important, though, to make such self-scrutiny from time to time and to note striking self-observations for later learning. And, most of the time, there is nothing wrong with feeling this way or that way, as long as we learn how to handle our feelings before their effects reach the patients. And there is no better way of learning that than by being clear about those feelings to begin with.

How Do I Know When I Should Stop It?

Remember the Four-Notch Scale

THE ISSUE is not "being permissive" versus "being punitive." It is rather choosing among the following four notches of possibility.

PERMITTING

Some behavior, even though uncomfortable to the adult, must be frankly permitted, and no maybe about it.

Example. In fingerpainting, it is perfectly okay to make a messy picture; it doesn't have to look like anything. Or in this joint they don't mind if you yell a lot during a running game.

TOLERATING

Some behavior must be tolerated, but the kids need not have the illusion that it is what we really want in the long run.

Example. Thieves in a treatment home know they won't be kicked out for having swiped something again, but they have no illusion that "Fritz permits us to steal."

Among the most frequent reasons for "tolerating" behavior are the following.

Learner's leeway. They have to have a chance to make mistakes while learning to spell, play, and so forth.

Age-typical behavior. A little kid has to be let crawl for a while, even though eventually we expect him to walk on two feet. Preadolescent kids have to have a chance to run around unscrubbed for a while, even though eventually we want them to learn better grooming.

Behavior that is symptomatic of a disease. They have to cough as long as they have chest colds; they have to throw tantrums as long as they are that sick; and so forth.

Strategic tolerating. Sometimes we tolerate something that we will later want to take issue with, simply so the kid doesn't think we are the same punitive bastards he had trouble with before or in order to avoid his purposeful distortion of our interference as "personal rejection."

INTERFERENCE

Sometimes behavior has to be interfered with. There are many ways of interfering and many degrees of insistence on stoppage, all the way from "signal interference" to bouncing or holding.

PREVENTIVE PLANNING

Sometimes behavior can be avoided ahead of time by planning a program, routine, policy, or whatnot in such a way that the misbehavior to be expected won't be necessary.

Example. We have often avoided the kids' running all over the place at the destination of a trip by building up in their minds more concrete expectations of the game they are going to play and by having props and game ideas all ready when they get there.

None of these four "notches" for interference is in itself better or worse than any other. To find the right combination is the real issue at stake.

Why Do We Want to Interfere to Begin With?

Here are criteria for whether or not to interfere.

Reality danger—to the kid or others.

Protection against psychological hurt (stopping the gang if its members get too merciless in their teasing).

To avoid the production of too much excitement or too much anxiety and guilt (protective interference against their own hyper-impulsivity).

To arrest a contagion chain (what this one does now isn't too bad, but, boy, if they all start in on it, then what will I do?).

To protect property (building, equipment, toys, props, from a certain point on).

To secure ongoing program activity (sometimes a group needs to be protected against having its activity or interest interrupted by a kid who is "high").

To "mark" an issue. In this case we interfere, not because the behavior in itself would be too dangerous or disturbing, but because interfering is the best way of pointing at a policy, value issue, rule, or whatnot that lies beneath the surface behavior.

Examples. Propriety areas of behavior (at the dinner table this does not go); interpretation of routines and rules; debunking delusions of omnipotence ("I am going to tear this joint apart and nobody can stop me"); demonstrating fairness and equal treatment of all (as all of us have to take turns, I cannot let you sit here now just because you want to); rubbing in the ceiling for the intensity of behavior (you can bounce the ball around, but you can't recklessly throw it at windows, lights, people, and so forth); forcing the real McCoy out into the open (one kid rushes madly at another kid out of rivalry excitement, and in this case you feel the ensuing fight will do nobody any good, that it is better to stop him and talk the real trouble over with him subsequently, whereas at other times you may feel it is wiser to let them "have it out").

To avoid conflict with the "outside world," to protect innocent bystanders and to protect public relations. Certain things are stopped if done to strangers in the elevator, which you might have tolerated toward yourself on the unit and so forth.

To protect your own inner comfort. Our own comfort is not the first thing that counts. Many times when we feel certain behavior makes us uncomfortable, the conclusion to be drawn is not that it has to be stopped but that we have to learn to be less uncomfortable with it if we want to treat this type of child. There is, however, a margin beyond which our own discomfort should not have to go. If it comes to that margin, it is better to stop the kid than to remain passive but start hating or avoiding the kid himself.

All these reasons why we may decide to "interfere" may be more relevant to some situations than to others. Obviously, we do not consciously go through all these steps each time we stop something. So much of the skill to figure what should be done becomes automatic, like a reflex, after a while. Whenever we have reason to doubt that a given action is wise or that we should do something else, this list of criteria for interference may come in handy in replanning our general course of action or in analyzing a given incident.

This Time We Should Not Interfere—But Why?

THE DILEMMA of the child-care worker often is that the child does something that, according to our list, certainly is among the things that ought to be interfered with. But under the special circumstances he is not so sure. After all, life is flexible, and it looks as if he ought to make an exception this time. In short, "I really would like to stop this. However, I think there is a good reason why, under the circumstances I better let it go by."

Question: Can I predict for what reasons you will most often find yourself in that predicament? I sure can. Here is a list of the most frequent ones.

Priorities for "Establishing Relationships"

This point takes in relationship either between the child and you, or between the child and the whole "outfit."

Examples. A new kid is obviously expecting you'll go berserk over what he does to provoke you. At a later date you might very well stop this behavior clearly right then and there. This time you figure it is more important that you gain ground with him, so you let this or that go by for awhile.

We have just made a rule: No comic books can be taken to school. We notice Tommy slip one in his sweater. We know, however, what interference will do to his feelings toward us and every other adult for the rest of the morning. It ain't worth it. Let's rather wait and see what he does and maybe interfere later.

The Fuss It Would Create Isn't Worth It

Sometimes the secondary confusion, aggression, and so forth that your interference would create would disturb the ongoing activity for

[349]

the child or the group beyond what interference at this moment is worth. In this case you would rather "let it go by" for the time being. This, of course, does not hold if the behavior is actually dangerous.

Examples. The kids are having their "stunt show," which they have worked up to for a long time. One of them, for a number of reasons, is getting way out of hand, and actually, under other circumstances, this might be a good occasion to stop it all and have it out with him in a life-space interview. Today, however, it would mean the whole thing would blow up for everybody. Obviously in that case it is better to try and keep things going as best you can, even though the one "gets away" with plenty.

The same principle is sometimes a counterindication for bouncing and issue rub-in of all sorts.

The Daily Interference Budget Is Already Brim Full

There is a limit beyond which interference, no matter how kindly and skillfully handled, has a negative effect. A kid can benefit from just so many "incidents" a day. If that budget is full, further misbehavior may have to be kept within certain limits, but clear-cut issue-marking interference is counterindicated.

Example. One kid is "restless" in a class or during TV today. You have already made several interference gestures and appealed to him several times. Again he starts crawling all over the place—he doesn't do anything more extreme than what you stopped him for previously, but he continues in the same vein. You begin to realize that "today he just will be restless, that's all" and give up further interference unless things get much worse.

You'd Better Wait Until It Is Clear Enough for Him and All to See

Sometimes *you* may know that, unless you stop this now, you will have more trouble later. However, you also know the kid (or the others) does *not* perceive his present behavior as anything worthy of being interfered with. He would just misinterpret your interference as hostility. So you wait until he gets a little bit more outspoken in his antics, so he too, when finally interfered with, has to "admit" the justification for your interference—at least soon after.

Example. Danny starts working himself up into the kind of mood in which he soon will pester the others enough to start a fight. You know you could stop this by bouncing him right now; it would save a lot of trouble for you and the group. However, Danny, at this early phase of his provocative antics, has no perception at all of the natural chain of events to follow. He would perceive your bouncing him as sheer unjustified attack. In that case, you had better let it get worse, enough so that anybody, including Danny, in a subsequent hash-over of the situation, would have to see that interference was clearly justified.

You'd Better Let Him Take the Consequences and "Learn from Experience"

Sometimes you figure that interfering too much doesn't give the kid a chance to "come to grips" with reality or the social consequences of his behavior. How can he ever learn that the other kids won't tolerate his teasing if you never let him do it long enough for them to retaliate? In that case you may purposely let some trouble brew, in spite of its discomfort for you and the mess it will create, to secure a learning experience or a chance to make it into one through the subsequent life-space interview.

Example. We have often discussed the dilemma we are in with Danny: We have to protect him from some of the consequences of his sado-masochistic taunting. On the other hand, don't we want him also to see what he does, and how is he ever going to see it unless we let him be exposed to some of the retaliation he gets? So from time to time we decide: This is a fight that should be had, even though of course we could foresee what would happen and could have stopped it.

Watch out for this one, though. People do *not* automatically "learn from experience," especially not our kids. The ground for this experience has to be laid very carefully; it has to be handled very hygienically, or no "learning" at all will result.

You Missed the Right Timing

By now things are too gummed up, and you had better forget about it. Sometimes you have a "beautiful incident," which, when interfered with, could lay wonderful groundwork for a rather fruitful life-space interview with the kid. But something else happens to mess up the ground for you, so you may just as well let this one go down the drain and wait for another opportunity.

Examples. One kid has been building up to get another kid infuriated for quite awhile. You have sort of "ignored" it, to let it become clear enough for all to see. Now he really goes too far, and you are just turning toward him to interfere strongly and make an issue. Unfortunately, by now his victim too has reached the breaking point. He throws a milk bottle at the kid and hits him square on the nose. Now throwing a milk bottle in the middle of the meal is a much more clear-cut "offense" in anybody's books than hard-to-demonstrate "taunting." So by now your kid has a wonderful prefabricated alibi against any argument you might want to raise about "unjustified taunting." You may as well realize it is too late to stop his taunting or for subsequent issue-making. You had better just handle that fight.

A kid has been "working up" to rather open defiance of your requests in a straight line but has never quite made it, has always stopped his defiance just in time. Now finally he carries through with it. He does grab that baseball bat you told him to leave alone and hops over the couch to try and get you to chase him. You have reason to know that strategy demands in this case that you "do something about it." However, just then somebody yells "Dinner's ready." The kid drops the bat and runs to the dining area with everybody else, and an entirely new "structure" surrounds the group. You may as well know that the timing to make an issue of the whole previous chain of mounting defiance is all out of joint. So cool off, forget it, and wait for another chance to come to the real point.

Part of a Pathological Episode

He couldn't do anything about it anyway, with or without your interference. You may as well ride it out. This is especially clear for obvious sickness-related symptomatic behavior: You can't stop a kid from "twitching" and so forth. We also know that, once a tantrum gets into a certain stage, it has to run its course and that all behavior directly connected with it must be free from interference or issue-making, except for the usual prescriptions of "hygienic holding" and the like.

Sometimes the pathology-related nature of a piece of behavior is not quite so clear, so we may be in doubt for awhile. Whenever we have reason to assume, however, that this behavior now is part of the kid's "basic pathology," our interference criteria make a strong shift.

Example. Some of our kids, when anxious or panicky, have a way of running, hiding, and flaunting our demands to stay put and are seemingly out to "provoke" us. Some of this behavior looks so much like the real McCoy of taunting that it took us time to tell it apart. Yet, the moment we know that this time Doug is not really "testing our power" but is hit by a whole chain of compulsive panic-assuaging and magic temper-containing rituals, our course of action will take a different turn.

You Are Just in Too Good a Mood to Get Serious About This Now

Remember we definitely said that our own feelings do not have priority. Decisions whether to interfere or not have to be made on the basis of what the patients need and what the situations and over-all treatment strategy require, not on whether *we* would feel better by doing one or the other thing.

This principle of the professional use of ourselves still holds. But, as with everything else in life, there is a limit. We said about interference that sometimes what the kid does will get you so scared or mad you will have to withdraw from him or hate him unless you stop it. In that case stopping him is the lesser of two evils.

The same principle holds here: Sometimes you are in such cheerful spirits or enjoy the "cute humor" of a situation so much you couldn't possibly be forcible enough or "nonphony" enough in a serious issue-making, no matter how hard you tried. Then maybe it is better to let the kid "get away with it" than to try to create an artificial issue you couldn't keep up anyway.

Note of warning: This, however, is only a temporary principle. If it happens too often that we "have to permit" against our better judgment or that we "have to interfere because *we* got too upset about something, no matter what the real issue," then this means we had better start doing something about our own feelings if we want to work with and help this type of child.

Example. One of my thieves at camp combined with his pathology such an amazing skill in turning on "humorous charm" and displayed such acrobatics of technique at handling *me* in an interview that I would sit there fascinated, studying the techniques used against me with so much enjoyment that I couldn't possibly manage to put on a clear enough front of concern about his bad behavior to make it stick. It got so bad I had to ask somebody else to do the "rub-in interviews" or "preadmission grilling" with that youngster. I think this was a better solution than if I had "tried" at that time. I couldn't have done well enough with such an expert diagnostician as an opponent.

All these nine issues related to "counterindications for otherwise justified interference" are to be taken as flexibly as the "criteria for interference" in the previous paper. If in doubt, do what comes naturally, and analyze afterwards, for use in the next incident.

Framework for Our Discussions on Punishment

I CAN'T WRITE A BOOK on punishment this week, and even if I could it would get too voluminous, you wouldn't read it anyway, and it would still not answer the concrete questions raised by day-by-day events. I might be tempted to suggest you have a look at what I wrote about this topic before, especially in *Controls from Within* and "Discipline in Classroom Practice." But it would also be a waste of time, for in these pages I had to argue with too many people from too many different backgrounds all at once by long distance, and, as I couldn't assume that they all had some experience with the type of kids we are surviving with, such as you have under your belts, I couldn't hit the issues there as close to home as I would have liked.

On the other hand, most discussions about what punishment might fit a kid or a situation at the residence this week have a tendency to get bogged down in the complexity of basic principles, therapeutic concerns, clinical theory, or the usual battle about people's private taste buds for life in general. Sometimes we even get caught in the sheer web of multiple meanings of terms—it happens in the best of families.

The following materials have one purpose only: to secure our important discussions about punishment from some of the pitfalls such discussions are known to get into and to hold before our eyes the basic principles involved in thinking straight about punishment issues. For, in my opinion, those principles as they apply to clinical work with disturbed kids are crystal clear, no matter how entangled their application to a situation here and now may become. In short, don't expect from this paper an answer to your question whether or not—or how—

Portions of "Framework for Our Discussions on Punishment" are found in "The Concept of Punishment," first published in *Conflict in the Classroom,* edited by Nicholas J. Long, William C. Morse, and Ruth G. Newman. © 1965 by Wadsworth Publishing Company, Inc., Belmont, California. Reprinted by permission of the publisher.

one of your kids should be punished when and if. For that decision, there is no substitute for concrete case thinking and situational analysis. No paper could do that trick. But I hope this one may draw out of the complexity of our concrete concerns the basic principle that should guide our actions and put it on the table as an issue in its own right.

Lest We Forget

Sometimes I am under the impression that it seems to us as though decisions about the use of punishments in the life of our resident kids constitute an entirely new angle and that we have to start all over again trying to find out just how one would search for answers in a concrete situation.

Fortunately, this is only partially true. Sure "punishment" introduces a few angles that the other "intervention techniques" we have discussed in so much detail over the years do not contain. But there is plenty in it that will be quite familiar once we give it closer scrutiny, and I think we can shorten our discussion if we remind ourselves what thoughts and doubts we have already been through. While I am at it, I might as well list some of the most frequent traps that I have seen discussions on punishment fall into in my previous life, so we can save ourselves some detours on the road.

First, punishment discussions have an amazing tendency to lure the participants into arguments about "permissiveness" versus "control." This is nonsense and a waste of time. The two topics are issues of separate meaning, each one important in its own right. "Punishment" is *not* a synonym for "control." It is only the name for one of several dozen techniques of *imposing* control. Whether or not and when permissivenes is indicated and whether or not and when controls should be planned we have always recognized as among the most important practical questions. They should be answered on their own merits from case to case. Whether or not "punishment" is indicated in a given case as one control technique preferable to the seventeen-odd others we have discussed in our training sessions is a question of entirely different scope. We may sometimes reasonably want to raise both these questions, but let's deal with them separately, for they are not the same.

Second, punishment is not a "more severe" interference in child behavior as such. The general layman's view, often enough creeping into professional discussions too, is that there is something like a line from "mild" to "severe," that "rewards" are on one end of the line and "punishments" on the other. Therefore, when challenged to defend an issue of punishment, most adults either find themselves apologetic and eager to assure us that they still mean well or are awfully "proud" of being tough rather than "soft." This is pure nonsense. Whether a punishment is experienced by the child as "severe" or not depends on a lot of things, and a "mild" form of intervention, like an attempt to motivate children by holding out rewards, can send some of them into a tizzy of fear that they might not get them, which certainly would be rougher on them than having to spend ten minutes in their rooms. If you still have doubts, remember the strong point we have always made in favor of holding a kid if he is really off his noodle and of assuring you that such intervention, if well handled, is not only not bad for him but may be the very thing he needs most to get over his fury and fright. Yet what goes on while I sit on a kid who tries to sink his teeth into my wrists for ten minutes is surely rougher and is felt by the kid as a more "severe" form of interference than if I had said to him, "today you go without your dessert." So severity-versus-mildness is no issue at all as far as defining the basic nature of punishment is concerned, and let's not waste any time on it.

Third, whether or not a given punishment "worked" or not must never be evaluated on the basis of surface behavioral effects alone. As with all the other techniques of behavioral intervention that we have discussed in so much detail, in the case of punishment too, the assessment of whether it worked or not must be judged, beside the immediate surface effects, in terms of the following questions.

What is going on simultaneously below the behavioral surface?

Example. Some kids seem to take their punishments "well" and go obediently to their rooms when asked but use their time in isolation for smoldering work-ups of their old delusions about the hostility of the world around them.

What are the "postsituational" side effects?

Example. Some kids go to their rooms all right, when chucked for longer periods of time, but they also develop tastes for passive daydreaming and lose their appetites for more healthy but behaviorally more risky normal recreational activities.

What is the affinity of the reaction produced in the kid to the basic treatment goal that we are after in a given phase of therapy?

Example. In a public school for delinquent kids in Detroit, they decided to allow the kids to smoke during intermission, even though there is a state law against it, which had to be reckoned with. The sole reason for this move was the recognition that they could never develop feelings of trust between kids and teachers if the first thing a teacher had to do in the morning was to frisk the kids for smuggled cigarettes when they came in. The punishments they had used for such smuggling before were relatively mild, but even so they gummed up the works for the major task of producing attitude change among kids toward school personnel.

How intact is the "ego equipment" a kid has available to cope with a punishment experience of a given kind?

Example. We may want to "teach the kid a lesson" for messing up in an activity by chucking him for the rest of the day. But if that kid is still in a state in which the "future" means nothing to him, in which he doesn't even perceive the benevolent intent of our action, or in which the mere sight of other kids playing while he is alone in his room stirs up unmanageable quantities of sibling rivalry in him—or if he is so restless and panicky that he can't cope with the anxiety produced by being in a room alone with not much else to touch but his body—even the most friendly and seemingly reasonable and well-deserved punishment of this sort ain't going to "teach" him anything at all. In all the cases in which we are tempted to argue that a given punishment ought to "teach" the kid a lesson, it is well to remember that no "teaching" takes place when the kid is not yet in shape to "learn."

What is the "contamination index" of a given form of punishment for a given kid? By this I mean that some punishments may seem all right from every possible angle we can think of, including those already mentioned here, but they may still be all off, either because they stir up the wrong things from the kid's past history or because they hit him too hard in terms of specific sensitivities of a given developmental phase he is in.

Example. For some kids, withdrawal of food, a relatively mild form of punishment in a setting like ours, would be wrong simply because food situations stir up much too much of the old mother-baby problem the child still hasn't coped with. Or having him sit it out in his room after he has been overexcited in a game and mad anyway may seem, on the surface, a pretty sound idea. But, with some adolescents the spectacle of being sent there by abrupt adult command, with the other kids looking on, becomes a matter of intolerable loss of face. In both cases, an otherwise reasonable form of punishment form is out because it is, for those specific cases, contaminated, either by the kids' past histories or by the specific developmental processes that are going on in them.

Fourth, the effect of punishment in a residential-treatment situation always should be calculated simultaneously on two entirely separate levels: What does it do to the individual involved, and what implications does it have for the life of the group? This, too, isn't a new speculation at all. It is not peculiar to "punishments" but is an issue of great relevance for all intervention techniques. I have called it in other places the "principle of marginal antisepsis," and we have been following it in all our discussions without bothering with a name for it, all the way from questions of routines, room assignments, and table and station-wagon arrangements to the selection of toys and arts-and-crafts props, to the planning of projects in woodshop or school, the question of bouncing from the dinner table, and even the question of just how much special affection or attention one counselor can give a child at a given time.

To find the right trick that does justice to both the individual impact and the group effect is not an easy task, and often enough we know that whatever we do will be better suited to the one than to the other angle. Yet we have always been eager to anticipate as best we can what the possible negative effect in the other direction might be, in order to take countermeasures and handle the spillover when it occurs. The underlying principle, however, remains unchanged, no matter how hard it may be to find the right procedure in a given case. To spell out my "law of marginal antisepsis" in somewhat more detail for whatever it may be worth: An intervention technique, well designed to meet the needs of the individual, should at least be "harmless" in terms of its effects on the group, or at the worst it should not produce more negative group effects than we can handle. Conversely, an intervention technique, well designed to meet the needs of a group, should at least be harmless in terms of its effects on the individual involved, or at the worst it should not produce more negative side effects for that individual than we can take care of.

In the complexity of life in a treatment home, the term "harmless" must, of course, be read with considerable leeway in mind, but this leeway has its natural boundaries. We have had many such discussions, especially around the issue of "bouncing."

Example. Unless Jon is bounced now, the program in school will go all to pieces, and the other kids are getting too much out of it to let that happen.

On the other hand, we had better provide for good coverage for Jon after he is bounced, so that somebody is there to take care of him and if possible even to help him make sense of the incident. Or, in the case of a new group, it is probably easier on the others if I bounce this one right now— and there is no problem so far as he is concerned because Phil is right out there and will take care of it all. However, I had better also remember that I need to spend some time with the group that is left, helping it see what we mean when we bounce a kid in this place here. Otherwise they may well misinterpret our basic attitude toward learning and toward kids or might develop "halo" or "scapegoat" reactions to the bounced kid when he comes back. This same principle, which has increased the complexity of our planning in so many other issues of our residential life, is just as valid when it comes to the discussion of punishments.

Example. Punishing a kid who raises hell at the dinner table and refuses, with great and publicity-eager glee, to cooperate on his room-cleaning project by excluding him from the work project next Saturday may seem a pretty good idea at the moment, especially if we know that the rest of the group won't want to have its earning capacity curtailed. So it might well be a measure fit to "get the rest of them in line." But what are the after-effects going to be with the kid in question, especially when we are so happy that he finally has gotten around, after many years, to developing a healthy interest in and some satisfaction from "work" at all? As a side piece to our illustration: A kid has been teased, mauled, and scapegoated by the group all day long, and we haven't been able to break into it very well yet. They are all high at the table now. Finally, this very kid throws some food around, and we figure he'd better "take the consequences" for a change. We have handled this kind of thing by all sorts of technique, including simple bouncing, long enough with him. Maybe this time he ought to find out that there can be worse consequences for his behavior. So we tell him we have had it. As he can't respond to anything, he had better stay home tonight; he can't go along on the shopping trip. Other things being equal, such a situation may well arise and, under some circumstances, may not look too bad as far as the kid is involved—we can handle it with him in a life-space interview after the other kids are gone. But how is the group going to take it? Isn't it just what the kids wanted anyway? Can we cope with its triumphant rub-in of his predicament, or will it perhaps consider our own swoop-down on the kid a blank check to "give it to the bastard" even more? Or is the group going to be happy to be rid of him for that store trip and maybe somewhat pacified by the idea that he got it from the adults anyway? Or, just to vary the theme a little, what if keeping kid A home involves a problem of muscle availability and means the rest of the group will have to be deprived of the trip just because of A?

In summary, tough as it may be on us, let's never look only at the effects of punishment on the group or *only* at the impact on the individual kid involved. Any one given form of punishment may be good or bad for either at the same time.

Let's Make Sure We Are Talking About the Same Thing

I have seen discussions on "punishment" lure even the most sophisticated and professionally trained discussants into the most obvious confusions through the simple accident of multiple use of words, more so than around any other topic I can think of. Although I don't at all intend to come to grips with the real problem of a "definition" of punishment that would fit both the value aspirations of the educator and the subsurface sensitivities of the clinician, I shall simply willfully define how I am going to use the term throughout this discussion. By the way, you don't have to agree at all that this is the way the term should be used, as long as we use it in the same meaning in all sentences or state openly whenever we think we have reasons to change the tag.

The colloquial use of the term "punishment" is very wide indeed. You can hear people say that their cars "took a lot of punishment" on that rough road; you may even hear me say, half humorously, that I sure deserved the "punishment" I got the other day for playing too exciting a game with such crazy kids just before bedtime. And most people will assure you that you had better know what "punishment" you will take next morning if you have too many drinks the night before. It seems then that, colloquially, we may use the word "punishment" to refer to any unpleasant consequence either that we have brought upon ourselves or that "destiny" or "mother nature" has visited upon us because we didn't respect her basic laws.

Coming closer to our topic, we also find the colloquial use of the word "punishment" includes most anything that people may do to kids that hurts them, apparently no matter what it is or what their reasons for doing it. Many adults refer to the beatings they give kids because of their own nasty tempers and lack of patience as "punishment," even though what they do is nothing but having temper tantrums of the worst sort. Or we may find adults "getting even" with kids for the discomfort they cause, on the principle of an eye for an eye, and calling that "punishment" too. In fact we may notice that adults have a tendency to say they "had to punish Johnny" just because they didn't know what else to do or found it easier to discharge their own fear or fury at the time and "couldn't think of anything else" at the moment.

It is important to admit that it is only natural for people to act that way when they are scared, unhappy, mad, helpless, desperate, or uncomfortable. Especially the feeling of being "helpless" and of not being able to communicate with a child seems to produce a lot of "punishments." In fact, it is my own impression that more of the really unnecessary or silly punishments occur not so much because a particular adult doesn't like kids or rejects a child but because he can't bear finding himself helpless vis-à-vis a problem he doesn't know how to tackle.

In short, in colloquial usage, adults have a tendency to call any behavior of their own that is designed to hurt in some form or other "punishment," provided a kid is on the receiving end of it. It is obvious that such wide use of language is totally inappropriate for professional purposes. We shall therefore in this discussion *not* use the word "punishment" for acts that are quite clearly outbursts of adult anger, vengefulness, or temper, in which the adults give vent to their own problems, using the children as props and trying to use the label "punishment" for a flimsy excuse. Not that we don't admit such behavior might happen to the best of us. All of us, I am sure, have caught ourselves at least in fantasies of "getting even" with kids who make life so hard for us or have acted so nasty just before. The temptation to sock a kid who spits us out of his room after we have come in with the best of intentions to communicate and who returns our saintly kindness with hatred and abuse must have tickled our muscle centers more than once. Yet had we given in to such temptations, which would be understandable enough, the right label for our behavior would still remain: "loss of temper," "getting even," "power showdown," or whatnot. It has nothing to do with what I am going to use the label "punishment" for in this discussion.

As educators or clinicians, it seems to me, our behavior toward children deserves the name "punishment" only if it is done with a clear-cut goal of helping the child. It is always a means to an end and is always employed for the sake of the basic welfare and growth needs of the individuals involved. Whether or not the actual punishment administered under this policy is correct or helpful, is stupid, mistaken, wrongly handled, or backfires in its intended effect is not the point when we first try to define our terms.

It is equally obvious that the use of punishment implies an attempt to produce an experience for the child that is unpleasant. It is based on the assumption that sometimes the affliction of an unpleasant experience may mobilize "something" in a child that gets him to think or change his behavior, a change that, without such a "boost" from without, would not occur. Tying together these two aspects of punishment, viewed in the tool cabinet of the professional educator or clinician, we might arrive at the following definition, which I think serves our purpose for the time being.

I refer by the term "punishment" to a planful attempt by the adult to influence either the behavior or the long-range development of a child or a group of children for its own benefit, by exposing it to an unpleasant experience.

The inclusion of the statement that it has to be a planful attempt for the children's own benefit excludes all simple outcroppings of adult sadism, bad temper, or personal vengefulness, as well as the use of the child as a prop to assuage one's own anxiety. The statement that all punishment aims at using the production of an "unpleasant" experience in the child marks this intervention technique as different from others. It also raises the crucial question that underlies all speculations about the wisdom of punishment as a tool in a given case: Just what is there to the underlying assumption that producing an unpleasant experience in a child is going to help him rally better to reason and control than he was able to before? For this is obviously the only assumption on the basis of which any educational or clinical use of punishment makes any sense at all.

Analysis of the Punishment Experience

"You can lead a horse to water, but you can't make him drink." This age-old saying is rather trite, but many a punishment discussion I have been in would have benefited had this been written in bold script on the blackboard before it started. For what counts most in punishment is not what we do to the kid but what the kid does with the experience to which we have exposed him.

WHAT HAPPENS WITHIN THE KID
IF THINGS GO WELL?

First, the kid experiences the displeasure to which we expose him. This "displeasure" can be the loss of a privilege or pleasure he took for granted or the exposure to something that is unpleasant or even "painful" in some way or other—or both. For instance, I can take away his dessert, I can sock him one, or I can insist that he stay in his room while he hears the others playing outside.

Second, whether or not the displeasure takes the form of frustration or pain on some level, it is bound to produce an upsurge of anger in the child. This anger may not be conscious, nor does it have to be strong. But it is normal for the human to react to frustration or pain with an upsurge of fury.

Third, the kid clearly perceives, at least after the first few moments, the difference between the source of his predicament and its real cause. The source of his predicament is obviously the adult who inflicts the punishment or the institution that makes him do so. The cause for his predicament, however, is equally obviously his own previous misbehavior, for otherwise the adult would not impose the punishment to begin with.

Fourth, the kid now directs the anger produced in him by his predicament, not against the source of his trouble but at its cause: He gets mad at himself and realizes he could have avoided all this had he only shown more impulse control and wisdom in his actions to begin with.

Fifth, he does, however, not only get a little "mad at himself"; he transforms this self-directed aggression into energy that can be used for his own benefit. By "transforms" we refer to a process by which what was originally personalized fury or self-hatred can be changed into neutralized energy available for a multitude of more sublimated ends.

Sixth, he uses this energy, drawn from his fury about his predicament, for two purposes: to force himself to regret what he has done and to force himself into a sort of "New Year's resolution" (I'll sure not be dumb enough to get myself into a situation like this next time).

Seventh, in a future temptation of similar kind, he can make use of the image left from the previous incident and can mobilize self-control *before* the act. The previous punishment experience has not only helped him toward better insight but has also left him with increased energies for temptation resistance.

These, basically, are the steps every kid goes through each time a punishment experience to which he is exposed is "handled well" by him—even though the steps are, of course, not really experienced clearly in the process. They are the conditions for constructive use of a punishment experience by a child.

HOW DO WE KNOW THIS CAN WORK?

It would be easy, with this outline in hand like a "map," to predict exactly just what could go wrong with the way a kid handles his punishment experience and what conditions must be met within a given punishment plan to make a successful ending most likely. It would be easy, but it would take me an estimated eighty pages to do it, so let's skip it for the time being. Let me select what seem to me the five most crucial items in this picture, leaving a dozen or so just about as crucial ones unmentioned for now.

First, from what we know about the kid, is the specific form of displeasure we select for a given punishment likely to be used by him as an incentive for concern, or is it either going to roll off him without impact or throw him into a tizzy of irrational response?

Examples. Some kids prefer to sit in their rooms and masturbate anyway, rather than to participate in competitive games with dubious results for them. Chucking such a one won't even be experienced as punishment, no matter what name *we* may want to give the procedure.

A real good moral masochist *loves* to feel sorry for himself and to nurse his grudge against the world that has "done him wrong." Most punishments do not hold much displeasure for him, and what little they hold he turns into self-pitying delight or juicy gratification of perverted needs.

Being sent to stay in one's room as punishment for some misdeed or other might, in itself, be a good "displeasure dose" to rattle a given kid into more thoughtful self-appraisal. But if we send him back while his neighborhood gang is just coming to pick him up for a ball game, the things we say are likely to make any self-respecting and emancipation-hungry teen-ager cringe with unconquerable shame.

Some kids are "allergic" to being alone in a small room. Being sent into one for punishment produces unbearable panic in them. They are allergic to this type of experience, so you can't use it on them no matter how well they may "deserve it."

Second, from what we know about the kid, is he going to be able to differentiate between "source" and "cause" of his predicament under the impact of the specfic punishment experience that we have provided for him? If the answer to that is "no," then we had better save our- selves the trouble. The punishment won't work, and whatever mo- mentary benefit we draw from it will be badly outweighed by the nega- tive side effects.

Examples. Very little children do not have such discrimination well de- veloped yet. A small kid, bumping his head against the table, is likely to turn around and hit the table in revenge for "what it did to him." He is in- capable of differentiating the source of his trouble (the contact with the table) from its cause (his own clumsy movements and not looking where he is going). Some older children regress to that level under the impact of displeasure or pain. If that is so, punishment has no chance to help.

Some people are quite capable of making such distinctions, but they don't *want* to make them. It is much more gratifying to hate the cop who gives one the ticket than to admit one wasn't driving as one should have. Espe- cially kids who are still in the grip of concerted efforts to view adults as hostile and to deny their own participation in the events of their lives will construe any experience of displeasure as a "personalized wrong coming from a hateful opponent," rather than considering it a challenge to revise their own styles of life. As long as they are in that stage, even the most clear-cut form of punishment is going to backfire.

Third, from what we know about the kid, is he going to be able to turn his aggression in the right direction under the impact of the punishment experience? By the "right direction" we mean, of course, toward that part of himself that makes him misbehave, instead of toward the punishing adult, the institution, the world at large, God, the universe—or the kid in the upper bunk.

Example. Some children are quite capable of knowing and admitting that they were in the wrong and "deserved what they got." Yet their egos are still totally incapable of coping with any amount of frustration or aggres- sion in constructive ways. Therefore, even when they are correctly mad at themselves, they will have to pour their fury on the people and things around them, or they will simply explode into orgies of diffuse and frantic aggression discharge. This is especially true for our type of kid: Even at the stage when he begins to feel guilty for what he does, as we hope he eventually will, he still has not developed enough ego skills to cope with guilt feelings adequately. So, even though kids know they are at fault themselves, their aggressions are still poured on the world outside them. As long as that is true, even otherwise well-planned "punishments" are of no avail.

Fourth, from what we know about the kid, is he capable of sifting and transforming the anger we produce in him through our punishment into the type of energy that can be used for increased insight and self-control? Among all the puzzles, this is probably the most serious one. For even if the kid gets correctly mad at himself instead of at the administrator of punishment or at the institution and its laws, the crucial question still remains: What is he going to do with the fury he now directs against himself? For the fact that aggression is turned against himself alone is not enough. It depends very much on just what he does with the aggression he turns against himself. Unless the "sifting-and-transforming gland" for internalized aggression functions well, a kid is not going to benefit from punishment received. "Sifting" and "transforming" refer to two separate tasks. By "sifting" I mean that the kid's ego must be able to decide just how much should be discharged as a waste product. Some kids, for instance, discharge all of it as a waste product—none of it sticks and is internalized. Others can't allow themselves any "waste-product discharge," so the full brunt of their anger is turned against themselves, which means they are flooded with much too much repentance, discouragement, and self-accusation. The normal kid has "glands" that operate well that way: When punished by an adult he can vent *some* of his anger by mumbling under his breath or slamming the door, *some* of it by a quickly produced "revenge fantasy against the punishing adult," *some* of it by diffuse discharge motions—restless pacing of his room, rough manipulating of a ball, and so forth—and only the right amount is then sent to the transformer to be turned into internalized energy for self-insight and self-control.

Example. Some kids know that they are to blame, but if the punishment, pain, frustration, or already-existing proclivities toward guilt are too strong they simply get paralyzed by their repentance and regret, drift into orgies of self-accusation, or end up feeling no good, incapable of ever amounting to anything, or not worthy of the adult's love or their own self-confidence. In such cases all the previous steps in punishment have worked well, for the kids should admit they are wrong as they do, and they should get mad at their own bad behavior as they do. But they go too far and in a totally ineffective way. For simply being mad at oneself is no good, unless one has the energy to do something about it.

Some kids get angry at themselves, as they should, but they puff out this anger in waste motions rather than in increases of energy available for self-control. That means they punish themselves by "slip" actions and "accidents," by losing their favorite toys, by breaking their prized possessions, but they cannot use their anger at themselves for more impulse control. No matter how "repentant" they seem in their immediate reactions to punishment, they are as helpless as before at the next onslaught of temptation. Whenever things are wrong with the sifting and transforming machinery in the kid's ego, a punishment experience cannot be benefited from.

Fifth, from what we know about the kid, is his ego in good enough shape to cope with the complications of the "time element" in punishment? In my estimation, the misfiring of punishments that are otherwise well designed because of this very factor of timing is the most serious trouble source in educational, as well as in clinical, practice. I guess I had better lay this one out in a little more detail. By "time element" I mean three entirely different issues, all of them, however, equally crucial to the constructive use of punishment by a child.

PUNISHMENT EXPERIENCE AND THE OFFENSE

Public opinion is wildly confused on the relationship between offense and punishment. It either assumes that the two should be in high proximity, so that the child will not forget what he is being punished for, or that they should be far apart, so that the "basic issue" has time to sink in and the adult has enough time to check on guilt and issues of justice and to get his machinery in motion. As is frequently the case, there is a kernel of truth in both extremes, but neither of them is it. Reality is more complex than either theory would like to have it.

In life with our children we have learned that there is great importance to the issue of timing, but whether proximity or distance is of the essence depends on many items in each case. Some kids' awareness that they did something wrong—or even of what they did—evaporates so fast that the punishment hits them after awareness has entirely evaporated. Then the displeasure felt during the punishment experience makes little sense and is likely to be perceived as rank meanness of an irritable adult rather than as punishment one has "deserved" for something one "did." On the other hand, some kids' "offenses" are entangled in so many issues, soaked with so much affect, anger, confusion, delusion, and so forth, that no punishment experience has much chance to do its trick, unless the confusion is untangled first.

Knowing this much about the ego of a kid will make it clear that certain forms of punishment that create complications in the time relationship between punishment experience and offense are by that very fact counterindicated.

THE TIMING OF EXPOSURE TO THE PUNISHMENT EXPERIENCE

The timing of exposure is of crucial concern. Some of our kids, for instance, might well "understand" that they deserve to be chucked to their rooms and might be able to "take" that part of it without distortion of the real facts, at least on occasion. The question to be asked next, however, is clearly what will they do with themselves while exposed to the punishment—staying in their rooms, paying for damaged items out of their pocket money, staying home while others go on a fishing trip, and so forth?

Many children's egos are not in good enough shape to take the time exposure involved in a given punishment. Then specific forms of punishment are counterindicated, no matter how good they may look from all other angles.

Public opinion, unfortunately, is caught in a hopeless confusion on this item too, which causes no end of trouble even in professional discussions on the issue. For it has assumed a fixed relationship between length of exposure and seriousness of offense. For a little offense in the swimming pool, one might assume that a kid should be chucked maybe for just five minutes. For a bigger offense, maybe it would be "fair" if he were told to stay out for two days. Well it may be "fair" all right, but what effect will it actually produce? As long as Johnny sits there watching the other kids splash around happily while he is sulking about his predicament, though still under the impression that he "had it coming" because of the freshness of the memory of what he did, all may be fine. The moment the self-perception of what he did has evaporated, though, the experience assumes an entirely different shape. From now on it is not "Too bad I had to get myself into this trouble" but "see, that bastard waterfront guy lets all those other kids have their fun; it's only me that doesn't get a break, hell with *him*."

In short, the psychological weight of a time issue has to be weighed on psychological scales, not on judiciary ones, and the psychology of timing belongs among the trickiest issues I can think of.

IMPACT ON FUTURE EVENTS

By "timing" we sometimes refer to the fact that the real test of the efficacy of a punishment lies in the question of whether or not a kid can make use of what he learns from it in the next temptation situation. Its major effect is hopefully its impact on future events. This, however, means no less than the question of whether or not a kid can learn from experience at all, especially from an unpleasant one. And beyond this, whether or not he can not only "learn" a lesson from the experience but also rely on his ego to supply him with the necessary control energies to make use of what he has learned when the next crucial moment comes around.

It ought to be clear by now that this is quite a lot to be expected, and I can't help being amazed time and again that adults are so naïvely anticipating all the time that a few little punishment tricks do not show such long-range effects. The question of whether or not a given kid has it in him to "learn" from a given punishment experience is an important one to assess correctly. For punishment, contrary to popular fantasies, does not teach a thing unless the recipient is in shape to do the learning. In the case of kids with severe ego disturbances, it is clear that this is one of the reasons why we should not expect much help from the punishment department. The ability to tie up a well-interpreted experience from one's past with an equally clearly perceived experience from the present and, on top of that, to mobilize just the right quantity of energy for self-control and send it in just the right control direction is obviously a test that a messy ego is likely to flunk. Yet the use of punishment in the present makes little sense unless we have some expectation that its impact can be utilized at some moment in the future.

In summarizing this issue of the "time element," we want to assess just how well a kid is likely to do in all three aspects: Can he take the time relationship between a given offense and a given punishment without getting confused? Can his ego sustain him for the duration of the punishment experience with all the specifics a given case involves? And is there a chance for some future usability of the experience to which we expose him now? If the answer to any of these questions is "no," punishment isn't worth the effort we put into planning and suffering through it, to say nothing of the complications in the lives of the kids.

The Problem of In-Situational and Postsituational Support

At this point, I hear you moaning: "Are you trying to tell us that punishment is as complicated as all that? What ever happened to the idea that it was a 'simple' technique, sort of clear cut, and very concrete, and much more 'definite' than most of the other intervention techniques we talked so much about?" The answer to that is: Yes. That's exactly what I am trying to convey. The idea that punishment is a simple, clear-cut technique belongs in the chapter on optical illusions. What the adult does in an act of punishment may be as simple and clear cut as a kick in the pants. What the kid does with this experience and how he reacts to it are anything but simple and clear cut. They involve the most sensitive and vital organs of his psychological self, as I have just tried to show. In this respect, punishment is much more comparable to a case of surgical intervention than to what you see happen when the guy at the delicatessen slices that salami for you with a sharp knife.

Unfortunately, I have to make it even more complicated, especially when we think of punishment in relation to a disturbed child. The prevalent thinking of the layman still puts most effort into finding the "best" form of punishment and having the educator impose it on the child—and from there on he expects the effect to be sort of automatic.

Fortunately, we already know better than that. We know that even a well-planned play experience for a child may need constant support during the time when the child is exposed to it or may need some postsituational follow-up. This principle again is not new. Remember the time we spent, not only on figuring what game should be selected in the evening, but also on just how to give the kids the support they need to live through the game successfully once it gets under way. Remember how important we felt it was, not only to hold a kid when that became necessary, but also to help him get through this experience without misinterpreting it? Remember how important it was to stick around all through his tantrums, even after we didn't have to hold him anymore, just so we could catch those moments when he needed or was ready for some activity he could hang onto and use to pull himself together again?

All this is as true of "punishments" as it is of other experiences in our children's lives. Our responsibility is not ended with the decision to chuck that kid into his room or to tell him he has to pay part of the damage he has done to the other kid's toy for the next two paydays. The safeguarding of the right *effect* of a punishment experience is a job that continues as long as that experience lasts, and the real help to make sense out of it all often occurs much later in a postsituational exploitation of the kid's reaction to it. Whenever we figure on any kind of punishment for our kids, therefore, it is important to plan just as much for situational and postsituational support as it is to decide what kind of punishment should be tried to begin with. Even a well-designed punishment will backfire badly if for some reason we are not able to give the kid the support he needs to go through it without distortions and to "learn" from it what we want him to learn. With the act of punishment our work with the kid on this issue does not end. It only begins.

In fact, sometimes we may even want to design a punishment experience primarily with the hope in mind that it will rattle the kid enough to allow us to have a better strategic "in" on the kid and the problem we want to help him work out. In any case, as much work by us with the kid is needed in punishment cases as in any other form of intervention. If you ever think of using punishment in some situations because it "saves trouble" or makes things work more simply, you'd better give that daydream up in a hurry.

Loose Ends for Sale

The "analysis of the punishment experience" with which I just bothered you is not meant to be a photograph. Only a map. It makes no pretense at answering your question of just what to do. It only tries to point out a few salient points you will run into if you get into this terrain. The task of discussing the various possible forms of punishment and their potential implications for our six individuals, for them "as a group," and for us is more than I can tackle now. But I may have space—and hopefully some of your patience—left to brush lightly past a few issues that I remember having come up in our staff discussions off and on.

RESTITUTIONAL RITUALS UNDER THE LABEL "PUNISHMENT"

The usage of the term "punishment" being as loose as it is, we often discuss under the same label situations in which we demand that a kid "make up" for a hurt he has inflicted or a damage he has caused. The form this restitution takes may vary. We may insist that he at least "apologize" or show he is sorry, we may want him to clear up the mess he has caused and that inconveniences the other kid in his cabin or room, we may demand partial payment for damage done, and so forth. I personally do not like to see these arrangements thrown into the same pot as punishments, for they have only a small part of the process in common with them. But I won't quibble about words at the moment. Suffice it to remember that such procedures are actually much more rituals for the restoration of the individual to the grace of the group or of his victim, including attempts to help him come to peace with himself. There are three major goals we have in mind when using this technique.

First, we may want to help the kid get the taste of some consequences of his behavior and at the same time offer him a way to do something about it that is apt to reinstate the *status quo*.

Second, by giving the kid a chance to "make up for it," we also help him to reduce his guilt feelings and to restore the previous relationship between him and the person or group against which he has offended.

Third, we also make it easier for the victim of the kid's misbehavior —be it individual or group—to "forgive" him, to terminate the victim's own wrath against him, and to stop whatever revenge measure the victim in turn might have in mind. We sort of offer the victimized kid or group members a pound of his psychological flesh as a premium for "forgetting" what has been done to him or them.

It must be obvious by now that this technique has a number of great advantages and may well be used at times to restore what had been disturbed, which may be a great relief to all concerned. It is also clear, of course, that this will work only when the offender has some guilt about what he has done to begin with, when he is clearly aware and admitting that he is in the wrong and basically ready to wish it hadn't happened, and when he is himself relieved at the idea of having it all "repaired." The major danger of the technique lies with the kid who not only has few guilt feelings but also defends himself against the development of such feelings by a system of "pay as you go" arrangements. Offering this type of kid too many opportunities to "pay for what he did" is inviting his exploitation of this technique to feed his own resistance against real insight and awareness of right and wrong. Great care must be taken in a case in which such "restitutional arrangements" seem feasible to see that the youngster gets all the help he needs to interpret his own "making up" correctly and that we make no mistakes in the nature and duration of the restitutional rituals we may choose.

PUNISHMENT—SAYS WHO? WE OR THE KIDS?

In our discussions about punishment occasionally we are concerned with whether or not the kids perceive correctly what we are trying to do. In the preceding phase of our residential treatment, when we planfully excluded any form of punishment because we knew the kids weren't ready to benefit from it, we were concerned lest they might misinterpret a benevolent intervention, like holding them during tantrums or taking them to their rooms when they got too excited about a game, and might think it was meant to be "punishment." Occasionally I also was under the impression that some of us felt that maybe it doesn't make too much difference whether we use punishments or not, because the kids will call anything unpleasant "punishment" anyway— including a therapy session. To be sure we don't get caught in this theoretical trap, let me just say a few words about it.

First, for the definition of punishment as an intervention technique and its differentiation from other intervention techniques, the question of what the kids think it is totally irrelevant. Once we define punishment, for instance, as I tried to in this discussion, as "a planful attempt by the adult to influence . . . by exposing [the child] to an unpleasant experience" in order to bring about a piece of insight or a change in his behavior, anything that falls within this definition is punishment all right. Whether the specific form of displeasure I use is correct or off the beam, has good or bad results, has nothing to do with the definition of my technique. Wrongly administered punishment is still punishment and as such is sharply differentiated from other techniques.

Second, confusion through the kids' labeling of what we are doing to them can, however, very well arise as soon as we step out of the strictly semantic area into a description of adult behavior that actually occurs in a given case. The confusion that can arise falls into two categories.

I, THE ADULT, MAY HAVE MISLABELED WHAT I DID

I may, for instance, think I "punished" the kid by chucking him to his room. A sound movie registering my actions, however, might very well reveal that my behavior did not fit my definition of punishment at all. I may have acted with such anger, personal irritation, whimsicality of command, or whatnot that for all practical purposes it was an act of revenge, loss of temper, or irritation, rather than anything else. In that case, the psychological reality to which the kid was exposed was not one of punishment but of adult loss of temper and so forth. If a kid happens to be shrewd enough to be as good on the uptake as the sound camera would be, he is right when he says I didn't punish, I just got mean.

THE KID MAY HAVE MISLABELED WHAT I DID

We sure know from our experience with holding and similar techniques how easily misunderstandings can happen. The use of punishments does not exclude this type of confusion. I may, for instance, have acted in every item totally according to prescription, and any sound movie camera would show that without a doubt. Yet the kid may be totally surprised by this kind of behavior and may not understand its difference from other forms of displeasure, or—and this is what we are most used to—he may have very good reasons of his own to distort the perception of our behavior as well as of its intent as a defense against change. In that case, he will call what we did "punishment," even though it was a perfectly correct psychiatric interview or holding situation. The psychological reality to which he was exposed, however, was still not one of punishment but one of interviewing or holding. The fact that the kid mislabeled it does not change the reality of the situation he was exposed to.

However—and here is where I assume we get together again—it is of course very important for me to know whether we or the kids mislabel what happens. Even if a kid clearly distorts my perfectly benign handling into its caricature and I can "prove" that "in reality" he was not handled in a mean way, the fact that he manages to make himself think so is a challenge in its own right. For the really beneficial effect of any well-used influence technique cannot come to fruition until its full impact and intent are correctly perceived by the kid. The argument in those cases, however, is not that we cannot use such a technique at all but that we have to *add* the attempt to secure a correct interpretation of the experience in the child.

In general it is a good guideline to avoid altogether if possible a technique that, by its nature and because of the pathology of the child, offers no chance even within months to be explained and made understood. On the other hand, it is also worthwhile to start with some techniques occasionally, even though there will still be confusion around them among the kids, and then, by the very caution with which they are handled and by special care in forms of in-situational support and postsituational interpretation, to work at their correct perception by the kids simultaneously. I think we have done a pretty good job of such interpretation on one of the most touchy techniques: physical restraint. All in all, most of the kids now "know" most of the time what we are doing. Our use of "punishments" is still new to them, and this is one reason why I want to use all the caution and care in the world in applying it only sparsely and with special attention to its design.

By the way, there is one more semantic confusion I want to hit while we are at it. That is the difference between "punishment" and "being punitive." It is most unfortunate that the same word roots should have been chosen for issues that are not only so different but also so contradictory to each other. To avoid another long theoretical harangue, let me just state it boldly and see how I can defend it when you challenge me next time: We can never afford to be punitive when we punish. For by the term "punitive" we usually convey the idea of hostility, meanness, lack of concern for the kids' feelings, and so forth. "Mean" or "hostile" would be better terms. From what we have seen about the conditions under which a punishment experience can be well handled by a kid, it is obvious that the exact opposite attitude is essential for a constructive effect to take place. Only if the kid is aware that even in punishment we are not "punitive" but have his benefit clearly in mind, that we aren't doing it because we want to get even with him but because we think it is the only way we can rattle him into the insight and control that he needs just now, is there any chance for the aggression released by punishment to be internalized. In fact, the more "incisive" our punishment, the less "punitive" must the atmosphere be in which punishment takes place. The seeming contradiction here is one of word usage only.

Well, I guess this is it. I have to stop somewhere, and I had better do it now while I am coming up for air. There are loads of basic issues I haven't even mentioned yet, as is all too obvious, and there are lots of "loose ends" that should be tagged on here, like the question of punishment by the group, punishment of a group, the problems of role implications for those in our kids' lives who do or do not have punishment power, and what such role distribution should be to begin with. Not to mention the host of specifics about particular forms of punishment like withdrawal of privileges, "chucking to their rooms," withdrawal of work and earning experiences, limitations on out-of-residence mobility, and so forth, including ones we would never even dream of using like physical punishment and isolation in a locked room.

What Do We Do About the "Facts of Life"?

       QUESTIONS ABOUT THE PROBLEM of handling sex talk, sex behavior, and sex curiosities of the children on the ward seem to be based on observations and thoughts around the issues to be listed in this paper. What is said here about each one is meant to be only a temporary policy guideline of the crudest type and does not even attempt to do justice to the complexity of the real problem and our long-range therapeutic plans. It is not meant to end, but to start, a more thorough and circumspect discussion of the matter.

Is This Still Normal?

What is and what is not "normal" cannot be answered in this short memorandum. Let's remember, however, two things about it.

Sometimes something is more or less "normal," as far as frequency of occurrence in the population at large is concerned. This does not mean, however, that we should let the kids go through with it. The question "Is this still normal?" and the question "Should we permit it?" are two separate issues.

Examples. A kid may have a most perverse sex fantasy and spend time daydreaming about it. His fantasy may be clearly pathological, but this does not mean the counselor should have to bother interfering with it, as long as he keeps it to himself. What to do with this is the therapist's long-range job.

Another boy may have a strong urge to assault sexually a pretty girl he sees. There is nothing "abnormal" about this urge. But it does not mean we let him go ahead and do it.

Sometimes when we call something "normal" or "abnormal," we think primarily of the question how "used a kid would be" to such things happening in his natural habitat versus how much of a "shock" such an event would be for him, judging from the milieu in which he grew up or usually lives.

Example. A youngster pushed around from institution to institution may have been exposed to a lot of sex talk or sex play, which goes on all the time where he lives. By now, knowing of or being mildly involved in such events may be an experience he is well used to and can easily discard; it holds no "conflict shock" value for him and therefore is hardly "traumatic."

Another youngster, although having curiosities or fantasies in the same line, would not expect to see or hear sex interest openly displayed; to be forced into it would constitute such an "unusual" experience that its shock value for him would make it much more of a "trauma" than for the first kid.

The whole question of what is "normal" in sex talk, sex behavior, and sex curiosity among youngsters is an important and interesting one, but our question of what we do about it is not based on labeling it "normal" or "abnormal" but on many other considerations. So let's separate for a while our "normality speculations" from the immediate problem of handling behavior on the ward.

What Can We Do About It?

Sex behavior, like all behavior, is important not only because it has to do with sex but also because it has in common with many other issues that it is overt behavior. So in many ways, the handling of sex behavior is often not primarily an issue of sex but should be viewed with what we have already learned about the handling of behavior anyway. Some of the policies we have arrived at for the handling of all behavior also apply to behavior in the area of sex.

The most important issues in the handling of overt behavior, let's just remember, fall into two categories.

First, the issue is not one of "permission" versus "punishment." We have learned to view all behavior on a four-notch scale: permitting, tolerating, interference, and preventive planning.

In a nutshell the same basic principles we have already applied to handling behavior are also at work in reference to sex behavior. Some of the questions around handling sex behavior are nothing new: what we have already discussed applies here too. The more detailed question—How do we know *when* we should interfere or not, and what are the various techniques of interference?—cannot be gone into at this moment, of course.

How About the "Sex" Part of It?

The questions raised by the staff seem to be concerned primarily with the following types of "sex" issues.[1]

MASTURBATION

SOLITARY AUTOEROTIC SEX PLAY

With the children we have with us now, a considerable amount of autoerotic sex play on varying levels all the way to straight masturbation is to be expected and has to be given an opportunity to occur in conflict-free ways. The concept of "privacy," which we respect in their lives with us in terms of undressing, defecation, and so forth, must be extended into this area. An attempt to make masturbation something that "may never occur" on this ward would be downright injurious to our therapeutic task in other areas of their lives. Therefore, their autoerotic solitary activities should be "ignored." If an adult walks in on one boy while he is engaged in more overt masturbation, he should react the same way as if he had inadvertently walked in on any other of the accepted privacy situations—he should tactfully withdraw. No speeches should be made; no theories or threats or warnings should be pronounced. And there is no need to go out of your way to reassure the boy, for it usually has the opposite implication if done at that moment. The incident should be noted and brought to the attention of the therapist. If there is reason to assume that the activity is of unusual intensity or that the child is conflicted about it, this is a matter for the therapist to decide and handle. Such decisions cannot be made on the spot,

1. The children on whom these discussions were based were between the ages of eight and twelve, and many of the policies suggested might have to be modified for much younger or much older groups.

and whatever handling is needed should have more specific planning anyway.

AUTOEROTIC SEX PLAY IN THE GROUP WITHOUT SEDUCTIVE INTENT

Sometimes children of that age play with their sex organs or indulge in rhythmic masturbation equivalents while they watch television, read comics and so forth. This too is to be "ignored" as far as the kid is concerned, as long as it is not drawing undue attention from the others or does not become an indirect excitation stimulant to the group.

GROUP AUTOEROTIC SEX PLAY WITH SEDUCTIVE INTENT OR AS "ADULT-TAUNTING"

In these cases, the adult needs to intervene. In the first, it is usually enough to tell the child to stop acting up like this, the implication being "leave the group alone" and "don't bother the others." In the second case, it has to be handled like any other group attack upon adult authority, depending on the degree and clarity with which it has become an issue. If the situation gets out of hand and leads to the ringleader having to be stopped more firmly, then a subsequent life-space interview with the counselor should clarify to the youngster again that "we cannot let you get the whole group wild and misbehaving just because you feel like it," and it has to be handled as any similar incident would be handled if the adult-taunting were on a clear aggression basis.

OPEN MASTURBATION IN THE GROUP AND MUTUAL MASTURBATION

With the children we have with us now, there is no reason why either should be tolerated. The children need to know that "we cannot let them do this," and we shall stop it when we see it happen. The implication with the first one should be thrown on the fact of its unacceptability right out here in the group with everybody around and having to watch you. The second one should simply be stopped on the basis of "this we cannot let you do" and is an obvious chance for the therapist to pick it up in an interview. The same policy holds for finding the kids in bed with each other in obvious sexual stimulation or making coitus movements, even though semiplayfully, or manipulating each other's sex organs, and so forth. This behavior has to be stopped. Do not get involved in arguments about why—they know and don't expect you to permit it. Don't argue about who started it or "we were really just playing, we weren't doing anything." They know the score on that one too. Simply insist quietly but firmly on stoppage, as you would with any other activity that had gone out of hand.

SEXUAL ASSAULTS UPON ADULTS

This behavior too needs clear but unexcited interference. You do not have to worry that our children will misinterpret such stoppage as lack of affection or friendliness on your side. They have so much opportunity for harmless and friendly mauling and wrestling with you that they know darn well themselves when they go overboard. Your firm warding off is in the long run a relief for them, even though it may lead to scenes or interference struggles at the moment. Sometimes, with a new child, you may be in doubt how much of this behavior is "naïve" and "well intended but clumsy" friendliness or when exactly it begins to fall into the other category. You have done well to be very patient with this, and you have been so overcautious not to hurt their feelings for so long that you do not have to worry any more at this time. You, too, by now have usually a very clear notion where the dividing line lies with a particular kid and can rightfully trust your judgment.

SEX LANGUAGE

EXPLOSIVE USE OF OBSCENE VOCABULARY

Explosive swearing is frequently not really a matter of "sexual assault," even though the vocabulary used may fall into the sex category linguistically. It often happens when children get excited, mad, frustrated, or panicky and has little direct intent toward you but is rather the sudden discharge of aggression or fear. With others, it is primarily a reflection of customs in their natural habitats, which they unwittingly imitate and use in excited states. As long as that is all there is to it, a lot of it should be simply ignored, especially when it happens in the midst of a tantrum, an interference struggle, or the excitement of a fight or a game. If it gets out of hand, it may be wise for somebody to have a life-space interview with the kid about it at some other time when he is in good shape and well related. On occasion, an undue mounting of this phenomenon might have to be handled in a group interview by somebody in a team-leader role or may be taken up with the kid by his therapist, as the occasion arises.

ASSAULTIVE NAME-CALLING

Assaultive name-calling, although the same words may be used, is really a horse of an entirely different color and has to be interfered with.

Sometimes kids get to the point at which they use it for planful taunting, paramount to hitting you, or they express their total defiance by putting you into the role of the contemptible sucker who can be ordered around as the whim dictates. Although you may not mind such insults personally, once they assume this flavor they must not be accepted. Being "tolerant" under those circumstances does not help the children and is not interpreted by them as a special sign of your affection and patience. On the contrary, it makes them feel helpless against the onslaught of their own wild impulses, seeing that nobody helps them in self-control. Groupwise, tolerating of sexually assaultive taunting is especially liable to lead to increased wildness and excitement and to a lowering of everybody's level of control; it becomes a signal for more collective outpourings of extreme and destructive behavior. The form of interference in such cases depends on the questions whether or not you are alone with the kid; if in the group, whether or not the rest of the members are aware of the behavior; whether or not it still is primarily a problem between the kid and you, even though the others are around; and, of course, how far gone their excitement is by now.

Specific advice on just what to say and do cannot be given in this paper but can be worked out in discussion from case to case. Often it is enough to repeat with firmness but without anger that you do not like to be talked to that way, though it may take several repetitions before it sinks in. By no means do for them what they ask you to do under these circumstances. If a kid says, for instance, "Get me another sandwich, you bitch," do not comply. I suggest that you say something like "I'll be delighted to get you another sandwich, but there is no reason for you to call me dirty names, and I don't like that." Further action depends on the kid's reaction to that one. Sometimes, in lighter cases, it is advisable to ignore for the moment some of the assaultive name-calling but to take it up with the kid soon after in a "postsituational aside" and make the point that you do not like him to talk to you that way and that there is no need for that kind of thing.

DIRTY JOKES

A certain amount of this kind of story or talk is unavoidable with our children and can be ignored. It is important, however, to intervene as soon as it looks as though you will be pulled into it as a partner. Our children need to know that some of this can be "tolerated," but it must not appear as though it were an adult-led program.

SEX QUESTIONS

It is impossible to condense a handbook on sex education into a few lines. Here are only the most urgent tip-offs in answer to your recent questions.

Some questions about sex simply need "short-order answers"; that's all that was wanted to begin with. Do not consider each question about sex as an indication that a long and exhaustive lecture or interview on the topic is indicated. This is especially true when they ask sex questions while busy with arts and crafts or at meals or other group activities.

Some questions about sex are meant to probe for more details or are confessions of ignorance or curiosity, but this is not the time to ask them. In that case, give them a short-order answer, but tell them that you will be glad to give them more details later—right now really isn't the time for a prolonged discussion. It is not true that children interpret all postponement of details as punitive ward-offs. They are perfectly capable of sensing the honesty of your intent. They have had so many punitive ward-offs in the past that they recognize one when they see it.

Some sex questions only look like sex questions; they are actually attempts to taunt you or are comparable to other ways of starting group-cohesive mischief against the adult. A short-order answer, if it is a real question, followed by a clear ward-off of the subsequent "dirty-talk bull session" is indicated. If even the question is already clearly a taunt, because they know that you know that they know, then you just tell them, "I know you know that anyway, so come on, let's get that plane painted now" or whatever the case may be.

Some sex discussion is a mixture of real questions and group mischief; it is usually couched in personal terms. In that case, promise them information on the general sex issue they have brought up, but pull it off the personal plane. You need not get into a discussion of your personal sex life or your sex experiences, nor do you have to answer questions like "Are you a virgin?" and so forth. A frank and honest approach to sex education does not imply a reversal of the interview table, and warding off curiosities about your personal life does not mean being "old fashioned and evasive about children's natural curiosities about sex."

In cases in which the kids seem to press you for more elaborate sex information than you feel should be given by you at the moment, it is often a good way out to tell them that you "know that Dr. X. (the therapist) will be very glad to give all the information" they want as an additional reassurance. Needless to say, for our records and for the therapist, all sex discussions or questions, including the "mischievous" ones, are important to keep track of, and it all needs to go into your records in as much original detail as possible.

Sometimes, I have known staff to be overly afraid that they might betray hesitation, embarrassment, or insecurity to the children when warding off a sex question at a given time. Do not worry about this. These kids live with you day in and day out, and the basic attitude and style of life that you establish with them can very well carry a few moments of insecurity or even counterindicated behavior.

How Good or Bad Is It to Get Angry?

POPULAR THEORIES about getting angry, like most of the "common sense and proverb" stuff, all have kernels of truth in them but so mashed up it isn't funny. It is easy to debunk them all.

The fact that anger scares kids may be quite okay. As long as the fear is well handled, comes in mild doses, and is well geared to reality, it can be a help to a child. But which anger scares him just the right way instead of producing panic, fury, counteraggression, or a feeling of being hated and no good? Ah, there's the rub.

Children may think adults don't like them—who says so? If anger is well modulated, clearly related to issues, and produced by a person who is otherwise known to love them, kids are perfectly able to interpret it correctly as a signal that their behavior is off the beam, not as a sign of rejection. In fact, nothing makes kids feel more uncared-for than a too cold attitude of disinterest in what they do. On the other hand, an irritable adult, flooded by aggressive anger and yelling at a kid who isn't so sure of his acceptance anyway, is hardly the best way to convey to kids that they are liked or what the issue is really about. As long as we remain so general, the whole issue doesn't mean a thing.

Getting angry at least shows them the limits—that is, does sometimes. But in innumerable cases it is quite obvious that there are more effective ways of showing limits than throwing temper tantrums, and the fact that they may show that the adult disapproves does not guarantee that they also help the children to identify with the values we get angry about or to control their behavior accordingly. How many people are well enough in shape to learn from experience by just having it rubbed in? For disturbed children especially, the sight of an angry adult is quite liable to stir up past images of that sort rather than awareness of the issues now at hand, and, for a repair job on the switches that operate the control system in a child, the adult's angry face or voice is definitely not much good.

It is understandable and normal to get angry—so what? It is normal to feel sentimental toward a neglected cute little ragamuffin; does that mean we should hug and coddle him while he snatches our purses? The "naturalness" of our feeling has nothing to do with the professional issue: How much of it should be shown to the child, and what action is really needed to help him in *his* life?

The real clinical problem around anger cuts right down into the core of education and mental health and cannot even be touched here. The following are just a few tips for applied thinking about it.

First, don't even talk about "the role of anger," without making sure you are talking about the same thing. There is a difference between

"irritation at the discomfort of Johnny's behavior, even though I know he can't quite help it now"

"fury at our own embarrassment for being so helpless even though we really ought to know better"

"vigor, in order to rub into the kid that this really doesn't go, that it is all wrong and totally unacceptable as behavior, even though of course we get so mad only because we love him and don't want him to act that way"

"indignant wrath at somebody's tampering with our values, and the hell with any son of a gun who does so"

"fury, as a direct result of our panic and fear, like the way you scream if you see a kid just barely escaping getting hit by a car after he disobeyed your warnings"

"the irritable disgruntlement of an adult who hates all brats to begin with and barks at anything that disturbs his comfort"

"the triumphant vengefulness of somebody who is engaged in a power struggle and now is eager to show the other guy where to get off"

"the impassioned demonstration to an invisible audience of other adults that we are really people who stand for law and order, even though our helplessness at the moment doesn't quite make that clear"

All these reactions are often meant when people talk about the "anger" of the educator toward a child. Let's make sure which is which, or we shall get nowhere.

Second, there is the problem, not of anger, but of "anger-flooding." When people raise the question of whether or not anger is okay, they forget to add the question of what an adult does with his anger. Even when anger may be natural, justified, or okay, the issue still remains: Should my anger be conveyed at this moment to the child? Should I allow my anger to decide what should be done at this moment?

These issues are entirely separate from the question of acceptability of anger itself.

Third, sometimes anger may even have to be "put on." In this case we mean by "anger" a mild quantity of forcible irritation, shown in order to mark the unacceptability of behavior to a confused child. A certain amount of such anger may have to be produced, even if we don't feel it. The ability to produce just the right quantity of constructively angry gestures without being swept away by them oneself in the process is an important educational skill in its own right.

Fourth, with disturbed children, always remember this point above all: Your anger may be "justified," and he may have it coming all right, but are we sure he can also make use of it?

Your anger may be justified, and, from your own point of view, quite "proportional." For a seriously disturbed kid, however, your face may look too damn much like that of one of the bastards who hated and mistreated him in his life before.

Your anger may be well intended, but from a certain stage of excitement on the child does not perceive it any more or uses it to feed his excitement and add to the already staggering amount of counter-aggression stirred up in him. Then where does it get you?

The heavier your actual interference is (taking something away, holding a kid), the less you can afford to show any anger at all. Interference and limiting already produce either panic or aggression, and with ego-disturbed children that makes any additional quantity totally inadvisable.

Even when it is perfectly all right for them to notice that "this makes even you, who are so patient otherwise, angry," the question of what should really be done or decided upon must never be answered on the basis of this anger. To be able to keep judgment free even with quantities of anger floating around in us is a prime prerequisite for this type of work. It is as important as a "steady hand" in surgery.

Fifth, feeling guilty about your anger shouldn't lead you astray, either. It is good for us to feel somewhat guilty if we let our anger interfere with what is educational and clinically wise. The reaction to such guilt feelings is quite obvious: Let's use them for better insight next time.

It is not advisable, however, to let this guilt about our anger interfere in our handling of the children. Most frequent mistakes possible along that line:

the adult who doesn't dare to interfere in time because he is afraid he might get angry;

the adult who is ashamed of having gotten too angry and therefore becomes overpermissive for the next three instances of mischief;

the adult who bothers the kids with his guilt problem to the degree of forcing situations of unnatural "apologizing," rationalizing, and so forth;

the adult who, in order not to have to admit that he feels rightfully ashamed of his anger-flooding last time, now has to defend his anger as "good for them" or deny it and argue it away in talking with the child.

Sixth, what do you do if you get angrier than you should? As we are all different, each one has to find his own kind of anger assuagement.

First-aid suggestions. Locate the life situations that are most likely to make you angrier than you know you should be. Knowing at least that "this is now *my* problem" makes it a lot easier at least not to let your anger interfere in important decisions.

Count up to ten, interfere before you get too mad, get out of there fast, take a day off, play hooky, or develop some not too unpleasant psychosomatic complaint. If none of that helps, make a speech or write a paper on "why we shouldn't have gotten angry"—double your ouput of write-ups of anger episodes in the kids for our special research files.

Part Five

Serious, But in a Lighter Vein

A peculiar misconception has crept in and lodged itself in the way of smooth communications among all of us who play important roles in children's lives in one way or another. If you are a theoretician or researcher, or at least are labeled as such, you are supposed to present your concepts and research findings in exactly the form in which they were cooked up—with all the tedious details and substeps you had to suffer through plain for all to see—with the result that the potential consumer of such findings gets bored or disinterested, puts them away half-read, but is duly impressed by your theoretical genius and methodological rigor. Your other alternative backfires just as badly: You talk to workers from the point of view of their task areas and about problems that really affect them, and they will think you don't trust them with the real McCoy, that you consider them less intelligent than your research colleagues, that you talk down to them—and probably that your concepts and facts don't stand up too well anyway, for why else would you not molest them with all your research trappings than that they are not even worth showing off?

I think it is time to rebel against all this, and those of us who can afford to ought to start, for the younger scientists and researchers can't—they would lose respectability in their own fields and in the applied fields to which they address themselves to boot.

In the following chapters I have gathered together a number of speeches and publications that fall into the category of this dilemma. The basic laws of human growth I discuss are, in my opinion, as well established and as respectable in their own right as even a most voluminous and boring compendium of experimentation, thought, and other people's readings could make them. Yet I have picked liberally from a variety of concepts and data that, in these combinations, would hardly appear within the same treatises or research reports, as long as they make sense to people who are directly confronted with action-geared tasks.

By the way, it is impossible and I think even wrong to keep professional lines clear in such endeavors. Some of these studies may seem to be addressed primarily to parents—intelligent and highly sophisticated parents, of course—yet how can one sharply differentiate a parent's concern about Johnny's peer associations from those of his teacher, a psychiatrist, or a ward nurse? Others are addressed more directly to group workers, social caseworkers, teachers, school principals—and even to psychiatrists, not in their roles as treaters of sickness, but as community advisers on plans for services. Again, some are directed more to those who have to make important decisions on staffing and implementing institutions for delinquents, yet aren't the issues involved here equally relevant for those who have to work in them after they have been set up?

In short, it is my conviction that it is not officially assigned professional functions or involvement in specific problems but the assortment of relevant issues, in terms of actual roles in kids' lives, that should be the basis on which selection is made. Whoever has participated in multidisciplinary teamwork related to the care and treatment of a group of children certainly has had this experience: The nurse on the ward may be a "nurse," with all that the term implies, but, when she has to decide what routines would be best to get those kids relaxed after hours, she had better discuss it in terms of group-psychological excitation clusters, plus issues of game selection, plus stopping emerging contagion chains. The psychiatrist who is supposed to help the attendant on the ward may officially be a research psychiatrist. But to help the attendant, who is stuck with the kids long after everybody else has left for the week end, he needs to worry less about the proper diagnostic phrasing of his case report than about the problem of invisible subgroup formation, activity patterns that are likely to soothe night panic in children's dormitories, stories that can be read and those that should be avoided, and how to talk with kids without either scaring, boring, or confusing them and without confusing this role with the role the psychiatrist himself takes at the weekly therapy sessions.

In short, it is wrong to assume that the subsequent papers are "less scientific" than the preceding ones. They differ only in the criteria for selection of issues and concepts, their relevance to specific roles in which people are likely to find themselves when confronted with kids.

This, by the way, is also the reason why only minimal attempts have been made here to avoid repetition of topics. It is one problem, for instance, to explore the concept of "behavioral contagion" or of "group-psychological intoxication" within the framework of psychoanalytic theory; it is another to help the nurse, teacher, parent, or caseworker to recognize it in the forms it assumes in the children's natural habitat and to deal with it there; it is still another matter to help the director of a camp or psychiatric ward to figure out what it may imply in terms of his tasks of staffing and program development or of his personal roles in children's daily lives.

The spread of themes, as well as of targets, has purposely been kept wide, and the original titles of the papers have been retained, in order to suggest the over-all frame of reference as well as can be done in advance.

Preadolescents—What Makes Them Tick?

THE PERIOD of preadolescence is a stretch of "no-man's land" in child-study work. By "preadolescence" I mean the phase when the nicest children begin to behave in the most awful way. This definition cannot be called exactly "scientific," but those who have to live with children of that age will immediately recognize whom I am talking about. This also happens to be the age about which we know least. Most of our books are written either about children or about adolescents. The phase I am talking about lies somewhere between the two—crudely speaking, between about nine and thirteen, in terms of chronological age, or between the fifth and eighth grades, in terms of school classification.

It is surprising that we know so little about this age group but there certainly is no doubt that it is one of the most baffling phases of all. Most referrals to child-guidance clinics occur around this age, and if you look for volunteers to work on programs in recreation or child care, you will make this peculiar discovery: You will have no trouble finding people who just love to bathe little babies until they smell good and shine. You will have a little more, but not too much, trouble finding people who are just waiting for a chance to "understand" adolescents who "have problems" and long for shoulders on which to cry. But the preadolescent youngster offers neither of these satisfactions. You won't find many people who will be very happy working with him.

Are preadolescents children? No. Of course, they still look like young children. Practically no visible change has as yet taken place in their sexual development. Their voices are about as shrill and penetrating as they ever were, and the personal pictures they present are still highly reminiscent of children—of about the worst children you have

"Preadolescents—What Makes Them Tick" is based on the article by the same title that appeared in *Child Study* (1939), copyright 1939, Child Study Association of America. Reprinted by permission of the publishers.

met but definitely not of the children they themselves were just a short time ago.

Are they adolescents? No. Although filled with a collector's curiosity about odd elements of information on human sex life at its worst, they are not yet really maturing sexually. Although they occasionally like to brag about precocity in their sex attitudes, "the boy" or "the girl" of the other sex is still something they really don't know what to do with if left alone with it for any length of time. Although impertinent in their wishes to penetrate the secrets of adult life, they have no concepts about the future, little worry about what is going to happen to them, nothing they would like to "talk over with you."

The reason we know so little about this phase of development is simple but significant: It is a phase that is disappointing for the adult and especially so for the adult who loves youth and is interested in it. These youngsters are hard to live with even when there is the most ideal child-parent relationship. They are not so much fun to love as when they were younger, for they don't seem to appreciate what they get at all. And they certainly aren't much to brag about, academically or otherwise. You can't play the "friendly helper" toward them either —they think you are plain dumb if you try it; nor can you play the role of the proud shaper of youthful wax—they stick to your fingers like putty, and things become messier and messier the more you try to "shape" children that age. Nor can you play the role of the proud and sacerdotal warden of the values of society to be pointed out to eager youth. They think you are plain funny in that role.

So the parent is at a loss and ready for a desperate escape into either of two bad mistakes—defeatism or tough-guy stubbornness. The teacher shrugs his shoulders and blames most of this preadolescent spook on the teacher the youngster had before him or on lack of parental cooperation—and hopes that somehow or other these children will "snap out of it." Even the psychiatrist, otherwise so triumphantly cynical about other people's troubles with children, is in a fix. For with these children you can't use "play techniques" any longer. They giggle themselves to death at the mere idea of sitting in one room with an adult and playing a table game while that adult desperately pretends that this is all there is to it. And one can't use the usual "interview technique" either. They find it funny that they should talk about themselves and their lives, that they should consider as "a problem" what has "just happened," that they should try to remember how they felt about things, and that they are constantly expected to have "worries" or "fears"—two emotions that they are most skillful at hiding from the self-perception process even if they do occur. Most of these youngsters seriously think the adult himself is crazy if he introduces such talk, and they naïvely enjoy the troubles they make, rather than those they have, and would much rather bear the consequences of their troubles than talk about them, even though those consequences include frustration or a beating or two.

Research, too, with very few exceptions, has skipped this period. If you study adolescence, you certainly can have graphs and charts on the rate at which the growth of pubic hair increases, the timing between that and the change of voice, and the irrelevance of both in terms of psychosexual development. Unfortunately, at the age we are talking about little of all this seems to take place. No drastic body changes occur, and whatever may happen within the glands is certainly not dramatic enough to explain the undoubtedly dramatic behavior of that phase. For a while some Yale biologist tried to discover an increase in hormone production around the age of eight, long before there is any visible sex maturation. However, they had trouble in making their research results useful for practical purposes. It took them weeks for one specimen of urine to be boiled in the right way to show the existence or nonexistence of these hormones, and in the meantime Johnny would probably have been kicked out of five more schools anyway. In short, research has discreetly left this phase alone and has retired from it, as it always does from things that are either too hard to demonstrate by statistical methods or too hot to talk about after they have been discovered.

Thus, the practitioner—the parent, the teacher, the counselor, or the group worker—is left to his own devices. Fortunately, most of the characteristic symptoms of this phase are known to us all.

Preadolescent Behavior—Bad and Improper

Here are some of the most frequent complaints adults raise in connection with their attempts to handle preadolescents: Outwardly, the most striking thing about them is their extreme physical restlessness. They can hardly stand still, running is more natural to them than walking, the word "sitting" is a euphemism if applied to what they do with a table and a chair. Their hands seem to need constant occupational therapy: They will turn up the edges of any books they handle; they will have to manipulate pencils, any objects near them, any one of the dozen-odd things they carry in their pockets, and even parts of their own body, whether it be nose and ears, hair, or parts of the anatomy usually taboo in terms of infantile upbringing. The return to other infantile habits is surprisingly intensive in many areas: Even otherwise well-drilled and very house-broken youngsters may again show symptoms like bed-wetting, soiling, nail-biting (or its substitutes, like skin-chewing, finger-drumming, and so forth). Funny gestures and antics seem to turn up overnight with little or no reason—such things as facial tics, odd gestures and jerky movements, long-outgrown speech disorders, and the like.

In other areas these youngsters do not return to exactly the same habits as those of their infancy, but they go back to typical problem areas of younger childhood and start again where they had left off. Thus their search for the facts of life, which had temporarily subsided under the impact of partial parental explanations will be resumed with vehemence and with the impudence and insistence of a news correspondent rather than with the credulity of an obedient young child. It is the oddity, the wild fantastic story, and the gory detail that fascinate them more than parental attempts at well-organized explanations of propagation, which they find rather boring.

Their old interpretation of the difference between the sexes is revived too. Girls seem obviously inferior to boys, who again interpret the difference in sex as that of a minus versus a plus rather than of a difference in anatomical function. Thus girls are no good unless they are nearly like boys; and, when direct pride in masculine sexuality is subdued, indirect bragging about the size and strength of the biceps takes its place and becomes the standard of evaluation for anybody's worth. The girls go through somewhat the same phase, accept the interpretations of the boys all too eagerly, and often wander through a period of frantic imitation of boyish behavior and negation of their female roles. What sex manipulation does occur at this age usually happens in terms of experimentation and is on a highly organic level and very different from the masturbation of later adolescent years.

The fantasy lives of youngsters of this age are something to look into, too. Wild daydreams of the comic-strip type of adventure, on the one hand, and long stages of staring into empty space with nothing going on in their conscious minds on the other, are the two poles between which their fantasy lives move rapidly back and forth. Often manipulative play with a piece of string or the appearance of listening to the radio covers long stretches of quickly changing flights of ideas, and youngsters who reply "nothing," when you ask them what they have been thinking about, do not necessarily lie. This description really fits the content as far as it could possibly be stated in any acceptable logical order and grammatical form.

The most peculiar phenomena, though, are found in the area of adult-child relationships. Even youngsters who obviously love their parents and have reason to do so will develop stretches of surprising irritability, distrust, and suspicion. Easily offended and constantly ready with accusations that adults don't understand them and treat them wrongly, they are yet very reckless and inconsiderate of other people's feelings and are quite surprised if people get hurt because of the way they behave. The concept of gratitude seems to be something stricken from the inventory of their emotions. The worst meal at the neighbors', at which they weren't even welcome, may be described more glowingly in its glory than the best-planned feast that you arranged for their birthday. The silliest antics, the most irrelevant possessions or skills of neighbors will be admired way beyond any well-rooted qualities and superior achievements of father and mother.

Daily life with Junior becomes a chain of little irritations about little things. The fight against the demands of obeying the rules of time and space is staged as vehemently as if he were one or two years old again. Keeping appointed mealtimes, coming home, going to bed at a prearranged hour, starting work, stopping play according to promise —all these demands seem to be as hard to get across and as badly resented, no matter how reasonable the parents try to be about them, as if they were the cruel and senseless torments of tyranny.

Lack of submission to parentally-accepted manners becomes another source of conflict. If these youngsters would listen as attentively to what Webster has to say as they do to the language of the worst ragamuffin on the street corner, their grades in English would be tops. Dressing properly, washing, keeping clean are demands that meet with obvious indignation or distrust. In a way, they seem to have lost all sense of shame and decency. Previously clean-minded youngsters will not mind telling the dirtiest jokes if they can get hold of them, and the most charming angels of last year can spend an hour giggling over the acrobatics a youngster performs with his stomach gas and consider it the greatest joke.

Yet, although they are unashamed in so many ways, there are other areas of life in which they become more sensitive rather than more crude: The idea of being undressed or bathed by their own parents may all of a sudden release vehement feelings of shame hitherto unknown to their elders, and open display of affection before others makes them blush as though they had committed a crime. The idea of being called a "sissy" by somebody one's own age is the top of shamefulness and nearly intolerable because of the pain it involves.

One of the most interesting attitude changes during this period is that in boy-girl relationships. The boy has not only theoretical contempt for the girl, but he has no place for her socially. Social parties that adults push so often because they find the clumsiness of their youngsters so cute and because it is so safe to have boys and girls together at that age are a pain in the neck to youngsters, who would obviously much rather have a good free-for-all or chase one another all over the place. The girls have little place in their lives for the same-age boys either. It is true that with them the transition through this pre-adolescent period usually is shorter than with the boys. But for a time their actual need for boy company is nil. The picture is different, though, if you watch the children within their own sex gangs. Then, all of a sudden, talking in safe seclusion with their buddies, the boys or girls will display trumped-up interest in the other sex, will brag about their sexual knowledge or precocity or about their successes in dating. All this bragging, however, though it is about sex, is on an entirely unerotic level; the partner of the other sex only figures in it as does the fish in the fisherman's story. The opposite sex, like the fish, serves only as indirect means for self-glorification.

What Makes Them Tick?

The explanation of this peculiar phenomenon of human growth must, I think, move along two lines. One is of an individualistic nature; the second is a chapter in group psychology.

EXPLANATION NUMBER 1

During preadolescence the well-knit pattern of a child's personality is broken up or loosened, so that adolescent changes can be built into it and so that it can be modified into the personality of an adult.

Thus the purpose of this developmental phase is not *improvement* but *disorganization;* not a permanent disorganization, of course, but a disorganization for future growth. This disorganization must occur, or else the higher organization cannot be achieved. In short, a child does not become an adult by becoming bigger and better. Simple "improvement" of a child's personality into that of an adult would only produce an oversized child, an infantile adult. "Growing" into an adult means leaving behind or destroying some of what the child has been and becoming something else in many ways.

The real growth occurs during adolescence: Preadolescence is the period of preliminary loosening-up of the personality pattern in order that the change may take place. It is comparable to soaking the beans before you cook them. If this explanation is valid, then we can understand the following manifestations.

First, during this "breaking up of child personality" period, old, long-forgotten, or repressed impulses of earlier childhood will come afloat again for awhile before they are discarded for good. This explains all that we have described about the return to infantile habits, silly antics, irritating behavior, recurring naughty habits, and so forth.

Second, during this period of the breaking up of an established pattern, we also find that already-developed standards and values lose their power and become ineffectual. Hence the surprising lack of self-control, the high degrees of disorganization, the great trouble these youngsters have in keeping themselves in shape and continuing to live up to at least some of the expectations they had no difficulty living up to a short time ago. The individual conscience of the child seems to lose its power, and even the force of his intelligence and insight into his own impulses is obviously weakened. This explains all we have said about these children's unreliability, the lowering of their standards of behavior, the disappearance of some of the barriers of shame and disgust they had established, and their surprising immunity to guilt feelings in many areas of life.

Third, during a period of loosening-up of personality texture, we should expect that the whole individual will be full of conflict and that the natural accompaniments of conflict will appear again, anxieties and fears, on the one hand, and compulsive mechanisms of symbolic reassurance, on the other. This is why so many of these youngsters really show fears or compulsive tics that otherwise only neurotic children would show. Yet this behavior is perfectly normal and will be only temporary. This explains the frequent occurrence of fantastic fears of ghosts and burglars in the dark, and it also explains the intensity with which some of these youngsters cling to mechanisms like the possession of a flashlight or gun as symbols of protection, or the display of nervous tics and peculiar antics that usually include magic tricks to fool destiny and assure protection from danger or guilt.

For a long time I thought that all this about finished the picture of preadolescent development, until a closer observation of the group life of preadolescents showed me that such a theory leaves much unexplained. It seems to me that there is still another explanation for a host of preadolescent symptoms.

EXPLANATION NUMBER 2

During preadolescence it is normal for youngsters to drop their identifications with adult society and establish strong identifications with groups of their peers.

This part of preadolescent development is of a group-psychological nature and is as important to the child's later functioning as a citizen in society as the first principle is for his personal mental and emotional health. This group phenomenon is surprisingly universal and explains much of the trouble we adults have with children of preadolescent age. To be sure that I am rightly understood, I want to emphasize that what happens during this age goes way beyond the personal relationship between Johnny and his father. Johnny's father now becomes for him more than his father: He becomes, all of a sudden, a representative of the value system of adult society versus the child, at least in certain moments of his life. The same is true the other way around. Johnny becomes more to his father than his child: At certain moments he isn't Johnny any more but the typical representative of *youth* versus *adult*. A great many of the "educational" things adults do to children, as well as many of the rebellious acts of children toward adults, are not aimed at the other fellow at all; they are aimed at the general group of *adults* or *youth* that this other person represents. To disentangle personal involvement from this group-psychological meaning of behavior is perhaps the most vital and so far least attempted problem of education in adolescence.

If this explanation is valid, then it seems to me that the following phenomena of preadolescent behavior can be well understood.

First, at no other age do youngsters show such a deep need for clique and gang formation among themselves as at this one. From the adult angle this is usually met with much suspicion. Of course, it is true that youngsters will tend to choose their companions from among those who are rejected, rather than approved, by their parents. Perhaps we can understand why the more unacceptable a youngster is on the basis of our adult behavior code, the more highly acceptable he will be in the society of his own peers. The clique formation of youngsters among themselves usually has some form of definitely "gang" character: That means it is more thoroughly enjoyed because it is somewhat "subversive" in terms of adult standards. Remember how youngsters often are magically fascinated by certain types of ringleader, even though this "ringleadership" may involve rather harmless though irritating activities—smoking, special clothes, late hours, gang language, and so forth.

From the angle of the adult and his anxieties, much of this seems highly objectionable. From the angle of the youngster and his normal development, most of it is highly important. For it is vital that he satisfy the wish for identification with his pals, even though or just because such identification is sometimes frowned upon by the powers that be. The courage to stick to his pal against you, no matter how much he loves you and otherwise admires your advice, is an important step forward in the youngster's social growth.

Second, in all groups, something like an unspoken behavior code develops, and it is this unwritten code on which the difference between "good" and "bad" depends. Up to now the youngster has lived within the psychological confines of the adult's own value system. Good and bad were defined entirely on the basis of adult tastes. Now he enters the magical ring of peer codes. And the code of his friends differs essentially from that of adult society. In some items the two are diametrically opposed. In terms of the adult code, for instance, it is good if children bring home high grades and take pride in being much better than the neighbor's children, in being better liked by the teacher, and in being more submissive to the whims of the teaching adult than are other people's children. In terms of peer standards things are directly reversed. Studying too much exposes you to the suspicion of being a sissy, aggressive pride against other children is suspiciously close to "teacher's pet" roles, and obedience to the adult in power often comes close to being a fifth columnist in terms of "the gang."

Some of the typically adult-fashioned values are clearly rejected by peer standards; others are potentially compatible at times but conflicting at other times; some of them can be shared in common. Thus, a not-too-delinquent "gang" to which your youngster is proud to belong may be characterized by the following code range: It is all right in this gang to study and work reasonably well in school. It is essential, though, that he dare to smoke and lie, even against his own father, if it means the protection of a pal in his gang, that he bear the brunt of scenes at home if really important gang activities are in question. At the same time this gang does not want him to steal, would be horrified if his sex activity went beyond the telling of dirty stories, and would oust him tacitly because it would think him too spohisticated for it. The actual group life of preadolescents moves between hundreds of different shades of such gang codes, and the degree to which we adults have omitted opening our eyes to this vital phase of child development is astounding.

Third, the change from adult code to peer code is not an easy process for a youngster but is full of conflict and often painful. For, although he would like to be admired by his pals on a peercode basis, he still loves his parents personally and hates to see them misunderstand him or have them get unhappy about what he does. And, although he would love to please his family and be again accepted by it and have it be proud of him, he simply can't face being called a "sissy" or be suspected of being a coward or a teacher's pet by his friends. In most of those cases where we find serious conflicts between the two sets of standards, we will find the phenomenon of "social hysteria." This applies to youngsters who so overdo their loyalty to either one of the two behavior standards that they then have to go far beyond reasonable limits. Thus you find youngsters so scared of being thought bad by their parents that they don't dare to mix happily with children of their own age, and you find others so keen to achieve peer status with friends of their own age that they begin to reject all parental advice, every finer feeling of loyalty to the home, and accept all and any lure of gang prestige even if it involves delinquent and criminal activity. It is obvious that a clear analysis by the adult and the avoidance of counter-hysteria can do much to improve things.

How to Survive Life with Junior

If these observations are true, then they should have an enormous impact on education. For then most of this preadolescent spook isn't merely a problem of things that shouldn't happen and ought to be squelched but of things that should happen but need to be regulated and channeled. Of course, you can't possibly just let Junior be as pre-adolescent as he would like without going crazy yourself, and you definitely shouldn't think of self-defense only and thus squelch the emotional and social development of your offspring. How to do both—survive and also channel normal but tough growth periods without damage to later development—is too long a story to complete in a short article. But here are a few general hints.

Avoid Counterhysterics

It seems to me that 90 per cent of the more serious problems between children and parents or teachers on which I have ever been consulted could have been easily avoided. They were not inherent in the actual problems of growth. They were produced by the hysterical ways in which the adults reacted to them. Most growth problems—even the more serious ones—can be outgrown eventually, though outgrowing them may be a painful process, provided the adults don't use them as springboards for their own overemotional reactions. This does not mean that I advocate that you give up and let everything take its course. I do suggest you study the situation and decide when to allow things and when to interfere. The problem is that, whatever you decide to do, the *way* you do it should be realistic, free from hysterical overemotionalism. With this policy in mind you can enjoy all the fun of having problems with your child without producing a problem child.

Don't Fight Windmills

Let's not forget that preadolescents are much more expert in handling us than we can ever be in handling them. Their skill in sizing us up and using our emotions and weaknesses for their own ends has reached a peak at this age. It took them eight to ten years to learn, but they have learned by thorough observation. While we were worrying about them, they were not worried about us, and they had ample time and leisure to study our psychology. This means that, if they now go out to prove to themselves how emancipated they are, they will choose exactly the tricks that will irritate us most. They will develop preadolescent symptoms in accordance with their understanding of our psychology. Thus, some of them will smoke, curse, talk about sex, or stay out late. Some will stop being interested in their grades, get kicked out of school, or threaten to become the type of person who will never be acceptable in good society. Others again will develop vocational interests that we look down on, will choose company we dread, talk language that makes us jump, or even run away at intervals.

But whatever surface behavior they display—don't fall for it. Don't fight the behavior. Interpret the cause of it first; then judge how much and in what way you should interfere. Thus, Johnny's smoking may really mean he is sore that his father never takes him to a football match, or it may mean he thinks you don't appreciate how adult he already is, or it may mean he has become dependent on the class clown. Mary's insistence upon late hours may mean she doesn't know how to control herself, or it may mean she is sore because her school pals think you are social snobs who live lives different from theirs, or it may mean she is so scared that her sex ignorance will be discovered that she has to run around with a crowd more sophisticated about staying up late, in order to hide her lack of sophistication in another respect.

In any case, all these things are not so hard to figure out. Instead of getting excited and disapproving of the strange behavior, just open your eyes for a while and keep them open without blinking.

PROVIDE A FRAME OF LIFE ADEQUATE FOR GROWTH

No matter how much you dislike it, every preadolescent youngster needs the chance to have some of his wild behavior come out in some place or other. It will make a lot of difference whether or not he has a frame of life adequate for such growth. For example, Johnny needs the experience of running up against some kind of adventurous situation in which he can prove he is a regular guy and not just Mother's boy. Cut him off from all life situations containing elements of unpredictability, and he may have to go stealing from the grocery store to prove his point. Give him a free and experimental camp setting to be adventurous in, and he will be happily preadolescent without getting himself or anybody else in trouble. All youngsters need some place where preadolescent traits can be exercised and even tolerated. It is your duty to plan for such places in their lives as skillfully as you select their schools or vocational opportunities.

WATCH OUT FOR PREADOLESCENT CORNS

Most people don't mind their toes being stepped on occasionally. But if there is a corn there, that is a different matter. Well, all preadolescents have certain corns, places where they are hypersensitive. Avoid these places as much as possible. One of the most important to avoid is harking back to their early childhood years. The one thing they don't want to be reminded of is themselves as small children and yourself as the mother or father of the younger children. If you punish, don't repeat ways you used when they were little. If you praise, don't use arguments that would please a three-year-old but make a thirteen-year-old red with shame or fury. Whether you promise or reward, threaten or blackmail, appeal to their sense, morals, or anything else, always avoid doing it in the same way you used to do when they were little.

I have seen many preadolescents reject what their parents wanted, not because they felt that it was unreasonable or unjustified, but because of the way in which the parents put the issue. There is something like a developmental level of parental control, as well as developmental levels of child behavior. The two have to be matched, or there will be fireworks.

IF IN DOUBT, MAKE A DIAGNOSTIC CHECKUP

Not all the behavior forms we have described are always merely "preadolescent." Some of them are more than that. After all, there are such things as juvenile delinquents and psychoneurotics, and we shouldn't pretend that everything is bound to come out in the wash.

Usually you can get a good hunch about dangerous areas if you check on these points: How deep is the preadolescent trait a youngster shows? If it is too vehement and impulsive, too unapproachable by even the most reasonable techniques, then the chances are that Johnny's antics are symptoms not only of growth but also of something wrong somewhere and needing repair. Often this may be the case: Five of Johnny's antics are just preadolescent, pure and simple, and should not be interfered with too much. However, these five are tied up with five others that are definitely serious hang-overs from old, never really solved problems, results of wrong handling, wrong environmental situations, or other causes. It will do no good to brush off the whole matter by calling it "preadolescent." In that case the first five items need your protection, and the other five need repair jobs done. Whenever you are very much in doubt, it is wise to consult expert help for the checkup—just as you would in order to decide whether a heart murmur is due to too fast growth or to an organic disturbance.

$\mathcal{O}$ur Troubles with Defiant Youth

$\mathcal{T}$HE TERM "DELINQUENCY" is generally used these days in vague and confusing ways. Clinically the behavior referred to as "delinquent" may cover a wide range of entirely different afflictions. Sometimes the word is as loosely applied as the popular term "belly-ache," which may cover anything from temporary upset after eating too much ice cream to stomach ulcers or acute appendicitis. Nobody in the medical field today would attempt to answer the question "what should be done about it" before finding out concretely just which of the afflictions gave rise to the "bellyache." Unfortunately, however, in the field of human behavior and mental health, the public has not yet reached so wise an acceptance of the variety of ills that may result in excessive aggression or as much respect for the need for specific diagnosis.

The concept of "defiant youth" does *not* coincide with the delinquency problem. Some "defiance" is part of the normal growth process. It may even be a desirable though an uncomfortable forerunner of a character trait commonly referred to as "integrity" or "spine." Other forms of defiance, however, do overlap with the kind of trouble usually referred to as "delinquency" and constitute a great strain on our communities. On the other hand, not all delinquents show overt defiant behavior. In fact some of the hardest-to-reach cases exhibit a very "slick" surface conformity as a safe cover for the cultivation of totally immoral outlooks on life or safe build-ups for long-prepared criminal "splurges."

These facts leave persons concerned with the behavior of today's youth facing two important questions: In what areas is confused public opinion on juvenile delinquency most seriously blocking clinical progress and preventive planning? What types of youthful defiance should be differentiated in order to begin wise preventive and therapeutic planning?

"Our Troubles with Defiant Youth" is reprinted from *Children*, January–February 1955, U.S. Department of Health, Education and Welfare, Social Security Administration, Children's Bureau.

Areas of Confusion

There are three main areas of confusion.

THE INDIVIDUAL AND THE SYMBOL

Most of us have been annoyed at one time or another by the fact that children go through a phase in which they suddenly consider us, their parents and teachers, as just general symbols of "the adult." They seem suddenly to have emptied us of all personal relationships with them. We stop being Mary's dad or Johnny's older friend and represent simply "those adults," the power group from whose grip they are trying to emancipate themselves.

However, we adults don't usually recognize that we begin to do the same thing to our children as soon as they enter the development phases of preadolescence and adolescence. In these periods Daddy does have moments of reacting to his son, not so much as a person, but as though he represented the "world of adults" pitched against "youth" that is getting out of hand. Dad's little boy suddenly becomes, not his son whom he knows and loves so well, but just an "example" of the way young people act when you don't "keep them in line."

This peculiar phenomenon, natural and harmless within limits, often becomes a real block to wise handling of youthful behavior. It is responsible for much avoidable antagonism between the generations. The more we feel threatened by what youngsters do, the more we fall into this form of stereotyping. As a result many a situation grows into a sham battle over a "cause," when the immediate problems could have been easily solved if the two adversaries had remained what they were to begin with: two *people* having it out.

SOME OF MY BEST FRIENDS ARE TEEN-AGERS

There seems to be a tendency in the adult world toward hostility to youth as such, which is in striking contrast to the fact that we all "like kids," especially our own or those entrusted to our care. Something seems to happen to the most child-accepting of us when we suddenly switch from personal involvement with a child to a collective view of the youth problem. This shift in focus tends especially to occur when a youngster becomes involved in some rather atrocious crime—although the act has so obviously grown out of extreme disorganization within the world surrounding him, such a long and involved chain of disturbing events that nobody could logically regard the outcome as "typical" youthful behavior.

A fourteen-year-old boy tries to defend his mother against the onslaughts of his drunken father and hits him a bit too hard with the piece of pipe he grabs in despair. Why are our newspapers so ready to call this a "teen-age crime"? By doing so aren't they implying that this boy is "typical" of the youth of our time or at least that something about being a "teen-ager" has brought about the unfortunate event that so obviously stemmed from the pathologies of the adults in the boy's life? On the other hand, do the papers write up as a typical teen-age deed the heroism of Bobby, an Eagle Scout, who rescued a little girl from drowning? On the contrary, Bobby Smith, aged fifteen, remains Bobby Smith, not a representative of his age, and the heroism is credited to himself. In other words, teen-agers are regarded as a breed suspect until proven innocent. Their bad deeds "redound" on the whole age group. Their good deeds point only to the exceptions that "prove the rule."

When public attitudes incline toward stereotyping of this sort there is cause for deep concern. Collective suspicion and negativism of one group toward another always backfire by engendering conscious or unconscious collective counteraggression and distrust from the other side. To increase intergroup tensions between the "world of grown-ups" and the "youth of our time" is the last thing we should do at this point in history. As we have paid such prices in the past for collective prejudices in the areas of race, religion, class, and caste, we should know something about the high cost of group-psychological pathology.

AN OPTICAL ILLUSION

Adult disgust with "youth" is easily aroused when the young people gather in mobs. Their boisterous and rather inconsiderate behavior gets on our nerves and reinforces our suspicious stereotypes. Thus, unfortunately, we are taken in by a kind of "optical illusion," for loud and thoughtless behavior is often more typical of the group situation individuals are in than of the individuals themselves. If you doubt this, just remember the last large convention held in your town. Many riotous teen-agers would have trouble living up to what otherwise dignified adults can do to hotel-room towels, ashtrays, and doorknobs when they are convening in somebody else's city.

Although much remains to be learned about the impact of group-psychological excitement on the behavior of the human individual, age, or "teen age," as such is not the main factor involved. The problem of how to predict which person's self-control and value system will melt under a certain amount of group-psychological heat and how to help individuals keep sense and control intact under free-floating contagion is one of the most urgent research issues before us. Instead of allowing ourselves to become irritated at an "age range," we should take steps to investigate thoroughly this larger problem of group pathology.

In summary, it seems as important for the fields of mental hygiene and preventive psychiatry to tackle the collective confusions about youthful behavior in which the present adult generation indulges as to cope with the problems of youth itself. We have made wonderful strides with analogous problems in the fields of physical medicine and health. Through the astounding successes of public-health education on a variety of levels, present public opinion is enlightened about the nature of invisible germs, accepts even unpleasant facts about the nutritive values of certain foods, and no longer quarrels with the wisdom of certain "first aid" directives even when they contradict deeply ingrained popular myths or personal feelings. But in the field of human behavior the major task of "deconfusing the public" lies ahead.

What About "Defiance"?

Without attempting anything as ambitious as an outline of symptomatology and etiology of the "defiant child," we can differentiate a few of the outstanding problems that usually sail under this heading. Here too conceptual confusion, although not the core of the difficulty, is a dangerous roadblock on the way to progress.

DEVELOPMENTAL DEFIANCE

In spite of all the talk about "adjustment," we would not really want children to "adjust" to everything all the time. If they did, we would think they lacked "spine." Healthy development on the part of a child is fostered by strengthening not only his ability to adjust to outside demands but also his ability to defend his own integrity against wrong demands made by others. We want Johnny to be respectful to his teacher, but we don't want him to run after the first designing bum that offers him candy just because the man is an adult and looks like a mixture of Abe Lincoln and Santa Claus. On the contrary, we want our children to retain the capacity for intelligent rebellion—courage to stick to what they believe in even against strong-armed pressure and the fear of becoming unpopular with the mob.

All traits that we want eventually to see in our children must grow through a range of developmental phases. "Intelligent rebellion," too, needs leeway to be learned and practiced. Of course, while being practiced it often looks anything but intelligent and can be very annoying to the adult who has to live with it. We know from our studies of child development that certain age ranges seem to be especially cut out for the practice of "emancipation acrobatics." The negativism of the child between three and five, as well as the strong "emancipation" efforts of the young adolescent, are normal phases in child development. Although uncomfortable for educator and parent, these rebellious phases are important as preparation for independence. We also know that defiance that is part of this developmental process is not habit-forming. It tones down by itself as soon as the character trait of integrity, for the sake of which it was displayed, is sufficiently secured.

Although we have many books that tell us how to cultivate "intelligent rebellion" in the well-adjusted child in relation to the child's dependence on individuals, we have little information on how to help him keep his integrity when confronted with gang and mob pressures. One of the nation's greatest problems at this time is to find out how to help our young people stick to what they believe in, even in defiance of whatever opinion or action might be popular at the moment with the rest of the youthful crowd. Actually a lot of behavior usually termed "defiance" is exactly the opposite. The sixteen-year-old who participates in an incident of vandalism because he is afraid of being called a sissy is not a defiant child. He is a coward, an overconformist, a spineless lickspittle for public acclaim. The fact that he is overdependent on the wrong opinions does not change the fact that submission rather than defiance is the real problem at hand.

Clinically speaking, then, we have to look a few inches below the surface before we can know what the problems in any specific "defiant act" really are. When behavior falls into the category of "developmental defiance," it presents us with an educational challenge, but we must not be fooled into regarding it as "delinquency."

REACTIVE DEFIANCE

Some youthful defiant behavior may be compared to the process of regurgitation. If you pour poison or stuff pins down somebody's throat, his organism will probably rebel by choking reactions to ward off the hurtful intrusion. Vomiting under such conditions is not symptomatic of illness. On the contrary, it is the defense of a healthy organism against hurt from the outside.

A lot of youthful "defiant" behavior falls into the same category. It is not the outcropping of a corrupt or morbid personality, but the defense of a healthy one against the kind of treatment that shouldn't happen to a dog but often does happen to children. At close inspection even many of the rather frightening and disgusting outbursts of youthful defiance are of this type. In a group of normal school children, bored beyond limit by stupid teaching methods, the intelligent ones will be the first to become "hard to handle." Their misbehavior is a defense against the demoralizing impact of excessive boredom. If a child with deep-seated anxieties is put into solitary confinement under frightening circumstances, the resulting temper tantrum will not be his "warped personality" coming to the fore but his desperate defense against total breakdown into mental disease. His frantic muscle spasms and aggressive mauling of the surrounding outside world are the expressions of his inward terror.

Such "reactive defiance" calls for consideration not only of what's wrong with the child but also of what is wrong with what we are doing to him. Every case of really pathological and dangerous defiance that I have had a chance to study closely has had its origin at some time in "reactive" defiance. Many people had to do the wrong things consistently for a long time to the children involved to produce such severe degrees of disturbance. This means that one of our greatest preventive opportunities lies in developing and applying greater knowledge about the most advantageous setting for growing youngsters and in helping adults toward maximum wisdom in their reactions to youthful behavior.

DEFIANCE AS A WRAPPING

Some defiant behavior is quite clearly "unprovoked," or at least seems so at first sight. Why should Billy, a well-loved and well-cared-for child, one day suddenly act up, hanging on to furniture and kicking and biting when you try to make him go to school? His unwarranted behavior toward you looks dangerously like the "rebellious child" in the making. It looks and feels like that until you learn that Billy has deep-seated fears of any "crowd" situation—fears that are irrational but extremely intense. The panic aroused in Billy's mind is in itself a "sickness," an anxiety neurosis. *This* is the affliction, not the "disrespectful disobedience" that he displays when confronted with it.

Other "defiant acts" by youthful offenders may be the secondary accompaniment of any of a variety of mental diseases. I once knew a child who, when compulsively hit by sudden intense spurts of fantasy images, would get up during class and wander around, impervious to threats of punishment. He seemed to do all this "just in order to spite authority." Yet nothing was further from the truth. At these moments, he did not even perceive the teacher's presence nor that of the world around him. He had no thought of being "spiteful." It would have been easier to help him if he had, for this child was out of contact with reality far beyond the normal degree of childish daydreaming. This sickness is worse than the usual "defiance." But the important point is that it is different and calls for entirely different treatment and preventive measures.

Defiance that comes as a "wrapping" around some other disease is especially frustrating because in such cases the techniques so often found helpful in dealing with other defiant children are totally ineffectual, and the adult's wrath at the defiant behavior is apt to be increased by his fury at his helplessness. The result is a loud cry for some form of physical punishment. Unfortunately, in these cases physical punishment is the most futile and most damaging technique we could use. When defiance is a "wrapping," no matter how smell-proof or loose, the only thing to do is to tackle the disease behind the wrapping. All other efforts are useless.

The Defiant Ego

By "defiant ego" I mean the ego that has thrown itself on the side of the child's impulsivity, defending it against reason and the voice of his "better self" with enormous skill and strength.

This, unfortunately, is the most neglected, although the most serious, form of defiance. Whereas from the outside it looks very much like other types of defiant behavior, at closer range it reveals itself as a most pernicious and serious affliction, which educator and psychiatrist are so far completely helpless to change.

Children with "defiant egos" act destructively any time they so desire because they enjoy it. If they want their "fun" they are going to have it. Either they have not developed those "voices from within" that would make them feel bad about "fun" that is unjustly had at somebody else's expense, or they have developed very skillful tricks for putting those "voices" out of commission should they tend to interfere. Diagnosis, however, is not easy. The size of the offense or the intensity of the defiance gives no clue to what type of defiance is involved. It is not true that rowdyism marks a child as sickest or worst, whereas milder or even "cute" forms of rebellion can be passed by as harmless. Nuisance value to others and intensity and degree of defiance are only a few of the criteria for sizing things up for what they really are.

I know of actions close to murder that had little to do with real defiance but were reactive or psychoneurotic in origin. I also know of cases in which as mild a symptom as polite withdrawal from arts-and-crafts activities—but always exactly when whim dictated and always accompanied by total disinterest and bland imperviousness to the per-suasions of others—proved to be the forerunner of very severe char-acter disorders that later blossomed into openly recognizable symptom displays.

A detailed description of the "defiant ego" is not possible in the space available. However, this is the type of affliction that may justi-fiably be classified as "delinquency," even if the defiance displayed does not seem to have any "legal" implications. The early recognition of such afflictions and the determination of conditions for preventive and thera-peutic work with them constitute some of the main themes upon which research is required today.[1]

Summary

The problem of "defiant youth" is complicated by the fact that the adult generation generally lacks conceptual clarity in discussing the issues involved. Furthermore, "defiant" behavior by children seems to

1. See Fritz Redl and David Wineman, *Children Who Hate* (New York: The Free Press, 1951); and Redl and Wineman, *Controls From Within* (New York: The Free Press, 1952).

bring out the worst in adults, provoking them to react with their own feelings rather than with deliberate thought. The collective "suspicious antagonism" that communities often display against "teen-agers" as a "caste and class" are likely to foster or increase a collective spirit of defiance among youth itself.

The actual phenomenon of "defiance" has many degrees ranging from "light" to "severe and dangerous," from "cute" to "morbidly obnoxious." Unfortunately, the degree does not indicate in any given case what lies behind the behavior. No matter which specific form of behavior defiance may take, it may derive from any one or a mixture of at least four types of affliction. The difference between failure and success depends on whether or not we gear our curative and preventive measures toward the type of affliction involved.

The answer to the problem of defiant youth must be sought in the direction of more practice-geared research, greater concerted effort toward the education of the public in the causes of defiance, and more courage to think straight even under the impact of panic and wrath.

$\mathcal{W}ho$ Is Delinquent?

$\mathcal{A}$ NEW GAME has been added to the recreational repertoire of the child-rearing population of our time. It is a game strictly for adults. It takes the most divergent and unrelated ideas and facts and shuffles them together so that in a short time nobody knows which is which any more. The name of the game? We might list it as the "Let's ask each other what is delinquency" game. I am sure many of you have played it or have watched others play it—both laymen and experts. I suspect you would like me to play it with you.

Well, I won't. Trying to define "delinquency" is not a game; it is a very important task. And, since people are using the term in such a sweeping way, maybe it might pay to pause long enough to mention what I at least do *not* mean by delinquency.

Let's not extend the word "delinquent" to all silly pranks, even if they backfire. Most youngsters get involved in something like youthful mischief at one time or another. Some of it may be harmless, even cute. It may elicit from us hardly more than strained smiles or somewhat embarrassed recollections of our own escapades. Some of it may be rather uncomfortable, more silly than it need be, or so thoughtless that it really isn't funny at all. Some of it may even backfire—through unfortunate circumstances or through the dangerousness of the props involved—and may result in more damage than the silly youngster had meant to produce.

From Pranks to Pathology

Now, I think, as you do, that communities should do a lot of planning on ways to keep the silly pranks of normal children and adoles-

"Who Is Delinquent?" is based on an article of the same title that appeared in *National Parent-Teacher* (December 1955), which is now published as *The PTA Magazine*.

cents within harmless limits. All I am suggesting is that this is a problem of a different order and should not be included under the "delinquency" label.

There is still a difference between "delinquency" and "juvenile crime." Some of the things you read and hear that "delinquents" are doing are so extreme, the problems they represent so severe, that they obviously belong in a chapter on advanced pathology. These actions are in no way comparable to what most people think of when they clamor that something should be done to prevent the rise of "delinquency in our neighborhoods." What you often read in the papers about the offenses committed by young arsonists, rapists, and inveterate sadists or about youngsters who suddenly go on killing sprees after having been bottled up for years behind fronts of blandly conforming passivity—all that belongs in a chapter of its own. Those youngsters are so sick that "delinquency" is much too loose a label to cover what they do. The same is true of the well-organized but extremely antisocial "young thug in the making." He is really a gangster or criminal who happens to start younger than most such people.

If we slice off "juvenile mischief" at one end of the line and "under-aged gangsters and severe mental cases" at the other, what's left? Enough. So much, indeed, that it would be hopeless to list the various types of childhood problem and disturbance in youngsters and their surroundings that need talking about. For our purposes here we had better stick to one question: Are there any general guidelines for the parent to follow when he gets worried and asks, "Does this mean that our youngsters are becoming delinquent?"

The Trouble They Cause Is Not a Safe Guide to What Causes the Trouble

Usually we expect that the seriousness of a youngster's problem can easily be detected from the seriousness of the offense he has committed or from his brazen defiance or penitent cooperation when confronted with his deeds. To most people the youngster who gets mixed up in a gang fight, which ends up with somebody's getting badly hurt or culminates in a wanton orgy of destruction, is a more serious case than the boy who is found hoarding pencils stolen from his little sister and burying them at regular intervals under his favorite tree. Also it is quite understandable that the profusely repentant sinner or the politely grateful receiver of just punishment would be considered a "good outlook," compared with the youngster who hits back when apprehended, clams up even in an interview with a friendly and well-intentioned adult, or bites the very hand that is extended in kindness.

Unfortunately everything we have learned through a thorough study of delinquent cases of all varieties proves that these general assumptions are wrong. Like most "common-sense generalizations" that are not based on research data, these theories do have a kernel of truth in them. It is important to know just what youngsters have done and how they act when confronted with capture, punishment, or reprimand. However, this is only one of the things we need to know to size up the seriousness of a case. It assumes meaning only after being put together with many more and many other data about the children's lives. Sometimes the "extremeness" of an offense or its consequences is the result of unfortunate complicating circumstances, and the youngster himself is not really a serious case.

On the other hand, our youngster with the pencil-burying ceremony may need help to learn how to solve life's problems in a less irrational way. Therefore he may actually have to be considered as more seriously disturbed. Similarly any experienced probation officer can cite dozens of cases showing how the most "hardened" psychopaths often manage to react to their punishments with the most urbanely charming attitudes of reasonableness and personal grace. He can also describe certain mentally sick patients who invariably produce the most convincing parades of penitence and conversion, whereas the observing expert knows already that the whole process is only a preamble for the next collapse. A child's "freshness" or his unreasonable attitude toward punishment may seem serious. Yet often it is but the attempt of a panicked soul to avoid hearing the voice of guilt and shame from his own conscience.

In short, things are not so simple as our "common-sense theories" would like to have them. Neither the severity of a youth's offense nor his behavior when captured, punished, or corrected is a safe sign of the severity of the delinquency problem involved.

Early Detection Is Tougher Than You Think

Among the preventive measures vehemently demanded at delinquency conferences is certainly this one—that parents ought to do more to detect delinquency early. I, too, would like to see more early detection, I can assure you. But the fuzziness and lack of precision with which we bandy this term around is severely blocking a reasonable, efficient approach to the delinquency problem. And, as far as the parents are concerned, in too many meetings and newspaper articles have I seen this very notion thrown in their faces as a punishment instead of being used to help them.

Two entirely different meanings are frequently confused in this cry for "early detection." By "early" some people are not thinking of time so much as they are thinking of the early stages of the problem. What they mean is that the parents should have done something about Johnny when he was a severe school problem instead of waiting until he ran away and then got into trouble with some older boys who gave him a ride in a stolen car. To other people "early" means early in time. They usually imply that Johnny's car thefts could have been avoided if he had been either thrashed or psychoanalyzed when he first came home from kindergarten with somebody else's toy. Both these concepts of early detection (and also early prevention) have a lot in them. But the real story is again much more complicated.

Some youngsters who are now in trouble did show problems earlier in their lives, problems that could be seen by their parents. But in many cases these children's problems were perfectly normal and had nothing to do with the trouble they are in right now. Many forms of "problem behavior" are quite typical of certain phases in a child's development and are not related to similar behavior that may occur at a later age.

It is normal for a two-year-old to try to solve his first problems of envy by seeking to destroy the toy of his rival. It is normal for a three-year-old to ignore blissfully the difference between fantasy and fact and to report imagined events with as much glee as though they had really happened. It is normal for a five-year-old to react with irritable vehemence when something interferes with his sole possession of Father's or Mother's attention. It is normal for an eight-year-old to gain status with his peers by bragging and to be quite ready to go much too far in an attempt to avoid being called a "sissy" or a "mother's boy."

It is normal for an adolescent girl to adopt for a while a "tomboyish" attitude before she is ready to accept the full impact of feminine behavior. It is normal for a young adolescent boy to form intimate friendships with his own sex as a defense against being with girls in situations too close to panic and fright.

The fact that your children did such things when they were young and you neither thrashed them nor had them psychoanalyzed does *not* mean that they will be delinquents. Your two-year-old will not have to become an extortionist mugger, nor will your three-year-old end up as a pathological liar or a passer of false checks. Your five-year-old will not try to do away with his parents or run away from home, and your eight-year-old will not have to become a professional "fence" for a gang of burglars. The tomboyish adolescent girl will not have to spend the rest of her life in sour-grapes contempt of men, and the young adolescent boy will not begin to seek the company of homosexuals and perverts. Of course there are many problems involved in handling each one of these incidents wisely, but eager "prevention" propagandists are all too likely to misinterpret them.

True, the psychiatrist may show you quite interesting connections between delinquent misdeeds and problems in earlier life. Some of these connections, however, are quite invisible to the naked eye, and nobody would expect to see them without a psychiatric microscope. Some youngsters "blow their tops," all right, when they are sixteen and often seemingly without reason. Yet the "earlier" problem signs that might have been detected when they were six were not wildness but its opposite: tearful overconformity, soundless submission to obviously stupid forms of punishment, inability to communicate and confess or to seek help when in trouble, and so forth. Neither parent nor teacher, if asked about the child's being a "delinquency risk" at that time, could possibly have seen those signs as the important clues.

The disappointing fact is that although in general later events are strongly influenced by what happens early in life, we still know very little about specific items. To predict the effect of what happens to and with Johnny now upon what happens ten years from now is possible only in the most obviously extreme cases. In the average ranges of normal family and neighborhood life, no conscientious expert would want to pretend too much magical skill.

All this should be cleanly and decently admitted by the professionals. Parents, instead of being made to feel guilty about their oversights, should be frankly told that experts, too, might not have known what to predict and what to do. Such an attitude could make better partners out of specialists and parents.

Wise handling of incidents when they happen is really the best prevention anybody can engage in, expert as well as parent and teacher. The only real answer to the detection problem remains the same as it is in all other forms of disease: hugely increased efforts at full-fledged and well-designed research.

What Can We Do Right Now?

Plenty. Let us assume that you suddenly find out that your youngster has been "involved in something" or that his attitude toward school, work, or authority makes you perk up and wonder if things aren't going wrong. What's the first thing to do?

KEEP YOUR EDUCATIONAL SHIRT ON

Some delinquent episodes in your youngster's life—and I exclude only the very serious ones from this statement—are blessings. Without them, how would you know that the formula needs changing? At least you are sure now that you need to do some thinking and replanning and that you aren't just getting jittery, nervous, or fussy yourself. So remember, the discovery that something is about to go wrong, no matter how upsetting for the moment, is probably the luckiest thing that could have happened to you. For if you had missed it much longer, how difficult it would be to get things back to normal!

CONTROL YOUR THEORIES

For many years I used to advise parents who came to me with delinquency worries to control their tempers. Amazingly enough, I don't have to do that quite so much any more. People have learned so much about the complexity of mental health, human emotions, and child development that only very tactless, ill-mannered, or sick adults still fly into rages at the discovery of specific problems in their children's lives. But I find now that people's inabilities to control their theories still block the path of reasonable educational and corrective planning. For even highly educated and otherwise well-informed parents, quite capable of counting up to ten as far as Junior is directly concerned, let fly with the most unwarranted, unexamined, half-baked, or downright stupid theories about his behavior and how to stop it!

My advice to you, then, is this: When suddenly confronted with the task of worrying about your youngster, please avoid *any* theories for the time being. This is not the moment to decide just which part of whose stock of knowledge applies best in your case. Your child is still your child, a person of a given age, of given characteristics, who has grown out of very specific circumstances into equally specific character patterns and is doing right now very unique and very specific things. You have to look at him and what he did long enough to know what is really going on inside and around him. In fact, I might suggest a moratorium on theory until you have the facts figured out. It is better to avoid going to delinquency discussions and reading newspaper reports on rapists and murderers and vandalism cases for a while. It is easier to see just what really is happening to John and Mary right now —and what their behavior means in the world they and you live in— if you don't compare them all the time with other people's cases.

CHECK UP ON WHAT IS RIGHT WITH THEM

Let me confess right off the bat that I don't consider a child's assets any excuse whatever for committing delinquent acts, nor does intelligence, ability, or social charm necessarily aid the task of prevention or repair. I know some crooks who know their psychology books, including their own case histories, better than their psychiatrists ever did. I know some youngsters who have a special knack for using all their assets as the main selling points for the rotten sides of their characters. And I know many parents who lull themselves into do-nothing attitudes under the cozy blanket of their children's good points.

When I demand a thorough investigation of what is right with a child I mean something quite different. I think I can show it best by a comparison from the field of medicine. As we all know, some diseases are simply matters for surgery. The diseased parts have to be cut out— of course, under very special and skillfully handled circumstances—and that's all there is to it. But many more diseases are not of that nature at all. There is nothing to cut out, or, if there is, cutting it out would never do. Some of these diseases have to be fought indirectly by "supportive therapy." That is, the healthy part of the organism has to be supported by special tricks, so that it can by itself do a better job of fighting off whatever would make it sick without such aid.

It is interesting but sad that when most people talk about delinquency they think of the surgical-operation type of thing first. Yet much remedial work in this area resembles the supportive-therapy approach. And to use this therapy we have to know just what it is that needs the support, what we have to build on. This is why we have to learn what is right with our children.

If a Symptom Disappears Too Miraculously, Run to an Expert Fast

I have seen more youngsters messed up because their parents are too complacent about surface results than youngsters whose parents wouldn't even try to tackle problems. The layman is still in love with quick cures. The real facts are harder to take. If a problem has developed in your child's life over a considerable period of time or if some extreme behavior outburst has occurred seemingly "out of nowhere," his course of recovery (after you have found the right thing to do) should be slow and gradual. Things ought to get a little better for a while. Then you should expect another outbreak of some trouble or other or a recurrence of the old. Then things ought to go uphill again for another stretch. After several such phases you may gradually rest assured that the real cause of the original problem is now being taken care of.

Whenever a youngster with a serious problem shows too much of a sudden "miracle change," you should try to find out just where the problem behavior went. For miracles, by the very definition of the term, are rare. If Junior's problems disappear just after you talked with him, thrashed him, or bought him a new football outfit, you have a right to be suspicious. The nearest social agency or child-guidance clinic will help you assess what is going on.

Stop Being Ashamed of Having "Delinquency Troubles" in Your Beautiful Home

We really ought to have learned this lesson from the history of medicine long ago. All the most vicious diseases couldn't even begin to be tackled until people lost their shame about them and faced them courageously. Not an inch of real progress was made in venereal disease, tuberculosis, epilepsy, cancer, and so forth until people stopped thinking that such things happen only in "homes not so fine as ours" or that these afflictions "can't happen here."

Many parents are still ashamed to admit to themselves the beginning of delinquent traits in their children because they still assume that delinquency ought to hit only the underprivileged. Research does not uphold such illusions. Like most afflictions, delinquency may strike anywhere. Sometimes it strikes families who could have helped it but didn't care enough to try. In most cases, however, things are not that simple. The most conscientiously observant parents, the most enthusiastically devoted teachers, may have rashes of it hit their homes or classrooms for reasons way beyond their grasp. There is nothing to be ashamed of. All you need to do is wake up and start grasping.

$\mathcal{S}$ex Education: Unfinished Business

THERE ARE PLENTY of good books and articles on what we know about sex education, but a book could be written also on what we don't know. Questions about just where we stand today and what we still have to learn are challenging ones. But all I can do in an informal little discussion like this is to think out loud about what bothers me most about the problem at this very moment. Remember, this is not a scientific compendium of present-day knowledge about sex; it does not promise to solve your problems with Junior. I don't pretend even that what I have to say is "new." But I repeat these are the things that bother me plenty.

The Devil at the Back Door

What we "enlightened adults" are proudest of in this field is that we have cast behind us a lot of the hellfire-and-brimstone approach to sex curiosity and sex behavior in growing children and have certainly become aware that it doesn't help to scare them and adopt a punitive attitude. In fact, we are even convinced that kids with quite obvious problems in that line, although in need of advice and control, are more helped by encouragement, reason, and moral support. Unfortunately, this changed attitude does not hold for all age groups of children. As so often happens, the old primitive "devil" manages to smuggle himself back into the picture, often by the back door during the very ritual that was originally meant to exorcise him. In this case, the devil has crept in through two back doors, really.

One is the concept of "traumatic experiences." Years ago, psychiatry discovered the importance of the fact that occasionally a single unfortunate experience might have the power to "fixate" a person on

"Sex Education: Unfinished Business" is based on the article of the same title that was published in *Child Study* (Winter 1954–1955), copyright 1954, Child Study Association of America. Reprinted by permission of the publishers.

an earlier development or to cause all sorts of hocus-pocus in the human soul that is hard to get rid of later. This concept is still a good one, and we have all been made aware of the fact that many adult neuroses or other mental afflictions may be traced back to things that happened in early childhood. But we have learned a few additional facts of life since this concept was first introduced. The general public, picking up psychiatric terminology at the original source, often forgets to note later modifications in the picture. We know now that the concept of "traumatic" experiences is not meant to be quite so rigid as it sounds. For some people have undergone exactly what for others was "traumatic," yet show few lasting ill effects. Some have even drawn later character strengths from what originally might have been expected to break their backs. We have learned that such things as the culture, the value system, and the subcultural background in which things happen have a lot to do with determining whether or not an experience is traumatic: We need to learn a lot more about what is normal for Johnny where *he* lives before we can be sure what a given experience will do to him.

Unfortunately, although the modern psychiatrist is quite aware of this, the public likes its borrowed concepts nice and rigid and is liable to stick to its old guns. We no longer make the *kids* afraid that a doubtful sex experience will wreck them for life. But we have got the parents scared stiff that Johnny might be doomed to becoming a homosexual just because he was involved in some smutty incident in the schoolyard. It would be silly, of course, to pass lightly over the possibility that an experience may have "traumatic effects," especially if it is accompanied by feelings of helplessness, anxiety, and guilt. The answer is not a vain "either-or" of terror or irresponsible dismissal but recognition that more organized research is needed. What really is the truth about this for the nation at large? And how can we help the parent in doubt to assess the meaning and impact of a specific incident with a specific child? No wonder young people complain we don't give them answers that are definite enough to offer guidance. How can we, as long as we indulge in either-or battles instead of making a constructive attack on the basic problem at hand?

The other back door through which the "devil" of hellfire-and-brimstone fear of sex comes into the picture leads right into the science and social-science classrooms of our schools. There, too, of course, the sly old devil uses the smartest disguise. What, to cover a superstitious belief, could be better than scientific terminology? But in giving children good scientific information we sometimes disguise our own motives. Of course, nowadays nobody would want to "wipe out" the sexual urge in his child or try to squash it with shame and fear. But are we really acting so differently if we try to squash it with semantic antics and scientific terms? Isn't a good deal of our talk about the importance of "sex information" and a "good, clean scientific vocabulary" based on the secret hope that we can somehow "educate" sex feelings out of our kids? I wouldn't be surprised if many children heard, not what the adult was saying about reproduction and so forth but another voice saying something like this: "Listen, none of this sex stuff is for *you*, understand? Of course, it is perfectly all right to *know* about such things or to name them—provided that Latin is the main language used for such nomenclature. So I'll give you all the correct terms and the slides and anatomical charts, even movies. But you must promise in return not to grin or smirk or giggle or smile. And, of course, none of that sexy stuff at all. If you promise to drop all sex *emotions* right here and now, that encyclopedia of sexual research on the shelf is all yours."

I hope I shall not be misunderstood. I am all for sex education in appropriate forms and at the developmentally right time. I am not complaining that we have too much of that. On the contrary, we have much too little. But I am complaining that the old devil of "scare the sex out of them" is apt to sneak back into our best efforts in the guise of enlightened "matter-of-fact" talk. Sex information is needed because knowledge is important in itself and because ignorance is the worst block to reason and control. It is meant to *aid* in the development of healthy sex attitudes, not to *substitute* for them.

Our Greatest Enemy: The Stereotype

We have, on the whole, become quite reasonable in our approach to the sexual development of the younger child. (Of course I'd rather you didn't force me to define just whom I mean by "we" at the moment or to count the number of people who should be included in such a statement.) But we still have trouble with the adolescents. Certainly some of our worries are justified and realistic. That is so obvious I hope I can skip over it lightly without being misinterpreted. Of course, some of the consequences of sexual behavior are more threatening when the youngster's body approaches physiological maturity and his actions are subject to much less parental control. Granting this, I still want to point out that we are getting to be quite irrational in our collective reaction to the problem of teen-age sex. No matter how much we may love our own youngsters or those entrusted to our care, the moment we talk collectively with the voice of "the adult," the youngster becomes "the teen-ager," and from then on it is clear that we think he is not to be trusted and that the only thing that stops him from acting out his terrible sex impulses is the watchful stare of the adult. There is another stereotype, of course, for stereotypes always come in pairs, like chimney decorations in a Victorian home. That is the illusion of the "nice, all-round kid," the real, red-blooded, sport-enthusiastic, "clean-cut" boy. All this boy is allowed of sex is the anatomical fact that he *is* a boy. Beyond that much concession to nature, he is not supposed to be interested in anything but plane models, baseball, and bottle-top collections. The female counterpart to this stereotype can easily be drawn by the reader.

What disturbs me about this naïve illusion of the black-and-white drawing is that it prevents us from giving solid guidance to the kids when they need it. When some kids become open sex problems, we are liable to get so disgusted and confused that we exclude them from the channels of therapy and adult life that they so badly need, whereas with the kids who seem to fit into the stereotype of the all-round boy we miss the boat because we don't feel right in assuming that they, too, have emotions and fantasies. Their adult sex life is supposed to just "pop out of nowhere," ready-made, so to say, with no trouble to us at all. Obviously, this is not the way the child grows to be a man or woman. How, then, in the face of our many mistakes do so many of them manage the transition with pretty fair success?

The Kids Themselves Do the Job

To answer that, I think we must first ask some other questions.

First, with all the trouble with sex problems and delinquency, is it true that the majority of youth is ending up as sex fiends or perverts?

Answer. No, nonsense. It is too bad that we only count the deviates and make no scientifically valid count of the normal youngsters. The majority of our youth, as the population figures show, seems to become quite capable of producing offspring, and, although a lot may be wrong in the daily life of many families, only a few of the parents break out into serious violence.

Second, is most youth given adequate sex education at the time when it needs it most?

Answer. No. Most schools do not face the problem at all, and most adults, even if they want to meet the sex-education needs of the youngsters, get there many years too late.

Third, if this is so, where do all the well-adjusted adults of this generation come from? If, as we well know, the adult generation is far from taking adequate care of sexual knowledge for youngsters and their introduction into the mysteries of love, who does the job?

Answer. The other kids.

I know this last answer sounds absurd, for isn't it a well-known fact that the kids tell one another the wrong things, that they often abuse the innocence of their age mates, and that the worst and filthiest stuff comes from what "that other kid told mine"? Granted. But where does the good information come from and the emotional relief of ignorance lifted and anxiety assuaged? It, too, comes from the other kids. In most people's lives there have been not only other kids who have told them the wrong stuff or teased them mercilessly about their ignorance. There have also been a few who had mercy upon them and told them what they obviously needed to know. And the mere fact that, in informal group bull sessions, even a frightening and shame-loaded subject may seem silly, funny, or at least less fearful must be counted as one of the "preventive psychiatric measures" that nature provided long before we invented "group therapy." In short, I really mean to insist that the major job of preventive psychiatry around sex knowledge and the sex lives of our youth is being taken care of by youth itself. The real psychiatrists for our children are the peer groups. Obviously there are silly or dishonest or exploitative "peers" and "peer groups" in our communities. But why count only them and not look at the terrific marvel that, by and large, the peer group of the American child, without any guidance or training and certainly with no help from adult society, is doing a passable job?

I don't insist that this is as it should be. Of course not. The "peer group" of the present-day adolescent world is as much in turmoil and confusion as is the world of adults—how could it help but be? It is not a good idea to relegate a job as important as the sex education of youth so much to chance. It is time that the adult generation takes the task seriously and produces adequate youth guidance on all levels. We might even learn much from a survey in which we tried to find out from youngsters how they have answered the sex questions of other youngsters and what experiences they themselves remember as recipients of such help.

Why Not More Confidence in Confidence?

We have done a lot of "parent education" on the sex issue over the last twenty-five years. Beside giving helpful aid, there is no doubt that we have also sometimes messed things up a bit. In trying to "unscare" parents about the sex lives of their children, we have inadvertently made some of them too light-hearted and unconcerned about youth's need for guidance. On the other hand, I think we have made other parents feel so responsible for giving sex education to their children that they constantly fear they have not done enough or have not done it in just the right way.

Among the insecurities we have helped to produce in the present parent generation there is one especially that I should like to single out for attention here. That is the frequent confusion about the meaning of "confidence." The fact is that the conscientious, psychiatry-loyal parent of today has a terrific need to be sure that his son or daughter develops enough "confidence" in him to share all secrets, including the most intimate problems of sex. This attitude is understandable because many conscientious parents themselves have gone through times of worry and confusion in their youths when they could not find any adults worthy of their confidence. The problem we are running into now looks something like this: In order to confide in one's parents— so we argue—about a delicate matter like sex, one must have a lot of confidence, a really deep "rapport" with them. True. But many parents now turn this insight around or overstretch it. What, then—so they argue—if my son or daughter does not ask me questions about sex, does not choose *me* as the one to turn to for such advice? This, they fear, is proof positive that they don't "mean anything" to their children. Why should "my own flesh and blood" turn to that "stranger" or that teacher in school, they ask, especially after "I have done everything always to let him know I love him?" In short, the ambitious parent of today is liable to tremble at the idea that his son's or daughter's sexual problems might be brought to other people or that kids might go through phases in which verbal help is not sought from parents at all.

Fortunately, we know it isn't necessary for the parent to feel so disturbed about this situation. It is well known that sometimes children go through a phase in which direct communication about sexual issues is the hardest to achieve with the people they love the *most*. Many children then turn to their peers or other adult friends or books, not because they have no confidence in their parents but because they feel so strongly and positively toward them that, in this area, the "home-grown adult" is, for the time being, taboo.

Parents are confused about the very concept of confidence itself. "Confidence," as used in this connection, clearly refers to some especially positive and intimate relationship of a child to an adult. But relationships can be manifold, and people have different types of relationship with different people, with much overlapping. Some children, for instance, like their psychologists. They have so much "confidence" in them that even matters hard to discuss are easily unpacked before them and put into their laps. At the same time, a psychologist suddenly turning up at camp or taking a kid to a department store may find himself amazed at how little influence he has on any other than the "let's share a secret" type of situation in the youngster's life. Even while he is with his most trusted "psychologist," Bobby may raise such mayhem in that department store that both get themselves bounced in no uncertain terms. At the same time, I have found children with terrific emotional affection for a teacher or camp counselor and with real "trust" in his judgment in direct life situations. Although these children would never dream of divulging to their beloved counselor what they have just confided to their psychologist in the last clinical interviews, they would stop being unmanageable and would come down off the roof in a minute if the counselor said to.

The moral of all this is that it is not true that, just because a child likes you, all the avenues of his life will be open to you. Some children will, on the basis of their love and trust, open up to you the avenue of shared secrets and will drop the barriers of shame and guilt. Others will open to you the avenue of "power over my actions" and will do things you demand without fear of loss of face. Both cases may imply that the child has "confidence" in you. Also we know that, with adolescent youngsters, very often the areas and ways in which they allow you an "in" on their lives shift rapidly.

I think it is important to remember this, partly so that parents need not feel guilty unnecessarily simply because, at a certain phase, other people are more "logical" confidants in matters of sexual guidance and partly because this confusion about "confidence" is often the cause of unwarranted jealousy between school and home. Many parents are afraid of asking educators, physicians, or psychiatrists to help in the sex education of their children, not because they really think they can handle it all alone, but because they are afraid that to call for assistance would reflect negatively on them and their abilities to win the children's trust. Getting rid of this illusion ought to make teamwork easier among all those who are needed in Johnny's or Mary's life.

Are You So Sure This Was Really "Sex"?

It is interesting to notice how often there is a great difference between what the experts say and what the general public hears them say and, even more baffling, how much of what experts say the general public entirely refuses to hear. It sometimes takes a few generations for these discrepancies to disappear.

Take just one of the smaller items out of the discoveries of Sigmund Freud. He sure said loudly enough for everybody to hear how often fantasies or feelings connected with sex may be involved even in seemingly "harmless" behavior, where the bare eyes of the layman might not expect to find such "hidden content" at all. The public heard that one all right. What Freud and all his disciples have *also* said, however, still seems to remain quite unheard: that sometimes it can be the other way around. The obviousness with which sex is involved in a given piece of behavior may be striking, yet the real problem in many such instances may lie somewhere else. Over the years, I have been called into many school situations in which groups of preadolescents had been caught in some form of sex play or other. It seemed to the authorities that those cases would naturally need sex counseling or might have to be referred for special treatment because of evidences of homosexuality or other perversions. In many of those cases it was soon obvious, though, that "sex" was only the surface reason for the behavior. The real problem lay elsewhere. Many of the little boys caught in what seemed to adults the purely sexual act of mutual masturbation were in reality primarily reassuring themselves about their eligibility to run with an "older and tougher group," accepting this ordeal as a social initiation rite with great strain, guilt, shame, and disgust. The literature of psychiatry is also rich in descriptions of prostitution among adolescent girls in which "sex" is actually the minor point—it is a weapon used in the revenge battle against rejecting or overstrict homes. In my work in the field of juvenile delinquency, I run time and time again into the "hardened case" of the supposed sex delinquent who blackmails or forces other youngsters into participation in his sexual acts.

No doubt there are plenty of youngsters with severe sex perversions produced by disorganized family and neighborhood life. Yet some of these youngsters are neither genuine perverts nor oversexed. What is wrong with them is their total lack of *control* over their impulses and their exploitative outlook on life, which makes any pleasurable act okay, regardless of the feelings of another person forced into it. The real damage to their personalities lies in the indecency of their basic philosophy of life or the absence of any feeling for "people." They need therapy, to be sure, but it is to their brains and their hearts that the therapy should be directed, not to their genitalia.

The deafness of the public to this important difference between the surface or overt behavior and the basic personality factors really involved is probably one of the most disastrous sources of failure in the proper guidance of the youth of today. Because of it, we are apt to apply effort in the wrong place and to miss the boat not only with the disturbed youngster but with the normal one as well.

Sometimes "Experts" Need Help Too

There are a few facts of which we—now I mean those of us in the fields of sex education, child development, psychology, and psychiatry —also should be reminded. Among them is one that was brought home to me several years ago when I was busy running a treatment home for particularly wild and uninhibited specimens of the preteenage generation. These kids were anything but physically overdeveloped; they had not even come close to the actual physiological stages one usually associates with puberty proper. However, their exposure, from early years of life on, to all the details and pathology of an open-door neighborhood sex life had made them rather peculiar in their outlook on sex. In a way, they were extremely "corrupt" as far as knowledge and sex terminology went, and the only reason I knew they hadn't read books on sex pathology was because they couldn't read. On the other hand, they had a deep need, from time to time, to go back and try to live out very early childhood attitudes that normal children get behind them before the end of their nursery-school years. The result was that I often was confronted with the sudden eruption of wild sexual behavior under conditions and in places where it obviously could not be afforded, even though much of what they did actually was quite "harmless" from the psychological point of view.

Whatever the details, the problem at the moment was to find ways to "stop that nonsense right now" without at the same time creating any feeling in their distortion-eager minds that we were opposed to sex, thought them depraved, or wanted to make them guilty or scared and without contributing to their outlook on sex as just so much smut anyway. I sought, at that time, advice on this matter from many sources —after I had exhausted what I thought I knew myself and had learned from experiences with such children over the years. This is the amazing thing I ran into at that time: I found all sources of advice most helpful in pointing out *why* those children might act the way they did. I also found these people most helpful when discussing just what we must "by all means avoid" in order not to add to the problem or create secondary trauma in those children. In fact, I found them so helpful because they all pointed out to me what I already knew. It seemed, however, they were as stuck as I was when it came to the question: How, while avoiding damage to the kids, am I going to *stop* them acting in this way before the cops come and cart them off to jail?

The despair in which I found myself has since given rise to my fervent interest in developing research into an "instrumentology" of interference techniques for child behavior, and I think this is needed on all fronts of the educational scene. Especially in the area of sex education, however, this experience has brought me up against one of the most serious gaps in our present equipment: We know a lot about the causes of sexual misdevelopment and about the nature of normal sexual development (though not quite so much), and we are beginning to learn about the techniques for long-range therapy for severe deviates. But as yet we know little to say when a sincere mother asks us, But what am I to do right now?

Fortunately, practice is, in this area, way ahead of theory and research. Most experienced specialists will be stunned by the abstract question, but, when you fill in for them the details about a certain child and a certain experience, they usually come through with the goods and deliver better than we really have a right to expect.

Let's Start Where We Are—But Where Are We?

Plenty of amazing progress has been made during the last few decades, not only in our actual knowledge about children and sex, but also in the spread of more enlightened attitudes among parents and in schools. The things we know best and that have been learned by the largest number of adults can be outlined as follows.

Many more people take more serious interest in the task of sex education for their children. We have learned a lot about what is to be considered "normal" in the development of sexual curiosity and sex behavior, certainly for the very young child. We have tried many techniques of sex information and sex education talks, and in the process of doing so we have gotten over most of the silly and strained efforts to find *the* "answer."

We have learned to consider more carefully just which of many approaches might be best for a particular child. We have learned that sex enlightenment, as well as sex education, is a task spreading into as many developmental phases as the child goes through, rather than something to "be got over with when he is five or fifteen." We have relaxed in our reaction to much child behavior that used to scare us, and at the same time most of us have got over jumping from an over-anxious and overmoralistic rejection of sex into an equally naïve illusion that all sex problems would be solved if parents only made nudist camps out of their homes or if kids were only allowed to act out their impulses.

We have come to recognize in some degree that many things about sexual growth, like the gradual development of sex roles, are quite as important to understand as are masturbation and menstruation. We now see that during transitional ages, especially in early adolescence, kids may have trouble "accepting their masculinity or femininity" and that such transitional growth pains are quite different from the real McCoy of homosexuality or perversion. We even have begun to listen to Kinsey, who tells us that a lot of the sexual experimentation that we previously relegated to textbooks on sex pathology is "gone through" by a much larger number of later quite normal adults than we had recognized.

Most of this—and a great deal more that would take too long to list here—can be taken for granted at this time, though it seems that quite a lot of people are taking an awfully long time to learn what "we" think "we know" in this day and age.

Where do we go from here? There is plenty yet to be done. In fact, the list would get so long it would bust the framework of this little study wide open. Therefore, let me restrain myself and limit this list to only three out of at least twenty-five possible points.

POINT 1

We still have, and search for, much too little knowledge about the problems of the adolescent and older youth. In fact, most of the books on direct sex education that are addressed to youth and have any claim to being frank and "talking turkey" are for the very young ages. We don't dare to "talk turkey" and be frank with the older kids. Why?

POINT 2

Our thoughtfulness about, and tolerance of, some unavoidable, "developmentally quite harmless" sexual behavior in kids stops around the seventh grade or so. Sex discussions from then on are definitely scary to adults, and we don't really know what to say or do. For a while we fool ourselves by telling adolescents what they wanted to know six years before—a process that gives us the illusion that we are providing "sex education" in some of our schools. But we are still quite ill-equipped to handle even the questions, to say nothing of the challenge for advice on action, of the older kids.

POINT 3

There is also the area of opinions that we are in danger of infecting youth with our own cowardice. The teacher who assists a kid in a rough sex problem still sticks his neck way out and is liable to be fired. The principal who allows too much advice to be given or sex education to go on in his school has to tremble in his boots every day even in the most "enlightened" community, as the effect of any crank objection is still terrific. This problem goes so far that we are even afraid to practice what we know because we can't afford to "take a chance." Many a coeducational program, for instance, that would dissolve pathological tensions in a given school in no time can only be "risked" with children who are very young. As long as the boys are so little that they want only to tease girls anyway or the girls are so big that they would despise these younger boys to begin with, coeducational programs are "safe." But at the time when they really begin to need each other in order to learn how to live with each other, we aren't so keen on it any more. Sometimes, too, we hesitate to help a kid who has developed a somewhat shady reputation, even though we know what he needs, because his rehabilitation might not be successful. We accept the fact that people sometimes may die even in well-planned operations, but we have no tolerance if a case of sex therapy backfires even a little bit.

Courage—In Conviction and Research

The answer to all this? More courage of our convictions, even the ones that don't happen to be popular. And more research, for, even with courage, how can we tell youngsters what they need to hear before we know what that really is?

In essence, then, the problem of sex development in the youth of our day is really a problem of the morale, brains, and stamina of the adults. Usually an adult generation has the types of problem with its youth that it deserves. If we could get together more on our own confusions about "values" as well as about psychologically correct procedures, we wouldn't find it quite so hard to face the problems with our kids.

Psychopathological Risks of Camp Life

$\mathcal{N}$o, I AM NOT debunking camping at all. On the contrary, just because I am so firmly convinced of the tremendous value of camping, educationally and also as a means of therapy, I can afford to discuss a topic like this without fear of being misunderstood.

This is what I mean. We are using camping on various levels to help youngsters grow up. We use the camp for character training, for supportive mental hygiene, for the treatment of disturbed children, and to stimulate normal values. But just because camping is such a powerful drug, it also shares the properties of all other powerful drugs on the market. It is risky, if the wrong person swallows it or if the right one swallows too much of it or at the wrong time. In short, the camp itself is not only something through which children are supposed to adjust better but also something to which they have to adjust.

This adjustment to camp life, which we take so much for granted, is not always easy, and sometimes the conflicts produced by the need for adjustment overbalance the values to be derived from its accomplishment. For the city child especially, large-scale group life far away from his home and exposure to what must seem to be "nature in the raw" without the protective comforts of the mechanized urban environment are sometimes quite a problem.

In most cases these difficulties can be counteracted, handled, adequately met. But we want to be sure that we meet them.

The following, therefore, is an attempt to analyze camp life in terms of its psychopathological risks for those who have trouble in making adjustments to this medium.

The word "psychopathological" refers only to camp life, not to the camper. I am not talking here about the problem child but about the average normal youngster who is exposed to this new medium for the

"Psychopathological Risks of Camp Life" is based on the article of the same title that appeared in *The Nervous Child*, VI, No. 2 (April, 1947), 139–147.

first time. If I list here the "psychopathological risks" of camping, then this limitation is due to the nature of our topic. I could write a much longer and more impressive list of the values of camping—and have done so in other places.

The Snake in the Grass or Nature in the Raw

The enthusiastic books on nature and its effects on our soul have all been written by people who have attained an appreciation of values that not everybody starts out with. Nature is all that people say in their books—and more. However, it includes much that they do not mention in their books. Let us remember the change from the overprotected city world, which constitutes the first exposure to camp life for a city child. The firmly built apartment house or suburban mansion is replaced by rustic log cabins or flimsy tents. And even the shack of the slum area child at least stands among other shacks in a familiar urban environment and therefore suggests much more security than does the camp cabin. The toilet smells, or the things that are supposed to prevent it from doing so smell worse. Animals and insects like spiders, flies, and ants intrude upon privacy at moments when the study of nature is not necessarily the main concern. That shady tree over there looks just like the one in that story book, under which the hero used to spin his daydreams. However, the child has hardly sat down under it when it seems as if half his zoology textbook is let loose on him. At night it gets dark. He never noticed darkness so much, especially darkness that is filled with a variety of entirely unfamiliar sounds. Sometimes he hears a wild racket way up in the skies, just like in some of those murder movies or thriller-radio plays. A storm is fascinating to watch, but he also has to listen to it, and maybe he has to step out into it to get to the washhouse or dining hall. There is an absence of all familiar noises like the streetcar, the automobiles on the drive behind his house, the street vendor. Maybe most of the new noises are less loud and "nerve-wracking," but they are certainly more frightening, for he has trouble identifying most of them, and the stillness of a nonmechanized world brings them out more threateningly.

City children have heard and read about storms, animals, and nature and have used these images as props in their nightmares and daydreams. What isolated contacts they have made with nature usually were in broad daylight or in the protective custody of father or mother on that car trip. Suddenly all nature is let loose on the child from town. It stirs up most of the half-forgotten childhood anxieties. Fantasy fears and real discomfort are mixed in a frightening blend. The result is that many children are frightened at camp much of the time. They may have to handle more anxieties in the first few camp days than during the entire school year—anxieties for the management of which routine, experience, and protective understanding have not been adequately developed.

The symptomatology of these anxieties is fascinating to watch. Few of them come out into the open in their direct forms, recognizable for what they are. Most suffer the destiny of "displacement" before they can be expressed. They assume all sorts of disguise—dissatisfaction with the cook, complaints about lack of cleanliness, opposition to the program, antagonism to the cabin. Or they assume a heavier disguise, the safest one they can assume, that of transformation into the opposite. Johnny's neurotic fear of nature in the raw is shown to you as an unreasonable bravado against all health and safety rules; his fear of the snake in the grass may be turned into a compulsive display of what looks like "nature-study interest."

The basic meaning of all this, however, is obvious and can be summed up in a simple statement: Johnny is exposed to a revival of some old childhood neurosis, or he is exposed to a new one in the making. In both cases he needs considerable help from you before the camp can really take hold.

Parents Through the Screened Porch

For many children the first camp experience also means the first decisive separation from the familiar life at home. This is, of course, true for those with somewhat overprotective but very happy family lives, but it is just as true for those whose home and family lives are really confused and unhappy. For even if the home environment is less pleasant than camp, it is certainly more familiar, and adaptive mechanisms to cope with its discomforts are well developed. Separation from home and the parents—even a temporary, voluntary, well-planned, and on the whole desirable one—cuts deep into the unconscious layers of Johnny's or Mary's case history. Some children love camp and enjoy every moment of it, but they know that Mother would really be quite disappointed to realize that Junior is so independent of her, and so this joy of camp life is tinged with guilt feelings in terms of early childhood loyalties. Other children go through feelings of discomfort at camp that they might be able to handle under their own steam. They know, however, that their parents really want them away—and this additional sting produces a conflict beyond their power to allay. Others again move through a happy phase of emancipation from home and enjoy their newly found independence for a while. With the next letter or package—or a letter or package for a cabin mate—the whole world of childhood conflict suddenly rises before their eyes, and the camp and whatever it tries to do may be engulfed. Some children enjoy the chance to unpack all the negative feelings they had piled up against family and home routine and to throw them rebelliously at the camp substitutes, indulging in pleasurable fights against the windmills of their case histories. Others withdraw from the threat of adjustment to camp into glorified nostalgic daydreams about home, painting pictures with colors they never possessed, and are in for rude awakenings on the first visiting day. In short, parents and home look different through the porch screen of the camp veranda. This experience of different feelings about home and the home folks is an upsetting experience for many youngsters, even when the outcome is to the good.

The symptoms of this phenomenon are varied. They are caught most concisely in the letters the children write, the stories they tell about camp. Most of them have little to do with the emotional and culinary reality of camp life. Most of them are designed to hit the consumer in a spot where it either pleases or hurts and to glorify some, to cover up other phases of real camp life. Camp directors would be horrified if they knew how often Johnny has to tell Mama he loves her by making the camp counselor out to be a torturing sadist and the camp director a parsimonious exploiter of little children's stomachs. And parents would be horrified if they knew how often that glorified description of the marvelous canoe trip really means an accusation against their own roles in life with Johnny at home.

With skillful planning, with good luck in the choice of camp counselors, and with unusual wisdom in the handling of moments of depression as well as of rebellion, Johnny and Mary will cope with this new experience in their lives. If the camp is less skilled or the home background just a few notches more confused or really wrong, this "adjustment phase" in the children's lives may in itself become the source of neurotic developments. Its proper handling is one of the things you hope for when you send Johnny to camp.

Ego Ideals for Rent

Most of us who invite children to come to our camps have deepseated ambitions to provide especially "valuable experiences" for them, to produce some changes or improvements in their character traits, in their value sensitivities, or at least in their abilities to bow in the right way before the altar of Emily Post. The camps that can claim serious consideration educationally certainly aim to make something of a "new person" out of Johnny, and if they succeed are proud of the way in which "he has taken to camp life." The ego ideal of the "good camper" has, as far as I know, not yet been studied by sociologists and anthropologists, and I certainly recommend it to them for study. I dare not bring up all the amazing things we would discover in such a study, but I should like to say this much: The ego ideal of the "good camper" is a special ethical standard developed in American society. Parts of it are derived from cultures that we conquered and exterminated (consider the heavy emphasis on Indian lore); other parts are nostalgic reminiscences of a world our nation has left behind (the lumberman at the campfire, the conqueror of mountains and streams, the skillful survivor against odds through crafty use of ax and bow and arrow). Some parts of this ego ideal are, of course, colored by the personal idiosyncrasies of the camp director or the people who give the money to run the camp (the different shades of religious philosophy or the varying styles of group life from autocratic militarism through various forms of cultist groups of "friendship for friendship's sake"). Some of the components of this camper ideal come from social pressures (a chance to teach Mary how to eat with fork and knife) and some from a simple urge to have the children stored during the summer vacation without too much risk of damage (the stress of being "good," constructive, adult-acceptable at all times).

For our purpose it is sufficient to remind ourselves that the exposure to this new ego ideal of the "good camper"—in whatever variety Johnny may meet it at any particular time—is a temporary one only.

This personality ideal is not for sale; it is only for rent, for your camp and the style of life to which you want Johnny to adjust run for only a few weeks. The style of life to which Johnny will have to return will vary to a considerable degree from this personality image of the good camper that you support with so much campfire glow. This temporary rental of special ideals, part of which we want to be incorporated for good, part of which we want Johnny to discard as soon as the camp train hits the city terminal, may sometimes constitute a problem of its own. Let me mention only a few from among the rich variety of pathological problems encountered along this line. If Johnny has too much trouble in adopting this ego ideal of the "good camper" for summer use, he will be a misfit in camp. He is doomed to be the scapegoat for the others and will be looked down upon by the camp adults—no matter what a genius he may be in his urban life—and all he can do is sit in the corner and either cry or pout or spin megalomanic daydreams against the group. If Johnny is too enthusiastic in becoming that 100 per cent good camper, he may sometimes bite off more than he can chew and end by becoming a failure in his own eyes, or he may really assume temporarily a tremendous amount of fame and "leadership" but on a basis on which it will not be granted to him when he gets back to his home town. Or he may push himself into a nostalgic ego ideal of woodsmanship and pioneerdom for which there is little use after his return to "civilian life," for only people who want to become camp directors themselves in their later lives, and a very few other exceptions can afford to turn into cultists of nature and permanent campfire enthusiasts. As for Johnny and Mary, we do not want them to swap their identifications with the complexity of urban occupations for these dated daydreams; we want them only to use some of the trappings of these ego ideals during the rental period for the inculcation of some of the values smuggled in under their romantic disguise.

It is interesting to discover that many very good city children do not make "easy campers" on that score, nor do some of the very bad ones. For them the new imagery of a mixture of "woodsman, pioneer, and Indian warrior culture" is strange, funny, or frightening. Instead of feeling secure and happy with us, they feel strange, lost, out of place. The semireligious ritual that the American camping movement has developed for the cultivation of this ego ideal as a substitute for a genuine youth cult is often rejected vehemently at the first exposure to camp. And some of the children who take too easily to these ideals, the so-called "natural campers," are sometimes prone to exploit them for pathological uses. Instead of being inspired by them, they smuggle their ego ideals home for permanent exploitation in terms of the easy superiority of the nature cultist to more realistic forms of city life, and they hide their inabilities to adjust to more complex structures of life behind the glorified and simple concepts of romantic escapist cults. The camps will do well to keep this phase of their life and work in mind. Sometimes our diet is too poor in terms of ego ideals, sometimes too crowded with them. Sometimes we do too superficial a job of rental; sometimes we try too hard to make permanent what is meant for use in summertime only. Sometimes we confuse the ritual form and the basic character content, and sometimes we fall so in love with our own ego ideals that we forget to study the consumer who is going to use them.

The resistance to, or enthusiasm for, these ego ideals sometimes produces a phase of conflict and confusion in our campers. To classify our stock of ego ideals, to help the youngsters who are confused about them, is an important phase of camp policy.

Can You Howl with the Wolves?

One of the great values of camping for many youngsters is that it shifts the emphasis from the adjustment of one child to the dominating adult pattern of life toward the task of adjustment to life with a group of other children his own age. This ambition to be a good member of a youthful group and to make a go of it even in the light of conflict and discomfort is a frequent theme of camp life. On the other hand, we should not forget that this very shift in developmental emphasis from "life with father" to "life with peers" is sometimes a difficult and painful one and that not all children are ready for it at the same time. In fact, this very desire to be popular with "the rest of the gang" is often in direct conflict with old, deeply ingrained demands of parental obedience. Thus many children are, through the philosophy of camping, often thrown into temporary conflicts between their ideal of being a "regular guy" with the group and their childhood concepts of what constitutes the earmarks of a "good little boy." I have, in my own camps, often seen children who are suddenly confronted by such problems. Johnny, for instance, was always so proud of being a good little boy and definitely not like "some other kids in his neighborhood" who didn't behave so well in school. Suddenly his father discovered that he was too "good" for his own taste and wanted him "toughened up" a little. The camp is supposed to do the job. Result: Johnny finds himself in a group of somewhat more emancipated boys, some of whom have what he considers a daredevil philosophy of life. Instead of imitating them, he is scared stiff by their behavior. Each independent act of the more sophisticated or more independent youngsters stirs up old guilt feelings in Johnny's father-identified soul. The result may be any of the following: fear of the other children whom he considers "bad"; wild imitation (overdoing it) of the worst of them so as not to be considered a sissy; indefinable feelings of confusion and irritation; anxiety attacks; lack of sleep; loss of appetite; a vague feeling of homesickness with crying spells. In short, in order to live in a pack, a child has to learn to howl with the wolves. What if he is afraid of them or doesn't want to be considered a wolf at that time or knows his parents really wouldn't like this howl if they heard it? The so-called "overprotected" child is the most frequent victim of this type of conflict. There is something like a vicious circle at work in his case. The parents send him to camp just because they know he is "overprotected." His very "overprotection" makes it hard for him to react without anxiety or guilt to the group life at camp. And if he does get over this, the hang-overs from his overprotected superego development make him feel nervous and guilty for the very accomplishment of the emancipation for which he was sent to camp.

Typical expressions of this problem are fear of other children, greed for popularity, extreme shyness, extreme clowning, unreasonable rebellion against even reasonable adults under the guise of pack loyalty, and open symptoms of neurotic fear and anxiety directly in relation to the group or in displaced forms. The most frequent of those are extreme forms of competitive pride and a mania for collecting prizes and badges as cover for lack of real adjustment to the things that count.

The Loneliness of Group Life

People who are enthusiastic about something are liable to talk themselves into such enthusiasm about the particular form of salvation they preach that they soon begin to think it is the only one. They tend to oversell a good thing, to pretend that the particular value they happen to sell is the only thing that counts, and to forget about all the other ingredients that go into a well-balanced and healthy diet. In a democracy, with its strong belief in group life, it is only natural that the camping movement sometimes falls into that mistake. For group life is the strongest medicine we camp people have to offer, and the uniqueness of the camp form of group life is our natural domain.

I have seen well-planned group life do wonders for children, but not everybody can stand equal amounts of it. Some children are suddenly exposed to group life before they are ready for it. Even if there has been too little chance for group play in Johnny's life at home, that does not mean he should have nothing else from now on. Like all good things, even good group life has its drawbacks and limitations, and people sometimes need vacations from it. First, group life is hard on one's standards of individual comfort, especially for twenty-four hours a day. Johnny is *not* antisocial just because he would rather take a shower or urinate by himself. And Mary is not an isolate just because she hates interrupting her morning daydream in favor of a flag-raising ritual. As for arts and crafts, let us not forget that none of the great symphonies was composed by a committee and that few great books have been written by people while they were dancing to the *Turkey in the Straw*. In short, although we often do a good job by offering chances for creative group life, we sometimes undernourish our customers in terms of opportunities for privacy and freedom from group exposure. Children need to learn not only how to be with a group and how to accept group pressures but also how and when to have the courage to be on their own and to defend themselves against the pressures of group and mob psychology. The result is that some children begin to overindulge in the delicacies of group life—some of them vomit them even before they enjoy them. Some of them go through the motions of group adjustment but feel terribly alone underneath. The necessity of adjusting themselves to so many people so much of the time makes it difficult for some children to make any deeper adjustments to a few. The threat of having to share friends—adults and other children—with so many or of being exposed to the constant dangers of rivalry and loss makes it hard for some children to dare to make any deep relationships at all. Although the group gives the numerical opportunity for many friendships, it often mars the psychological chances for all of them. I do not say that the group necessarily has this effect, but I do maintain that I have seen it happen, and this in itself we should recognize as an important pathological risk. I have seen children "opened up" for the enjoyment of group life through a summer's camp experience. I also have seen children acquire deep hatred for all group life through one summer's experience. So we had better remember how important it is for us to figure out which way we can swing them. Skillful programing and group-psychological antisepsis in the choice of leadership techniques are the best safeguards against this risk.

What Can We Do About All This?

My list of psychopathological risks of camp life is not only incomplete, but it is also barely a scratch on the surface. In addition, I have restricted myself to selecting a few illustrations only out of the field of "individual hazards." There is an even wider area of ·pathological risks of camp life that I have not even mentioned—the psychopathology of group life. Instead of expanding into this field, I had better make a few remarks on the question of just what we can do about pathological risks.

Of course, there is no specific answer to a general question. Real help can be given the parent, camp director, or child only on the basis of a specific analysis of Johnny and his present development and of a situational analysis of the troublesome incidents in camp life. I think, however, a few general suggestions can be offered even in as short a statement as this one.

AVOIDING MULTIPLE SHOCK

Many children can stand adjustment to one or two new and difficult items at a time. Before you send them to camp, figure out just which phase of camp life is liable to be traumatic for them. Some will enjoy life with nature, but adjusting to a gang of strange children will be hard for them. Others will like everything except that they have never been away from Mother before. Others again will like the company, but the athletic angle of outdoor life is going to be quite a shock, and they will worry if anybody finds out they wet the bed.

Make your selection strategically. Pick the camp that promises most understanding and help in the area in which Johnny's contact with camp life is liable to be the most difficult.

Do not send the child if you expect more than two essential aspects of camp life to be traumatic. For instance, do not send Johnny if he is scared of the dark and also of other children and also has never lived away from home before. Or if you do, send him to a camp that promises unusually skilful and professional handling of most of these problems.

PSYCHIATRY FOR THE UNINTERESTED

Camps, with few exceptions, are frightened of anything that even approaches psychiatry or mental hygiene. In some, this is because of the personal idiosyncrasies of the camp directors or sponsors. Others would like psychiatric help, but they are afraid of what the parents would say if they knew. In short it is difficult for psychiatric knowledge to infiltrate the field of normal camping with normal children, where it is needed most. I am trying to point out that if you want to avoid psychopathological risks for your normal children, you have to train your staff so that it is aware of what it is supposed to detect and avoid. You need special consultants who can warn you of the risk areas of your clientele, and you need good in-service training for your staff so that they can discover and handle whatever pathological risks they unearth.

THE MIRACLE OF GROUPING

Many children have trouble with their first camp adjustment. Whether they can handle this trouble or not often depends less on them than on the group to which they are assigned. For instance, Johnny is not quite ready to howl with the wolves. The question arises of how loudly his cowolves howl. If Johnny is exposed to a group of boys who are just slightly more athletic than he but in their personal behavior violate none of his individual value standards too badly, he will be all right in a few days. But if he is placed in a group in which some of the boys have the precocity of young adolescents whereas he is barely emerging from the phase of "young child," you have an insoluble problem on your hands. The skill of antiseptic grouping is an involved one. I am fascinated by the increased interest the public and private camping field has shown in this aspect, but I am equally impressed with the paucity of organized and usable research available.

THE IMPORTANCE OF TIMING

Many parents confuse the question of what a child should become eventually with what he is able to take right now. They may say that

Johnny "needs" a camp experience. What they mean is usually, "I saw a good camper the other day; I wish my boy would show more of that attitude than he does now." The question of the period in his development at which he is ready for camp experience to take effect is an entirely different one. A badly timed camp experience, even though the camp itself is superb, may do more harm than good. And in such a case the camp is not to blame.

THE PROGRAM AND THE HUMAN EQUATION

Program and routine are really only frozen forms of human relationship. There is no such thing as a "good" program or "good" discipline as such. Your pathological risks are lowest if there is a free flow between programing and disciplinary policies, on the one hand, and the total atmosphere of human relations and your child, on the other. The amount of thought that goes into relating the two is the best safeguard against pathological risks.

THE PROTECTIVE COATING OF A GOOD "CAMP ATMOSPHERE"

Some of the difficult experiences Johnny and Mary meet during their first camp exposure are not as "traumatic" as they might be, provided the total atmosphere of the camp is one of happy personal relationships. In a camp where Johnny feels at ease with the adults, his fear of other children, his worry about the threats of nature, his difficulty in making a success of his role in the group will not upset him too much. Even if it does, he will show this in one way or another and give you a chance to observe it, or he will go to you with some vague complaint that you will have no trouble in relating to the real issue. And you need not be afraid, either, that Johnny will not "know" how helpful you can be to him. Children have astounding intuitions of this very factor in human relations and are much better at sensing it than we are in figuring it out and putting it into scientific terms. Just what constitutes the healthiest and most protective group atmosphere, one that really provides a safeguard against potential pathological risks, is more than this short paper can undertake to describe.

The Furious Children in the Library

This paper is part of a larger piece with the same title, in which I and the
   library staff at the National Institute of Mental Health Clinical Center participated. I have selected here only those issues that are of wider
   theoretical concern in library design and library training and function.
   The children involved were our patients at the Child Research
   Branch, in a closed ward for psychiatric treatment of disturbances involving extreme forms of aggressive acting out. In the phase of treatment discussed here, the children were still considered unready for any
   but a closed-ward living arrangement.

THE MAIN THING I can add to discussion of this topic[1]
is a deep regret that we didn't have sense enough to insist on a chance
for a much more thoroughly organized and more solidly supported
research project on the full range of the book-and-library experience
of our children, from the day we started out all the way through. As it
stands now, all we can do is hope that others may take our warning to
heart after reading about our trials and tribulations and build a full-
fledged research—and service—design along the library line into any
residential-therapy project they may have the opportunity to undertake.

Two questions, though, seem to me especially urgent, and in need
of being pulled into the limelight right now: Just what is it that the
"library experience" can contribute to the over-all therapy design for
the hyperaggressive and ego-disturbed child? What does it take to bring
it all about?

To tackle the second question of what it takes on "our side"—the
side of the librarian and the rest of the treatment staff—would fascinate

1 For further details on this project see Margaret C. Hannigan, "As the Librarian
Sees It"; Florence Glaser, "The Library as a Tool in Re-Education"; Joel Vernick,
"Use of the Library in a Psychiatric Setting"; Edith M. Maeda, "Link between
Hospital and Community"; and Fritz Redl, "What Can We Do for Them Right
Now?" all in *Top of the News*, March, May, and October 1960. These articles are
available in one binding from the American Library Association.

"The Furious Children in the Library" is based on "This Is What We Can Do
for Them Right Now," *Top of the News* (October 1960), American Library
Association, Chicago.

me no end, but it seems to me an issue so important and so involved that I cannot hope to manage even part of it in a short space. As for the first question about the actual "clinical value" of our children's library experiences, I shall try to remain less loquacious while simply summarizing the highlights.

It seems to me that on any tentative—and of course most incomplete—list of "what we know right now," the following items include essential "chances" for the library in its therapeutic role with "children who hate."

A Piece of the "Outside World"

With child patients like ours, it is absolutely essential that we create a "closed" framework for their lives. Although rich in program and activity opportunities, affectional supplies, and wise clinical and educational handling, a "closed ward" still remains—and purposely so —shut off from the rest of the world. For some of these children such a state of affairs has to continue for months or even years. It must be obvious what price we may pay for keeping them in such "clinically airtight" life space for such a long stretch. So naturally, as improvements set in, we are eager to find ways in which to puncture this clinical tightness and to let the outside world in—and our kids out—without paying too heavy a price in terms of therapeutic risks.

It is the library of a hospital or treatment center of this sort that seems to have the best chance to become this "first door into the outside world" for many child patients. In the case of our youngsters, this was quite visibly so. At a time when more or less "normal" interactions with other people—even on our guarded trips and excursions outside the hospital—were quite impossible or very rare, it was our N.I.H. library that provided such a chance. There they met "adults" who were not perceived by them as part of their more narrow "home-base treatment team" at first: librarians or other patients of many varieties, not psychiatric patients only. There they met other children who had been hospitalized for different reasons and with whom they were not yet able to manage any reasonable play life on their own ward. The fact that our N.I.H. library was geographically still part of our larger life frame, yet free from the too "treatment oriented" excitement of daily ward life, made the uniqueness of this experience possible.

Exposure to High-Structure and High-Status
Patterns, Yet Tax-Free from Otherwise
Battle-Loaded Demands

Of course our children were exposed to books, to situations in which they were required to sit quietly (for a change and for a while), and to a wider variety of limitations of their behavioral desires in many other places in their ward and school life with us too. But our school, in order to have any chance at all, had had to lower its "status" assumptions as well as loosen its structural patterns, in order to accommodate the severely disturbed pathological needs of these children. The same was true of their daily program on the ward. In short, the ward program and school, during this phase of their treatment, had stopped being representative for them of a world in which "books and learning" were revered for their own sake, and these situations had become for them much more battlegrounds in the daily struggle between educational challenge and pathological defiance, with all the fireworks this entails.

What I am trying to point out is the fact that, although all this was necessarily going on, it was the library that could remain an outfit with its own unique goal and atmosphere. It was not "just" there for the therapy of our child patients; it had a purpose and a value system of its own, well maintained and clearly "oozing" from its book-studded walls. Yet this specific library didn't just "ooze" its values at innocent customers. While offering all the "kudos" that come from being a proud consumer in such a "high-falutin' joint," this specific library could afford to smile tolerantly on a considerable range of inappropriate behavior and usage without having to challenge it too much. The experience for our child patients was something like this: "Look at us, here we are, in this fancy place with all them books and stuff around, and moving around in this like any regular guy or even grown-ups—even the adults who bring us here change a little bit when they enter this joint. And yet, while there are lots of books and it is quite obvious these gals would like us to read them, they still don't really "mind too much" if we don't —they like us enough to have us around even if we don't do much more with their stuff than play with it, or put these books in and out without really reading anything. They only let our counselors bounce us back to the ward if it gets too rough, and even then they seem sorry to see us go."

In short, our children had a chance to visualize themselves as people sane enough to go to a library with a real library air in it, not just "one of those things the therapists make up for us to destroy to begin with," without at the same time being tested too seriously on the degree to which they could live up to such a role. And all this in a phase of their treatment in which such an experience of even allowing themselves to be seen by themselves as normal and sane was quite unthinkable in the rest of their lives. To provide for them—though only for short durations at a time—this opportunity to experience themselves in much more "worthwhile roles" than they were able to live up to for long is one of the trickiest clinical maneuvers known in residential therapy. For us, it was our library that helped us come close to it when we could hardly produce it anywhere else.

Taste Preparation for Post Situational Use

Some of the books our kids would finger during their library visits remained nothing but the manipulative discharge props of the moment. Yet sometimes they would begin to drag books with them. True, at first with not much serious intent and certainly with no intention of "reading them." However, these books were lying around in their playrooms, in their bedrooms, on their bunks. And sometimes they didn't remain just "any books." They were books "their librarian had allowed them to take out." They still had the smell of that generous gesture with them and that aftertaste of an experience of "trust"—never mind all the other smells to which they had been exposed in the meantime.

Occasionally, some of this would pay off. In idle or empty—and angry or sad—moments, some of these books would suddenly remind them of the "feeling tone" of that library visit the other day. An accumulation of such events would finally get them to change some of these books from the "play gadgets we wheedled out of those adults," which they had become, back into books. Anyway, it seems to me—though I have no decently recorded "evidence" to prove all this—that this factor might also explain why most of the borrowed library books received so much better treatment from our kids than we had any reason to expect. Also, during their visits in the library, they could pick up an image of the "person as a reader," without being prematurely forced into that role. I think that the acquisition of this image, through their library experiences, had something to do with their ability to find and accept themselves in such roles earlier than we could otherwise have hoped.

Emergence of the Concept of the "Benign Guardian" of Societal Treasures

According to the way our kids naturally looked at life, anybody who guarded anything—from a museum statue to the gadgets in a gift shop to the paints the teacher might keep locked up when not in use —was seen by them in either of two ways only. He was seen either as a stupid, pompous ass ("Who does he think he is anyway?") who didn't like kids to finger his prized hoard and deserved to be outwitted by ruse, or as a hostile, kid-devouring ogre who hated people in general and kids in particular and had only one aim in life, to "protect his precious stuff from being enjoyed by anybody else, the dirty S.O.B."

In our life with the children on the ward, in the therapy hours, and even in school, we had to avoid this image and relinquish our "guardian" roles as much as we could afford, just to make ourselves understandable as benign facilitators rather than as preventers of enjoyment or of the use of tools. By the very necessity of doing that, though, we had also surrendered—or at least blurred—our images as "guardians" in their eyes. In the library, however, we could manage to maintain both: the reality role as "guardians" of toys and tools and the benign attitude toward their consumption and toward the enjoyment of what we were guardians of.

Such an achievement is possible only if librarian and child-caring adult (counselor, nurse, attendant, teacher, psychiatrist—whoever was with the children on their library visits as part of their "ward personnel") function as a well-organized team. We took great care to protect the librarian from interventions in child behavior that would have been too damaging to the children's perception of her "benign role." We— those of us who lived with the children all the time—could afford more easily to draw upon us their temporary wrath at interruption or whatever other anger was produced in the unavoidable melee of behavioral interference. For we could "live down" in the rest of the hours of a given day whatever hostile feelings a bouncing or other intervention incident might have drawn upon our heads. It was through this carefully planned "division of labor" that we were able to help the librarians remain in the role of "friendly enablers of fun with books." Their role, whenever things did get out of hand, thus remained limited to that of the person who only points out where the limits are, while we loaded ourselves with the task of enforcing them. However, this is only half the story. For, in order for this "role protection" to work, it was also essential that our own intervention in the children's library behavior, no matter how drastic, remain totally benign and nonpunitive. Had we, for instance, punished the children for library misbehavior—however wisely or deservedly—the anger at this experience would still have fallen on the librarian's head as the one whose fault it really was that they got punished by us. As our interventions—including bodily removal from an excited scene—were always of the nature of "marginal situational restraint" (with all the cautions that such policy demands on clinical grounds) and as even such situations were usually picked up for later discussion in life-space interviews, any contamination of the children's perceptions of the benign intent of the librarian was avoided. The wonderful spectacle of at least one "uncontaminated" and "correct perception of an adult's benign role in their lives" emerging in their messy minds was well worth the temporary loss of relationships that we had to take upon ourselves through such strategy. I, personally, have no doubt that the wonderful team arrangement between our life-space staff and the librarians in our project made it possible for those children to elevate their perceptions of the benign-guardian roles of the librarians to the level of a model that later helped to decontaminate even other "guardian" roles from pathological distortions in their subsequent return to the community and its libraries and schools.

Refuge from Unbearable Stress

I was worried at first, when I noticed how much emphasis our librarians, as well as the rest of my staff, put on the benefits our kids derived from using our library as a "refuge and haven" from the stresses of life, as a welcome niche for "escape." What worried me a bit was not the issue as such but the danger that this type of statement might be misread as meaning that the library experience for a sick child might primarily be viewed as "just an escape if things get too tough" on the ward and nothing more. So I would like to hasten to add the following argument as a defense of the "refuge" argument. First, if we call our children's use of the library or of books and reading in general occasionally a "defense" or an "escape," we do not mean to imply that this is all there is to it or that this is one of the major "goals" of the library experience to begin with. We do, however, imply that, in the treatment of children as severely disturbed as ours, even a gain as little and "low down" as this one may be of great importance clinically. If librarians worry that the most important values their medium has to contribute seem to be blurred through these statements about "escape," I should like to remind them that even a long detour is very much worthwhile if it eventually leads a kid closer to accepting the more important goals we may really have in store. In short, what I am trying to say is this: No matter how devoted you are and how proud of the treasure you are trying to insert into people's lives, never mind if you see it temporarily "abused" for ulterior motives or "wasted" on "subordinate subgoals." Those who can't stand to see their religious symbols abused or ridiculed —or even misused at times—had better stay in their home-town churches. They certainly wouldn't do much good as missionaries with a tough heathen tribe. You have to be willing to have your best books somewhat abused and your valuable atmosphere for reading and contemplation "wasted" occasionally on something as trivial as "escape from the stress of the day," if you hope at all to find a pathway into your child patient's soul for your more lofty goals.

Second, though, I also want to stick up for the clinical value and therapeutic realism that lies in the use of anything—even a library— for really effective temporary relief and escape whenever pressures from within or without become too much to bear. It is our experience that there are many moments in the process of growing up and therapy when the ability to find an escape that works without doing clinical damage is not only something to be "indulged" in but is an essential condition for the continued treatment process as such. As far as our kids are concerned, what was wrong with them was not only that they were escaping many of the issues of real life that they should have faced but also that they were quite unequipped and unable to find constructive escapes for those pressures that they were not ready to face at a given time anyway. In fact, if I had the time and space to do it in, I would like to show you in detail how much the treatment success with this type of child depends on the skill to teach them how to escape constructively instead of meeting a stress situation in a sick way. In short, for the stretch of therapy that we are talking about now, we needed, as one of the important offerings that a good library could supply, its ability to be perceived by the child as an uncontaminated haven from unbearable strain. The fact that, after this therapeutic phase had been gone through, other functions became more important in their lives is a story in its own right but does not deduct from the clinical value of the "refuge service" to the child, who often needed a nice, psychologically clean haven from the inner and outer stress of reorientation to a new life.

What holds for many people in their ordinary lives is certainly true for life in a psychiatric ward, especially a closed one: There is no hiding place down there. The hiding places the kids have brought with them are no good and can only support and prolong their sicknesses. Life without a hiding place, even in the best "therapeutic milieu" is more than any child patient can take. To find "hiding places" that we can clinically afford and that are therapeutically clean yet perceived as effective by the child is probably one of the most urgent—and still sorely neglected—challenges in all residential-treatment strategy.

In conclusion, as librarians as well as in your roles as therapists, you may now be angry with me for closing my list of "library benefits for the hospitalized child" right here instead of going further down the line and arriving at more lofty, more "library conscious," and also therapeutically fancier points. But I do not mind too much having to stop so soon. For I have no doubt that the librarians among you are all aware of the "deeper" levels of what a library and its books—and the people who mediate between them and the patients—have to contribute to the over-all therapeutic task. It is the "little things," which become paramount in survival with patients who have library-obnoxious symptoms and are ridden by a book-alien type of pathology to begin with, that we have neglected for too long. Also I have a hunch that any one of the points we have listed in this sequence might strike a familiar chord in all those librarians who do not deal with hospital populations of "furious children" undergoing residential therapy but who are trying to be of help to the normally library-consuming child population in open community life. For what we saw emerge, in condensed and often grotesquely distorted form, with the children in our ward might well turn up as an occasional problem here and there in library life with the "normal child," especially during periods of developmental change or environmental stress. We hope that the strategies and techniques we had to evolve to help our kids make the grade as future library citizens may be thought stimulants for the more community-embedded librarian too.

The Virtues of Delinquent Children

IT IS A REAL ART to produce a delinquent. It requires persistence and perseverance in making the same fatal mistakes all over again, in piling injury upon insult, in combining personal rejection with wrong handling or sentimental coddling with outbursts of punitive righteousness. And even then you are liable to fail unless destiny comes to your rescue and also exposes the youngster in question to wrong handling by other people, to undesirable influences through prestige-loaded age mates, criminal adults, or the boredom of insufficient and inadequate recreational facilities. And still you may be licked unless you happen to put your child into a neighborhood with a high degree of delinquency lure and unless the school complies by refusing to give your youngster personal guidance in his first great conflicts with life or bores him into truancy.

This is not a joke. I mean every word of it. I have seen plenty of normal, as well as delinquent, children, and I have seen their case histories unfold before my eyes with more specificity than the average observer is allowed to watch. The results of all this can be embodied in two statements.

First, most children have such an astounding resistance to wrong handling and wrong settings, that only elaborate efforts to do everything wrong consistently and have them live in the wrong emotional "climate" altogether can make them "good and delinquent."

Second, even then, your success in making a delinquent is limited. I have not seen any "delinquent" yet who quite deserves this name. What you get at best is a personality with certain *areas* of delinquent behavior trends or character malformations. In many other aspects this same child is entirely intact, healthy, or even virtuous indeed. The confusion comes from the habit of wrong name-calling: Instead of talking about

"The Virtues of Delinquent Children" is based on an article of the same title that appeared in *Understanding the Child* (April 1963) and is reprinted here by permission of the National Association for Mental Health, Inc.

"the delinquent," we should talk about "youngsters who have developed delinquent trends." Except for these trends, they are still "youngsters" like any others, and, although much is wrong with them, something is always also in good repair.

If even part of this is true, then it may pay to modify temporarily our approach to those suspected of delinquency: Instead of asking What is wrong with them? let us ask, for a change, What is right with them?

To safeguard myself against misunderstanding by the righteous and indignant, I had better say it in so many words: Of course, we want to know what is wrong with them, in order to be able to do a good repair job when it is needed. However, let us not stop there. Too often we are satisfied with asking this one question and then shooting "against" a youngster's wrong traits, not quite realizing what this does to the kid himself. All I suggest is: Add to this study of what is wrong with your youngster another, equally careful, study of just what is dead right with him. And support your findings with adequate action. You will be surprised.

A really good study of the good traits in delinquent children has not been made. It might also be hard to find a publisher for it. This is not the report of such a study but an invitation to start one. The following are chance impressions gained from professional contact with delinquent adolescents in school work, clinical work, and camping.

Group Loyalty

Oddly enough, the so called "antisocial" youngster often shows the desirable characteristic of group loyalty most emphatically. Of course, it depends on which group you are talking about. Johnny may refuse to "cooperate" with his teacher's request to keep his mouth shut, sit quiet, and hand in assignments on time in class. He may even pinch the wallet of another kid in the same classroom. However, the Johnny I am thinking about will only steal from people who are group-psychologically meaningless to him. Toward people who belong to "his gang" he sometimes displays more courageous self-sacrifice, good-natured helpfulness, and enthusiastic support than does many a goody-goody boy who wouldn't condescend to do anything wrong ever.

What is wrong with the Johnny I am speaking of is that he steals. What is dead right with him is that, under group-psychologically favorable conditions, he is the best sport, the most reliable friend, the most unselfish pal under the sun.

Your task is to cure him of stealing. Your other task is to give his marvelous qualities a climate in which they can unfold. Look at the temperature in your classroom. Then look at the human closeness of his gang. You can learn something.

Healthy Independence of Growth

Growing up means moving away from secure and safe paths of childhood and experimenting with the puzzling and mysterious forces of the "world outside." Growing up for a healthy kid means trial and error, experimentation, experience. A yearning for the insecurity of the new life situation is as normal to an adolescent as is the oft-quoted need for "emotional security." Here is George. Who the heck gives him a chance to "grow and try out new things"? The slightest deviations from his childhood submissiveness are fought at home as though they were the makings of a jail bird. Social experimentation with other kids in school makes noise, leads to trouble, and gets him the reputation of being a "bad kid."

Many a youngster before George has turned coward and chucked the fight, has become a model child, has chosen the easy way out, and has refused to grow up in fear of the punishments put upon such attempts. Not so George. He feels he's got to do things, to find out what other people do, *if*, to learn what it feels like to be in bad with everybody, to see if he can manage this or that task alone without the "guidance" of an overdominating adult. To fulfill this task, he finds little challenge at school or at home. So off he wanders into the unknown, and how can he find out whether or not he is brave unless he takes a chance? How can he be brave unless it is against somebody? So George becomes brave against the adult," trespasses against whatever symbol of infantile restrictions he can discover or invent, and soon is one of those silly truants with petty thievery, mischief, robberies, and escapades that are so well known to juvenile courts and detention homes.

This is what is wrong with him. What is right with the George I am talking about is this: He sure has guts. Compared with him, many nice children are cowardly in their childhoods. He knows how to rough it. He has gone without the amenities of life many children are spoiled into needing for quite a while in order to stick with his silly plans. He also has weathered many a storm of guilt feelings, of homesickness, of the awful sense of being in the wrong and being alone at the same time, without going neurotic over it. This is far more than many more pleasing kids can say about themselves.

Your task is to cure George of the silliness of his revolts, of the inadequacy and futility of his adolescent attempts at self-assertion. Your other task is to do this without breaking his spirit, without making a boring conformist and a moral coward of him, to challenge his spirit of emotional and social pioneering in a constructive way.

Justice and Fairness for All

All youngsters make the discovery of inequalities and injustices, of meanness and misunderstanding, of undeserved rewards and unwarranted punishments at some time in their lives. Some of them are lucky. They make it in an atmosphere of acceptance and friendly guidance that helps them to intellectualize. It makes them searchers for solutions, eager students of what schools have or do not have to offer on the ways of human nature. Others are egotists to begin with, so what do they care? They take this discovery as just one of those things, make the complacent "adjustment" they see their elders making, and stop thinking. There is a third group, though. It develops a sharpened sense of injustice and unfairness and a hankering to discover and fight it tooth and nail. In times of revolutions or wars, such youngsters furnish a goodly number of the heroes to be written up in history books later. In times of peace or before they are old enough to be granted the right to fight for what they believe in, they are bound to become delinquents.

For their criticism is taken as revolt, and it soon becomes revolt for revolt's sake. The futility of anything they can do lures them into matching it with an equally silly futility of action. So they soon develop the habit of attacking, not wrongdoers, but the symbols of such (other colored kids, other white kids, other Jews, other teachers than the ones they really have gripes against). From there on the way into a search for chances for combat is wide open. The misinterpretation of their first referrals stamps them as violent characters, as bad men, and from there on the ideal of the lone wolf and the big shot has an easy way to grow.

Here is Bob. This is exactly what he is doing. He is the wildest one in his "neighborhood gang." This neighborhood gang originally developed out of the rejection of the lower-income-and-relief group by the more ambitious and goody-goody middle-class youngsters. This sociological origin of the fight has long been forgotten. Now it is the tough boy against the "nice kids from better families."

This is what is wrong with Bob: He is a gang leader, brutal, with a love of violence that is highly disturbing, cruel, and thoughtless to those who don't belong to his gang. Enticed into gang leadership at an early age, he has also developed all the negative traits of a boss, bully, and big shot. This is what is right with him: He doesn't do all this just for egotistical gain. It is the event of the fight he is after, not so much the damage that is done. He is proud and would rather die than give in or admit that he is wrong. He sticks to what he thinks is right, however distorted his thoughts may be about that. Your task is to cure him of his violent character, his lack of sympathy with anyone who doesn't happen to belong to his crowd, his big-shot bossiness and lack of civilian standards of manners and decency. Your other task is to give him a chance to be a strong guy in other ways, to organize, to fight for something, to stick up for his way of life instead of having to submit to adult standards of evaluation. Give him a chance to be *against* something that is worthwhile and *for* something that is worthwhile, and forget about the language he uses in the process.

This is but a glimpse of what I mean. There are a couple of hundred different combinations of positive and negative traits found in "delinquent" youngsters. I am as far from wanting to sentimentalize the delinquent as anybody can be, and I also want it understood that the "good traits" in delinquent children do not excuse their bad ones. It isn't a question of "excusing" or even "justifying" anything; it is a question of doing a good repair job. The only contentions I make are that, for a good repair job, it is important to discover and support the already existing "good traits" in a youngster, instead of trying to force him into virtues that don't fit his size or shape; and that we don't, at the moment, use up half as much typewriter ribbon to describe and discover the less visible positive traits in delinquent youngsters as we use on their sore spots. As it only means to open our eyes and strain them in the right direction, there is no reason why we couldn't all begin doing just this—and doing it right now.

"Disadvantaged"
—and What Else?

$\mathcal{W}$HEN I BEGAN to consider my topic, "disadvantaged
—and what else?" I was especially eager to focus on the "what else."
But then it became obvious that the "what else" would be so long and
involved that there was no hope of covering even part of it in a brief
discussion. So please forgive me if this proves to be a sequence of odd
comments rather than an orderly, well-organized, and "research-
sounding" discussion.

First, a few "irritational statements," purposely overstated a bit, to
make you a little uneasy, excited, angry—and interested.

Irritational Statement Number 1

I don't like the term "disadvantaged." I think it has an awful odor,
to phrase it politely. However, we are stuck with it, and most other
labels smell no sweeter, but at least we ought to remember each time
we use it—or its relatives—that we should look twice to be sure we
know what we are talking about or what others mean when using the
term. For nothing is more tempting than a new label to cover our
ignorance or to hide the fact that we may be referring to widely differing conditions. "Disadvantaged" means little without something added.

DISADVANTAGED—IN TERMS OF WHAT?

You, in all likelihood, do not have everything you want or need.
But does that mean you are "disadvantaged" in every respect? Don't we
limit our use to such people as the youngster who is not doing well in

"Disadvantaged—And What Else?" is based on an article of the same title that
appeared in C. W. Hunnicutt, ed., *Urban Education and Cultural Deprivation*,
Syracuse University School of Education, 1964.

a specific learning or character development that we are supposed to support? May not the same "environmental conditions" that make him disadvantaged in these respects actually hold advantages valuable to his later life tasks, even though they may not show right now?

One year, in a camp for disturbed children, I had reason to be especially grateful to one youngster—let me call him "David" (his real name)—who was a rather rough customer. When I caught on to some of his special talents, I was green with envy. For, although he wasn't good in school matters—in fact, he couldn't read—he had some skills that it would take a year of intensive work in a seminar for young psychiatrists to approximate. To be even franker, he had some skills that I couldn't match at all, with all my years of training and experience and just plain age in my favor. One day I found David rifling through my filing cabinet. Under the letter "C" he had pulled out a bottle of cognac kept there for purely medicinal purposes, of course, and was about to take a slug from it. I grabbed it away from him and said, "Listen, brother, this isn't coke!" His answer: "Can I help it if I can't read?"

This kid's real skill, though, in spite of his retardedness in matters of schooling, lay in the direction of uncanny diagnostic and even prognostic know-how. This became apparent during one of the episodes one is bound to run into when one gathers a bunch of thieves to run a camp for. For a week, flashlights had been disappearing, and, even though our staff was pretty good at sleuthing by that time, we never could find out what happened to them. After a while we caught on to their system. If an older kid swiped a flashlight, he would go over to the younger boys' "village," pick out a kid from among those playing around in front of their cabin, and say, "Listen, little boy, want to play with my flashlight for a few days?" And, of course, the little boy, being quite aware of what he was in for, would say, "Oh, sure." As nobody was searching there, the stolen loot would be quite safe until it could be retrieved from the "temporary loan" arrangement without risk.

Now, luckily, David and his accomplices sooner or later were also bound to make a diagnostic mistake, which is how we caught on to the whole thing.

What bothered me, however, and even more now, was the question, just how do they know which kid to pick so they will be safe? David did not know these younger kids, and the turnover that year was considerable. I had all their case histories, and with all the stuff in them and the tests I could not have done so well. So I asked him. His answer made me mad, for he said, "Oh, you just know those things." That is exactly what we do in professional situations when we can't explain something.

So I decided I couldn't let him get out of it that easily and took him down to the little boys' village and challenged him, "Okay, show me how." I pointed to a group of kids playing around the cabin. True enough, he pointed at one without much hesitation. I said, "But why this one; why not that one over there?" This made *him* mad. He said: "But, Fritz, you must be crazy. That one you pointed at would never do. He wouldn't be safe at all!" Now I was really eager to get the details on that diagnosis. And I got it: "Fritz, if I would pick that one, you know what would happen? Of course he will say yes, on account he is scared. Of course he won't blab, on account he knows what would happen to him. But then, one of these days there will be a thunderstorm, and the kids will come home late from a rained-out overnight or something. And the counselor will sit on his bunk to read a story. The kid will feel kind of cozy and good because he likes her. What will happen? He will fiddle around with his flashlight, he will drop it, and then the counselor will suddenly wonder where it came from, because it wasn't in his laundry check, and she will ask him how he got it, and he won't say, but she will know, and I will be in the soup!"

Brother, what a fantastic prediction! How did he know? Not only what the youngster's characteristics were—that I could also find out from his case history, his Rorschach and what have you, and the pile of psychiatric evaluations I had in my green files. How did he know which character trait would melt under the impact of a specific experience and, if the resolution not to blab melted, what specific form it would take, namely an "unconscious slip" type of betrayal? Remember, David had not read Freud—I can prove that; he couldn't read.

Now, if that is what he could do, then I say: David was disadvantaged all right, in many ways, but this does not mean that everything in his life had operated to his disadvantage. Unfortunately, he wasn't advantaged enough to be able to make positive use of his unusual skill, except in battle-relevant areas. He was not able to translate into constructive forms his skill at casing the joint and casing the personnel, his close-to-genius level of diagnostic and prognostic skill. By the way, even if he had been able or willing to do so, there was no market value for this type of psychiatric expertise at his age level and where he lived. However, and this is why I bother you with this story to begin with, it does raise a point: If we say "disadvantaged" and if we insist that a given "setting" in which a kid operates and grows up is inappropriate, we had better pause for a moment, become more specific, and also ponder just what potential *advantage* it may contain, which, if we only know how to discover and build on it, may become an asset rather than a hindrance in a kid's life.

DISADVANTAGED—ON WHAT BASIS?

The term "disadvantaged" needs a second addition. Here, I am afraid, we sometimes take our own professional frame of reference too much for granted. For instance, if we are sociologists or anthropologists, we are rather sure we know what "disadvantaged" means. Yet, no matter how well based in general research our interpretation of the sociological or anthropological meaning of "disadvantaged" may be, how do we know whether or not all this has anything to do with the specific issue we confront in a given youngster?

I remember a kid who had a learning-problem. The visiting teacher had tried hard to be helpful. The boy was also emotionally disturbed, but, in spite of this, the teacher had done well as far as the youngster himself was concerned. She had gotten "through" to him all right, and theoretically there should have been no reason why this boy could not be helped.

Yet the case was hopeless. For this kid was disadvantaged not only for the reasons you suspect after my introduction but also for an additional reason: He had a father who was a blustering fool and a conceited sadist. Now never mind how his father got that way. I am as ready to "understand" that as you are. In a case like this, the fact is, however, that the kid is now stuck with his old man, and we are stuck with both. The result is that nobody who tries whatever remedies may seem advisable can get anywhere. Even if we could find a place where the kid can be treated, the money to take care of costs, and so forth, when the teacher came to consult the father, he would refuse even to talk with her. For he knows it all; he knows "schools are hostile, and the hell with them, and what do silly people like teachers know to begin with?" and so forth. I am sure you know the line. In fact, although mercilessly cruel to his child in cases of misdeeds, he defended him against anybody outside who might criticize.

In short, the point of this crudely abbreviated description is that such a child is "disadvantaged" but not only in the basis of an economically, socially, or culturally inappropriate environment. He is disadvantaged on the basis of a characterological accident in his family: His father is a blustering fool and a conceited sadist.

Now this variable is highly independent of sociological or subcultural milieus. To put it differently, we produce the same type of characterological miscreation in any setting, not only in the so-called "underprivileged" ones. Details and forms of parental behavior will vary of course. When we encounter the same basic situation, for instance, high in the "upper mobile" class, in a family that has just moved into a fancier neighborhood because that goes with the professional promotion and the need to live in appropriate high-society circles, the same style of father would not consider the school "hostile." Rather, he would be more angry at the kid than at the school because the kid had embarrassed the family in its social prestige. He would ward off a teacher who might dare to suggest "treatment" with equal anger, but his anger would be based on the hurt dignity implied in such a suggestion. "Who are you, an underpaid employee of the school system, to suggest that a member of our fine family is emotionally sick? And, by the way, if you talk about silly fads and frills like clinics and such in our community, you are probably subversive anyway, and we had better call the board of education about it, for we don't want that kind of talk in our fine community."

What I am trying to convey is this: If we talk about a kid being "disadvantaged," we should remember that the basis on which we make such a statement may transcend the variables usually associated with this term. Even when many items in a particular environmental setting may suggest anything but the term "disadvantaged," other issues like characterological properties of important figures in a child's life or other "accidents" like death in the family may be equally crucial. In short, whenever we use a term like "disadvantaged" or "culturally deprived," let's remember that we have a rather hot terminological potato in our hand, and let's not become too complacent, even though at first sight the variables we happen to be able to isolate look logically clean and sociologically respectable.

Irritational Statement Number 2

Let's watch out for the return of the obsolete. Nothing is more dangerous when we suddenly find a "new interest" emerging and being implemented than to forget what we have learned the hard way. In a new situation we may make the same mistakes that it took us years to get rid of in the old one. Each time, for instance, that a new science develops, it usually goes this way. It may take us twenty to thirty years to rediscover what everybody already knew. Just one illustration may firm up this point.

When "group therapy" started to become popular and began to be taken seriously even in more rigorous professional circles, we returned to a state of naïveté we had long abandoned in the field of individual treatment. We lulled ourselves into the idea that it would be a cheaper and easier shortcut because the well known and bothersome phenomenon of "resistance" could be ignored. The "group" was naïvely expected, for a while, to do it all so much more easily.

It took a few decades until we realized that the old issue is still with us, that the complexity of "resistance phenomena" cannot be forgotten. The forms they take in group leadership are different from those in the "therapy room," but we are stuck with meeting them and with finding new ways to do so. There is no return to the obsolete concept of therapy without the complex technology of dealing with "resistance" phenomena.

There are three types of concepts regarding the "disadvantaged child" that I think are definitely obsolete but that seem to sneak back into practice under the pressure of contemporary fashions.

OBSOLETE MODEL 1910

By this I mean a model that I consider *sociologically naïve*. The chronological date, by the way, is rather willful and should not be taken too literally. I am talking about the time when one thought the misbehavior in children was simply the result of moral turpitude or of disease. Never mind the specific styles of the environment, factors of social class and caste, or any of the "subcultural mores" issues of which sociologists and anthropologists have since made us so aware. At that time, for instance, it was hard to convey the idea that some "hyperaggressive" youngsters did not need to be "analyzed" because their behavior was not primarily a clinical issue but had to do with the value-standard discrepancy between their neighborhood mores and the middle-class morality of their classrooms. Now, by the way, this way of thinking is totally gone. I wish sociologists and anthropologists were aware of how completely successful they really have been in puncturing social and cultural naïveté in the healing professions! I do not know a single psychoanalyst, for instance, who does not know all the things that sociologists are so eager to publicize. In fact, sociologists have been so successful that I find many of my younger psychiatry students not even aware that the emphasis they are getting on "socioeconomic and subcultural data" in their case-history writing was not originally part of psychiatric lore but has been introduced through infiltration from sociological and anthropological research! By the way, I still find people in sociological and anthropological ranks who seem unaware of the educational success of their sciences, so this should provide a "happy ending" for them. In short, what I am trying to say is this: There seems to me no danger that Obsolete Model 1910 is likely to return, for even those who took their time in modernizing don't remember the old pattern.

OBSOLETE MODEL 1940

By this term I mean a model I consider *clinically naïve*. Again, my chronological figure is only crude and not meant too literally. But there was a trend accompanying the blissful ascendance of anthropology and sociology to assume that tracing environment and culture involved in disorganization or disease was all that was needed. Of that obsolete model I say two things.

First, of course, all the factors isolated are important, but that is not always all there is to it. After all is said and looked at from that angle, there remains a *difference between sickness and health,* at least from a certain point on. If people think that, just because somebody has developed fantastic delusions or a paranoid system of thought, he can become a medicine man in a primitive tribe, that somebody is very much mistaken. Even though it is true that, up to a point, what in a given society would be considered schizophrenic fantasy might be considered legitimate religious belief or lore in another, this only reaches that far. Beyond that point, even in the same society or culture, some guys would be considered plain screwy and would never make it as medicine men.

Second, even when we come closer to our topic, some of this needs to be remembered. In work with children, for instance, I find we still sometimes try to smuggle in the obsolete concept of the "cleanly sociological delinquent," whose only difference from everybody else is that he has absorbed a delinquent value system as a legacy from his environment, instead of a neatly middle-class one.

Unfortunately, I haven't yet found such a kid. Maybe that is my fault, but I have a suspicion that this pure case does not exist. For even children in a tough and delinquent neighborhood *live under a double standard.* Those who work with such kids will remember how often we find this neatly demonstrated. Remember the cases in which members of a tough older gang have somebody's younger brother trailing around with them? He certainly is exposed to a lot that doesn't fit his age, but there invariably comes a cut-off point. His older brother will object, "Shut up, you can't say that in front of my little brother; he ain't old enough for that yet." For somewhere along the line, there are rather clear dividing points between what goes for a kid and what goes for an adult. Even the parents, by the way, who in their own lives may be liberal with tough talk or actually train their kids to steal, don't want them to swipe within the bosom of the family and won't "take that kind of talk" from them until they are "old enough" for it.

In short, even children in reasonably clear-cut delinquent subcultures are expected to develop guilt feelings, embarrassments, and concerns, producing anxieties not visible on the behavioral surface. Psychiatrically, this often makes for a very complicated diagnostic problem. For all practical purposes, some of our swaggering toughies look just like the real McCoy. Some of them, at closer inspection, and after you shave off some of the tough defenses a bit, turn out to have nice clean neuroses buried under their delinquent skins. They are just as nice and value-conflict-conditioned as any we used to make so efficiently in the upper classes in Vienna at the turn of the century. But where they live they can't afford it, so they have to put a heavy layer of the opposite over it for disguise.

I am afraid I discover a certain illusory hope in much of the recent discussion about "disadvantaged youth" that we can return to this oversimplified and seemingly pure sociological model and save ourselves the complications of clinical work and therapeutic implementation.

OBSOLETE MODEL 1966

This one worries me most, for it looks as though it were new, but it is already obsolete even before we flood the market with it. It is, in my opinion based on a phenomenon that, out of politeness, I am willing to call *implementational naïveté*.

It, in turn, appears on two levels. At level 1, we sometimes show a lack of recognition for the specialized knowledge, training, experience, and skill that a given job requires in changing a kid, a group, or a neighborhood. We usually admit how complex our own sciences are, be they anthropology, sociology, psychiatry, education, or whatnot. But we have a tendency *to consider complex essentials of our neighbor fields expendable or even silly luxuries*. For instance, why should we need trained people: Can't any bum cured by Alcoholic Anonymous who happens to smell of the same flophouse other people come from be used as a therapist, with the additional advantage of being "one of them"? Now there is no question about the importance of a certain amount of familiarity with class differences, with the body odor of different neighborhood styles, and so forth. Also, there is no question that the ability to translate oneself into somebody else's value and style domain is essential and has limits beyond which we cannot go. There is also no question in my mind that the judicious use of volunteers on all levels could be increased. However, any such increase also requires an *increase in implementation with trained staff, supervisory time, well-screened work situations, and so forth,* in our field as well as in any other. I am afraid I hear in some recent statements a note of nostalgia for the obsolete idea that an increase in volunteers would "solve the problem" and that our sister disciplines' standards can easily be done away with as an urgent compromise. Such a return to this type of obsolete model of services would, in my opinion, have most disastrous results.

On the second level I mean by "implementation naïveté" the lack of essential conditions for doing a specific job. Under conditions I include size of staff, space arrangements, tools needed, and time available for work and communication among the workers, beyond the usual concept of "environmental" factors.

In physical medicine we are more realistic about this. If you want to take an appendix out, there are certain conditions that have to be guaranteed or else. You can't say: "After all, let's not be fussy. The charwoman is friendly; let her help with this or that. You can't have everything, can you? And you don't have to wash all that stuff in expensive antiseptics. After all, do you think money grows on trees?" Doctors have enough guts to say: "Listen, that's what it needs. It costs that much to get it; there is no way around. Or else we could not expect the operation to succeed."

Unfortunately, in the tasks I am likely to undertake, I cannot count on so much financial realism. If it comes to reforming kids or changing neighborhoods, we frequently are not courageous enough to speak up loudly for what we need. If, for instance, we set up a classroom for emotionally disturbed children—and I have recently been through this many times—we know by now what is needed and what a successful design requires for implementation. Yet we find ourselves continually confronted with the suggestion, "Let's just put some kids together, and never mind whether their disturbances click or not." Children who don't fit elsewhere get dumped into the same pot, even though the natures of their problems may be as different as foot disease from scarlet fever. On top of that, I am invariably hit with the argument, "We haven't enough teachers, and of course a visiting teacher is just a naïve fad and frill." The teacher they have doesn't even have time to go to the john until 3:30, to say nothing of her need to keep records, communicate with other teachers, talk with parents, and so forth. Yet we have the cheek to call such designs "classrooms for emotionally disturbed children." I think this is an obsolete model of special services that, unfortunately, even professionals frequently don't have the guts to yell about. And professionals of "other professions" frequently watch this kind of disaster without raising their voices, for after all, the problem is no skin off their specialties' noses.

Now all this is obviously disastrous. If you really want to do something that is effective for the children you call "disadvantaged," no matter what caste or class or neighborhood they breathe in, you must recognize that obsolete models of whatever sort have to be fought against with more vigor than does the disease itself. *Psychological reality is as real and unrelenting as is the reality of the gadget world.*

We finally arrive at the topic of the day: "disadvantaged—and what else," and I should start talking about three issues: What else should we know about children to change things and to communicate with them? What techniques do we have to develop in order to do the job? What designs do we need, and which ones do we have to create beyond those now known in order to do our jobs?

Unfortunately, this is obviously more than I can possibly manage even to list properly in the remaining space. So let me switch instead to something different, though related, an issue I should like to get you worked up about. Unfortunately, I have to give it a fancy name, for it is an issue all too frequently swept under the rug, and I must mark it with some kind of headline, or it will get too long to unfold.

The Secondary Characteristics of Primary Action Relevance

This concept really is very simple, but with all its simplicity—or perhaps because of it?—it is one of the most sorely neglected problems I could list.

Let's assume somebody has a beautifully classic anxiety neurosis as we made them in the upper social crust of Freud's Vienna. We don't produce many today. Our kids are much too disobedient to pick a classical symptom. They mix their syndromes from all over the map, hopelessly ignoring our psychiatric textbook prescriptions. However, let's assume we have found a pure one, say a boy in China. Let's also assume that this boy somehow gets together with an expert psychoanalyst who has been longing in vain for just such an affliction. Let's assume there are no financial handicaps to prevent doing what is obviously duck soup. We know all about this affliction and how to handle it; all it takes is time and money, and we have both. But our neurotic boy talks only Chinese, whereas the therapist knows only English. See what I mean? The linguistic barrier is obviously entirely irrelevant clinically, yet it blocks the child's therapy as much as if he had come with an unknown disease!

This example is a bit oversimplified. Let's move to one somewhat closer to our concern: I have a kid who finally, in tenth grade, gets interested, motivated, and eager to change. He was a no-good delinquent bum before I got hold of him. It took a year to move him to the point at which he stopped hating me and is ready to give me a chance to become a change agent in his life. In short, he is with me and wants what I want him to grow into. Yet it so happens he can't read. Even with all my therapeutic conceit, I don't think whatever I do with him will be enough, unless somebody helps me take that hurdle. He reminds me painfully of a classroom observation I made years ago.

Twelve kids were in a classroom with a nice young girl supposed to bring them up in reading skills. It was the craziest assortment you could think of. Here was one little girl, in the front row, looking like seven but probably nine, with blond braids, and looking like the kind of kid with "prince and princess"-type daydreams of the preschool age. In the row behind her were three really rough and tough customers, about thirteen or fourteen, though one looked eighteen. Each time they put their hands in their pockets dice fell out. You know what I mean.

The teacher had language material "on their reading and comprehension level." It was the story of the princess and the pea. Our blond little girl listened with rapt attention. She obviously was eating it up. The three lugs at first were wide-eyed with incredulity and then of course gave up. That anybody should have such a dermatological affliction that one little pea (watch the spelling, by the way, I wasn't so sure they got that right either) buried under twenty eiderdown mattresses would produce a rash was more than they could find appealing. Besides, why should they worry about peas and eiderdown mattresses? Two of them slept on the same couch, and one of them was a bedwetter. There were only two beds in the whole family to begin with. Besides, if that kid is so sick, why the hell don't she go to a school-nurse to begin with?

The point I am trying to make is that, if I can't find well-implemented remedial reading services for the youngster I started this story with, all my therapeutic skill will remain wasted. His reading problem is not part of the clinical syndrome for which he came into therapy, but it may become an unmanageable block unless the program is implemented by designs appropriate to reading. A cured delinquent who cannot read can hardly find the gratifications that would induce him to stay on the straight and narrow path that leads to middle-class and job respectability for his adult existence.

One more illustration before I start on my list: Let us assume I have youngsters with anxiety states, and there are plenty of them, hidden or not hidden. Yet, for some reason, the youngsters I am now considering have no ability at all to talk about any of their problems to a guy in an office too far away from the original scenes of their lives. In short, although they have the type of disturbance we know how to treat or counsel in an interview situation, they cannot fit our usual interview design. Talking about what happened last Friday on next Wednesday at 3 P.M. is totally useless. It makes no sense to them; there are no revivable memory traces of last Friday's experience left. Besides, talking to people who seem like artifacts in their lives is unbearable to them; it makes no sense, and they won't have any of it. So, while you can drag them there, you cannot make them "relate."

The fact is that most of our "therapeutic- or counseling-interview situations" have been designed on a model that was first developed for the psychoanalysis of children with rather special types of neurosis and personality structure. For them it is ideal; it has to be sharply separated from their ordinary lives. The therapist's role has to avoid anything that could smack too much of teacher or parent roles. He must be free from any need to interfere in behavior beyond a certain unavoidable minimum, so that a clean "transference neurosis" can blossom into therapeutically usable forms.

It so happens that the kids I am now referring to are different. Although the anxiety states for which they need treatment are practically identical, other parts of their personalities, especially their so-called "egos" are allergic to the usual treatment milieu. They need interviewing in high proximity to the settings in which the symptoms bother them most, in close time proximity to the events themselves, and by people who are perceived by them as part of their usual "life space." This allergy to our usual interview design and the ability to use only life-space interview patterns are not part of their diseases nor are they likely to be caught in the usual diagnostic work-up procedures. Clinically speaking, they are of *primary* importance. Never mind how well equipped you are to understand or treat anxiety states in such children; you can't get at them unless you can produce the high life-space proximity-of-treatment design. In short, inaccessibility to a specific mode of therapy in itself, although not part of the disease to be treated, may be of primary relevance when it comes to the question, Who can be changed and by what process?

Now, at last, a few illustrations for the long list of secondary characteristics in kids who need help, which may become of primary treatment or action relevance.

Supercharging Reality-Geared Issues with Overdoses of Symbolic Valence

Yes, you are right, this does sound funny and fancy. However, it is really quite simple. Simple to understand, I mean. Handling it is another chore!

DEVELOPMENTAL-PHASE PRESTIGE

Sometimes, for a kid, the haircut he has, the pants he wears, the language he uses, or the question of whether or not he carries a specific gadget like a knife, cigarette, or whatnot may assume a valence way beyond anything we would expect and totally out of line with reality. You try to tell him he can't bring or wear this or that in school, a perfectly reasonable request, which, by the way, he doesn't really question at all. However, just watch the reaction you get. The reason for this overreaction: The issue packs more than we expect; it is *symbolic of something else.* What the kid reacts to is not the issue, only the symbolic valence it has assumed in his own life. Symbolic of what? In this case, not even of anything fancy way down deep in the unconscious. Just of the issue of having left behind a certain phase of early childhood and being now engaged in adolescence. The behavior of the adult toward him has become symbolic of the amount of "emancipation" from infancy a youngster has reached or the degree to which we seem to deny it. So what started as a harmless demand by the adult suddenly seems to have loads of TNT packed into it, because for the kid it has become an issue of finding his emancipation questioned or challenged. "I am not a baby any more; you can't treat me like that," seems to be what he is trying to say.

This issue is especially important to remember for those of us who work in the trenches of daily behavioral warfare with children in classrooms, clubs, groups, institutions—and we had better remember that any issue, no matter how simple it may seem to us, may for a given kid suddenly assume this overdose of symbolic valence.

By the way, this issue seems highly independent of the much-quoted issues of socioeconomic or subcultural factors. Just *what* it is that kids are so allergic to is certainly codefined by the social milieus in which they grow. The question, however, *whether* or not a given kid will pack so much symbolic valence into a given situation has nothing to do with sociology or anthropology. It is not found only in the so-called "lower-lower disadvantaged" areas; you find it just as much in the so-called "upper-upper" socioeconomic strata. It is a function of childhood history and much else, not of psychosocial locus.

SOCIAL-LOYALTY ISSUES

Sometimes youngsters react to situations, not in terms of what they really hold, but in terms of what they seem to imply regarding the group the youngsters come from. To illustrate: Anybody may remember kids coming back to an institution after a runaway or because they have just been brought in by the police. They are miserable, cold, dirty, tired, bedraggled. The first person they meet is a big-bosomed, motherly matron, who is full of love and pity, eager to engulf them in an affectionate embrace, and as a gesture of kindness she offers them a shower or a bath. "Come on, sonny, it will make you feel better." For some of these kids this is about the worst insult you could inflict upon them. Far from even perceiving the good intention behind the offer, they see it as a symbol of hostility to them and their kind. "Of course she wants to scrub us, for she thinks we stink. Of course that bitch makes us wash; she don't like our folks either; she thinks we all stink. The hell with her, I want nothing to do with her any more, ever." In short, what started as a benign gesture ends up as a symbolic clash between two hostile camps.

By the way, these facts as such are well known. What we have trouble recognizing is the potential symbolic valence in a given moment of intervention in a child's life. Just remember how many such confusions on the basis of symbolic valence lead to tension in any class room any hour of the day, and we don't even smell what is going on, despite all the clever research and fancy books we read just before we meet the kids.

RELEASE OF SURPLUS AGGRESSION

A third type of "supercharging reality issues with an overdose of symbolic valence" seems to go in the direction of enormous quantities of surplus aggression released at even slight degrees of frustration or behavioral intervention on the part of adults.

To illustrate: Camps or institutions frequently consider depriving a youngster of dessert or sending him away from the table rather mild forms of punishment, especially when the over-all tone of the place is warm and friendly, the kids know they are liked, and their bellies are already stuffed with more sweets than is good for them. Yet, amazingly, even under such favorable conditions, we sometimes find that children react with totally irrational quantities of rage, panic, fury, or revenge. It seems that sometimes even relatively mild punishments or quite reasonable and unavoidable frustrations—like the request to stop playing and come to lunch—release in some of them emotional upsets certainly worthy of greater causes. Therefore, if you work with children who have some problems and are prone to "supercharge," regardless of background or neighborhood, it is important to learn their *special indexes of vulnerability to this item.* Although irrational in nature, it becomes a forcible issue for those responsible for the children's upbringing and care.

THE GANG UNDER THE COUCH

A second illustration of the point that clinically secondary issues sometimes assume primary importance when it comes to figuring out what to do with kids is even more peculiar. My title "The Gang Under the Couch" is, of course, only meant figuratively—and, by the way, I am not really thinking of a "couch" either. However, it may suffice as a caption for an issue too complex to squeeze into short space.

Here is what I have in mind. Sometimes you want to have an "interview" with a youngster, either as part of long-range therapy or in order to talk over with him an issue that has come up in his life. You think there are just the two of you in a room, the kid and you. Sometimes that is all there is to it, of course, but sometimes the physical pair really turns, psychologically speaking, into a very different situation. You have the whole "peer group" sitting in. For instance, your talk with the kid starts off on a friendly note. In a short while, you suddenly notice you get an amount of defiance, resistance, hostility, stubbornness, and denial, far beyond anything you had reason to expect. What do you conclude? Ordinarily, you assume that one of three things is messing it up for you: The kid doesn't like you personally or is mad at something you said or did. If you happen to be a psychiatrist, you assume that he is in a phase of "resistance to change." If you are a sociologist, you are likely to assume that probably your middle-class body odor bothered him.

Whatever it may be, and sometimes all three and several more assumptions may be correct, in the cases I am talking about none fits. What is really going on has little to do with you as a person or with the kid's relationship with you. What is really bothering our youngster is the fear of what his gang might think if it saw him now. He may like you and accept what you are trying to point out, but how can he possibly give in to an adult without a battle? He would be considered a potential traitor or fifth columnist in the eyes of his pals. Even if he is ready to "give" eventually, he must at least obey the unspoken "dueling code" that his peer group would expect him to uphold before surrender. The specific content of that "peer-group code" of brave behavior in an interview with an adult is, of course, different from group to group, from social or subcultural milieu to milieu, and so forth. But the phenomenon as such may become an important technical issue in work with kids on any level at all. I have had kids sit in my office at camp, with their stolen loot hanging right out of their pockets, with full awareness that nothing would happen to them if they told me what had happened, and even with perfectly "good" interpersonal relationships and well-established "role trust" between them and me. Yet they would rather die than come through with the real story, without making me jump through the whole gamut of their subgroup's dueling code first. They still would insist: "Honest to God, Fritz, I swear on a stack of Bibles, I wasn't even there, I ain't done nothing." Yet they knew I knew, and both the kids and I were quite comfortable with the eventual outcome. But how could they go back to their group and live with it—and with themselves—if they had "given in" without first making me fight hard for their surrender?

This one, too, is not a function of social caste and class—only the specific content of a given code may be. It does not hit us only in work with kids from the so-called "disadvantaged areas." I meet it with kids from way up on the social ladder, kids of parents with a lot of dough, powerful and willing enough to fix any ticket for them. Here they sit, in Mr. Psychiatrist's office, basically miserable and in obvious need of help. Yet they would rather die than accept a treatment relationship. They have to maintain, in the eyes of their peer groups, the image that "my old man only makes me come, for otherwise he would take my car away from me." It may take you months before you get them out of it. In fact, for practical purposes you might as well have the peer group sit right in that room. It couldn't be much more difficult to handle, and maybe you could get some of the other customers on your side in the meantime. It is important to remember that this type of "resistance" is not what we usually assume. It is not the kid's resistance to you or to change but his desperate battle to maintain a group image he cannot afford to lose. It is really a group-psychological phenomenon, even if it happens in a room with just the two of you in it.

RESEXUALIZATION OF OTHERWISE SEX-DETACHED FORMS OF EXCITEMENT

As you know that I am a Freudian, you would expect me to bring sex in somewhere anyway. So why not save you the trouble of trying to find out where I hid it and pick it up where it counts most in daily warfare with child behavior? This is what I have in mind with this rather complicated sounding title: For practical purposes and in the ordinary way of speaking, certain forms of "elation" and excitement in kids are really "nonsexual." They are quite "naïve"; the kids themselves would be surprised and angry if you tied them up with sex. They just enjoy rolling on the floor, wrestling, tickling one another, playing hide-and-seek, packing into tight corners, chasing one another in tag games with increasing wildness quite visible to anybody who looks at it. In ordinary language, they are right; it is quite a "legitimate" enjoyment of physical contact, of bodily excitement, and of all that goes with it. Only just let it go on a little too long, and you will find that either it gets really closer to open sexual stimulation—where they grab each other now is quite below the usual requirements of a tag game—or, even if overt sexual behavior is missing, the degree of elated wildness that develops is more comparable to that of people in states of un-controllable sexual excitement than that of kids involved in quiet and harmless play. If you ever have to interrupt such a scene, you will know what I mean; it is hard to calm them down, as if they were really in a clearly sex-excited elation. Unfortunately, some kids are especially vul-nerable to this switch from normal play into "resexualized" forms of excitement. Worse even, their case histories contain no warnings. For they are not kids with sex problems at all; it only so happens that the elation and excitement of even harmless activities are likely to re-sexualize them into getting uncontrollably high. I find that in practical work with youngsters this is an especially important issue and that educators have a lot of trouble with it. Just because it is *not* obviously "sexual" in the usual meaning of the term, the adult dislikes interfering in "harmless body-contact pleasure," and may let it go beyond the point of easy return to normal. As many kids who are not sex problems at all are prone to this type of "resexualized state of overexcitement," we are likely to miss the point. Besides, it is not only kids with "poor controls" who are likely to get into that state. I really am convinced that it is an independent variable. I have seen kids with very poor con-trols and plenty of obvious sex problems who are unaffected by this type of elation. I have run into kids with excellent controls and no overt sex problems at all, whose drifting into this type of "resexualized elation" constitutes an enormous hazard. For the parent, teacher, or child-care worker, it is important to recognize this transition of normal and harmless fun into more orgiastic wildness and to learn how to intervene before it gets too messy. Unfortunately, neither sociologists, anthropologists, nor psychiatrists have so far given us the kind of research that would be helpful in this task.

SLAVERY UNDER THE IMPACT OF THE "DARE"

This phenomenon is well-enough known. Under some conditions —details are too long a story for the remaining space—and, of course, especially under some situations with a lot of "group-psychological excitement" in them, kids are likely to display nearly slavish dependence on anybody who "dares" them. And, even more important to remember: Once in the grip of the "dare psychology," even the nicest and otherwise most reasonable and self-controlled kids are likely to do the most stupid, dangerous, silly, or even mean and nasty things. In short, the "dare" situation throws some kids into the same state of disorganization that we otherwise find only in drunkenness and mob psychology. Historically, we know the phenomenon well from the German fraternity of the late nineteenth century and its dueling code. If somebody wants a fight, all he has to do is to go up to you and "dare you" in some form or other. From then on, the course of events cannot be changed; you have to pick up the "dare," or you are dishonored forever after, even if your or anybody else's career or life is wrecked. When I came to this country I was naïve enough to think I would never again have to witness this type of mental disease. How wrong I was! Our kid cultures somehow have developed a very similar type of "dare" and "dueling code"; only the form varies from subculture to subculture. By the way, the general idea that this is true only in more or less delinquent circles is all wrong. In fact, I have found some rather obviously delinquent kids who had developed high degrees of immunity to this dare psychology. They knew how to set it off, but they were by no means helpless when exposed to it themselves. Yet, probably to all our surprise, I could show you loads of very nice kids with excellent self-control, reasonable, well-intentioned, with good superegos and well-identified with the values we cherish, who, the moment somebody "dares" them, are totally helpless. This, by the way, is one thing we ought to learn more about; for the question of whether or not it is safe for a youngster to go for a ride with a group of kids does not depend only on his own driving skill or on the kids he is with. It depends on his own inner resistance to situations that constitute open or unspoken "dares." This is a characterological variable in its own right, independent of many other issues, and it is highly unexplored!

Some youngsters, furthermore, have developed special skills in setting off this "dare psychology" in others and in retaining enough sense themselves to remain uninvolved, to vamoose from the scene before it gets too rough, and to leave others to act out to the bitter end what they have so skillfully engineered. For those of us who have to work with kids in groups, this is a most important "characteristic." I should like to know who is slavishly vulnerable to dares and in which situations and who has the uncanny skill to create "dare slavery" in others without being obvious about it.

It so happens that this "variable" or "characteristic" is obviously not a disease in its own right and therefore will hardly turn up on the list of psychiatric or other evaluations, nor will most case histories on kids we are supposed to help have any clear reference to it. Yet, although "secondary" in terms of educational or psychiatric assessment, it certainly becomes of primary relevance for anybody who has to decide what to do or is involved in the daily action scene with Junior. In fact, why do you always insist on telling me whether Johnny was or was not born with instruments or—if you are more sociologically inclined—the income level and status symbols of his neighborhood? True, I may want to know that too. But if you invite me to teach a class, run a playground or an institution, or plan for community change and prevention, I'd rather have you tell me first about the "dare" index.

In closing, and it hurts me to leave my list of "characteristics of primary action relevance" so dismally short, I should like to remind you of the two most important issues for projects you may plan in work with the "disadvantaged child or youth."

First, we must develop more courage to help people over "complexity shock" and see to it that we don't get stuck in it ourselves. There are some things that cannot be done more cheaply, quickly, easily, without skill and trained staff and appropriate means. Whenever we know this to be so, we had better speak up.

Second, we must increase our sensitivity to what I should like to call "implementational stench." At the risk of being called "fools" and "eggheads" or of being considered "uncooperative" or "starry-eyed," we had better make our observations known whenever we run into projects, programs, or designs that are obviously miserably implemented, no matter how fine and worthy the basic ideas may originally have been. For work situations with children and communities that are not decently implemented stink. Period.

Publications by Fritz Redl

1931

"Erziehungsberatung in der eigenen Klasse" ("Counseling Work in One's Own Homeroom"), *Zeitschrift für Pädagogische Psychologie*, 11:425–501.

1932

"Erziehungsberatung, Erziehungshilfe, Erziehungsbehandlung" ("The Three Functions of Guidance Work"), *Zeitschrift für Psychoanalytische Pädagogik*, 12:523–532.

"Die Erzieherischen Aufgaben des Klassenvorstandes" ("The Educational Duties of a Homeroom Teacher"), *Die Wiener Schule*, 12.

1933

Einführung in die Psychologie (*Introduction to Psychology*), Vienna: Deuticke (with Franz Häussler).

"Wir Lehrer und die Prüfungsangst" ("The Teacher and the Psychology of Examination Fear"), *Zeitschrift für Psychoanalytische Pädagogik*, 11: 378–409.

1934

Einführung in die Logik und in die Grundfragen der Philosophie (*Introduction to Logic and Philosophy*), Vienna: Deuticke (with Franz Häussler).

"Zum Begriff der Lernstörung" ("The Concept of Learning Disturbances"), *Zeitschrift für Psychoanalytische Pädagogik*, 9:319–349.

"Die Wirkungen einer Phimoseoperation" ("Conclusions from a Case of Mental Trauma through Circumcision"), *Zeitschrift für Psychoanalytische Pädagogic*, 8:319–349.

1936

"Der Mechanismus der Strafwirkung" ("The Mechanism of Punishment"), *Zeitschrift für Psychoanalytische Pädagogik*, 9:221–270.

"Pansexualismus und Pubertät" ("Pansexualism and Puberty"), *Zeitschrift für Psychoanalytische Pädagogik*, 9:342–359.

Kleines Mittelschullexikon (*Educational Guide on Practical Problems*), Vienna: Deuticke (with Franz Häussler and Anton Klieba).

"Schule und Haus" ("Home and School Relationships"), in *Wissen und Können, Lexikon des Praktischen Wissens*, Vienna, pp. 63–104.

"On Examination Fear," *The New Era in Home and School* (March).

"Working Together," *The New Era in Home and School* (November), pp. 205–211.

1937

"Adolescence and the Parent," *Child Study* (May), pp. 235–236.

"No Grudge Left?" *National Parent-Teacher* (May), pp. 14–15.

"Parents I Have Known," *Yearbook of the Ethical Culture Schools*, New York.

1938

"Discipline," *The New Era in Home and School* (July-August), pp. 199–202.

"The Chances for Success in Guidance Work," *Visiting Teachers Bulletin* (January), pp. 1–9.

1939

"Techniques of Sex Information," *Child Study.*

1940

These publications are available in mimeographed form from the American Council on Teacher Education, Division on Child Development and Teacher Personnel, 5835 Kimbark Avenue, Chicago, Illinois.

"A Method of Determining Training Needs for Teachers."

"The Concept of Adjustment."

"The Use of the Terms Normal and Abnormal."

"The Concept of Maturity."

"The Culture Concept and Its Place in Education."

"Group Psychological Aspects of Classroom Teaching."

"The Need-Concept and Its Place in Educational Thinking."

"Exercises in Applied Thinking."

"Suggestions for a Method of Discussion of Child Study Materials."

1941

"Mental Hygiene," in *Encyclopedia of Educational Research*, New York: Macmillan.

"Adolescent Changes as a Factor in Delinquency," *Probation and Parole Progress Yearbook*, pp. 191–209.

Helping Teachers Study Their Children, The Michigan Cooperative Teacher Education Study, No. 3.

What Should We Know About a Child? The Michigan Cooperative Teacher Education Study, No. 2.

1942

"Scientific Study of Developing Boys and Girls," in *General Education in the American High School*, Chicago: Scott, Foresman.

"The Role of Camping in Education," *The American Camping Magazine* (February).

1943

"Delinquency Prevention and the Role of Love," *Childhood Education* (December).

"Group Psychological Elements in Discipline Problems," *The American Journal of Orthopsychiatry* (January).

"Clinical Group Work with Children," in *Group Work and the Social Scene Today,* New York: American Association for the Study of Group Work.

"Zoot-Suit, An Interpretation," *Survey Midmonthly* (October).

1944

"Deviations Tending Toward Delinquency," in *Child Growth in an Era of Conflict, Yearbook of the Michigan Education Association, Elementary.*

"Diagnostic Group Work," *The American Journal of Orthopsychiatry* (January).

"Problems of Clinical Group Work with Children," in *Psychotherapy with Children and Group Therapy,* Chicago: Institute for Psychoanalysis.

1945

Contributions to *Helping Teachers Understand Children,* Part I, Washington, D.C.: American Council on Education (in cooperation with Caroline Tryon and Daniel Prescott).

1946

The Case Worker's Manual, Detroit: Detroit Group Project Summer Camp. These publications are available in mimeographed form from the Detroit Group Project, Wayne University, Detroit, Michigan.

"Individual Behavior Log."

"Group Study."

1947

"Discipline and Group Psychology," *Journal of the Deans of Women* (October), pp. 3–5.

"The Preadolescent," in *Childcraft,* Vol. 9: *The Growing Child,* Chicago: Quarrie, pp. 114–130.

1950

"The Use of Sociometric Data in Research on Group Treatment Processes," *Sociometry,* 13:39–62 (with Norman Polansky and Ronald Lippitt).

Understanding Children's Behavior, New York: Bureau of Publications, Teachers College, Columbia University.

1951

"Hypertrophic Ego Functions, a Neglected Factor in the Pathology of Delinquents," *The American Journal of Orthopsychiatry* (April).

Mental Hygiene in Teaching, New York: Harcourt (with William Wattenberg).

Children Who Hate, New York: Free Press (with David Wineman).

1952

Controls from Within: Techniques for the Treatment of the Aggressive Child, New York: Free Press (with David Wineman).

"The Dynamics of Power, A Field of Social Influence Techniques," in *Readings in Social Psychology*, New York: Holt, pp. 626–636 (with Ronald Lippit, Norman Polansky, and Sidney Rosen).

1953

"Leaders and Followers," in *An Introduction to Social Science*, Philadelphia: Lippincott, pp. 264–275.

"Are Parents Worrying About the Wrong Things?" *Child Study*, 30:4–8, 47–50.

1954

"Child Study in a New Setting," *Children* (January-February), pp. 15–20.

"What Is Normal for Children?" *Casework Papers 1954 from the National Conference of Social Work*, New York: Family Service Association of America, 99–109.

1955

"Can 'Nice' Children Be Delinquents?" *Woman's Home Companion* (April), p. 7.

"The Therapeutic Ingredients in the Group Work Program in a Residential Treatment Center for Children," in Harleigh B. Treacher, ed., *Group Work in the Psychiatric Setting*, New York: Morrow, pp. 43–47.

"Teenagers Don't Have to Be a Problem," *McCalls* (July).

1956

"What Makes Children Misbehave," *McCalls* (August).

"Child Psychiatry: Hospital Aspects," *Mental Hospitals*, 7:38–41 (with G. Wilse Robinson, Jr.).

1957

"Research Needs in the Delinquency Field," *Children*, 4:15–19.

"The Camp Milieu and Its Immediate Effects," *The Journal of Social Issues*, 13:40–46 (with Paul Gump and Phil Schoggen).

"What Do We Do When They Fight?" *Parents' Magazine* (September).

The Aggressive Child (combined edition of *Children Who Hate* and *Controls from Within*), New York: Free Press (with David Wineman).

1958

"The Impact of Game Ingredients on Children's Play Behavior," New York: *Fourth Conference on Group Processes,* Josiah Macy, Jr., Foundation, pp. 33–81.

"Implications for Our Current Models of Personality," *Fourth Conference on Group Processes,* New York: Josiah Macy, Jr., Foundation, pp. 609–612.

"The Emotionally Disturbed Child and the Classroom Teacher," *NEA Journal* (December), pp. 609–612 (with Stanley Jacobson).

1959

Consultant contribution to *Psychiatric Aspects of School Desegregation,* New York: Committee on Social Issues of the Group for the Advancement of Psychiatry, Report No. 37.

Mental Hygiene in Teaching, 2nd ed., New York: Harcourt (with William Wattenberg).

"Some Ecological Considerations in Child Drug Research," in S. Fisher, ed., *Child Research in Psycho-Pharmacology,* Springfield, Ill.: Thomas, pp. 81–96.

1960

"Why Children We Love Make Us Angry," *Parents' Magazine* (February).

"What to Do When They Make Us Angry," *Parents' Magazine* (March).

1962

Technical Assistance in the Public Schools, Washington, D.C.: School Research Program, Washington School of Psychiatry (with Ruth Newman and Howard Kitchener).

1963

"Residential Treatment for Emotionally Disturbed Children" in Albert Deutsch, ed., *The Encyclopedia of Mental Health,* New York: Franklin Watts, Inc., Vol. 5, pp. 1769–1781.

1964

Consultant contribution to *Psychiatric Aspects of the Prevention of Nuclear War,* New York: Group for the Advancement of Psychiatry, Committee on Social Issues.

"Education and the National Conscience," in *Education Conference Report,* New York: Bank Street College of Education.

"Our Children—Where Do They Go From Here?" in *The Future of the American Family,* New York: Child Study Association of America.

"Problems of Cross-Cultural Communication," Foreword to Helen B. Redl, *Soviet Educators on Soviet Education,* New York: Free Press.

1965

"Dehumanization, A Composite Psychological Defense in Relation to Modern War," in Milton Schwebel, ed., *Behavioral Science and Human Survival,*

Palo Alto: Science and Behavior (with Viola Bernard and Perry Ottenberg).

"Fritz Redl on 'Den Heiligen Nikolaus,'" in Adriaan de Grott, *Saint Nicholas, A Psychoanalytic Study*, Hague: Mouton.

"Pathogenic Factors in the Modern Child's Life" and "Comments on Kibbutz Education," in Peter Neubauer, ed., *Children in Collectives—Child Rearing Aims and Practices in the Kibbutz*, Springfield, Ill.: Thomas.

"Management of Discipline Problems," in *Proceedings of the 8th annual Conference of the Virginia Council for Exceptional Children*, University of Virginia, pp. 41–62.

Index

Accidents, 368
Acting out, 18, 27
Action
    initiatory, *see* Initiatory acts
    interpretation of, defined, 144
    secondary influences on, 477–87
    threshold of, 325–27
Activeness of leaders, 180
Activity
    "preparatory" therapeutic, 37–38, 44
    protection of, 347
    structure of, in milieu therapy, 87–88
Adjustment, 48, 412
    to camp life, 440, 446, 448
    demands for, 103
    new tools for, 45–46
    problems of group, 188–89
Adolescents, 74–75, 224, 292, 422
    groups of
        favored group types, 187–88
        group codes, 296
        group composition, 238, 246–47
    leaders of, 163–64, 166–72
    "serious," 107
    sexuality of, 121, 429–30, 435, 438
    use of term, 10
    See also Delinquency; Preadolescents;
        Youth movements
Adult roles, *see* Roles—adult
Age, *see* Child development
"Agency guilt, resurrection of," 15
Aggression, 56, 157, 248
    discipline for, 278
    due to guilt, 137
    frustration, 129, 287
    toward group leaders, 167–68, 169–
        70, 177–78, 182, 185–86
    holy, 192–93
    from punishment, 366–67
    release of surplus, 481–82
    See also Fights; Hostility

Alexander, Franz, 197
Alibis, 113, 122
Ambivalence, 96
    toward self-image, 113
    toward youth, 10
Analysis, *see* Psychoanalysis
Anger
    of children, 296
        children in libraries, 452–60
        emotional first aid, 48–49
        moral indignation, 163, 165, 167
        punished children, 364, 366–68
    of guiding adults, 13, 386–89
        anger over improvement, 100, 115
        provocation of anger, 218–19
        punishment and, 377
    of parents, 361–62, 471
    See also Aggression; Fights; Hostility;
        Quarrels; Resentment; Tantrums
Anthropology, 313, 473
Antisepsis, marginal, 264–65, 272, 359
Anxiety, 131, 163, 208–9, 414, 478–79
    discipline and, 296
    guilt, 137
    impulsivity and, 143
    nature producing, 442
    prevention of, 347
        central persons preventing, 169–71,
        173
    See also Fear
Anxiety neurosis, 61, 242–43, 415
Armed services, 192–93, 257–58
Artificial relationships, 61–62
Arts, 145, 207–8
    subgrouping for, 250
Assaults, sexual, 382
Athletics, competitive, 74
    See also Games
Attitudes
    change of, 268–74
    improved, 117

Attitudes (*Cont.*)
  observation of, 334–37
  of staffs, 86
Autocratic pressure, 293–94
  See also Patriarchial sovereigns; Tyrants
Autoeroticism, *see* Masturbation
Autonomy
  limits on, 91
  of decision-making, 113, 117–18
  through trust, 122
Aversions, observation of, 336, 342
  See also Hatred

Bathing, 39, 400, 481
Berman, Leo, 309, 312, 317–18, 326–27
Bethesda project, 74, 330
Betrayal, 49
Bettelheim, Bruno, 84
Blackmail, emotional, 112, 291–92
Blasphemy, 205–6
  discipline for, 276, 279–80
  sexual, 382–83
Books, 452–60
Boredom
  classroom, 288, 296–97
  contagion and, 319–20
  defense against, 414
Borrowing, 51

Camps
  adult roles in, 54–55
  Detroit Group Project, 128, 141, 216
  psychopathological risks of, 440–51
Caseworkers
  in Pioneer House project, 140–41
  psychiatric, 23, 57
"Casing the joint," 128
"Caste" systems, 120
Central person, defined, 160–61
Change, 105–6, 108
  of attitudes, 268–74
  resistance to, *see* Resistance
  strain and sudden, 296–98
  in superego, 323–24
  See also Improvement; Transition
Character
  of family figures, 471
  strength of, 428
Child analysis, *see* Psychoanalysis

Child development, 37, 346
  defiance in, 412–13
  education and, 287, 294
  group composition and, 245–47
  healthy independence of, 463–64
  parental development with, 310–11
  premature, 107
  prestige in, 480
  problem behavior in normal, 421–22
  sexual development, 427–30, 437–38
  stages of, *see* Adolescents; Preadolescents
  therapy appropriate for, 74–75
Child-guidance clinics, 23
  community, 12–13
  delinquents in, 233
  teams for, 23–24
  See also Mental hospitals
Child Research Branch, 65–66, 98, 452
Children Who Hate (Redl and Wineman), 48, 125
Choice, *see* Decisions
Clinical elasticity, 75–76, 91
Clinical group work, *see* Group therapy
Clinical resilience, 90–91
Clinics, child-guidance, *see* Childguidance clinics
Cliques
  as discipline problems, 289
  subcliques, 84–85, 343–44
  See also Gangs
Clowning, 263–65
Codes, *see* Groups—codes of
Collective disease, *see* Community disease
Commitment, fear of, 111
Communication, 422
  institutional, 82
  intuitive, 213
  maintained in relationship decay, 49
  professional, 330
  about sex, 433
  sympathetic, 48
Community disease
  hatred for youth as, 11–12
  implementational psychopathy and, 12–17
Community services, *see* Mental-health services
Competition, 136
  climate of hostile, 292

professional, 118–19
in sports, 74
See also Rivalry
Comradeship, 165, 167, 177
See also Friendship
Confidence in parents, 432–34
Conflicts, 56, 81, 190, 289, 348
aid in, 48
central persons preventing, 169–74
competitive, 119
contagion and, 193–96, 204–5, 208–10
displaced, 219–20
group, 113
impulse-ego, 143
of normal children, 62–63
of overprotected children, 447
preadolescent, 401–2, 404
Confusion, 127
Conscience, 156
"group," 204
preadolescent, 401
See also Superego
Constituent performances, 87–88
Consumers, 103
Contagion, behavioral (infectiousness), 84–85, 193–213, 319–21
factors determining, 201–5
group composition, 237–38, 241–44, 249
group-psychological factors, 201–3
personality factors, 203–5
by group leaders, 172–74, 193–96
implications of, 210–13
index of, 129
indirect, 206–10
observation of, 343–44
prevention of, 347
Contempt for group therapy, 311–12
Control, 401
contagion and, 204
depersonalized, 144
loss of, 206–7
ego control, 129–30
fear of loss, 110–11
see also Impulsivity
punishment and, 356, 364–65
sexual problems and, 484–85
Control groups, 18–19

Controls from Within (Redl and Wineman), 355
Convalescence, psychic, 31–32
Counseling, 29, 65
depth-oriented, 57
seeking of, 46
Counterhysterics, 405
"Countersuspicion," 105
Counting machines, 17–18
Cowardice, emotional, 165, 171, 463–64
toward sex education, 438–39
Crafts, 145
Crime, *see* Delinquency; Gangs; Murder; Prostitution; Theft
Criticism and improvement, 110
Culture, 92
American, 103
backgrounds in, 74–75
differences in, 155
peer, *see* Peer groups
seeping into institutions, 89

Dare psychology, 485–86
Davis-Dollard-Warner studies, 181
Daydreams, *see* Fantasies
Deals with pseudonormal children, 115–18
Death wish, 95
Decisions, 247, 326
emotional first aid for, 51
improvement and, 113–14, 117–18
Decontamination of experience, interpretive, 144
Defenses, 132
contagious, 320
defiance as, 414
of delinquents, 224, 227, 229–32
against improvement, 105
of intelligent patients, 101
against mental health, 96
against professional conscience, 8–9
withdrawal as, *see* Withdrawal
See also Resistance
Defiance, youthful, 409–17
types of, 412–15
See also Delinquency; Rebellion
Delinquency, 128, 139, 189, 224–35
codes of, 226, 228–32

Delinquency (*Cont.*)
    dare psychology in, 485
    defiance and, 409–11, 416
    degrees of, 211
    determination of, 418–26
        early detection, 421–23
    as "dog-bone" issue, 16
    four types of, 224–25
    sexual, 435
    special classes for, 270–71
    treatment of, 232–35
        illiteracy and, 477–78
        special treatment techniques, 139–40
        supportive treatment, 424–25
    virtues combined with, 461–66, 474
    See also Detention homes; Gangs; Reformatories
Delusions
    accusatory, 137–38
    escape into, 147–48
    megalomaniac, 47
Dependency
    defiance and, 413
    discipline and, 292, 300
    exaggerated, 132
Depersonalizing symbolization, 230–31
Depression (despondency), 47, 296
    with improvement, 109–10
Destruction, contagious, 203–4
Detention homes, 13, 203, 233
    See also Reformatories
Detroit Game Study, 87
Detroit Group Project, 128, 141, 234
    club program of, 216
    life-space interviews for, 58–60
    Summer Camp, 128, 141, 216
Development, *see* Child development
Developmental defiance, 412–13
Deviation tolerance, 341–42
Dignity of teachers, 295, 303
Disadvantaged children, 467–87
    definitions of, 467–71
    obsolete models of, 472–76
    secondary factors affecting, 477–87
Disappointment, 63
Discipline
    attitudes toward, 335
    classroom, 166, 254–308
        defined, 260–61

discipline as teacher value, 162–65
    preventing discipline problems, 280–302
    strict discipline, 185
    teacher personality and, 302–6
    three disciplinary headaches, 261–80
    See also Interference; Punishment
Disease, *see* Illness; Psychopathology
Dissatisfaction in schoolwork process, 286–88
"Dog-bone Complex," 15–16
Dollard-Davis-Warner studies, 181
Drive, 157, 159, 181
    central person as object of, 165–70
    ego support through, 169, 173–75
    support of, 194
    sympathy with adolescent, 163–64
    See also Aggression; Needs; Sex
Drug therapy, 26

Education, 24, 37, 476
    counseling and, 57, 65
    crisis in, 3, 8–9
    of disadvantaged children, 470–71
    discipline for, *see* Discipline—classroom
    elasticity of, 76
    group composition for, 246
    group emotion and
        educational applications, 184–90
        group leaders, 162–74
    life-space interviews and, 67
    lowered status of, 454
    medical, 28–29
    psychoanalysis and, 147–51
    rules governing, 50
    sex, *see* Sex—education about
    special, 25
    technical skills in, 302–5
    therapeutic, 79–81
    See also Illiteracy; Learning
Ego, 36, 45, 50, 479
    decisions made by, 326
    defiant, 415–16
    defined, 125–26
    disturbances of, 44–45, 125–46, 225
        deficient concept of disturbance, 126–28
        types of disturbance, 128–33

identification of, 177
improvement of, *see* Improvement
proximity to, 53
punishment affecting, 358, 366–70
support of, 125–46
   central figure as support, 168–75
   conflict and, 194
   defined, 133–35
   emotional first aid, 48–49
   games supporting, 88
   gangs supporting, 228
   healthy child under strain, 62–64
   implications, 139–42
   supportive techniques, 135–39,
      142–46
Ego ideals, 156–57, 164, 323
   of campers, 444–46
   of delinquents, 225, 229
Ekstein, Rudolph, 147
Elasticity (flexibility)
   clinical, 75–76, 91
   of program, 250
   of routine, 251–52
Elation (overstimulation), 143, 296
   with improvement, 109–10
   resexualization of, 484–85
   See also Clowning; Hilarity
Emotion
   blackmail by, 112, 291–92
   cowardly, *see* Cowardice
   distance of, 296
   first aid for, 42–43, 47–52
   group, 155–96
      defined, 159–60
      educational applications, 184–90
      emotional currents, 142
      initiatory acts, 190–93
      spatial repetition compulsion, 192–
         96
      ten group formations, 162–84
   in interpersonal relations, 288–90
   strain on, *see* Stress
   See also specific emotions
Employment, *see* Work
Environment, 38–39, 141, 473–74
   awareness of, 150–51
   of camp, 441–44
   See also Milieu therapy
Envy, 177, 192

Equipment in milieu therapy, 88
Erikson, Erik, 93
Erotic play, 380–82
   group, 381–82
   preadolescent, 398, 435
   solitary, 380–81
Escape
   from guilt, 219–20
   library as, 457–59
   into love, 217–18
   into virtue, 221–22
   See also Withdrawal
Estrangement from peer groups, 112–14
   See also Ostracism; Outcasts
Examples (central persons), *see* Influence—of central figures
Exculpation magic, 178, 190–93, 228
Expectations
   professional over-expectations, 114–
      15, 120
   role, 144
Experience
   interpretive decontamination of, 144
   learning from, 351
   punishment as unpleasant, 363–64
Exploitation
   of group-psychological securities, 138–
      39
   of improvement, 114–15

Face, loss of, 45, 53, 358
   See also Shame
Failure, 101
   improvement and, 110
   of teachers, 304–5
Fairness, 348
   acceptable code of, 45
   for all, 464–66
Fantasies, 49, 200, 421
   delusional, 137
   of gangs, 187
   observation of, 336–37
   Oedipal, 95, 208
   pathological, 415
   preadolescent, 398–99
   revenge, 367
   sexual, 378, 434
   See also Delusions
Fatigue, 288

Favoritism, 120
Fear, 291, 447
    of adult anger, 386
    of classmates, 165
    of commitment, 111
    of crowds, 415
    initiators free from, 205, 210
    of loss
        loss of control, 110–11
        loss of security, 163
    observation of, 336–37
    preadolescent, 402
    of water, 243
    See also Anxiety; Phobias
Feelings
    inferiority, 265–66
    paranoid, 78
    See also Emotions; Sensitivities
Fenichel, Otto, 155
Fights, 53, 84
    classroom, 268–69, 278–79, 283, 289,
        293
    gang, 464–65
    of normal children, 63
Films, 89
Finances
    of beginning psychiatrists, 29
    for community services, 14–15
    of Pioneer House, 141
    for research, 19–21, 31
    of special schools, 476
First aid, emotional, 90, 389
    life-space interviews as, 42–43, 47–52
Fixation, sexual, 427–28
Flexibility, *see* Elasticity
Foster homes, 25–26
"Freeze-up," referral, 15
Freud, Anna, 133, 150, 167n, 194, 311–
        12
    *The Ego and Its Mechanisms of De-
        fense*, 189
    emphasizes "preparatory" activities,
        37–38
    *Introduction to the Technique of
        Child Analysis*, 69
Freud, Sigmund, 95–96, 101, 125, 177,
        193, 312–13, 318, 326
    *Group Psychology and the Analysis of
        the Ego*, 156–57, 164, 195–96

imitation viewed by, 319
    on leadership, 160–61, 165–66
    on sexual fantasies, 434
Friction, teacher-pupil, 290
Friendship
    adolescent, 189–90, 422
    autocratic, 263–64
    as discipline problem, 289
    as resistance, 218
    sharing of, 448–49
    See also Comradeship
Fringe-area treatment goals, 76–77
Frustration, 115, 137, 297
    aggression from, 129
    drain-off of acidity of, 48, 54
    punishment as, 364
    over schoolwork, 287
Fury, *see* Anger

Games, 71, 143–44, 181
    constituent performances in, 87–88
    See also Athletics; Play therapy
Gangs
    adult, 113
    formation of, 180, 465
        exculpation magic, 190–92
        psychology of formation, 224–35
    individual therapy blocked by, 482–
        83
    preadolescent, 186–87, 191, 247, 400,
        403–5
    pseudo-improvement of, 222
    taxation powers of, 324
    See also Cliques; Delinquency
German Youth Movement, 178
"Germophobia," 244
Gossip, 208, 210
    about adult leaders, 240–41
Gratification (satisfaction)
    chart of group, 344–45
    of delinquents, 226, 229
    forgotten, 143
    through group libido, 183–84
    guarantees of, 145
    improvement and, 111–13, 121
    substitute, 288; *see also* Sublimation
    of undesirable drives, 169–70
"Gripe sessions," 206–7
Group therapy, 13, 133
    life-space interviews rooted in, 58–60

psychoanalysis and, 309–27
  challenge, 317–27
  changing attitude toward group therapy, 311–17
residential, 140–46
resistance in, 214–23
Groups
  behavioral contagion in, *see* Contagion
  campers as, 446–49
  classroom discipline for, *see* Discipline —classroom
  codes of, 144–45, 296
    acceptable games, 144
    contagion and, 201, 211
    delinquent groups, 226, 228–32
    depersonalized code, 78
    dueling code, 485
    exploitation of code, 138–39
    powers of taxation, 323–25
    preadolescent groups, 403–4
    professional observation, 340–42
    religion and, 205–6
    therapy blocked by codes, 482–83
  composition of, 236–53, 450
    discipline and, 298–301
    homogeneous, 245
    importance, 211
    remedies for ill-matched groups, 248–53
  control, 18–19
  dynamics of, 214–15
  emotions of, *see* Emotion—group
  individual punishment affecting, 359–61
  leadership of, *see* Leadership
  loyalty to, 462–63
  observation of, 338–45
  peer, *see* Peer groups
  personnel psychologically impregnated by, 144–45
  processes of, 84–85
  psychological intoxication in, *see* Intoxication
  psychological security in, 138–39
  psychological suction in, *see* Suction
  roles in, *see* Roles—group
  sexual activity in, 169, 381–82
  See also Cliques; Gangs; Group therapy
Growth, *see* Child development

Guardians, concept of benign, 456–57
Guilt, 136–37
  over anger, 388–89
  camp life and, 443, 447
  emotional first aid for, 48–49
  exculpation magic for, 192
  initiators free from, 204–5, 210
  over loss of control, 207
  preadolescent immunity to, 401
  prevention of
    prevention by group codes, 228–29
    prevention by group leaders, 169–70, 173
    prevention by interference, 347
  punishment and, 367, 373–74
  "resurrection of agency," 15
  taxation and, 324
  See also Shame
Gump, Paul, 87

"Hang-over" effects, 135–36
Hatred, 387
  for adults, 240–41
  as discipline problem, 289
  contagion and, 208
  gang, 230
  for group life, 449
  of leaders, 165, 167, 177, 219
  of male rivals, 166
  of social class, 275
  for youth, 9–12
  See also Aversions
Health
  mental, *see* Mental health
  observation of, 337
  See also Illness
Helplessness
  toward group-psychological suction, 46–47
  punishment and, 362
Heroes (central persons), 170–72, 175
Hide-and-seek, flashlight, 88
Hilarity, 130–31, 296
  See also Clowning; Elation; Humor
Hitler, Adolph, 178–79
Hitler Youth Movement, 178
Homesickness, 209
Homosexuality, 195, 422
  of group libido, 183–84
  pairing and, 189–90

Hospitals, mental, *see* Mental hospitals
Hostility, 74, 209–10
    admission of, 96
    climate of competitive, 292
    contagious, 320
    frustrations producing, 48
    improvement and, 106, 112, 115
    reinforced by punishment, 116
    repressed, 10, 165
    of schools, 470–71
    See also Aggression
Humor
    dirty jokes as, 383, 400
    sense of, in teachers, 303, 306–7
    See also Clowning; Hilarity
Hurt, psychological, *see* Pain
Hypertrophy of ego, 128
Hypothesis complex, 19–20
Hysteria, 61
    counterhysteria, 405
    social, 404

Id, 36, 128
    conflicts over, 194
    of delinquents, 140
    See also Impulsivity; Libido
Ideals
    central figures as, 182
    ego, *see* Ego ideals
Identification
    absence of, 144–45, 166–68
    of delinquents, 226, 228–29, 231–32
    Freudian concept of, 157, 177, 195–96
    with leaders, 163, 165, 170–71, 174, 177–78, 185, 189
    libido and, 183, 188, 217–18
    of preadolescents, 402–3
Illiteracy, 468–69, 477–78
Illness, 6–7
    community, *see* Community disease
    convalescence after, 31–32
    maladjusted, 61
    mental, *see* Psychopathology
Imitation, 447
    in contagion, 206, 319
Implementational psychopathy, 12–16
Implementational stench, 486–87
Improvement, 95–124, 218–19, 221–22
    cost of, 107, 109–23

defined, 102–5
    determining real, 105–8
    directives for handling of, 117–18
Impulsivity, 50, 84, 110, 127, 130–31
    contagion and, 204–5, 210
    controlled, 129
    drainage of, 142–43
    protection against, 116
    sexual perversion and, 435
In-situational support of punishment, 371–72
Incest, 183
Individualization, educational, 255–56, 262–68
Infectiousness, *see* Contagion
Inferiority feelings, 265–66
Influence
    awareness of, 303
    of central figures
        bad influence, 172–74, 180, 185–86, 190
        durability of influence, 181
        good influence, 173–74, 190
        solution of conflicts and, 193–96
"Informality," classroom, 275
Inherent structures, 130–31
Initiatory acts, 169–71, 199
    group status and, 201
    guiltless, 204–5, 210
    magic of, 179, 190–93
Insecurity, longing for, 463
Insight, 171
    improvement and, 110–11, 113
Insulation
    group-psychological, 211–12
    subgroup, 248–49
Intake, institutional, 252–53
Interests (tastes)
    observation of, 336, 342
    preparation of, 455–56
Interference (intervention), 120, 133, 295, 347–54
    anger and, 388–89
    criteria for, 347–48
    marginal antisepsis in, 359
    protective, 143, 347
    refraining from, 349–54
    resistance to, 144
    responsibility for, 456–57

restraint as, 116, 357, 376
severity of, 357, 388
signal, 136–37, 347
Interpersonal relations, *see* Relationships
Interviews, 144, 382, 479
"expressional" group, 250
life-space, *see* Life-space interviews
marginal, 40–42, 64–65, 141–42
psychiatric, 57, 64
Intimacy, fear of, 165
See also Friendship; Sex
Intoxication, group-psychological, 84–85
ego control lost in, 129–30
prevention of, 143
Issue clarity, 53

Jealousy, 177, 192, 265
Jokes, dirty, 383, 400
Justice, 464–66
Juvenile delinquency, *see* Delinquency

Kinsey, Alfred C., 438

Language
blasphemous, *see* Blasphemy
primitive, 191
sophisticated, 247
of teachers, 287
Lay therapy, 26–30
Leadership, 133, 150, 256–59
gang, 176, 465
group emotion and, 155–96
educational applications, 184–90
initiatory acts, 190–93
spatial repetition compulsion, 193–96
ten group formations, 162–84
mistakes in, 293–96
tensions of, 84–85
Learning
deficient, 77, 468–69, 477–78
improvement in, 102
See also Education
Le Bon, Gustave, 319
Lewin, Kurt, 41
Libido, 188, 195, 217–18
group, 182–84
toward parent surrogates, 323
Libraries, 452–60

Life-space interviews, 32, 35–69, 113, 381–82
as clinical exploitation, 42, 44–47
components of, 64–66
concept of, 39–42
as emotional first aid, 42–43, 47–52
as group therapy, 58–60
as innovation, 66–67
for normal children, 62–64
See also Marginal interviews
Limitations, reality, 131–32
Loaded transactions, 51
Loneliness, 447–49
Loss
of control, *see* Control—loss of
of face, 45, 53, 358; *see also* Shame
of security, 163
Love, 45, 132, 433
adolescent, 189–90
in code of delinquents, 231–32
conveyance of, 116–17
crisis in, 9–12
as drive, 157
as emotional blackmail, 291
escape into, 217–18
of leaders, 162–67, 177–78, 185, 195
See also Libido
Loyalty, 480–81
gang, 229–32
group, 462–63
"tests" of, 113
to youth movements, 181
Luck, 107–8

Machines, counting, 17–18
Magic, 179, 402
exculpation, 178, 190–93, 228
"seductive," 227–28
"Maladjusted diseases," 60–62
Manageability
of moods, 55
observation of, 343
See also Discipline; Manipulation
Manipulation, 105
healthy children affected by, 63
of "hang-over" effects, 135–36
managerial, 268–74
"milieu," 37
Manners, 107
Marginal antisepsis, 264–65, 272, 359

Marginal interviews, 40–42, 64–65, 141–42
  See also Life-space interviews
Mascot cultivation, 84–85
Masochism, 206–7, 365
Masturbation, 365, 380–82, 435
  group, 169, 381–82
Maturity
  organizational, 247–48
  pseudomaturity, 107
Medical degrees, 26–30
Megalomaniac illusions, 47
Mental health
  delinquency and, 224
  professional dislike of, 30–32, 95–97
  See also Improvement; Normal children
Mental-health services, 3
  obsolete models of, 22, 24
  research vs., 20–22
  volunteers for, 475–76
  See also Child-guidance clinics; Mental hospitals
Mental hospitals, 13–14, 27, 30, 41n, 80
  crowding in, 7–8
  social structure in, 82
  See also Child-guidance clinics
Mental illness, *see* Psychopathology
Middle Ages, 191–92
"Milieu manipulation," 37
Milieu therapy, 36–40, 41n, 68–94
  components of, 81–91
  therapeutic aspects of, 72–81
  traps in, 70–72
Minority groups, 25
  Negroes as, 236, 275
Misbehavior, group attitudes toward, 163–64
  See also Discipline
Moods
  group, 202–3, 340
  interference and, 353–54
  manageability of, 55
  of normal children, 63
  "positive," 107
  See also specific moods
Morbidity, 96–97
Motto, Rocco, 147
Murder, exculpation magic for, 192–93

Muteness
  in group therapy, 320
  improvement, 118

Naïveté, 134, 221
  clinical, 473–74
  implementational, 475–76
  relapse into preclinical, 119–20
  sociological, 472–73
Narcissism, 166
  of delinquents, 225
  toward leaders, 164
  professional, 101, 118–19
National Institute of Mental Health, 41n
  Child Research Branch, 65–66, 98, 452
  Clinical Center, 452
  library of, 453
  Research Grant Division, 197
Nature, 441–42
Needs
  basic coverage of, 73–74
  contagion and, 201–2
  See also Drives
Neglect, crisis in, 9–12
Negroes, 236, 275
Neurosis, 127, 148, 310, 428
  anxiety, *see* Anxiety neurosis
  camping and, 442, 444
  classical, 61–62
  delinquency and, 225, 474
  environmental influence on, 150–51
  reticence, 17
  "sputnik," 8–9
  "transference," 479
"Newness" panic, 110–11
Normal children
  as problems
    discipline problems, 288
    problem behavior, 421–22
  pseudonormal children, 115–18
  under strain, ego support for, 62–64
Nostalgia
  homesickness, 209
  for pathology, 111–12

Obedience, *see* Discipline
Observation
  delinquents' skills of, 128

professional, 333–45
  group observation, 338–45
  realm of observation, 333–37
  See also Perception
Obsolete models, 22–26, 472–76
Occupational therapy, 73–74
Oedipal fantasies, 95, 208
Open cottages, 81, 89
Opposites, assertions of, 96
Optimism, professional, 117
"Optimum distance, law of," 246
Order, educational, 162–64, 260–61,
  303–4
Organization
  classroom, mistakes in, 293–96
  maturity in, 247–48
Organizers (central persons), 168–69,
  175, 185–86, 228
Orphanages, 24–25
Orthopsychiatric teams, 23
Ostracism, 113
  See also Estrangement; Outcasts
Outcasts, 120, 167, 292
  See also Estrangement; Ostracism
Overstimulation, *see* Elation

Pain, psychological (hurt)
  prevention of, 347
  punishment as, 361–62, 364
Panic, 75, 78
  emotional first aid for, 48–49
  improvement, 95–124
  "newness," 110–11
  separation, 106
Paranoid feelings, 78
Passivity of leaders, 180
Pathology, *see* Disease; Psychopathology
Patriarchal sovereigns (group leaders),
  162–63, 178, 181, 185–86
Pecking order, 71, 82
Peer groups, 105, 121
  codes of, 226, 482–83
  estrangement from, 112–14
  preadolescent, 187
  sex education through, 431–32
  shame before, 45
  See also Cliques; Gangs
Perception, 212
  of inherent structures, 130–31

intuitive, 468–70
  See also Insight; Observation
Permission, 346
Permissiveness, 132–33, 356, 389
Personality, 85–86
  "constellation" of, defined, 194
  developed in groups, 188–89
  disorganization of preadolescent, 401–
    02
  improvement of, *see* Improvement
  of leaders, 178, 180
  obsolete models of, 22–26
  threatened balance of, 209–10
  of teachers, 302–7
Perversion, 435
  See also Homosexuality; Masochism;
    Sadism
Phobias, 209, 244
Pessimism, professional, 104
Pictures, 89
Pioneer House, 128–31, 145
  described, 140–41
  ego support in, 134–36, 139
  resistance studies at, 216
Pity, 171
  moral, 164
  self-pity, 365
Plato, 196
Play therapy, 57–58, 75, 77, 396
Postsituational support of punishment,
  371–72
Practice
  educational theory and, 255–59
  research vs., 21
Praise
  improvement and, 110
  for preadolescents, 407
Preadolescents, 107, 395–408
  formulas for dealing with, 405–8
  gangs of, 186–87, 191, 247, 400, 403–
    05
  improper behavior of, 397–400
  improvement of, 121
  revolt of, 168, 170–71
  school problems of, 188–89
  sexual development of, 201, 396, 398,
    400, 434–35
Prejudice, 230–31

"Preparatory" therapeutic activities, 37–38, 44
Preventive planning, 347
Pride, climate of group, 292–93
Primitivism, 191–92
Privileges
    with improvement, 117, 120
    loss of, 364
Program distortion, 121
Progress
    technical, 6–7
    therapeutic, *see* Improvement
Projection, 113, 290
Promises, 115–18, 295
Props, 325–26
    in life-space interviews, 56–57
    in milieu therapy, 88
Prostitution, adolescent, 435
Provocation
    defiance as, 415
    interference and, 352–53
    by name-calling, 382–83
    protective, 218–19, 280
    sexual, 381
Psychiatric caseworkers, 23, 57
Psychiatric interview technique, 57, 64
Psychiatrists, 71, 135, 141
    camp, 54, 450
    child guidance and
        guidance clinics, 12–13
        guidance teams, 23
    of delinquents, 232–34
    educational, 258–59
    medical, 27, 29
Psychoanalysis, 57, 133, 156
    conditions for classical, 69–70
    education and, 147–51
    group therapy and, *see* Group therapy
        —psychoanalysis and
    life-space interviews and, 36–37
    sociology and, 158–59, 313
    See also Psychiatrists
Psychoanalytic Study of the Child, The
    (periodical), 313
Psychopathology, 11, 346, 420
    in camp life, 440–51
    community, *see* Community disease
    defiance and, 414–17
    episodes of, 352–53
    interacting of, 85

improvement of, *see* Improvement
juvenile pranks and, 418–19
"maladjusted," 60–62
milieu therapy absorbing, 76
nostalgia for, 111–12
prepsychotic, 281–82
slips and accidents as, 368
See also Neurosis; Psychopathy; Schizophrenia; Symptoms
Psychopathy
    implementational, 12–16
    punishment and, 420
    values and, 45
Psychosomatic symptoms, 209
Psychotherapy, 25, 471
    defense against, 105
    for delinquents, *see* Delinquency—treatment of
    escape and, 458–59
    goals of, 36
    improvement through, *see* Improvement
    lay, 26–30
    mental health and, 30–32, 95–97
    for preadolescents, 396–97
    secondary factors blocking, 477–79, 482–83
    for sexual perverts, 435
    terrain and props in, 56
    See also Group therapy; Life-space interviews; Play therapy; Psychoanalysis; Psychiatrists
Punishment, 69, 193, 355–77, 420
    absence of stupid, 72
    adult feelings accompanying, 86
    analysis of experience of, 363–71
    avoidance of, 115–16
    defined, 361–63
    disciplinary, 259, 261, 276, 279–80, 290–91, 292, 295
    improvement and, 106, 110, 112, 117–18, 120
    for preadolescents, 407
    provocation of, 218–19, 280, 415
    restitutional rituals as, 373–74
    of ringleaders, 191
    support of, 371–72
"Punitive referrals," 15

Quarrels, 51, 84

Rapport, "positive," 134
Rationality, 131–33, 179
Reaction formation, 208–9
Reactive defiance, 414
Readers, image of, 455–56
Reality, 143, 145, 347
  internal, 111
  limitations of, 131–32
  principle of, 131
  Platonic, 196
  psychological, 476
  reshuffled, 137–38
  rub-in of, 44, 53, 143–44
  supercharged issues of, 479–82
  testing in, 31–32, 79–81
Rebellion, 240–41
  absence of, 165, 167
  adolescent, 121, 435
  against injustice, 464–65
  intelligent, 413
  preadolescent, 168, 170–71
Recidivism, 31, 97
Recreation, 107
  program of, 74
  therapeutic, 77
  See also Athletics; Games
Re-education, therapeutic, 79–81
Referral "freeze-up," 15
Reformatories, 242–43
  See also Detention homes
Regression, 99
  in healthy children, 63
  improvement and, 112, 115, 120–22
  partial, 132
Regrouping, 252
Regulations, 71, 122, 143, 306, 348
  on behavioral traffic, 50–51, 89–90
  of clinical resilience, 90–91
  emotional need for, 247
  excessive, 294
  of games, 87
  in milieu therapy, 84
Reinforcement, 50
  of delinquency, 227–28
  of hostility, 116
Reiss-Davis Seminars and Institutes, 149
Relationships
  artificial, 61–62

  decay of, 49
  emotional unrest in, 288–90
  preadolescent, 399–400
  priorities for establishing, 349
  See also specific relationships
Religion, 205–6
Repetition compulsion, spatial, 193–96
Repression, 53
  of hostility, 10, 165
  of joy at improvement, 118
  of libido, 183, 195
  shock effect and, 207–8
Research, 97
  animal, 31
  on preadolescents, 397
  search needed in, 17–22
Resentment, 49, 54, 90, 287
Residential therapy, 140–46
Resilience
  clinical, regulation of, 90–91
  of ego, 109
Resistance, 53, 56, 112
  to adult interference, 144
  of delinquents, 227, 232–34
  to improvement, 100–2, 114–15
  to mental health, 96
  peer group code as, 482–83
  in therapy groups, 214–23, 314–15, 320
  to wrong handling, 461
  See also Defenses
Respect for teachers, 306–7
Restitutional rituals, 373–74
Restlessness, preadolescent, 397–98
Restraint, physical, 116, 357, 376
Reticence neurosis, 17
Revenge, 387
  on adults, 105, 367
  of teachers, 295
Revolt, *see* Rebellion
Rewards, 116
  absence of professional, 99
  disciplinary, 292, 295, 357
  improvement and, 110, 117–18
Rituals
  in milieu therapy, 84
  restitutional, 373–74
Rivalry, 166, 177, 292
  See also Competition

Roles
  adult, 127
    compatibility, 53–54
    consistent, 144
    distribution, 82
    role confusion, 220–21
    role protection, 457
  group, 289–90
    observation, 335, 339
    mascots, 84–85
    suction, *see* Suction
    see also Leadership; Scapegoating
  of leaders, 168
Rorschach test, 85
Routines, 348
  attitudes toward, 335
  concessions in, 250–52
  ego-supportive, 138, 143
  in milieu therapy, 84
Rules, *see* Regulations
Russian education, 9

Sadism, 178, 206
  of parents, 470–71
  of teachers, 164, 167, 171, 291
Satisfaction, *see* Gratification
Scapegoating, 84–85, 200, 278
  in camp, 445
  contagion and, 207, 208–10
Schizophrenia, 128
Schooling, *see* Education
Security
  appeal of, 247
  group-psychological, 138–39
    gangs, 187
    lack of classroom security, 294
    leaders causing security, 163, 174
  symbols of, 145
  See also Insecurity
Seduction
  by central persons, 169–70, 172, 175–
    76, 180
    Hitler as seducer, 178
    teachers' views of seducers, 185–86
  "magical," 227–28
  sexual, 381
Segregation, 280, 236
Self, 51
  ambivalence toward, 113
  expression of, 207–8

  manipulation of boundaries of, 46–47
  schizophrenic perception of, 128
  See also Ego
Self-appraisal, institutional, 252–53
Self-government, educational, 271–74
Semrad, Elvin, 317
Sensitivities
  adult, 86, 295
  preadolescent, 400, 407
Separation
  panic over, 106
  from parents, 442–44
Services, *see* Mental-health services
Sex, 194, 247, 378–85
  adolescent, 121, 429–30, 435, 438
  discipline and, 282–83
  education about, 287, 427–39
    peer-group education, 430–32
    role of confidence, 432–34
    sex questions, 384–85
  excitement and, 484–85
  in feudal societies, 314
  infantile, 95
  normal, 378–79
  parental, 69
  preadolescent, 201, 396, 398, 400,
    434–35
  unconflicted, 209
  See also Homosexuality; Erotic play;
    Incest; Masturbation
Shame
  toward delinquency, 425–26
  before peers, 45
  preadolescent, 400
  See also Face, loss of; Guilt
Shock, 85
  avoiding multiple, 449
  "complexity," 486
  effect of, 206–13, 243–44, 319–21
    implication, 210–13
    indirect contagion and, 206–10
  improvement, 95–124
  See also Trauma
Sifting, 367–68
Skills
  diagnostic, of disadvantaged child,
    468–70
  grouping according to, 250
  observation of, 336
  teaching, 302–5

Slavery to dares, 485–86

Slips, psychological, 368, 469

Smoking, 168, 358
discipline of, 270–71
preadolescent, 406

Snobs, 292

Social class, 25, 475
grouping and, 300
hatred of, 275
values of, 181

Social structure of milieu therapy, 82–83

Social traffic, regulation of, 50–51, 89–90

Society, use of term, 225–26

Sociology, 71, 83, 86, 473
delinquency and, 16
psychoanalysis and, 158–59, 313

Sociometric study, defined, 344

Soviet Union, education in, 9

Space
action-threshold impact of, 325–27
in milieu therapy, 88
repetition compulsion in, 193–96

Specialized handling, 249–50

Spontaneity, limits on, 91

Sports, *see* Athletics

"Sputnik neurosis," 8–9

Status
adolescent, 121
group, 201
patterns of high, 454–55

Stereotypes, 225
negative, toward youth, 10–11
of sexual development, 429–30

Stories, 89

Stress (strain), 114, 133
on healthy children, 62–64
refuge from unbearable, 457–60
sudden change and, 296–98

"Strong-man theory," 178

Structures
inherent, 130–31
patterns of high, 454–55
social, of milieu therapy, 82–83

Subclique formation, 84–85

Sublimation, 131, 186
of group libido, 182, 183–84
improvement and, 112–13

Success, 101
improvement and, 110
of teachers, 304–5

Suckers, 46–47, 248

Suction, group-psychological role, 84–85
helplessness toward, 46–47
power of, 321–23

Sulking, 42–43

Superego, 36, 136, 205–6, 225
changes in, 323–24
conflicts over, 194
defiance of, 415–16
of delinquents, 128, 228–29
incorporation of leader's, 163, 165
repair of, 78
suppresses undesirable drives, 170, 173–74
See also Conscience

Superstition, *see* Magic

Suspicion, 177
"countersuspicion," 105
about group therapy, 311–13

Swapping, 51

Swearing, *see* Blasphemy

Symbols, 479–82
depersonalized, 230–31, 410

Symptoms
disguise of, 117
droppage of, 30–31, 103, 221, 425
estrangement from, 44–45
living with, 47
psychosomatic, 209

Taboos
on code-dangerous identification, 231–32
sexual, 282

Tact, lack of, 294

Tantrums, 127, 144, 209, 352
as defenses, 414
emotional first aid for, 49
holding children in, 116
in school, 267

Tastes, *see* Interests

Tattling, 321–23

Taunting, *see* Provocation

Taxation, psychic
freedom from, 454–55
group powers of, 323–25

Teachers, *see* Education

Teen-agers, use of term, 10–11
See also Adolescents

Television, 89
Temper tantrums, *see* Tantrums
Terrain in life-space interviews, 56–57
Theft, 220, 284–85, 346, 468
  contagious, 200
  life-space interview for, 59–60
  morality and, 462–63, 474
  pathological, 420
  preadolescent, 406–7
Therapeutic communities, 80
Therapeutic milieu, *see* Milieu therapy
Therapy
  drug, 26
  group, *see* Group therapy
  milieu, *see* Milieu therapy
  occupational, 73–74
  play, 57–58, 75, 77, 396
  psychotherapy, *see* Psychotherapy
  residential, 140–46
Threats, verbal, 295
Tics, preadolescent, 398, 402
Time
  to come home, 406
  repetition in, 195
  scheduling of, 88, 136, 143
Timing
  of camp experience, 450–51
  of interference, 351–52
  of life-space interviews, 55–56, 61
  of punishment, 368–71
Tolerance, 98, 346–47
  deviation, 341–42
  public, 123
Tomboys, 422
Tools, mental
  bargaining, 111–12
  salesmanship for new, 45–46
"Total living," 13–14
Toughness-shyness line, 248
Toys, 130–32
Trading, 51
Traffic regulations, behavioral, 50–51, 89–90
Trait clusters, 85–86
Transactions, loaded, 51
Transference, 86
  goal of, 36
  in group therapy, 314–15

  of improvement, 105–6, 108
  of neurosis, 479
  "spillover" of, 76
Transformation of punishment, 367–68
Transition, 194
  "hang overs" in, 135–36
  to psychoanalysis, 37
  See also Change
Trauma
  improvement and, 106, 108
  protection from, 72
  sexual, 379, 427–28
  See also Shock
Treatment-relevant facts, 19–20
Trust, 122
  lack of, 165; *see also* Suspicion
Tyrants (group leaders), 164–65, 170–71, 185–86, 189
  Hitler as, 178

Umpire services, 51, 89–90
Unconscious, 148
  discovery of, 95–96
  primitive, 192
Underdeveloped countries (in children's fields), 5–9
United States, children's fields underdeveloped in, 5–9
Unity, group, 177

Valence, symbolic, 479–82
Values, 58, 78, 387, 401
  elasticity as, 75
  of leaders, 162–65
  massaging numb areas of, 45
  in milieu therapy, 83–84, 93
  moral, 171, 174
  social-class, 181
  See also Groups—codes of
Vienna, Austria, 155

Ward bosses, 54, 72
Warner-Dollard-Davis studies, 181
Wineman, David
  Children Who Hate, 48, 125
  Controls from Within, 355
Withdrawal, 209, 218, 242, 248, 416
  borderline of psychotic, 49

Work
 group emotion and, 163–64
 therapeutic, 73–74

Youth movements, 178, 181, 187

Zeitschrift für Psychoanalytische Pädagogik (periodical), 156, 313